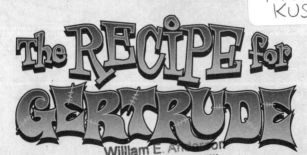

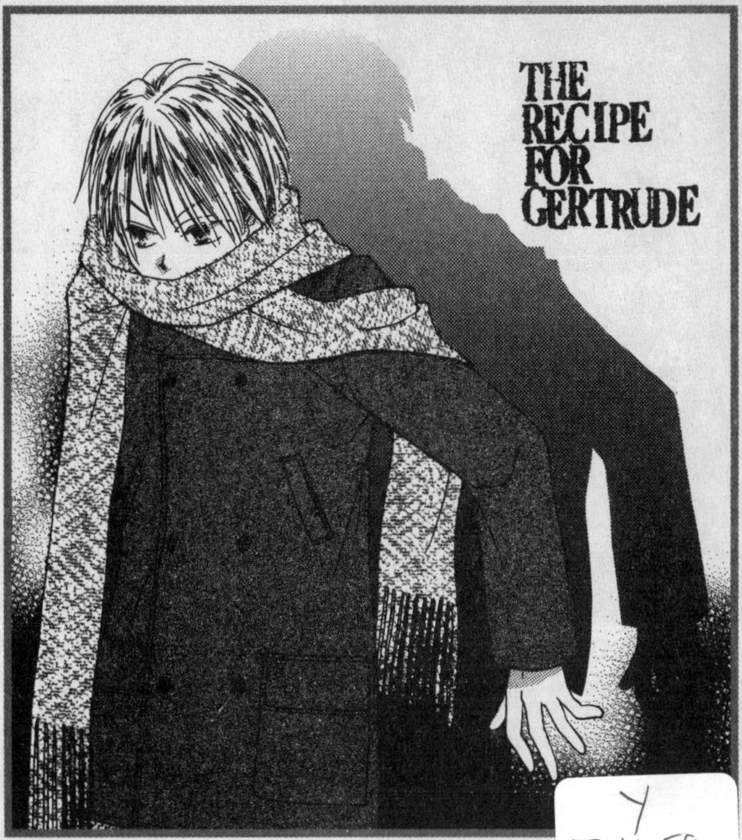

THE
RECIPE
FOR
GERTRUDE

The RECIPE for GERTRUDE

By Nari Kusakawa

Volume 2

CONTENTS

STORY SO FAR

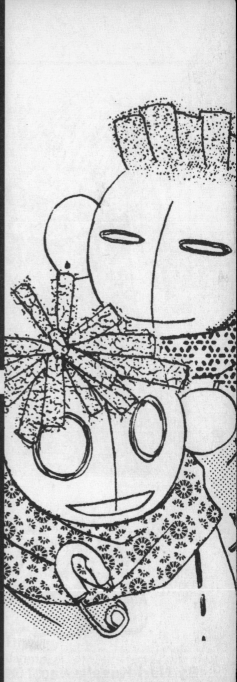

Gertrude, a 100-year-old manmade demon (who looks pretty good for his age), met Sahara, a girl who is not quite as normal as she seems. Gertrude was built from the stolen parts of various other demons, and some of them want those parts back. He (yes, Gertrude's a guy) figures that he won't find any peace until he locates and destroys the "recipe" that was used to make him. Gertrude's not the only one trying to find it, but at least he has Sahara and a couple of funny looking demons named Puppen and Mariotte to help him.

CMX

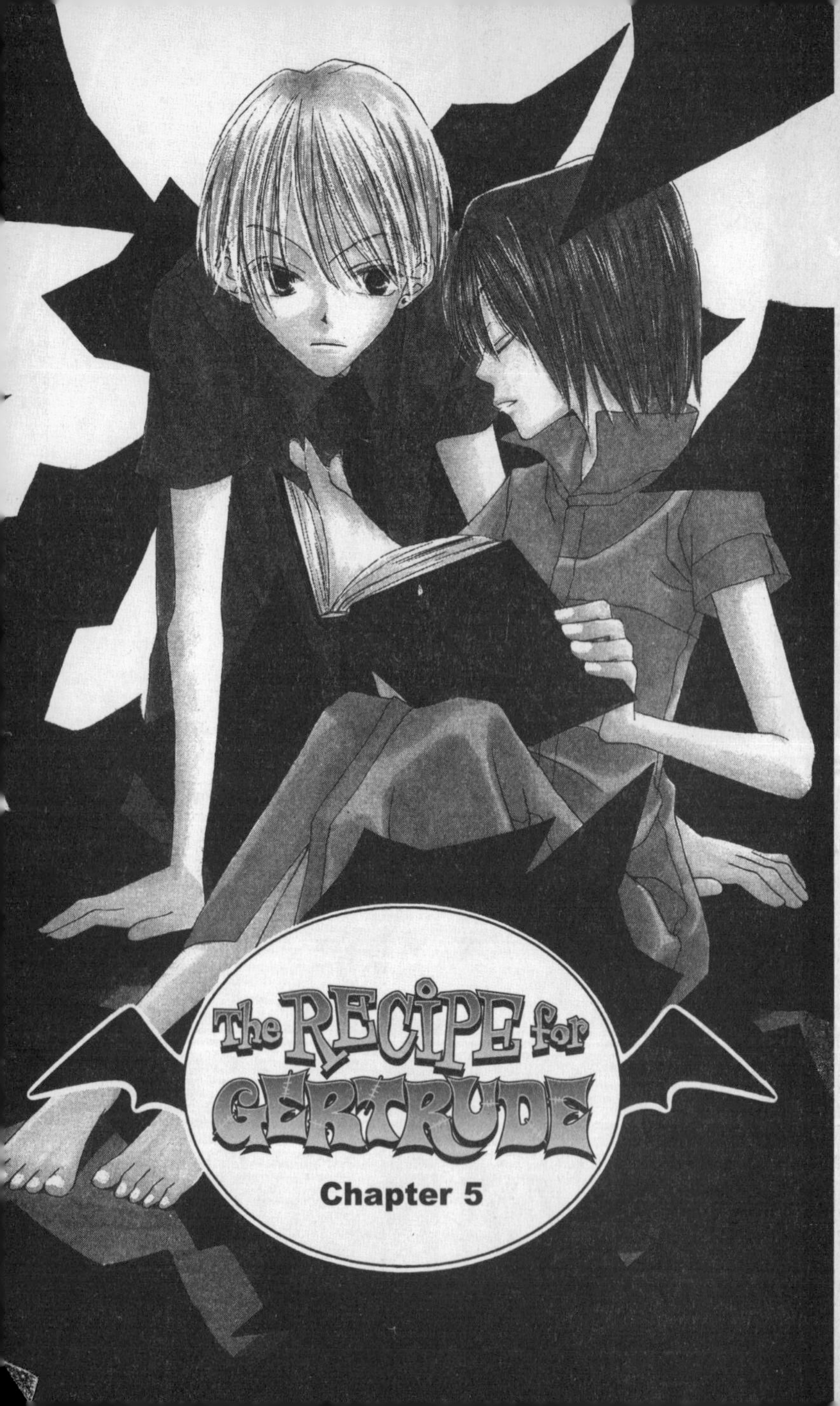
The RECIPE for GERTRUDE
Chapter 5

IT'S YOUR BROTHER. SOMETHING'S NOT QUITE RIGHT.
WHILE LOOKING FOR THE INSTRUCTION MANUAL ON HOW TO MAKE A MANMADE DEMON...
"THE RECIPE FOR GERTRUDE..."
...I BECAME INVOLVED WITH AN EXTRA-ORDINARY PERSON.
HEY, SUSUGI, HERE'S LUNCH.

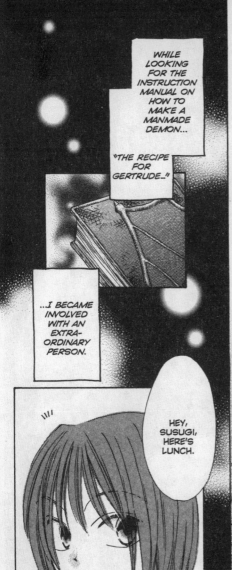

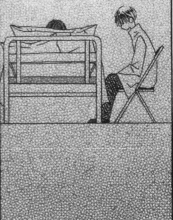

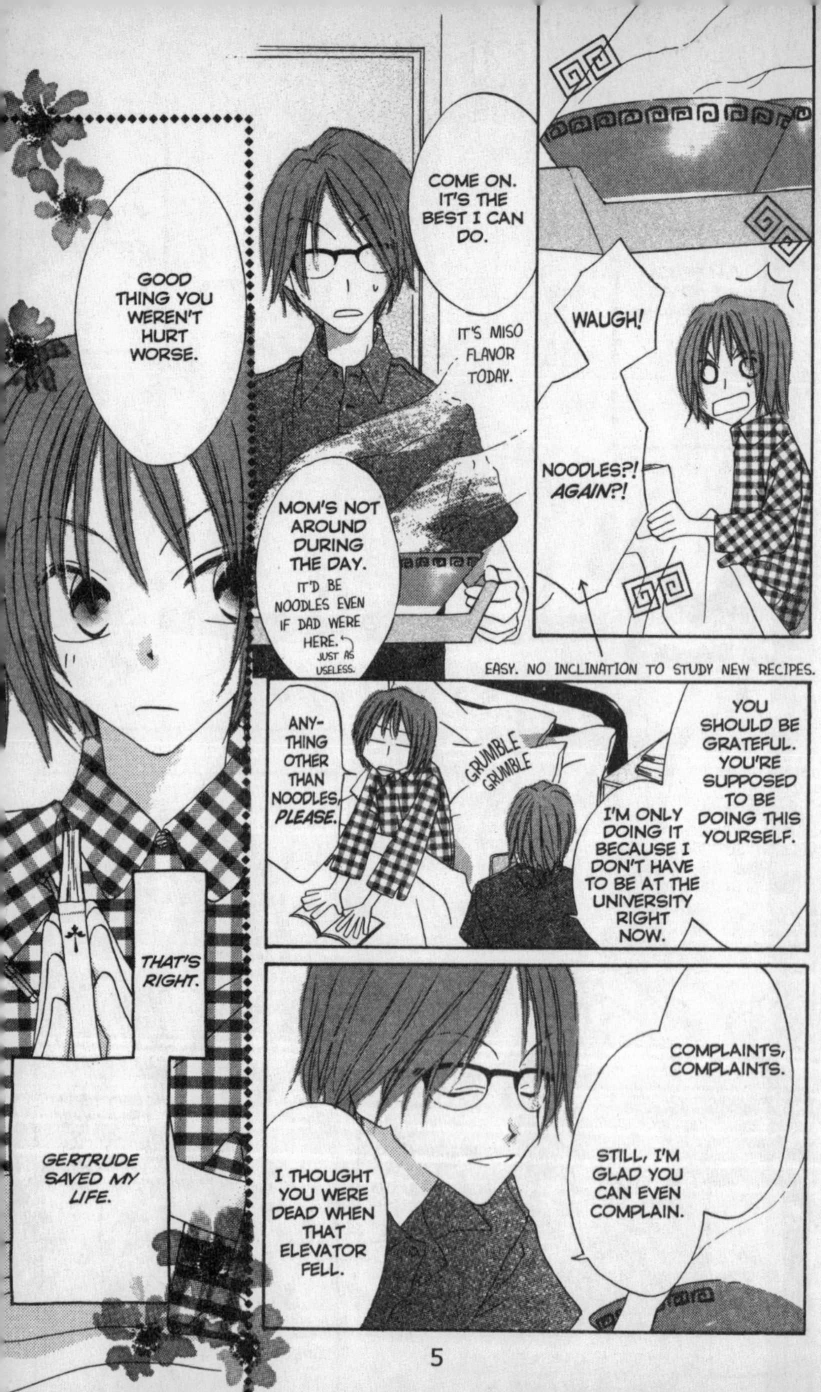
WAUGH!
NOODLES?! *AGAIN?!*
EASY. NO INCLINATION TO STUDY NEW RECIPES.
COME ON. IT'S THE BEST I CAN DO.
IT'S MISO FLAVOR TODAY.
MOM'S NOT AROUND DURING THE DAY.
IT'D BE NOODLES EVEN IF DAD WERE HERE.
JUST AS USELESS.
YOU SHOULD BE GRATEFUL. YOU'RE SUPPOSED TO BE DOING THIS YOURSELF.
I'M ONLY DOING IT BECAUSE I DON'T HAVE TO BE AT THE UNIVERSITY RIGHT NOW.
GRUMBLE GRUMBLE
ANYTHING OTHER THAN NOODLES, *PLEASE.*
COMPLAINTS, COMPLAINTS.
STILL, I'M GLAD YOU CAN EVEN COMPLAIN.
I THOUGHT YOU WERE DEAD WHEN THAT ELEVATOR FELL.
GOOD THING YOU WEREN'T HURT WORSE.
THAT'S RIGHT.
GERTRUDE SAVED MY LIFE.

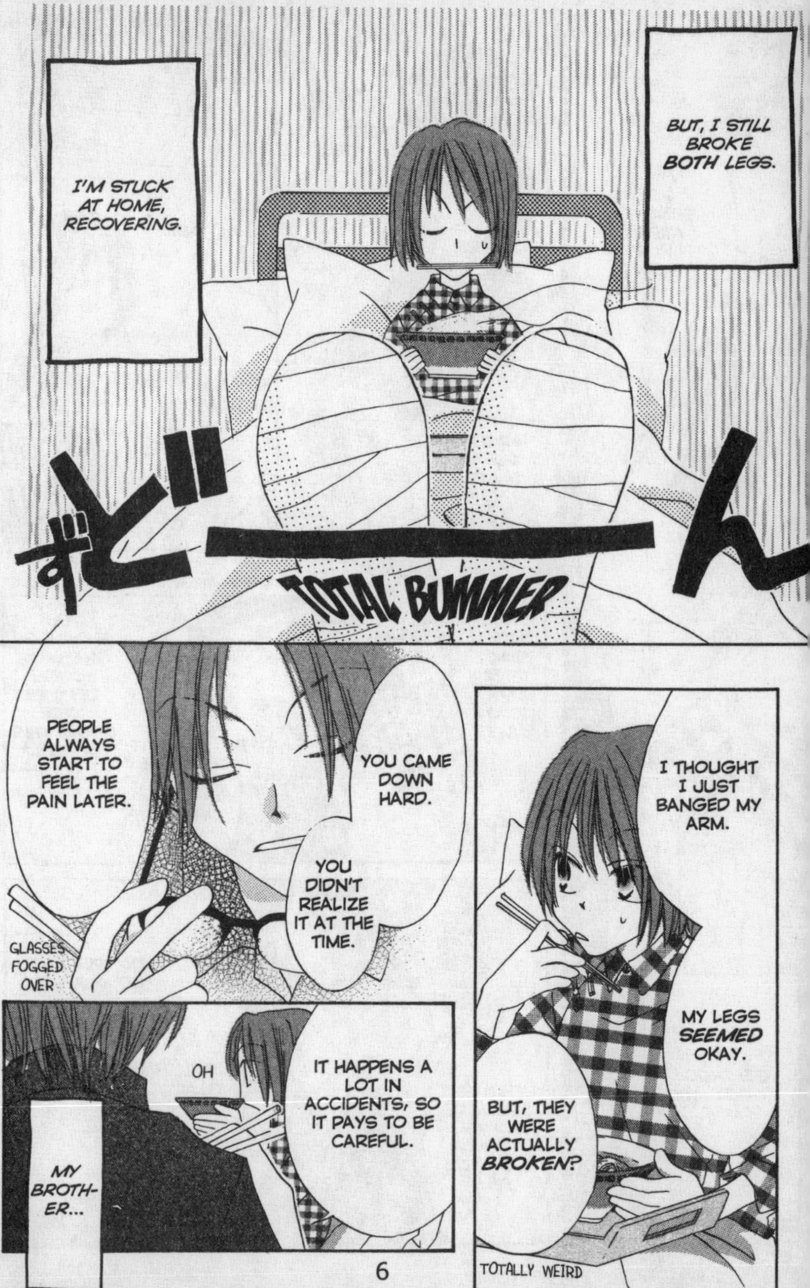
BUT, I STILL BROKE BOTH LEGS.
I'M STUCK AT HOME, RECOVERING.
ずどーーん
TOTAL BUMMER
I THOUGHT I JUST BANGED MY ARM.
MY LEGS *SEEMED* OKAY.
BUT, THEY WERE ACTUALLY *BROKEN?*
TOTALLY WEIRD
YOU CAME DOWN HARD.
YOU DIDN'T REALIZE IT AT THE TIME.
PEOPLE ALWAYS START TO FEEL THE PAIN LATER.
GLASSES FOGGED OVER
IT HAPPENS A LOT IN ACCIDENTS, SO IT PAYS TO BE CAREFUL.
OH
MY BROTHER...

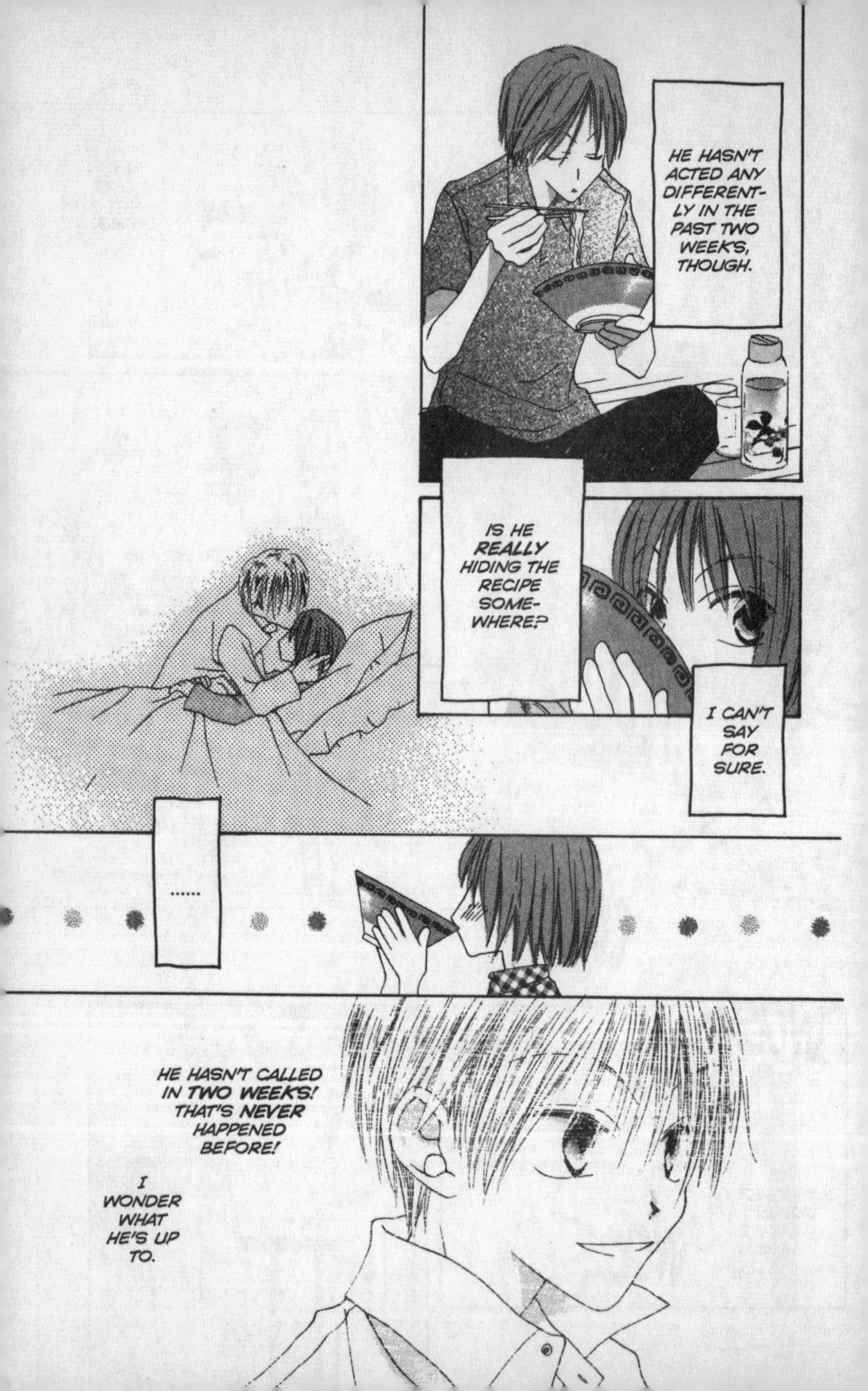
HE HASN'T ACTED ANY DIFFERENTLY IN THE PAST TWO WEEKS, THOUGH.
IS HE REALLY HIDING THE RECIPE SOMEWHERE?
I CAN'T SAY FOR SURE.
......
HE HASN'T CALLED IN TWO WEEKS! THAT'S NEVER HAPPENED BEFORE!
I WONDER WHAT HE'S UP TO.

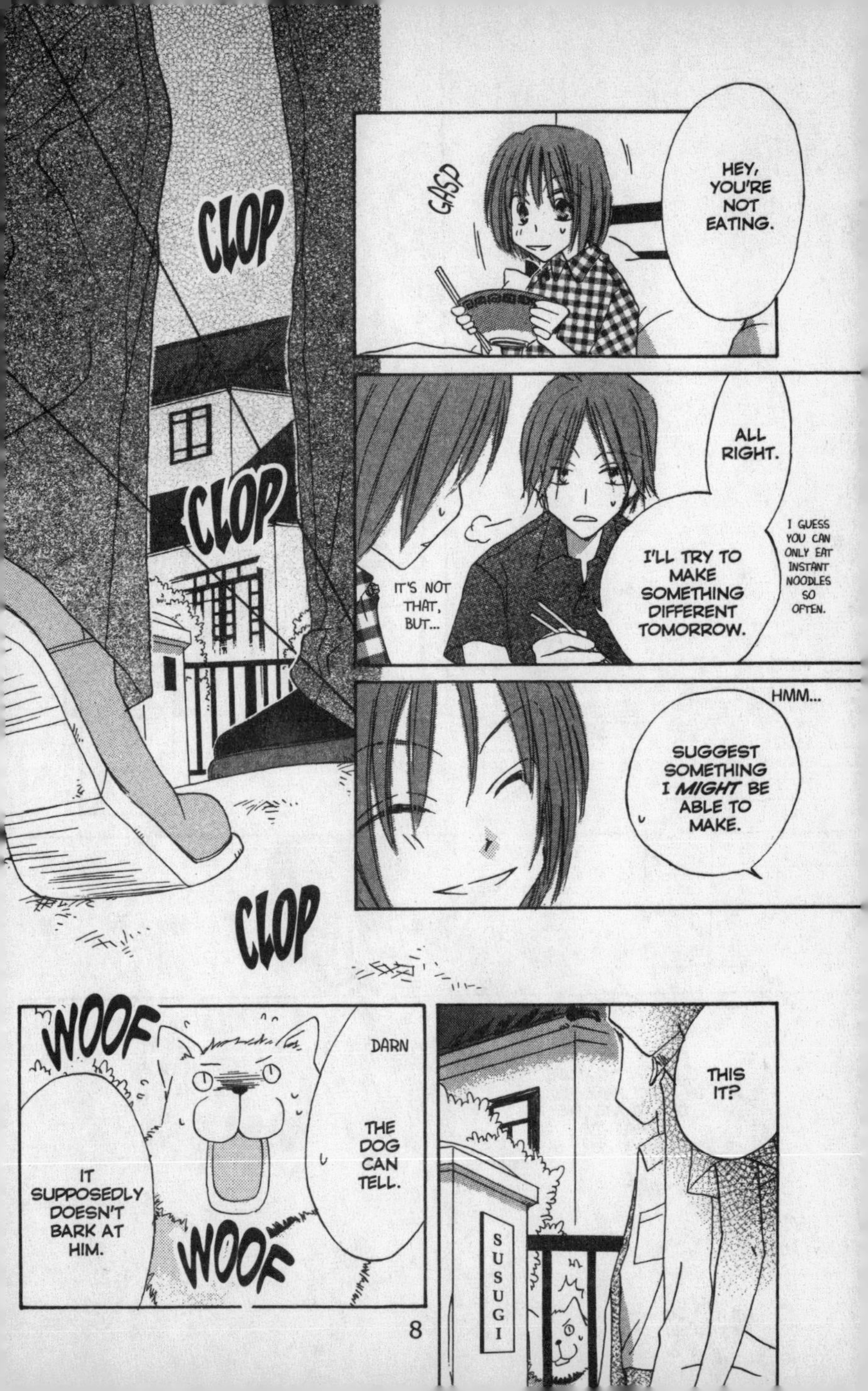
HEY, YOU'RE NOT EATING.
GASP
ALL RIGHT.
I GUESS YOU CAN ONLY EAT INSTANT NOODLES SO OFTEN.
I'LL TRY TO MAKE SOMETHING DIFFERENT TOMORROW.
IT'S NOT THAT, BUT...
HMM...
SUGGEST SOMETHING I *MIGHT* BE ABLE TO MAKE.
CLOP
CLOP
CLOP
THIS IT?
SUSUGI
DARN
THE DOG CAN TELL.
WOOF
IT SUPPOSEDLY DOESN'T BARK AT HIM.
WOOF

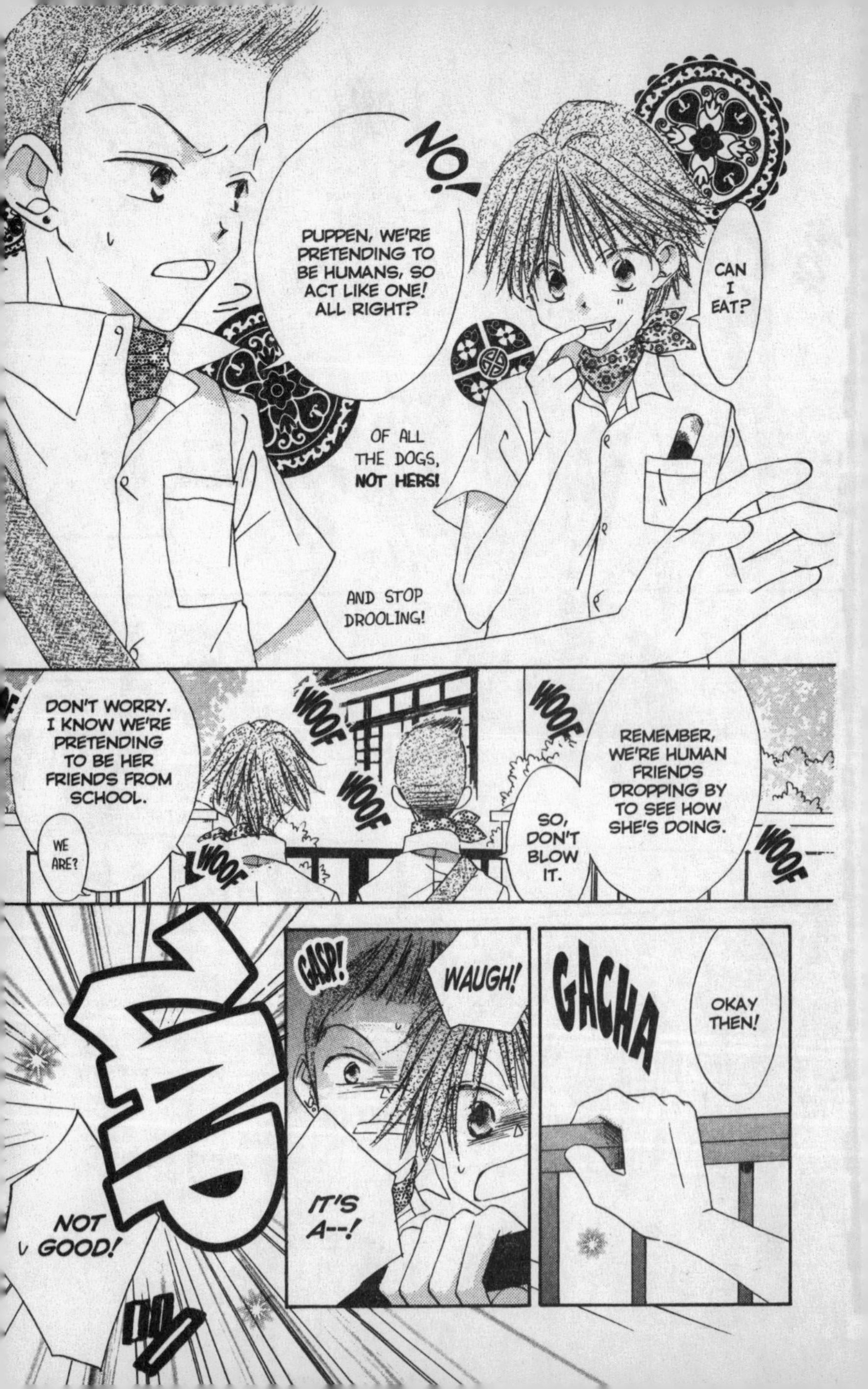
CAN I EAT?
NO!
PUPPEN, WE'RE PRETENDING TO BE HUMANS, SO ACT LIKE ONE! ALL RIGHT?
OF ALL THE DOGS, **NOT HERS!**
AND STOP DROOLING!
WOOF
REMEMBER, WE'RE HUMAN FRIENDS DROPPING BY TO SEE HOW SHE'S DOING.
WOOF
SO, DON'T BLOW IT.
WOOF
WOOF
DON'T WORRY. I KNOW WE'RE PRETENDING TO BE HER FRIENDS FROM SCHOOL.
WE ARE?
WOOF
OKAY THEN!
GACHA
WAUGH!
GASP!
IT'S A--!
ZAP
NOT GOOD!

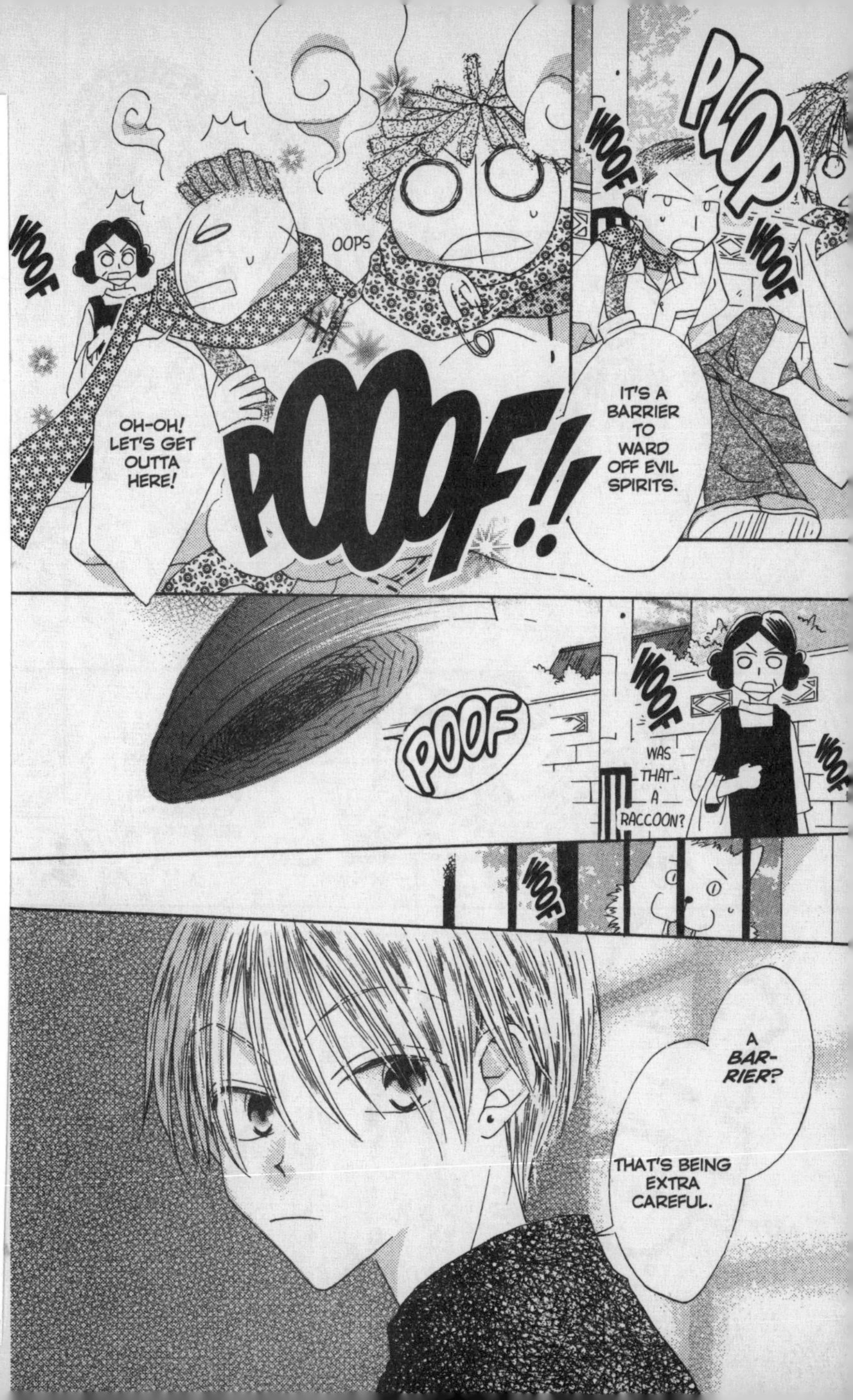
PLOP
WOOF
WOOF
WOOF
IT'S A BARRIER TO WARD OFF EVIL SPIRITS.
POOOF!!
OOPS
OH-OH! LET'S GET OUTTA HERE!
WOOF
WOOF
WOOF
WAS THAT A RACCOON?
POOF
WOOF
A BAR-RIER?
THAT'S BEING EXTRA CAREFUL.

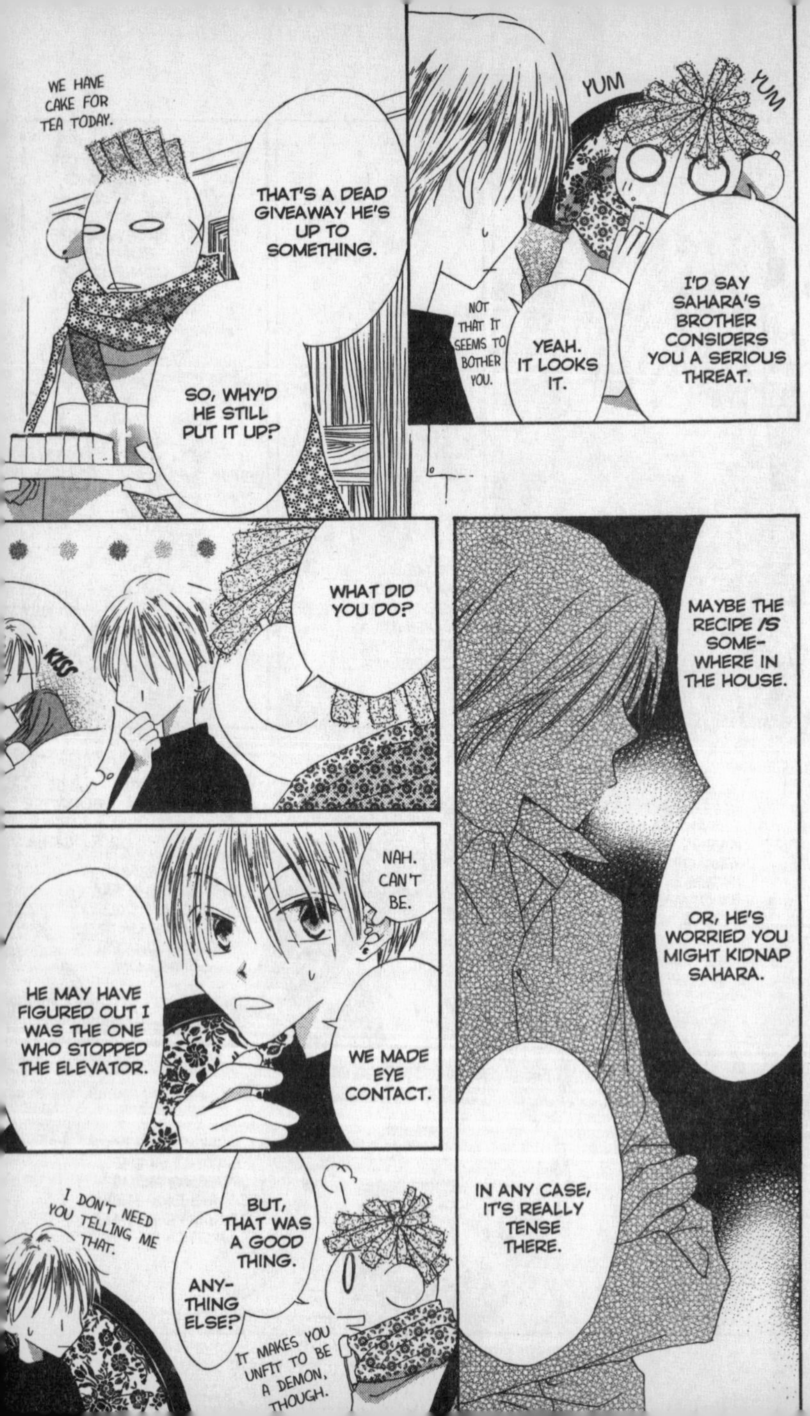
YUM
YUM
I'D SAY SAHARA'S BROTHER CONSIDERS YOU A SERIOUS THREAT.
YEAH. IT LOOKS IT.
NOT THAT IT SEEMS TO BOTHER YOU.
WE HAVE CAKE FOR TEA TODAY.
THAT'S A DEAD GIVEAWAY HE'S UP TO SOMETHING.
SO, WHY'D HE STILL PUT IT UP?
MAYBE THE RECIPE IS SOME-WHERE IN THE HOUSE.
OR, HE'S WORRIED YOU MIGHT KIDNAP SAHARA.
IN ANY CASE, IT'S REALLY TENSE THERE.
WHAT DID YOU DO?
KISS
NAH. CAN'T BE.
WE MADE EYE CONTACT.
HE MAY HAVE FIGURED OUT I WAS THE ONE WHO STOPPED THE ELEVATOR.
BUT, THAT WAS A GOOD THING.
ANY-THING ELSE?
IT MAKES YOU UNFIT TO BE A DEMON, THOUGH.
I DON'T NEED YOU TELLING ME THAT.

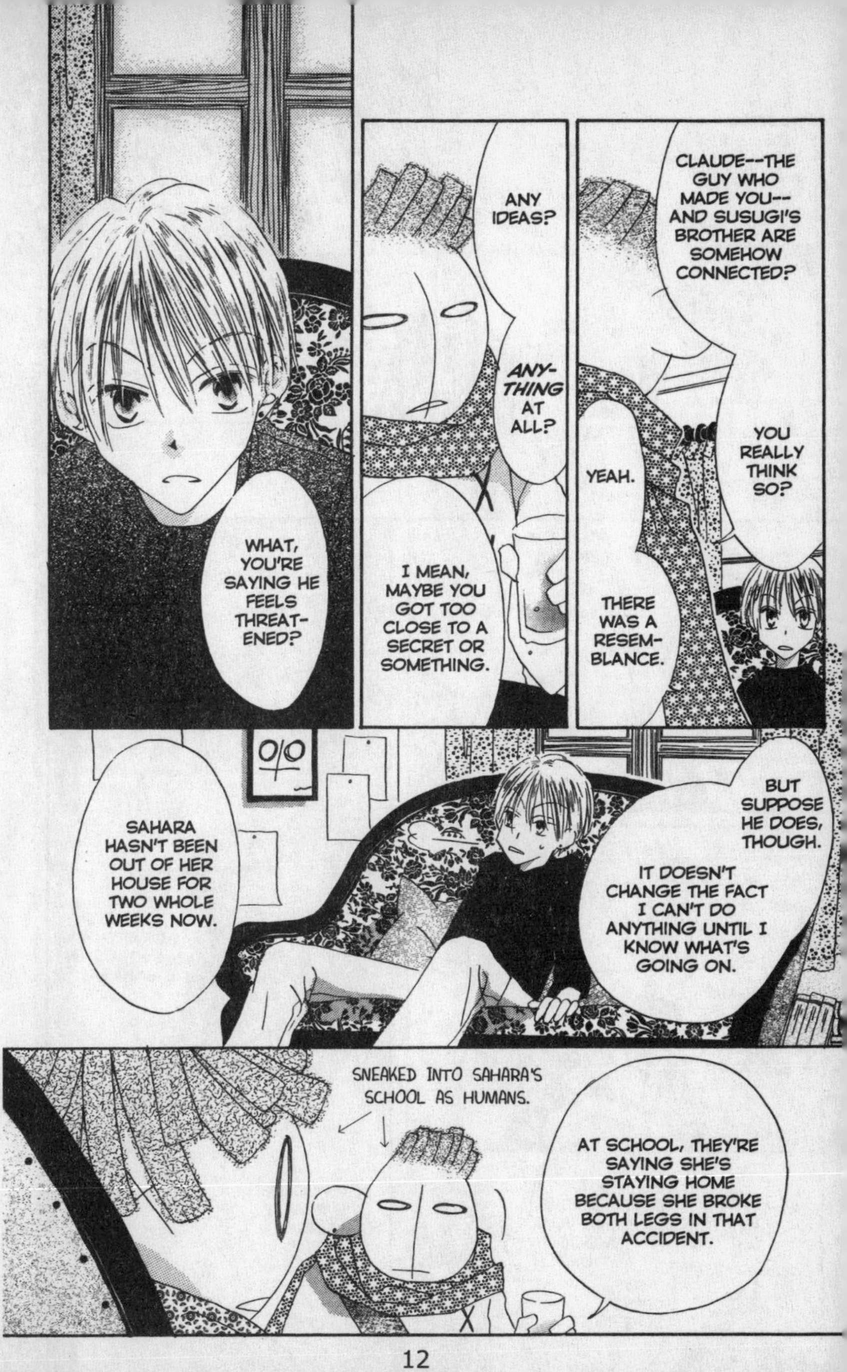
CLAUDE--THE GUY WHO MADE YOU--AND SUSUGI'S BROTHER ARE SOMEHOW CONNECTED?
YOU REALLY THINK SO?
YEAH.
THERE WAS A RESEMBLANCE.
ANY IDEAS?
ANYTHING AT ALL?
I MEAN, MAYBE YOU GOT TOO CLOSE TO A SECRET OR SOMETHING.
WHAT, YOU'RE SAYING HE FEELS THREATENED?
BUT SUPPOSE HE DOES, THOUGH.
IT DOESN'T CHANGE THE FACT I CAN'T DO ANYTHING UNTIL I KNOW WHAT'S GOING ON.
SAHARA HASN'T BEEN OUT OF HER HOUSE FOR TWO WHOLE WEEKS NOW.
AT SCHOOL, THEY'RE SAYING SHE'S STAYING HOME BECAUSE SHE BROKE BOTH LEGS IN THAT ACCIDENT.
SNEAKED INTO SAHARA'S SCHOOL AS HUMANS.

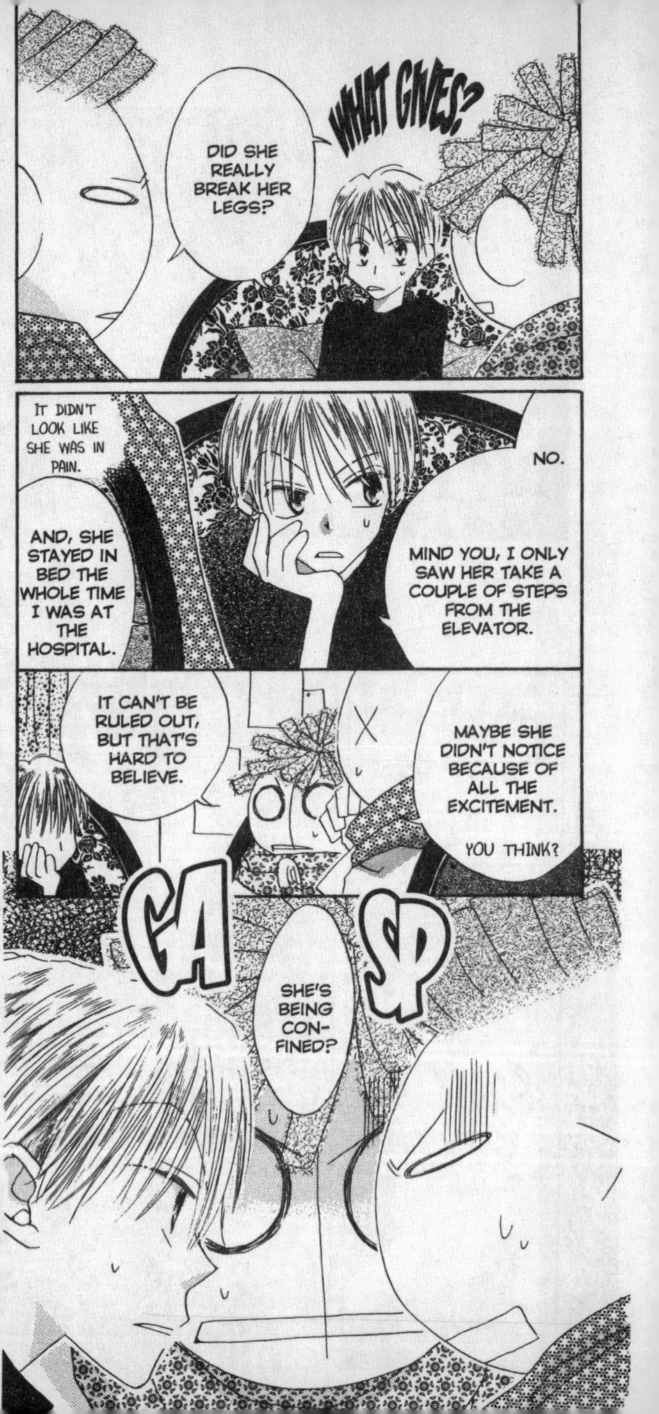
WHAT GIVES?
DID SHE REALLY BREAK HER LEGS?
NO.
MIND YOU, I ONLY SAW HER TAKE A COUPLE OF STEPS FROM THE ELEVATOR.
IT DIDN'T LOOK LIKE SHE WAS IN PAIN.
AND, SHE STAYED IN BED THE WHOLE TIME I WAS AT THE HOSPITAL.
MAYBE SHE DIDN'T NOTICE BECAUSE OF ALL THE EXCITEMENT.
YOU THINK?
IT CAN'T BE RULED OUT, BUT THAT'S HARD TO BELIEVE.
GASP
SHE'S BEING CON-FINED?

01

THIS IS VOLUME TWO.

I quit my part-time job and became an artist full time. My health suffered for it. I've never ever been fit, but it's pretty ridiculous when your body aches just from weeding the garden. I keep telling myself to go swimming, but half a year has already gone by and I still haven't gone. I can only swim about 80 feet, but I think swimming will be less hard on my knees than running and stuff like that.

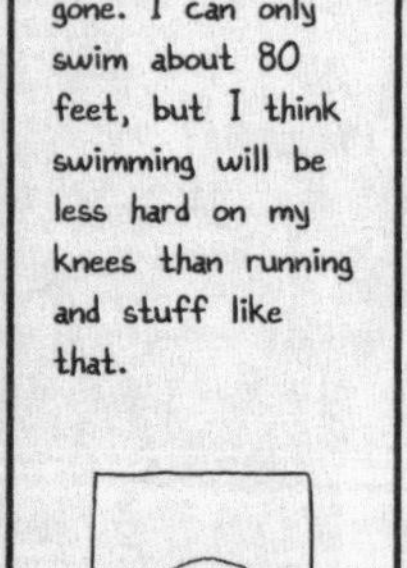

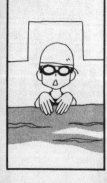

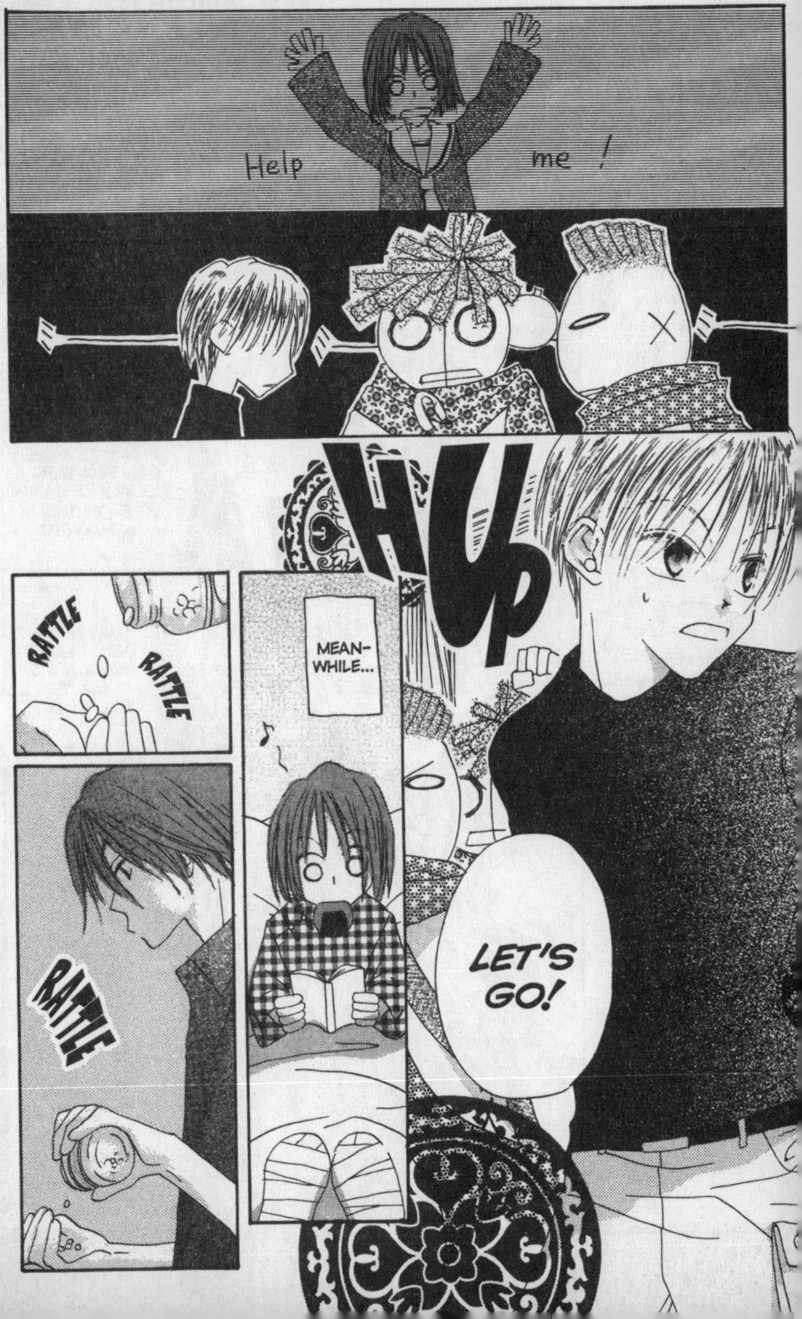
Help me!
HUP
LET'S GO!
MEAN-WHILE...
RATTLE RATTLE
RATTLE

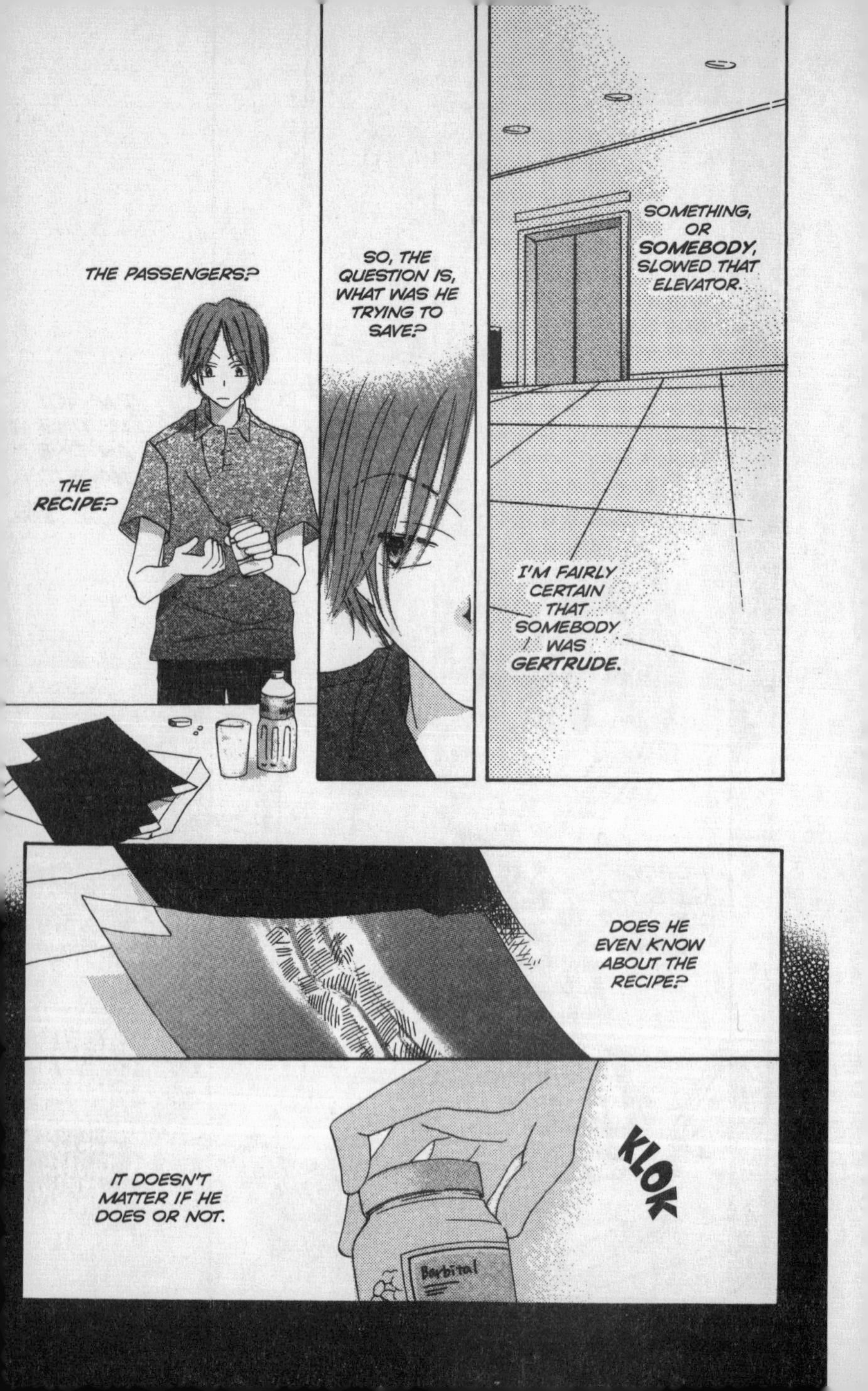
SOMETHING, OR SOMEBODY, SLOWED THAT ELEVATOR.
I'M FAIRLY CERTAIN THAT SOMEBODY WAS GERTRUDE.
SO, THE QUESTION IS, WHAT WAS HE TRYING TO SAVE?
THE PASSENGERS?
THE RECIPE?
DOES HE EVEN KNOW ABOUT THE RECIPE?
KLOK
IT DOESN'T MATTER IF HE DOES OR NOT.
Barbital

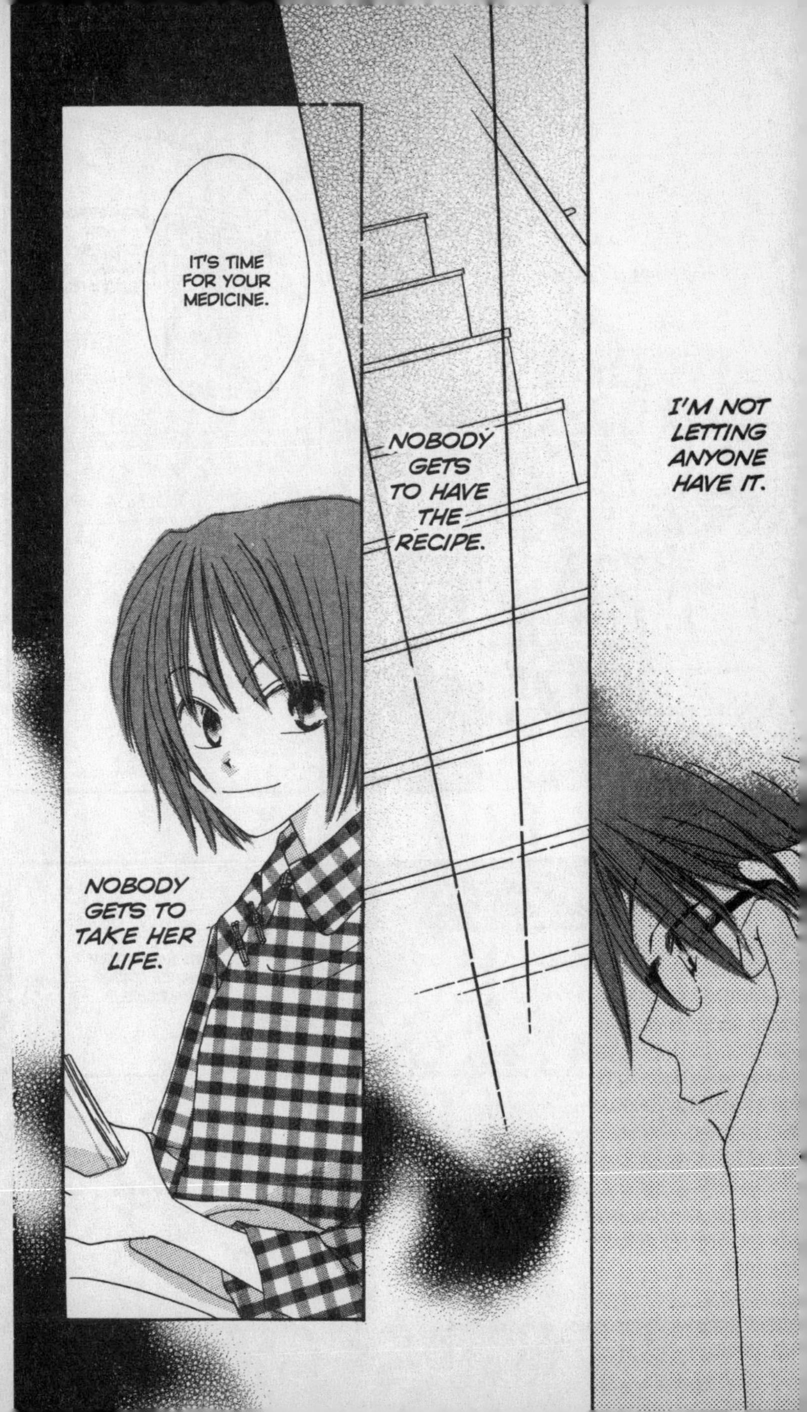
I'M NOT LETTING ANYONE HAVE IT.
NOBODY GETS TO HAVE THE RECIPE.
IT'S TIME FOR YOUR MEDICINE.
NOBODY GETS TO TAKE HER LIFE.

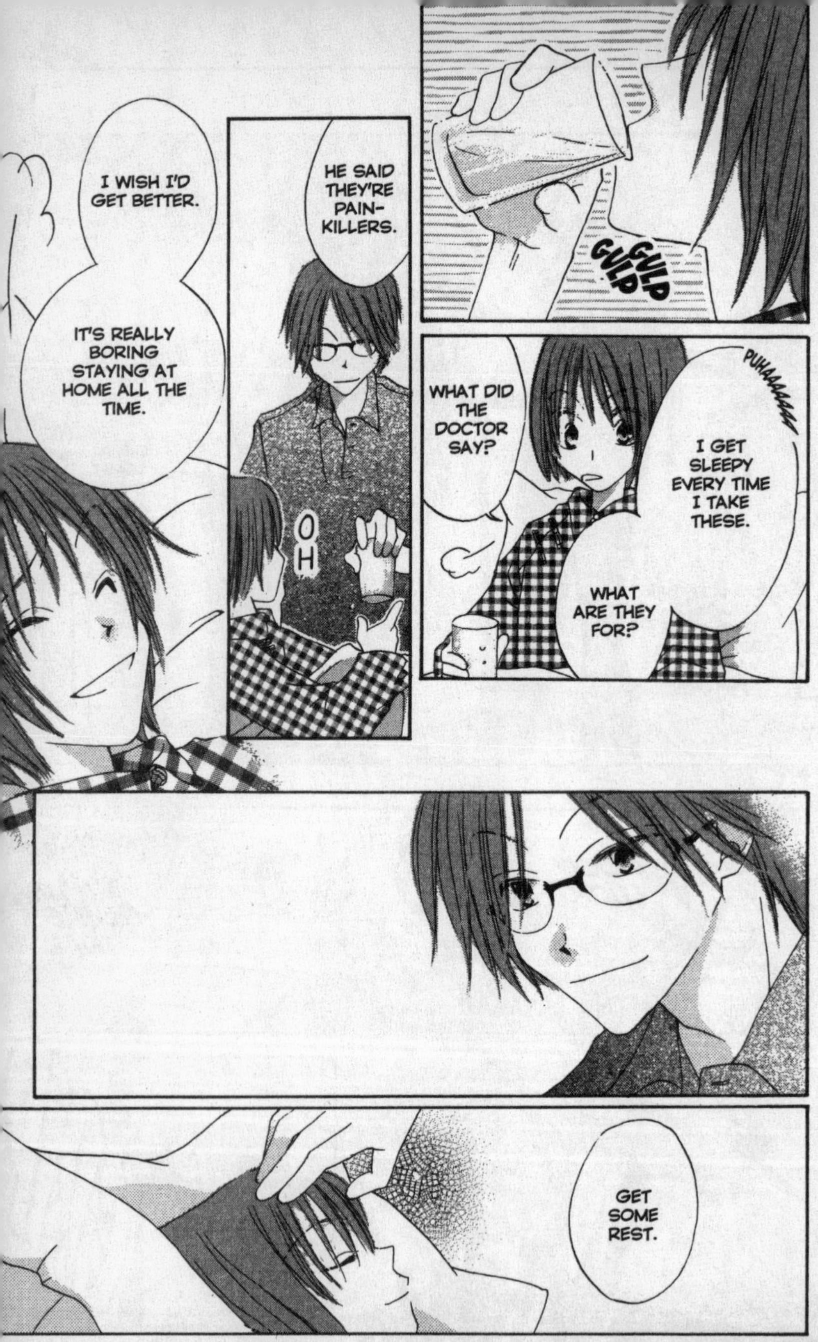
GULP GULP
PUHAAAAAAAA
I GET SLEEPY EVERY TIME I TAKE THESE.
WHAT DID THE DOCTOR SAY?
WHAT ARE THEY FOR?
HE SAID THEY'RE PAIN-KILLERS.
OH
I WISH I'D GET BETTER.
IT'S REALLY BORING STAYING AT HOME ALL THE TIME.
GET SOME REST.

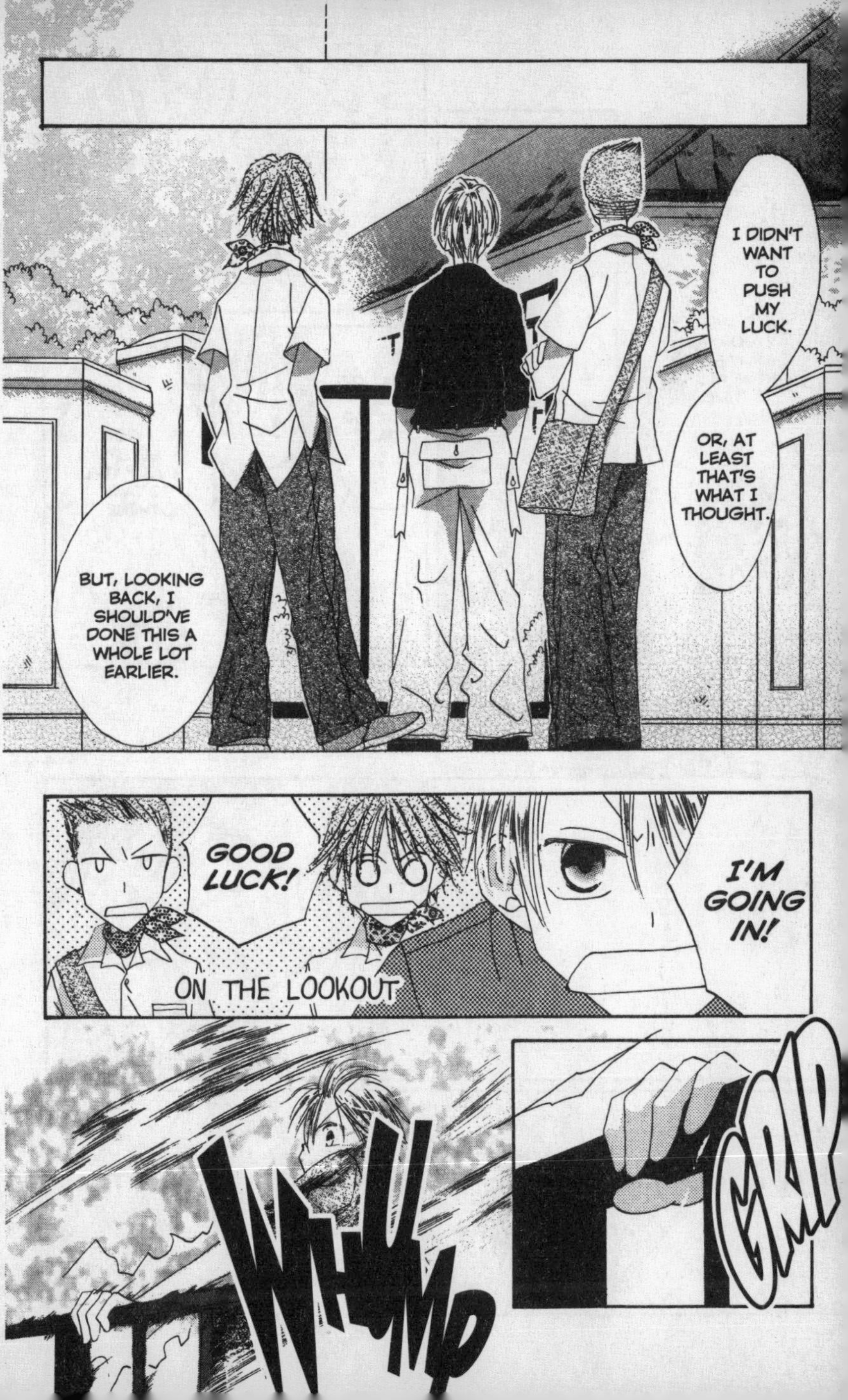
I DIDN'T WANT TO PUSH MY LUCK.
OR, AT LEAST THAT'S WHAT I THOUGHT.
BUT, LOOKING BACK, I SHOULD'VE DONE THIS A WHOLE LOT EARLIER.
I'M GOING IN!
GOOD LUCK!
ON THE LOOKOUT
GRIP
WHUMP

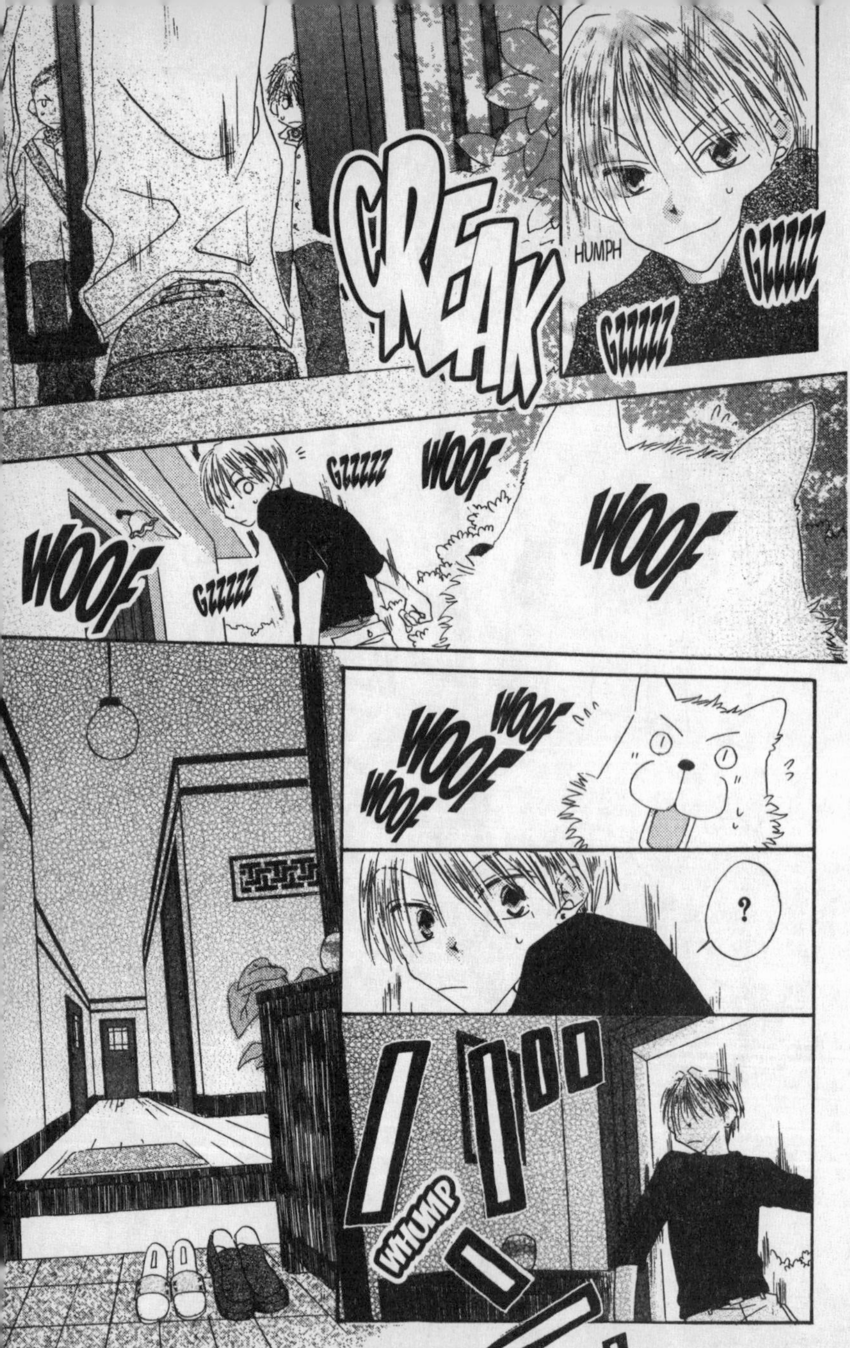
HUMPH
GZZZZZ
GZZZZZ
CREAK
WOOF
WOOF
GZZZZZ
GZZZZZ
WOOF
WOOF
WOOF
WOOF
?
WHUMP

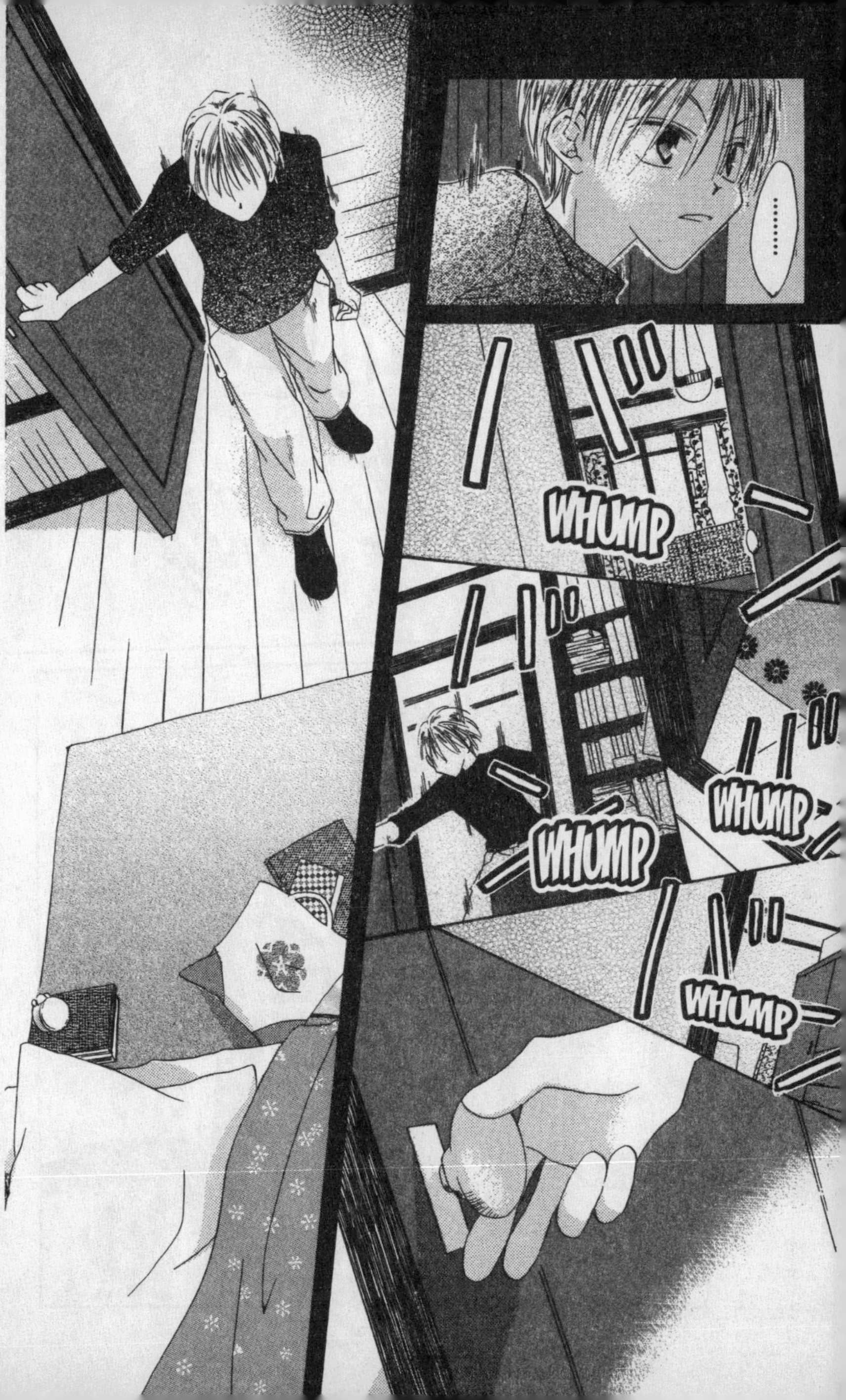
......
WHUMP
WHUMP
WHUMP
WHUMP

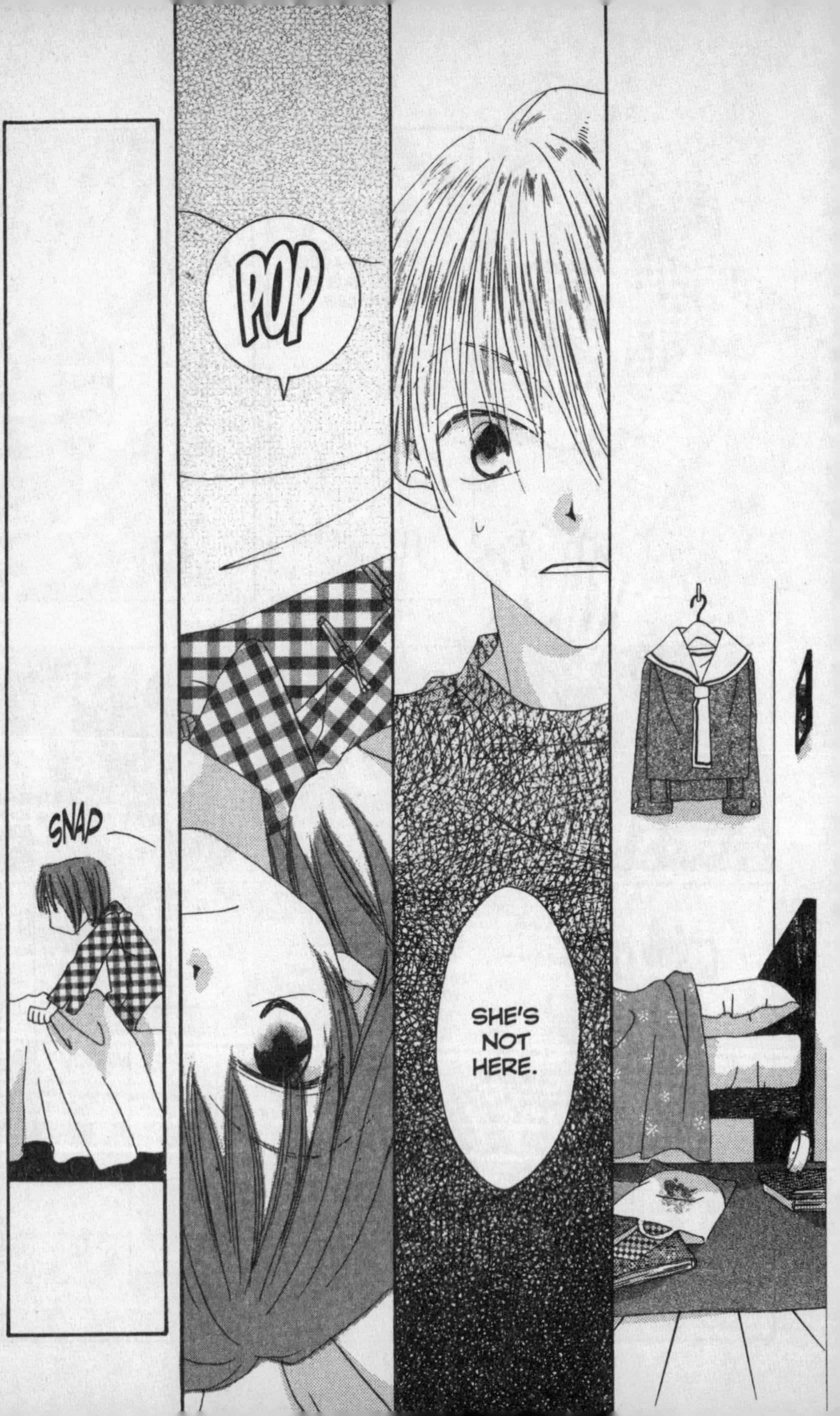
SHE'S NOT HERE.
POP
SNAP

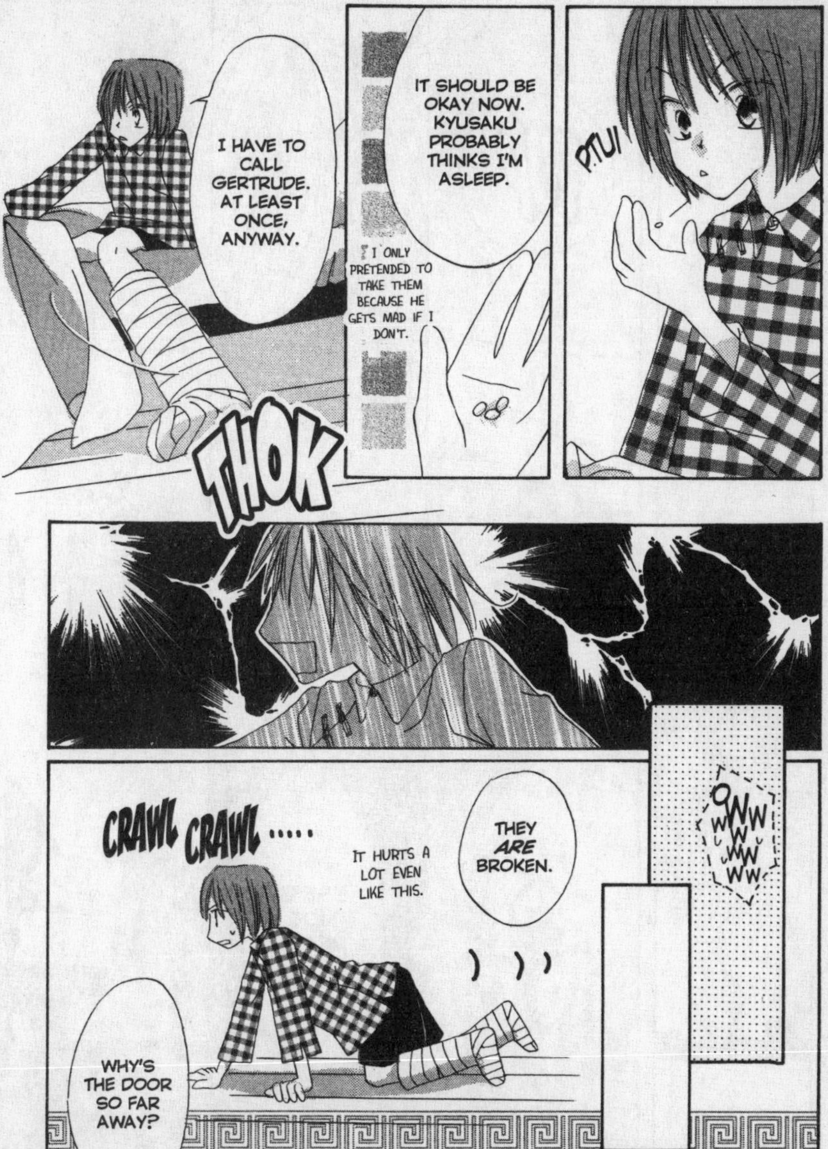
P.TUI
IT SHOULD BE OKAY NOW. KYUSAKU PROBABLY THINKS I'M ASLEEP.
I ONLY PRETENDED TO TAKE THEM BECAUSE HE GETS MAD IF I DON'T.
I HAVE TO CALL GERTRUDE. AT LEAST ONCE, ANYWAY.
THOK
OWWWWWWW
THEY *ARE* BROKEN.
IT HURTS A LOT EVEN LIKE THIS.
CRAWL CRAWL .....
WHY'S THE DOOR SO FAR AWAY?

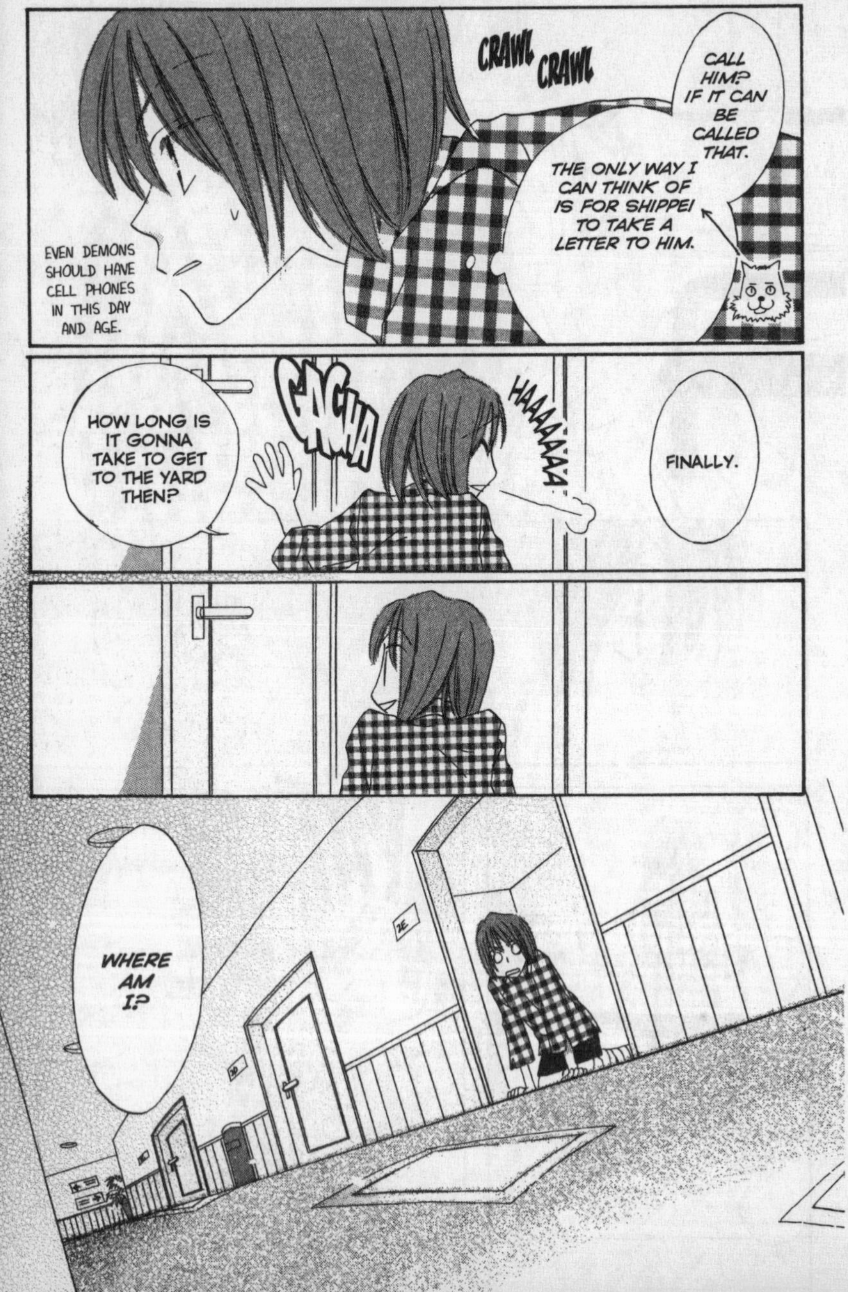
CALL HIM? IF IT CAN BE CALLED THAT.
THE ONLY WAY I CAN THINK OF IS FOR SHIPPEI TO TAKE A LETTER TO HIM.
CRAWL CRAWL
EVEN DEMONS SHOULD HAVE CELL PHONES IN THIS DAY AND AGE.
FINALLY.
HAAAAAAA
GACHA
HOW LONG IS IT GONNA TAKE TO GET TO THE YARD THEN?
WHERE AM I?

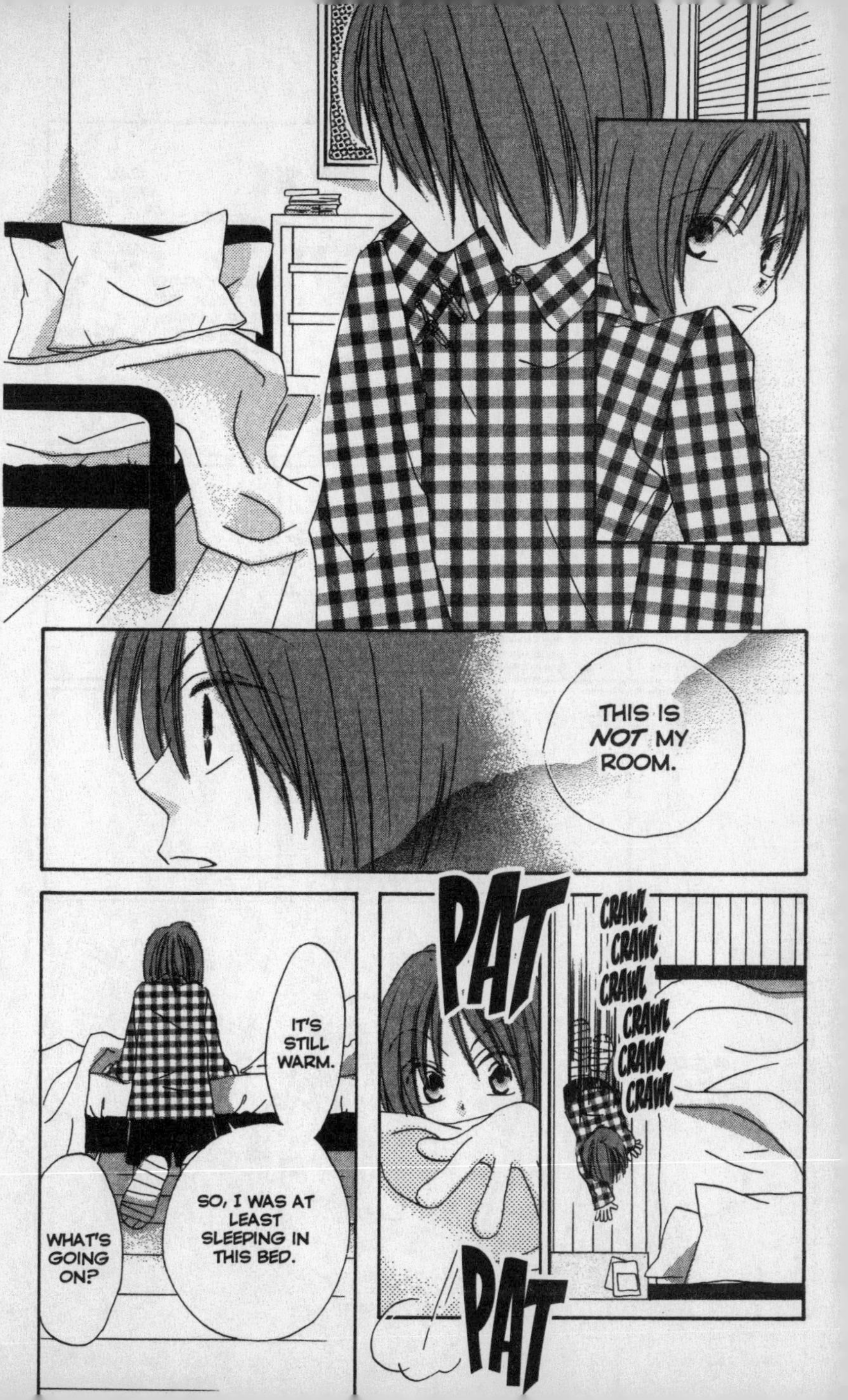
THIS IS *NOT* MY ROOM.
PAT
CRAWL CRAWL CRAWL CRAWL CRAWL CRAWL
PAT
IT'S STILL WARM.
SO, I WAS AT LEAST SLEEPING IN THIS BED.
WHAT'S GOING ON?

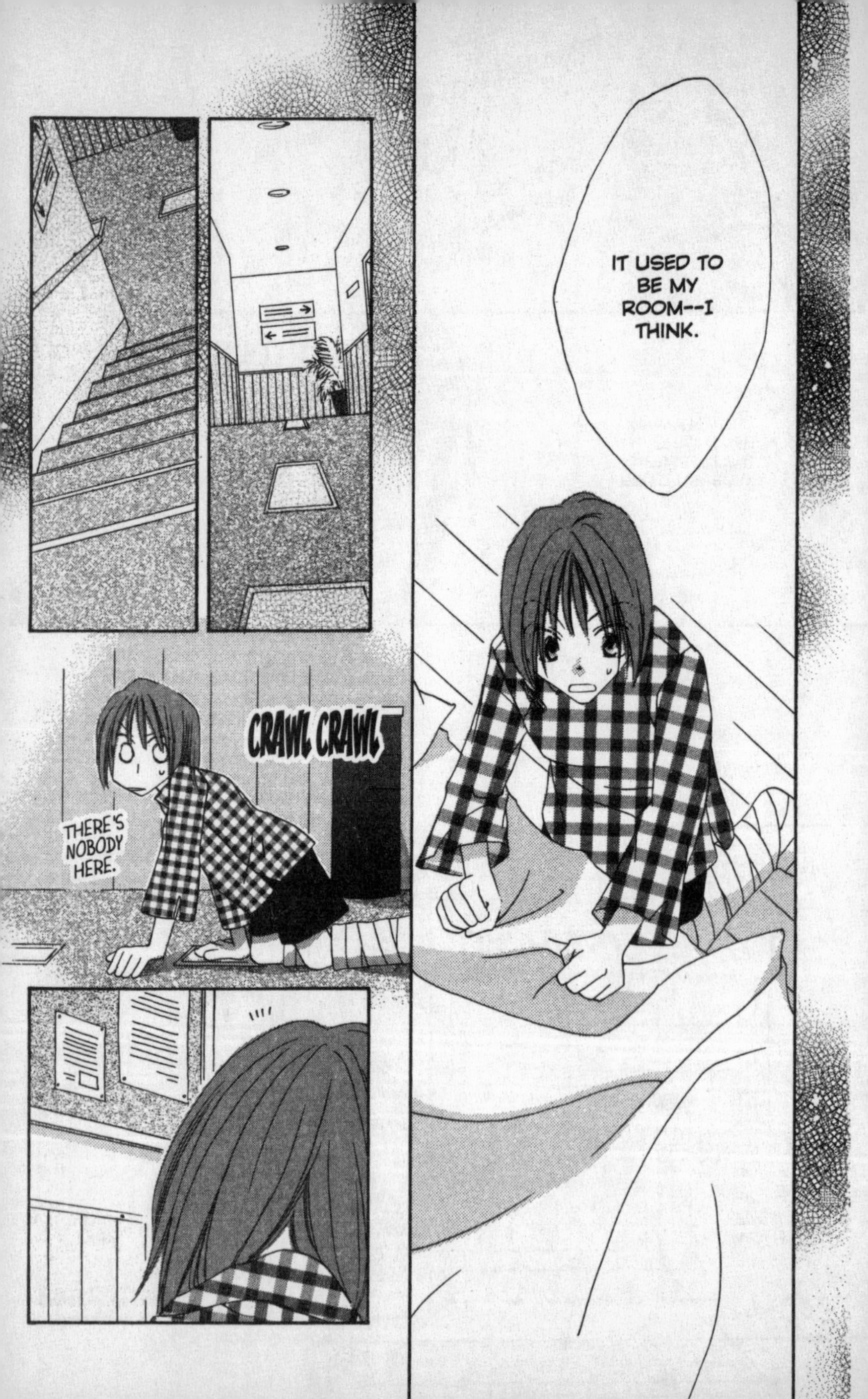
IT USED TO BE MY ROOM--I THINK.
CRAWL CRAWL
THERE'S NOBODY HERE.

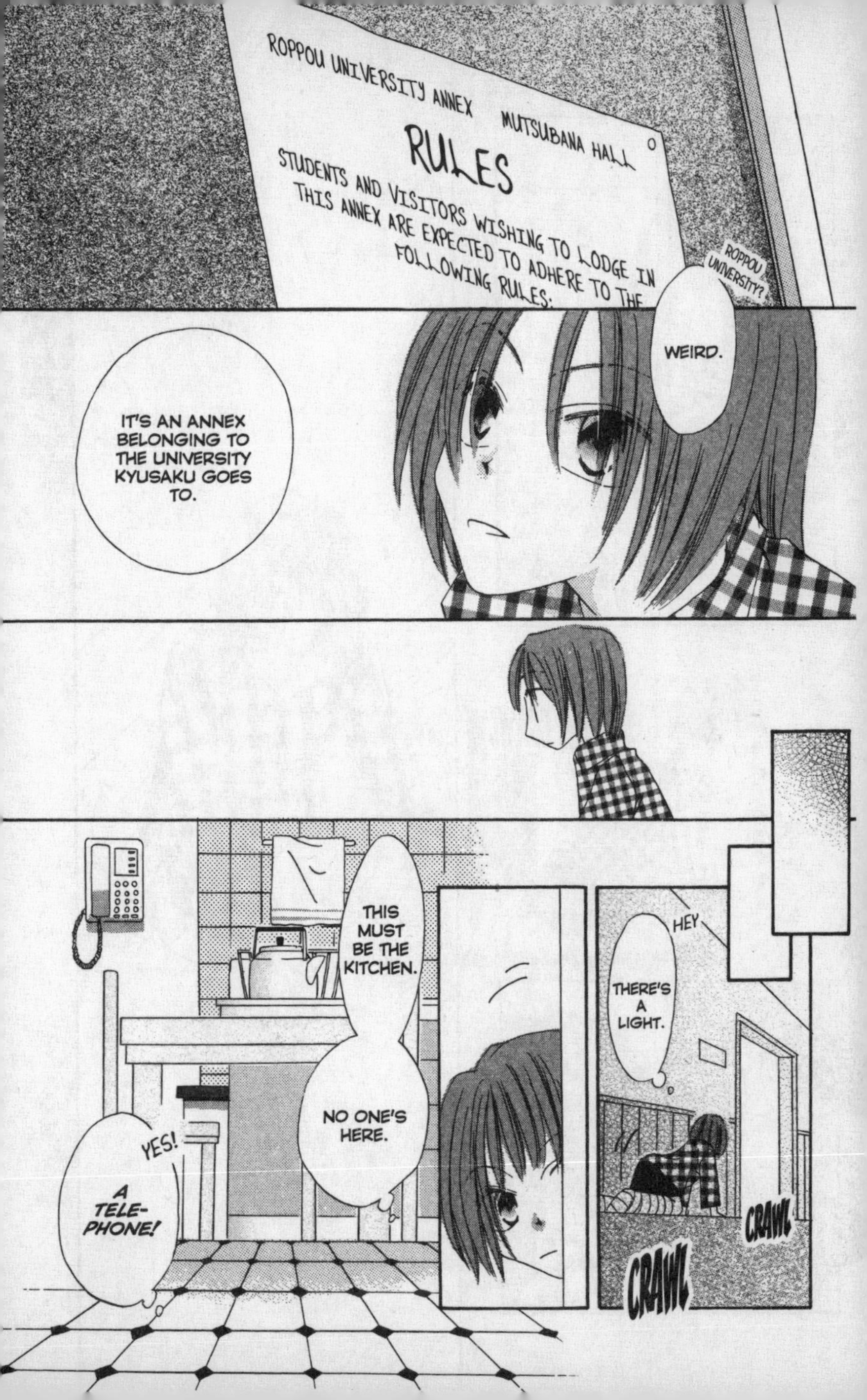
ROPPOU UNIVERSITY ANNEX MUTSUBANA HALL
RULES
STUDENTS AND VISITORS WISHING TO LODGE IN THIS ANNEX ARE EXPECTED TO ADHERE TO THE FOLLOWING RULES:
ROPPOU UNIVERSITY?
WEIRD.
IT'S AN ANNEX BELONGING TO THE UNIVERSITY KYUSAKU GOES TO.
HEY
THERE'S A LIGHT.
CRAWL
CRAWL
THIS MUST BE THE KITCHEN.
NO ONE'S HERE.
YES!
A TELE-PHONE!

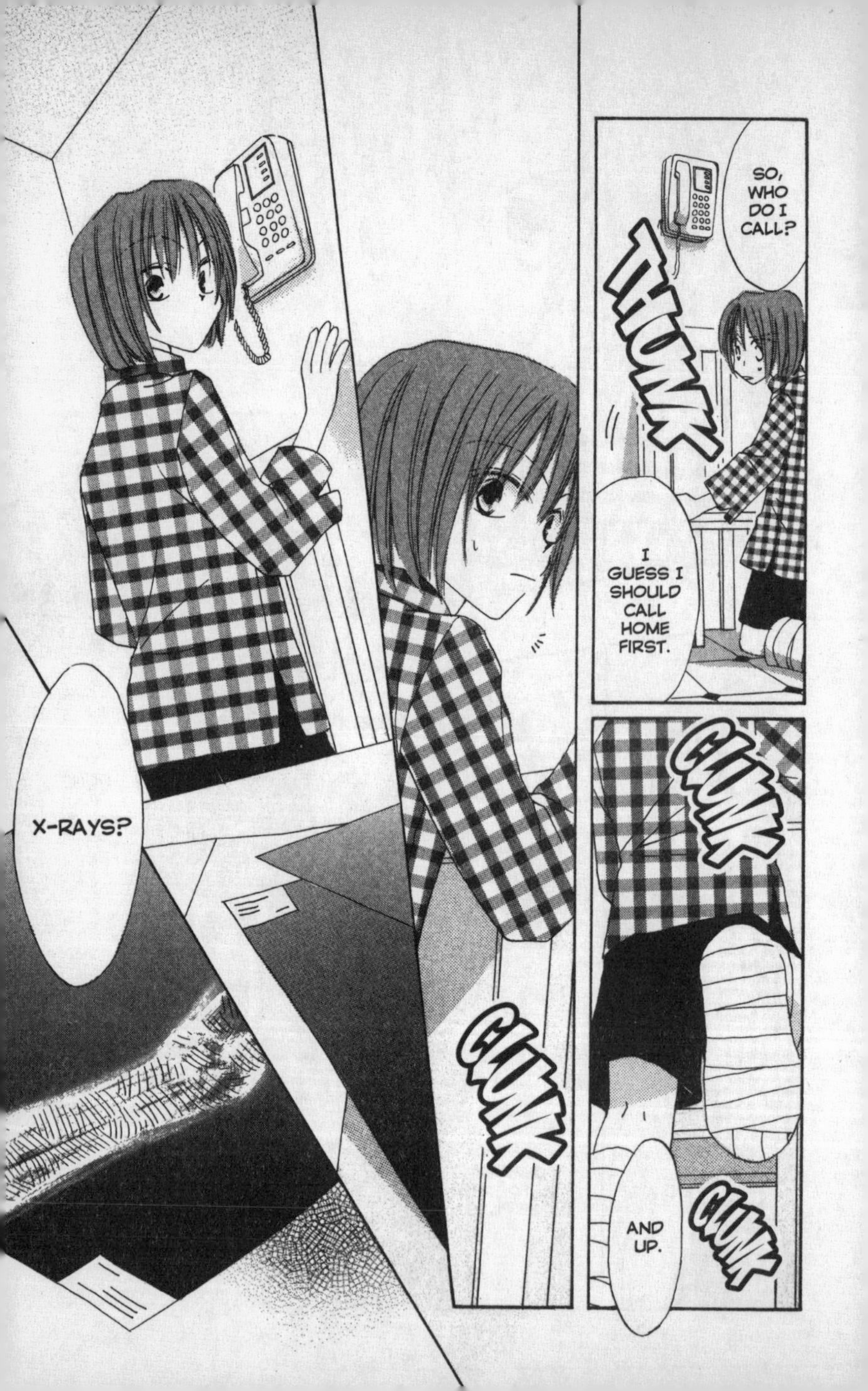
SO, WHO DO I CALL?
THONK
I GUESS I SHOULD CALL HOME FIRST.
CLUNK
CLUNK
AND UP.
CLUNK
X-RAYS?

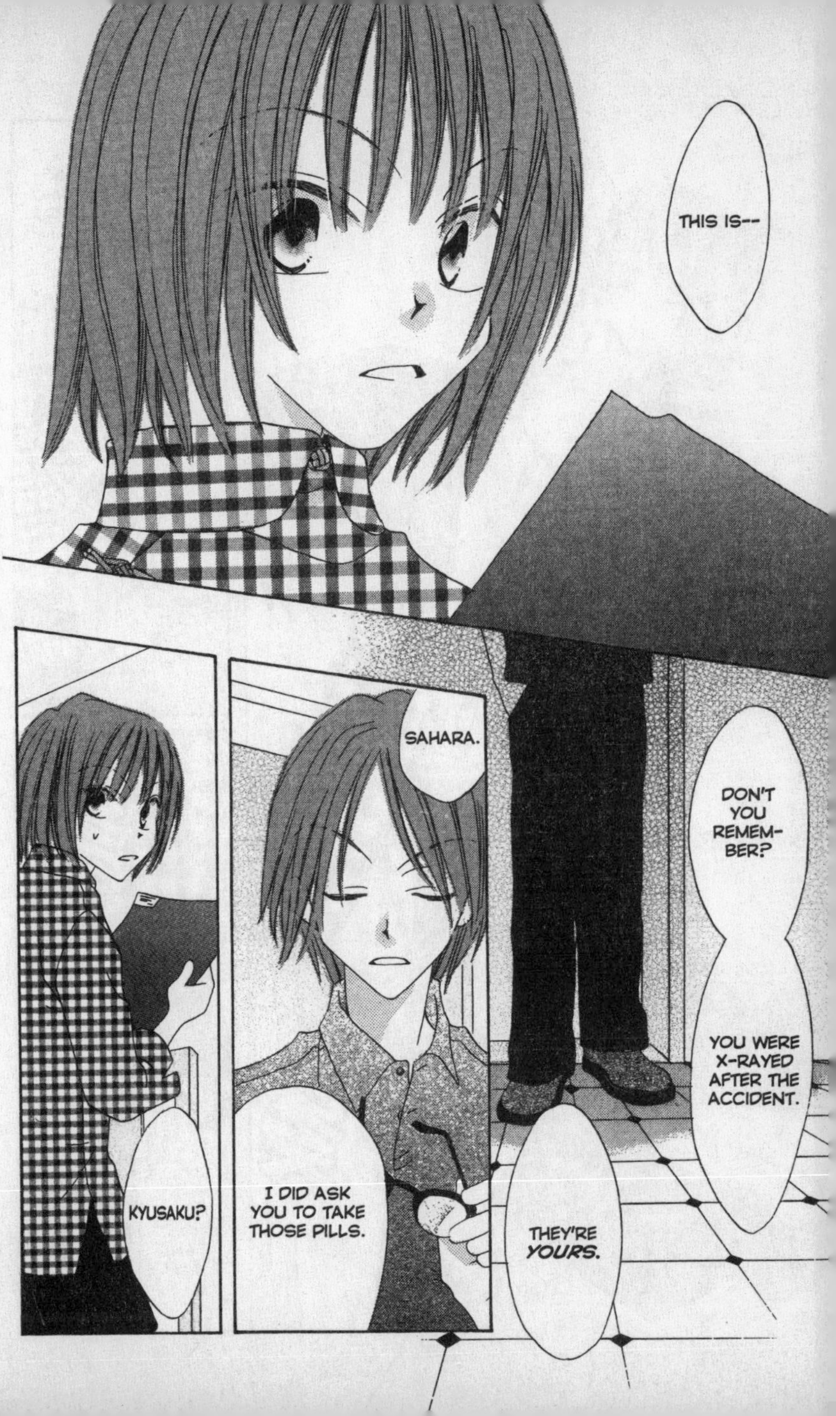
THIS IS--
DON'T YOU REMEM-BER?
YOU WERE X-RAYED AFTER THE ACCIDENT.
THEY'RE *YOURS.*
SAHARA.
I DID ASK YOU TO TAKE THOSE PILLS.
KYUSAKU?

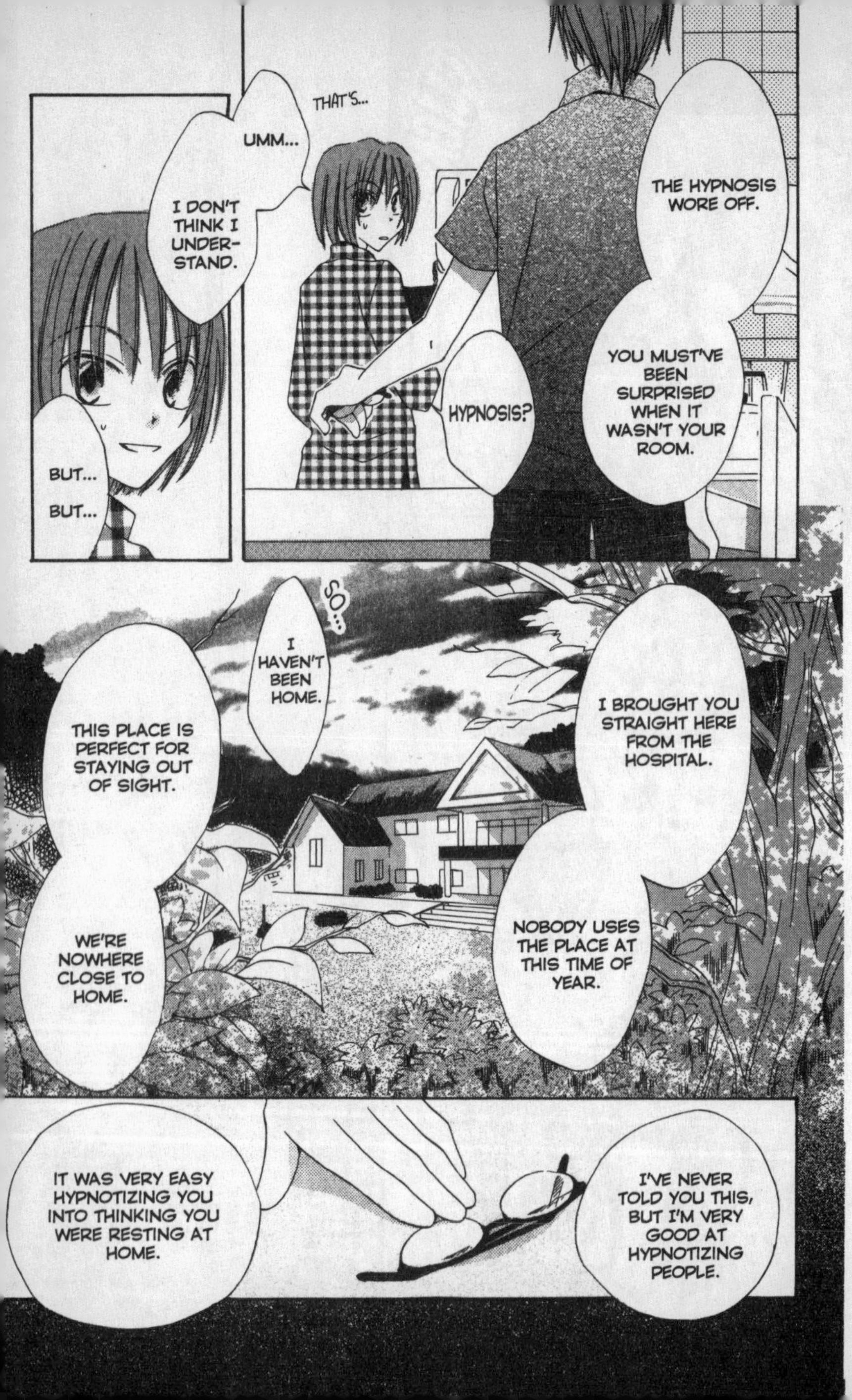

THE HYPNOSIS WORE OFF.
YOU MUST'VE BEEN SURPRISED WHEN IT WASN'T YOUR ROOM.
HYPNOSIS?
THAT'S...
UMM... I DON'T THINK I UNDERSTAND.
BUT... BUT...
I BROUGHT YOU STRAIGHT HERE FROM THE HOSPITAL.
NOBODY USES THE PLACE AT THIS TIME OF YEAR.
SO...
I HAVEN'T BEEN HOME.
THIS PLACE IS PERFECT FOR STAYING OUT OF SIGHT.
WE'RE NOWHERE CLOSE TO HOME.
I'VE NEVER TOLD YOU THIS, BUT I'M VERY GOOD AT HYPNOTIZING PEOPLE.
IT WAS VERY EASY HYPNOTIZING YOU INTO THINKING YOU WERE RESTING AT HOME.

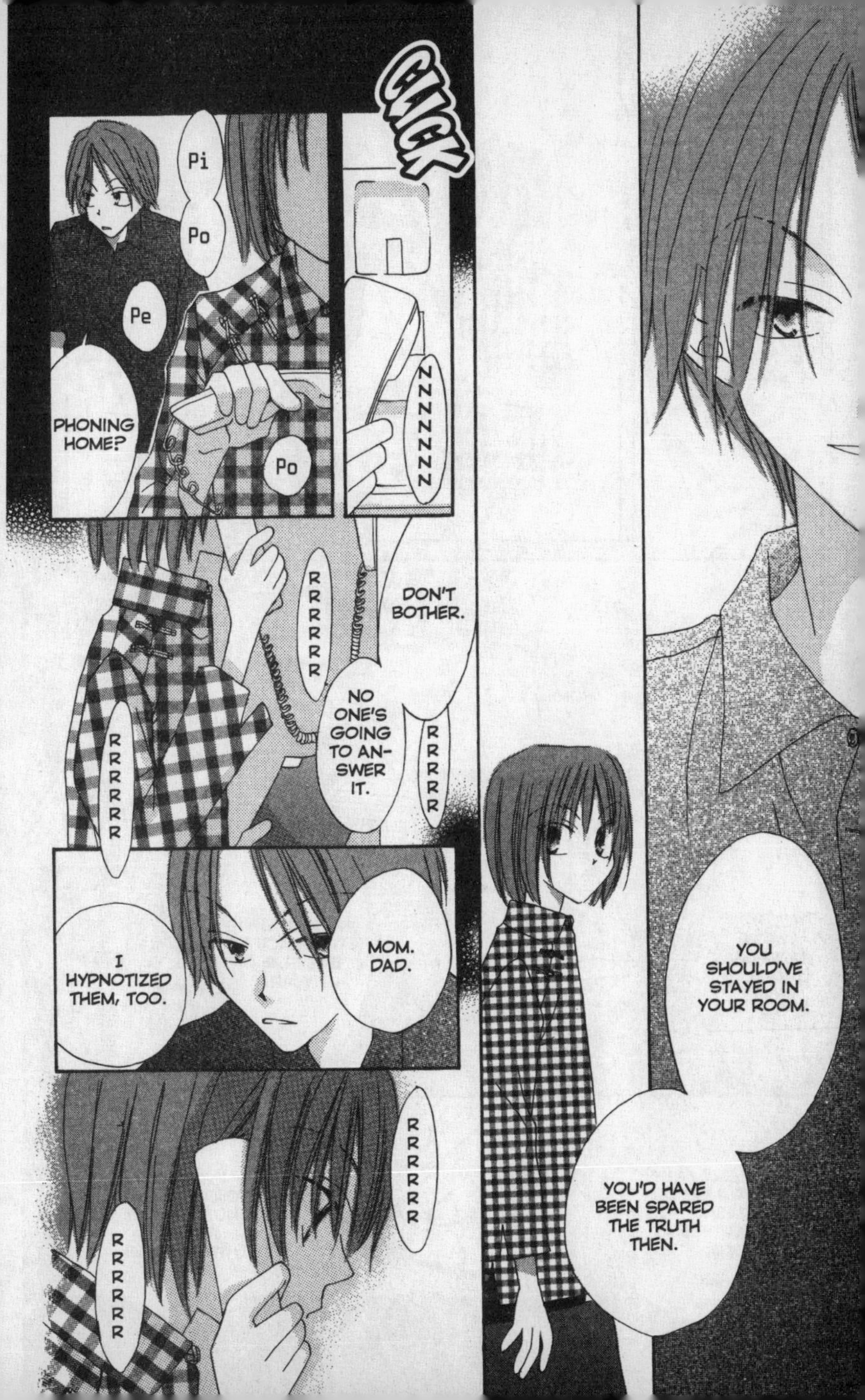
YOU SHOULD'VE STAYED IN YOUR ROOM.
YOU'D HAVE BEEN SPARED THE TRUTH THEN.
CLICK
NNNNNNN
Pi
Po
Pe
Po
PHONING HOME?
DON'T BOTHER.
RRRRR
NO ONE'S GOING TO AN-SWER IT.
RRRRRR
RRRRRR
MOM. DAD.
I HYPNOTIZED THEM, TOO.
RRRRRR
RRRRRR

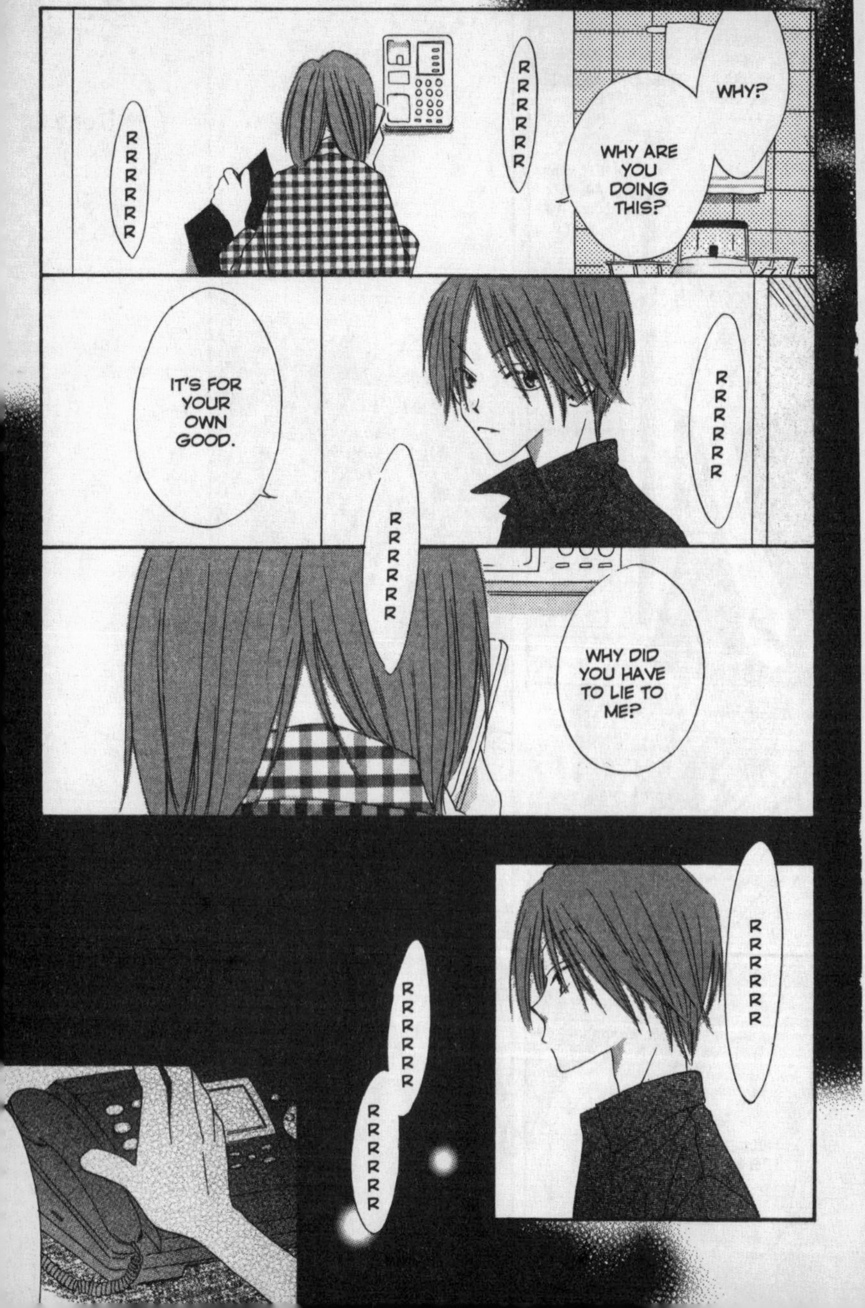
WHY?
WHY ARE YOU DOING THIS?
RRRRRR
RRRRRR
RRRRRR
IT'S FOR YOUR OWN GOOD.
RRRRRR
WHY DID YOU HAVE TO LIE TO ME?
RRRRRR
RRRRRR
RRRRR

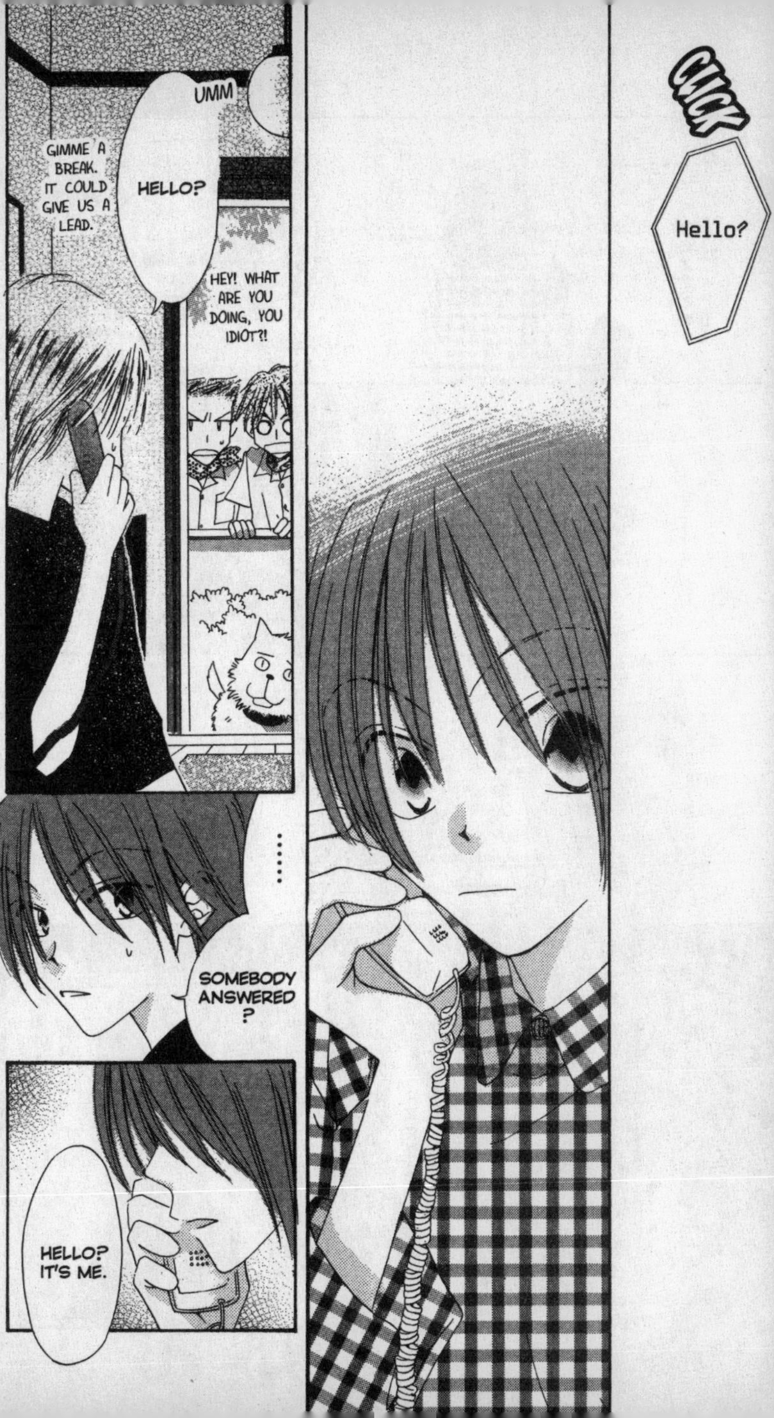
CLICK
Hello?
UMM
HELLO?
HEY! WHAT ARE YOU DOING, YOU IDIOT?!
GIMME A BREAK. IT COULD GIVE US A LEAD.
......
SOMEBODY ANSWERED?
HELLO? IT'S ME.

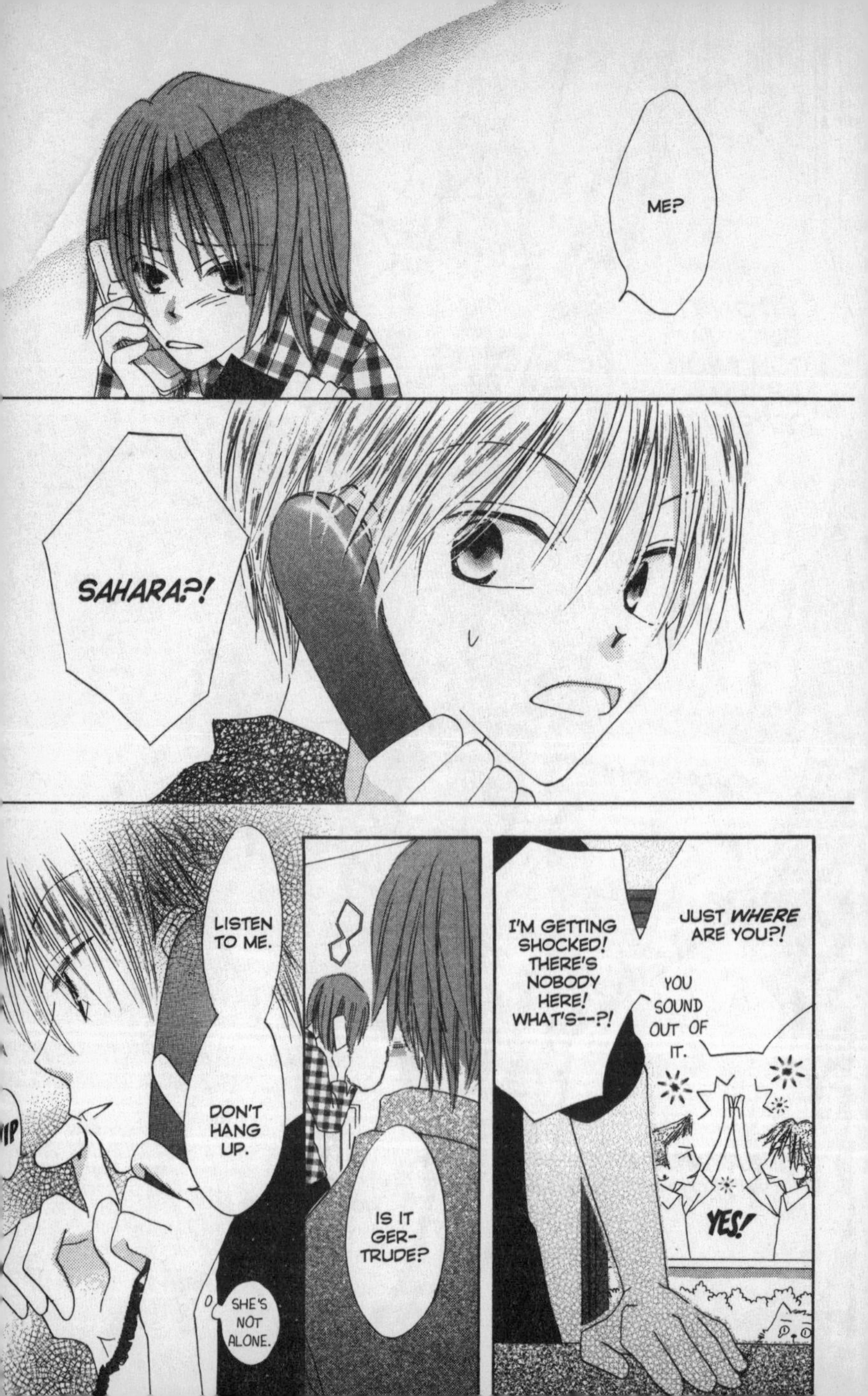
ME?
SAHARA?!
JUST *WHERE* ARE YOU?!
I'M GETTING SHOCKED! THERE'S NOBODY HERE! WHAT'S--?!
YOU SOUND OUT OF IT.
YES!
IS IT GER-TRUDE?
SHE'S NOT ALONE.
LISTEN TO ME.
DON'T HANG UP.

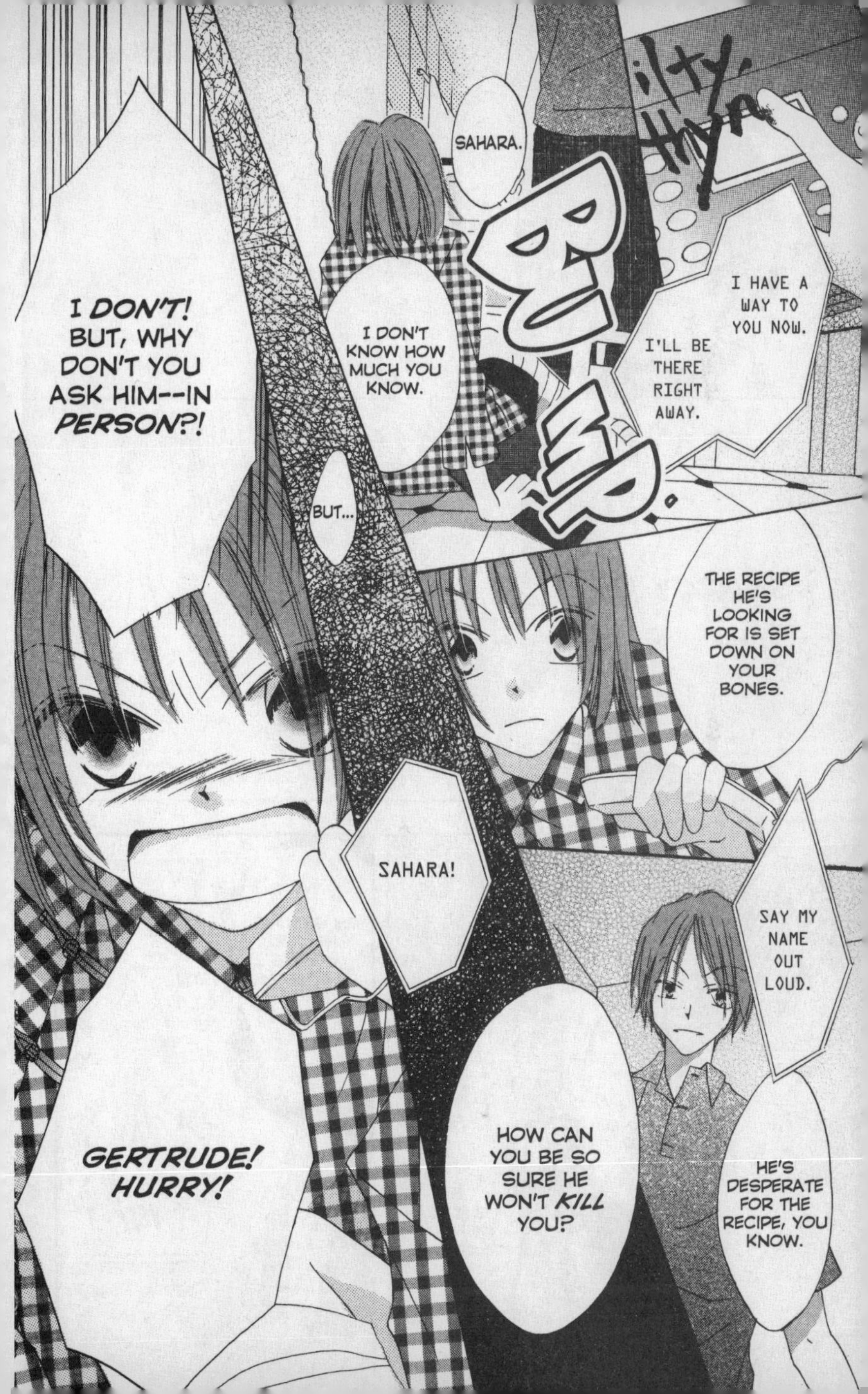
SAHARA.
I HAVE A WAY TO YOU NOW.
I'LL BE THERE RIGHT AWAY.
BUMP.
I DON'T KNOW HOW MUCH YOU KNOW.
BUT...
THE RECIPE HE'S LOOKING FOR IS SET DOWN ON YOUR BONES.
SAHARA!
SAY MY NAME OUT LOUD.
HE'S DESPERATE FOR THE RECIPE, YOU KNOW.
HOW CAN YOU BE SO SURE HE WON'T *KILL* YOU?
I *DON'T*! BUT, WHY DON'T YOU ASK HIM--IN *PERSON*?!
GERTRUDE! HURRY!

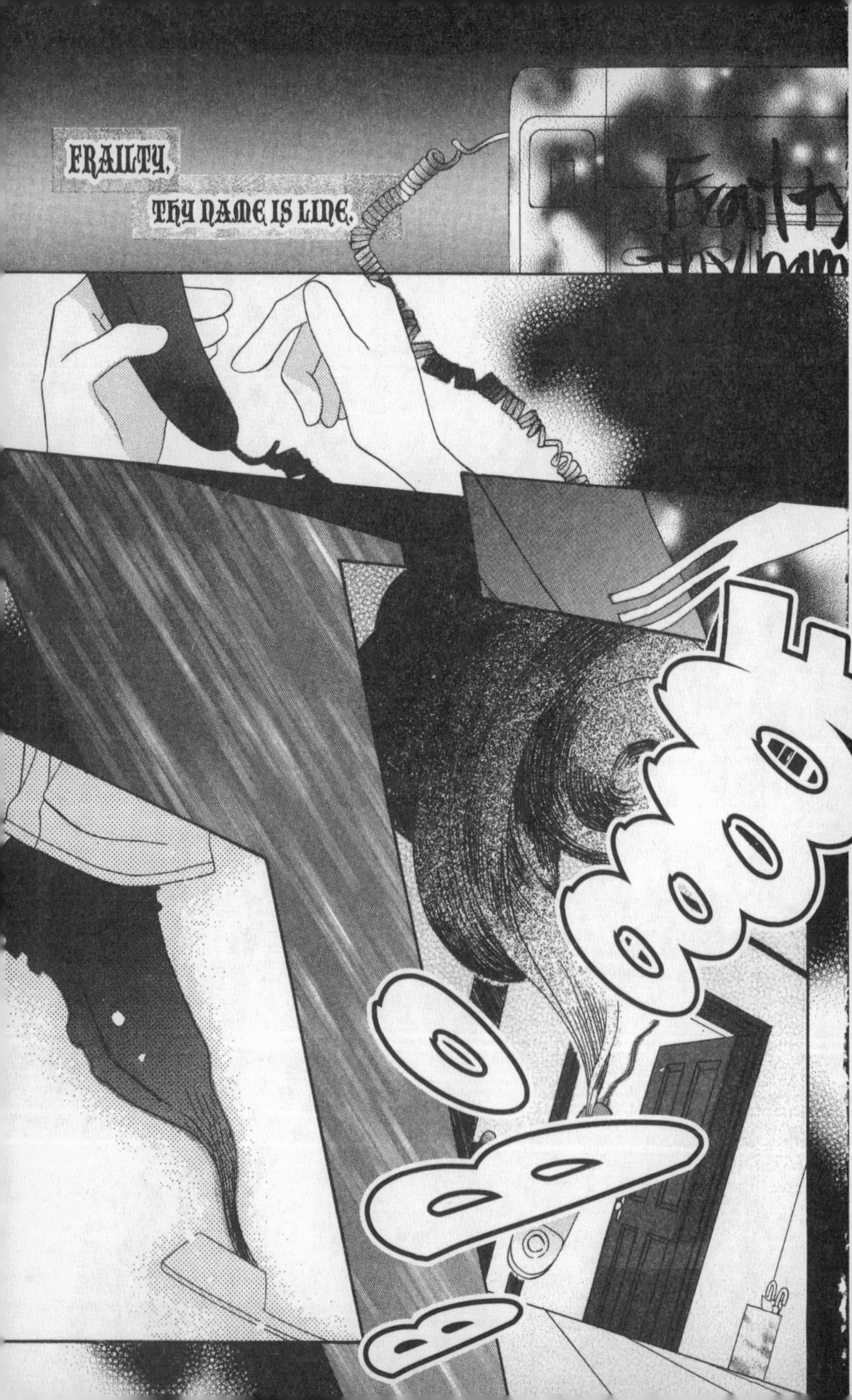
FRAILTY,
THY NAME IS LINE.

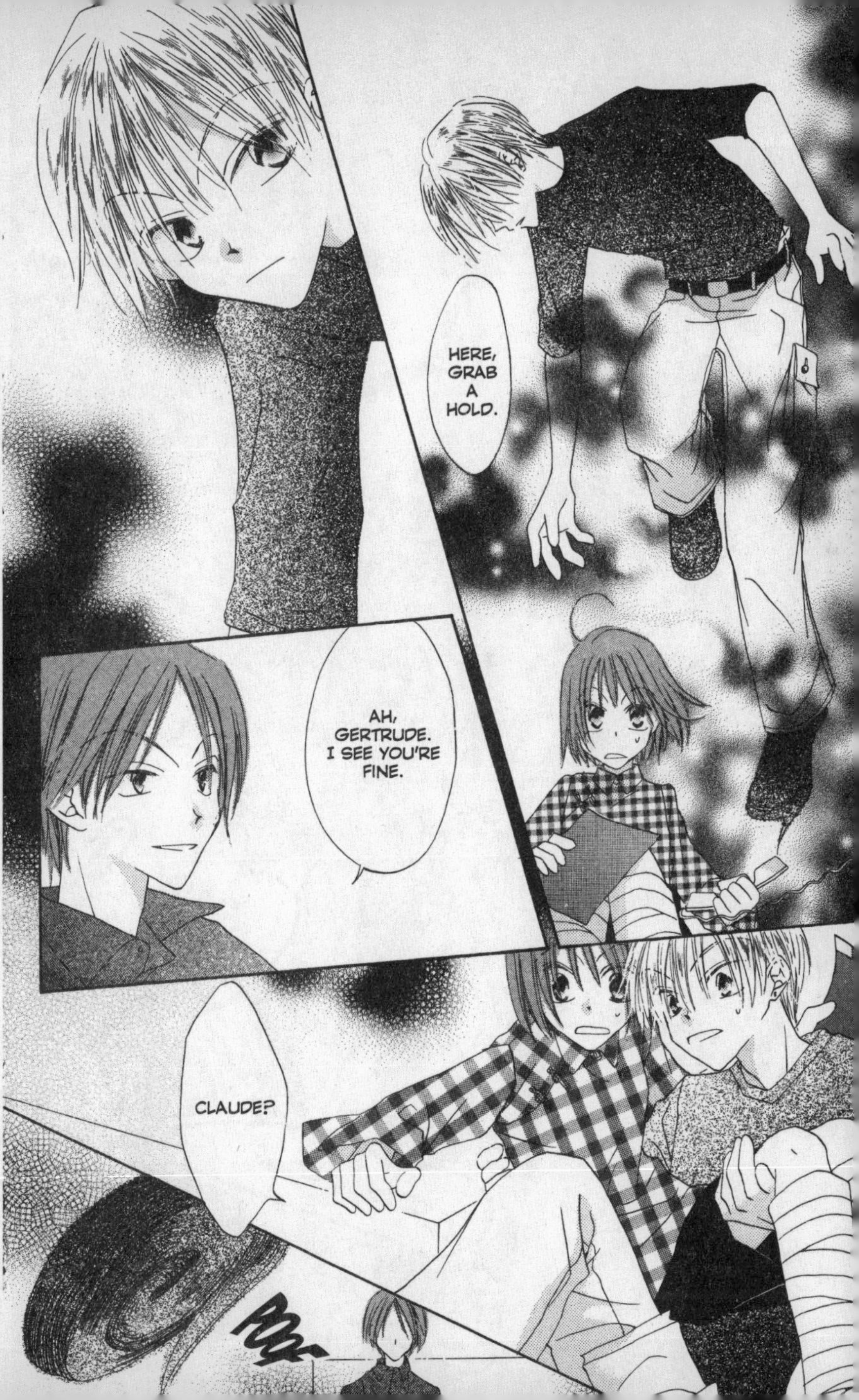
HERE, GRAB A HOLD.
AH, GERTRUDE. I SEE YOU'RE FINE.
CLAUDE?

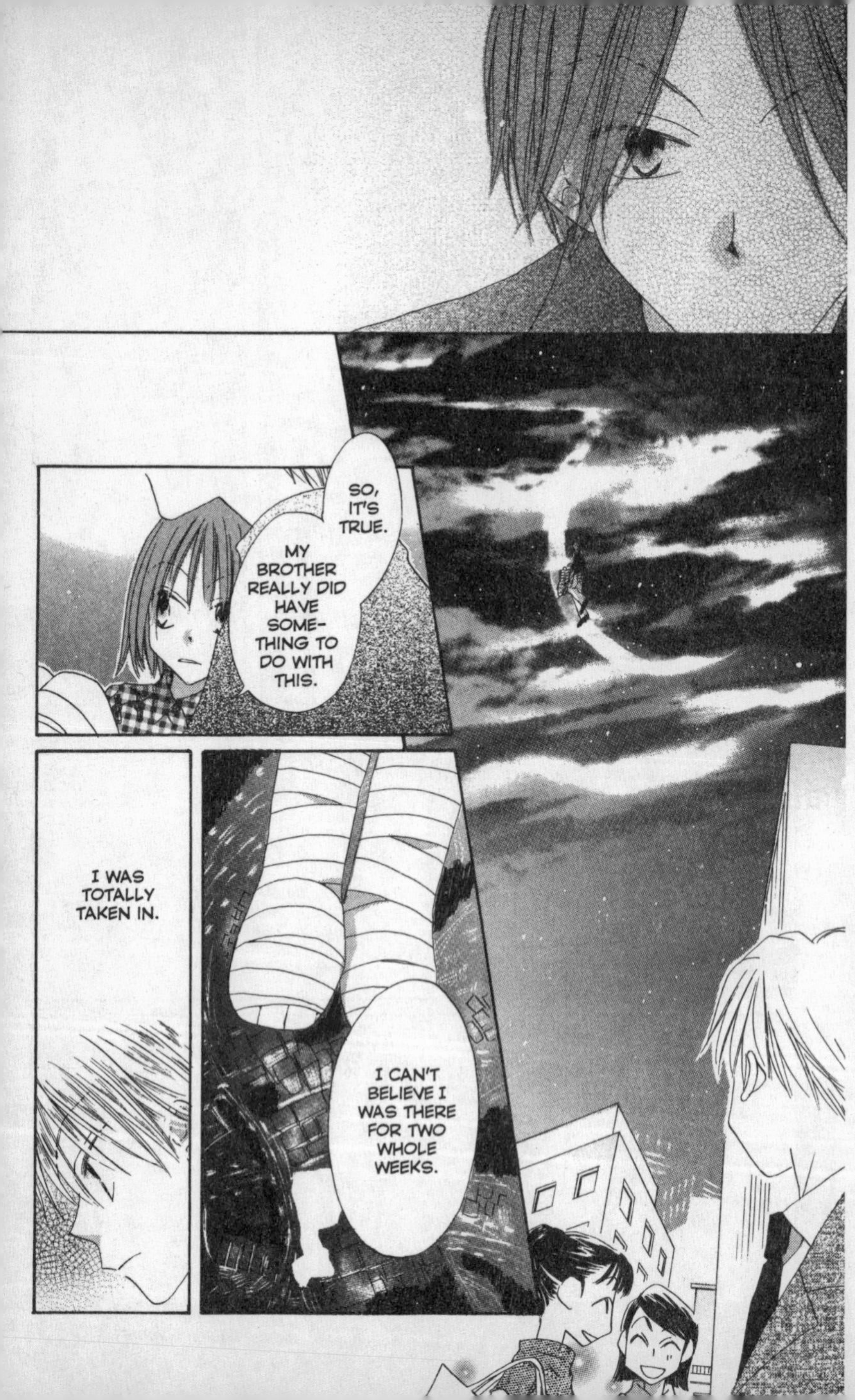
SO, IT'S TRUE.
MY BROTHER REALLY DID HAVE SOME-THING TO DO WITH THIS.
I CAN'T BELIEVE I WAS THERE FOR TWO WHOLE WEEKS.
I WAS TOTALLY TAKEN IN.

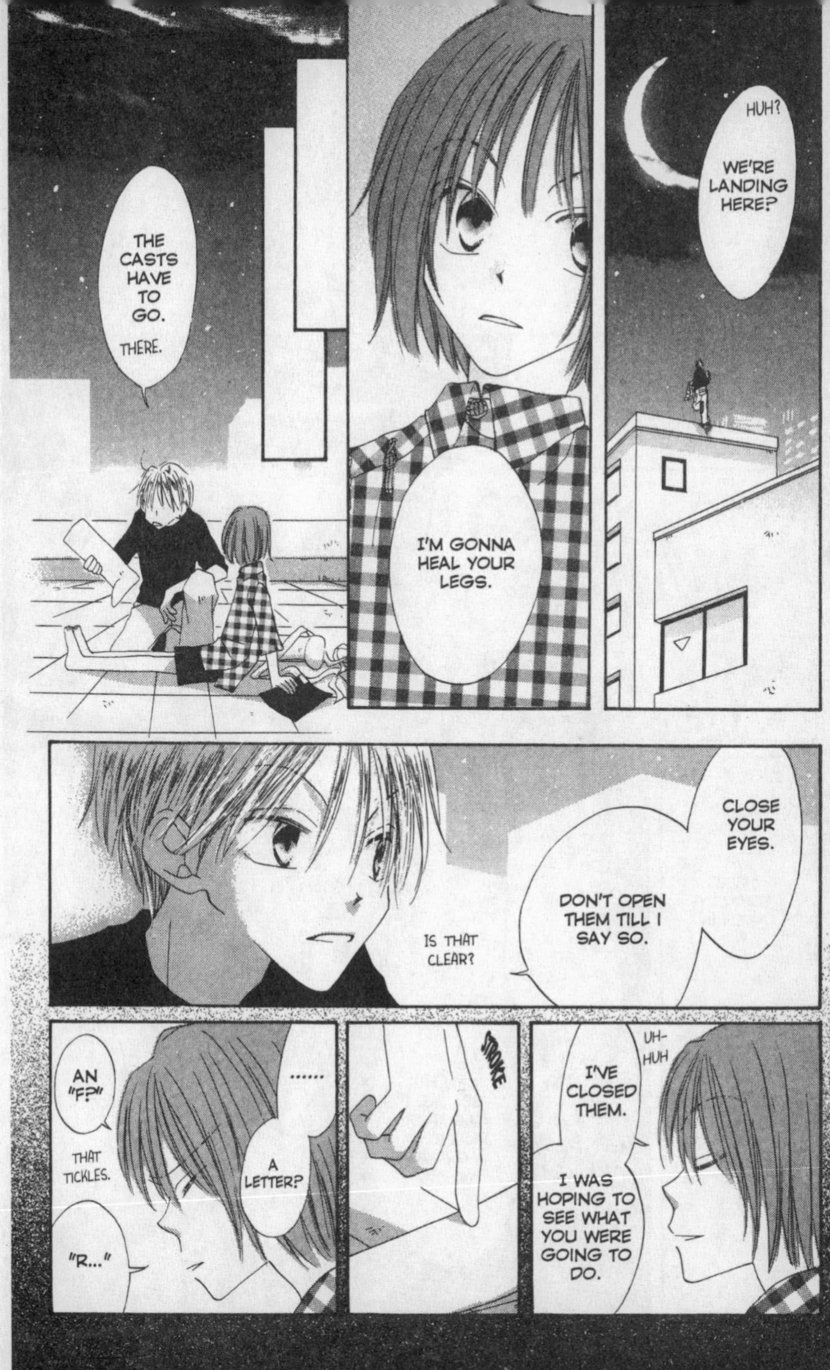
HUH?
WE'RE LANDING HERE?
I'M GONNA HEAL YOUR LEGS.
THE CASTS HAVE TO GO.
THERE.
CLOSE YOUR EYES.
DON'T OPEN THEM TILL I SAY SO.
IS THAT CLEAR?
UH-HUH
I'VE CLOSED THEM.
I WAS HOPING TO SEE WHAT YOU WERE GOING TO DO.
STROKE
......
AN "F?"
A LETTER?
THAT TICKLES.
"R..."

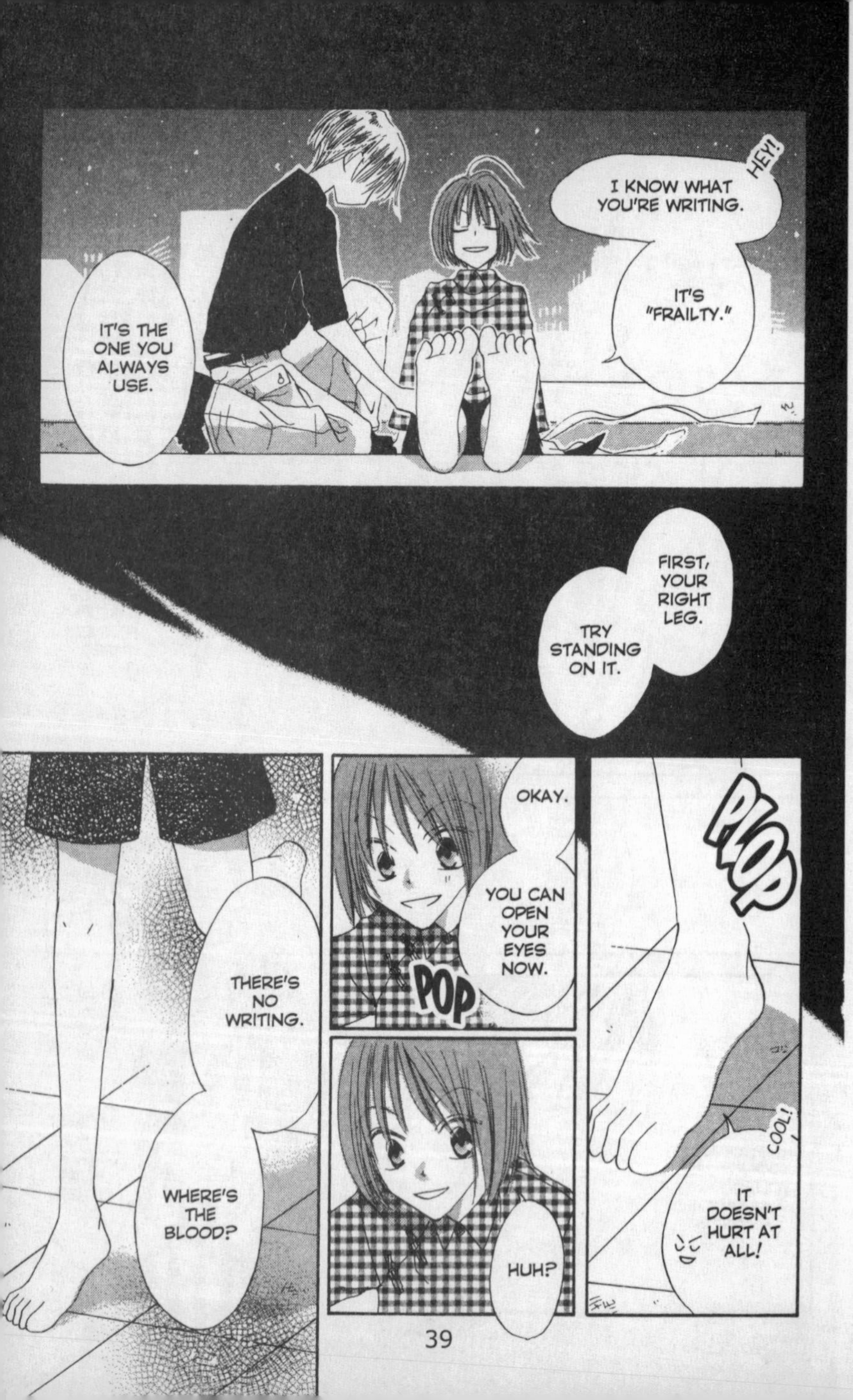
HEY!
I KNOW WHAT YOU'RE WRITING.
IT'S "FRAILTY."
IT'S THE ONE YOU ALWAYS USE.
FIRST, YOUR RIGHT LEG.
TRY STANDING ON IT.
PLOP
COOL!
IT DOESN'T HURT AT ALL!
OKAY.
YOU CAN OPEN YOUR EYES NOW.
POP
HUH?
THERE'S NO WRITING.
WHERE'S THE BLOOD?

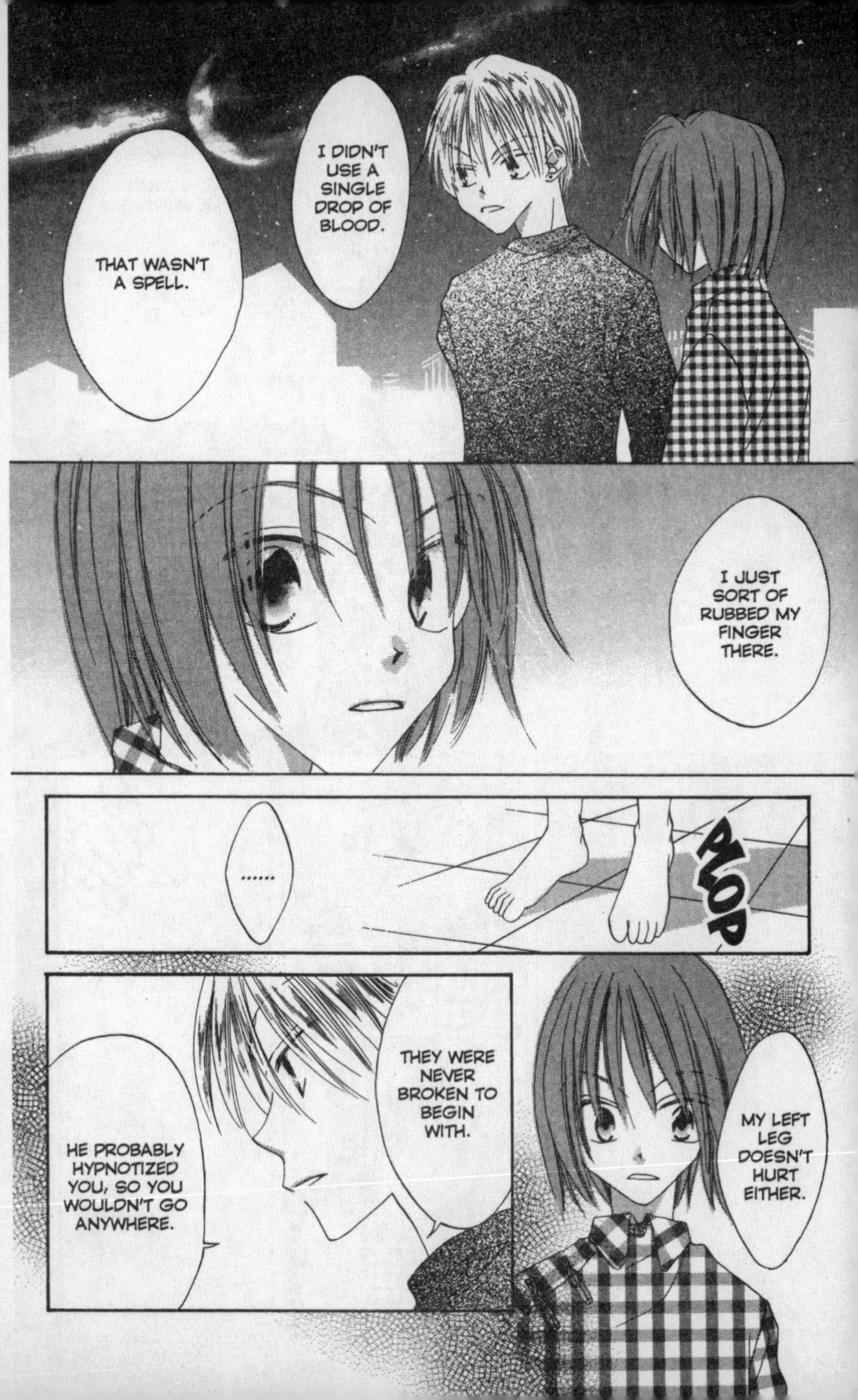
I DIDN'T USE A SINGLE DROP OF BLOOD.
THAT WASN'T A SPELL.
I JUST SORT OF RUBBED MY FINGER THERE.
PLOP
......
MY LEFT LEG DOESN'T HURT EITHER.
THEY WERE NEVER BROKEN TO BEGIN WITH.
HE PROBABLY HYPNOTIZED YOU, SO YOU WOULDN'T GO ANYWHERE.

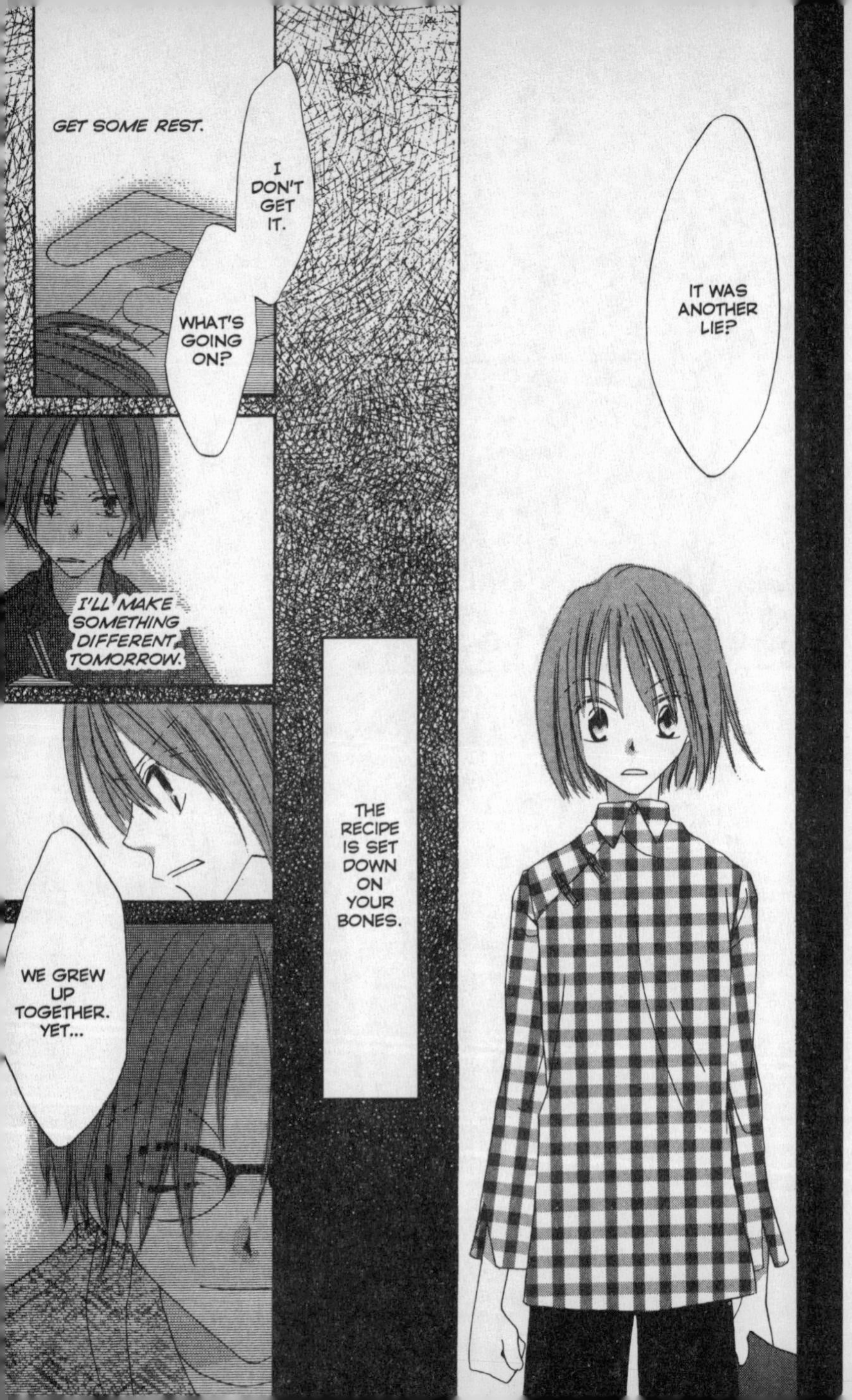
IT WAS ANOTHER LIE?
THE RECIPE IS SET DOWN ON YOUR BONES.
I DON'T GET IT.
WHAT'S GOING ON?
GET SOME REST.
I'LL MAKE SOMETHING DIFFERENT TOMORROW.
WE GREW UP TOGETHER. YET...

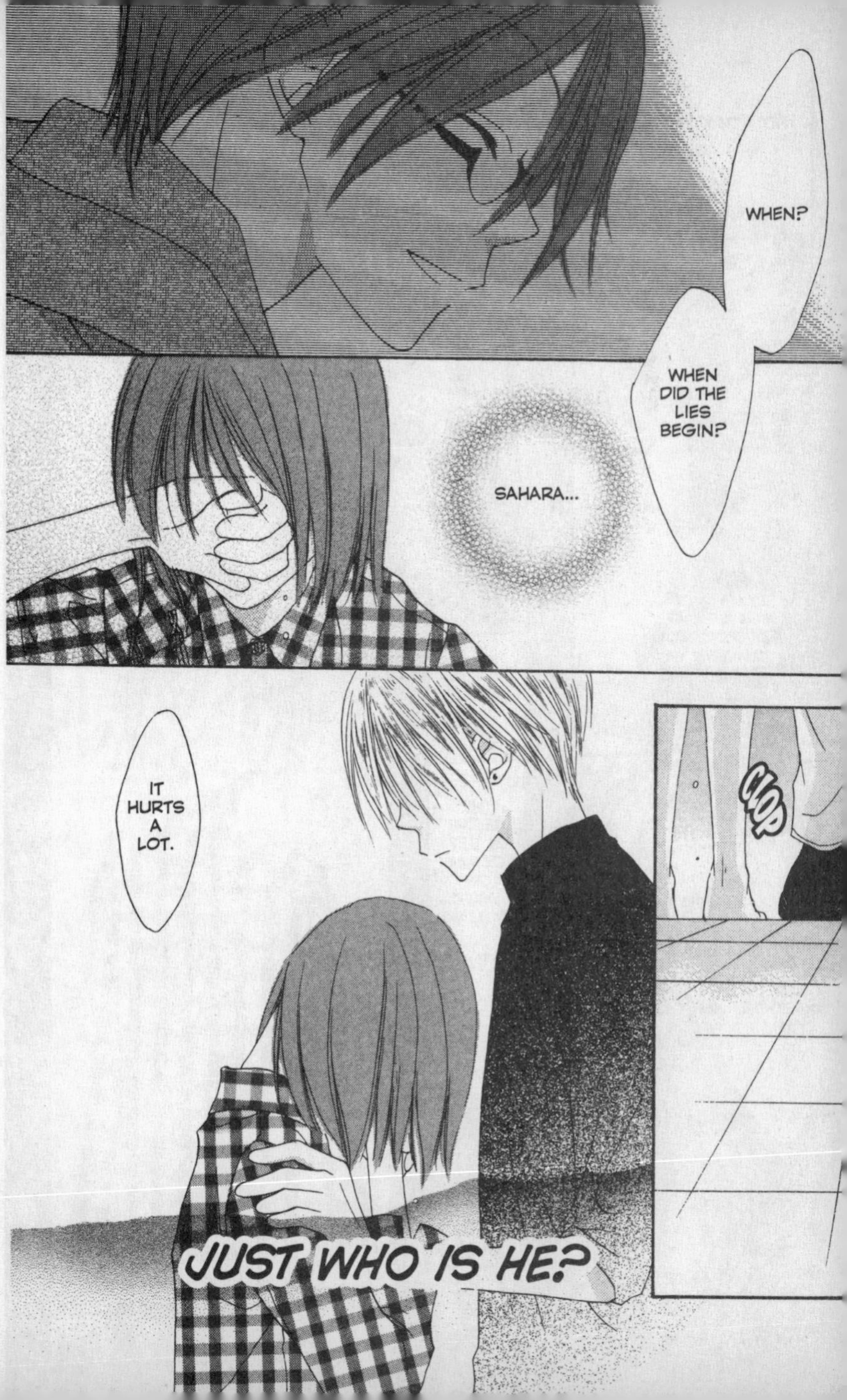
WHEN?
WHEN DID THE LIES BEGIN?
SAHARA...
CLOP
IT HURTS A LOT.
JUST WHO IS HE?

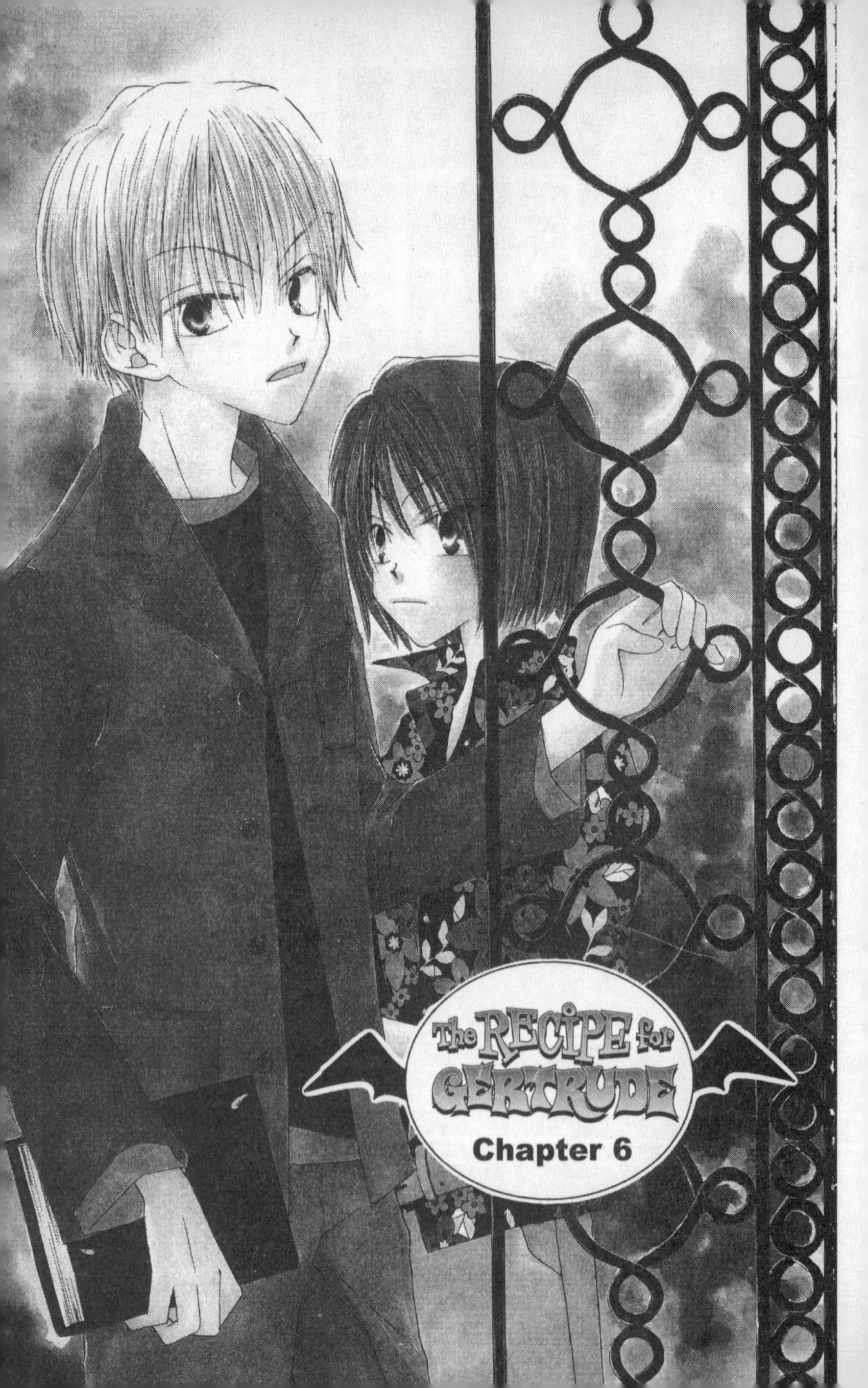
The RECIPE for GERTRUDE
Chapter 6

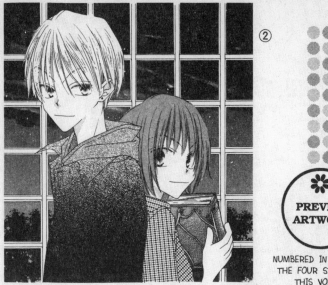

PREVIEW ARTWORK

NUMBERED IN ORDER OF THE FOUR STORIES IN THIS VOLUME.

②

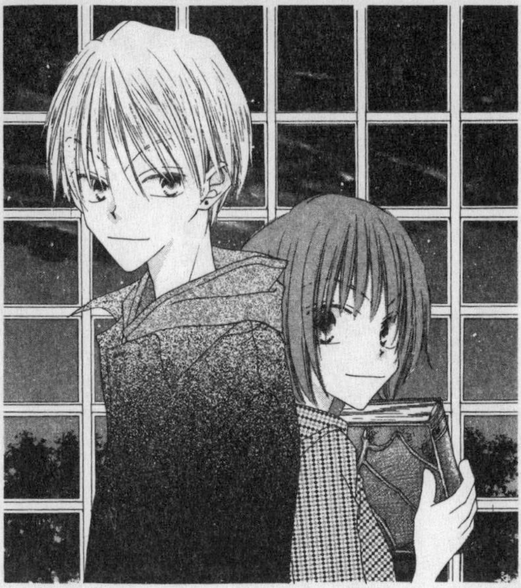

①

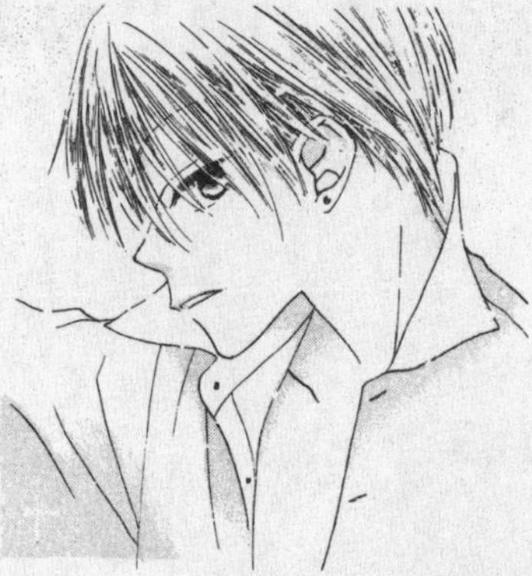

③

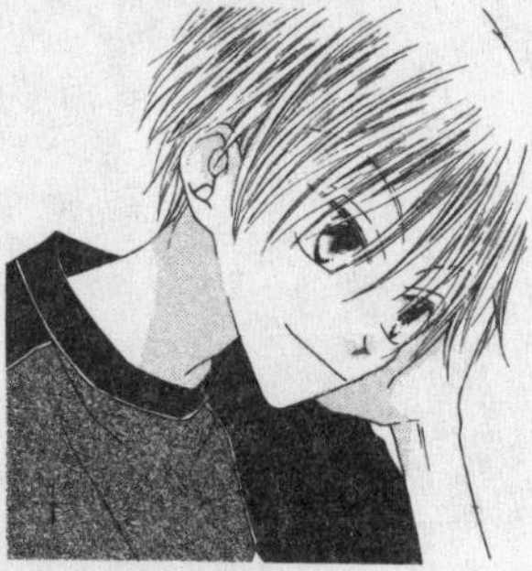

① I opted for a breezy look because it was almost summer when the story appeared in the anthology.

② Preview drawings and cover art always take time because the ideas are never there. It took me a long time to figure out what to do for the background.

③ I often have him resting his head on his hand, like here.

④ I reversed the two. The amount of hair Puppen has is shocking.

④

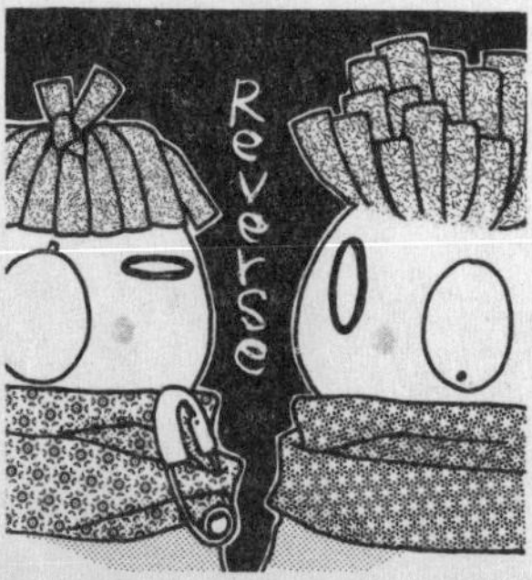
Reverse

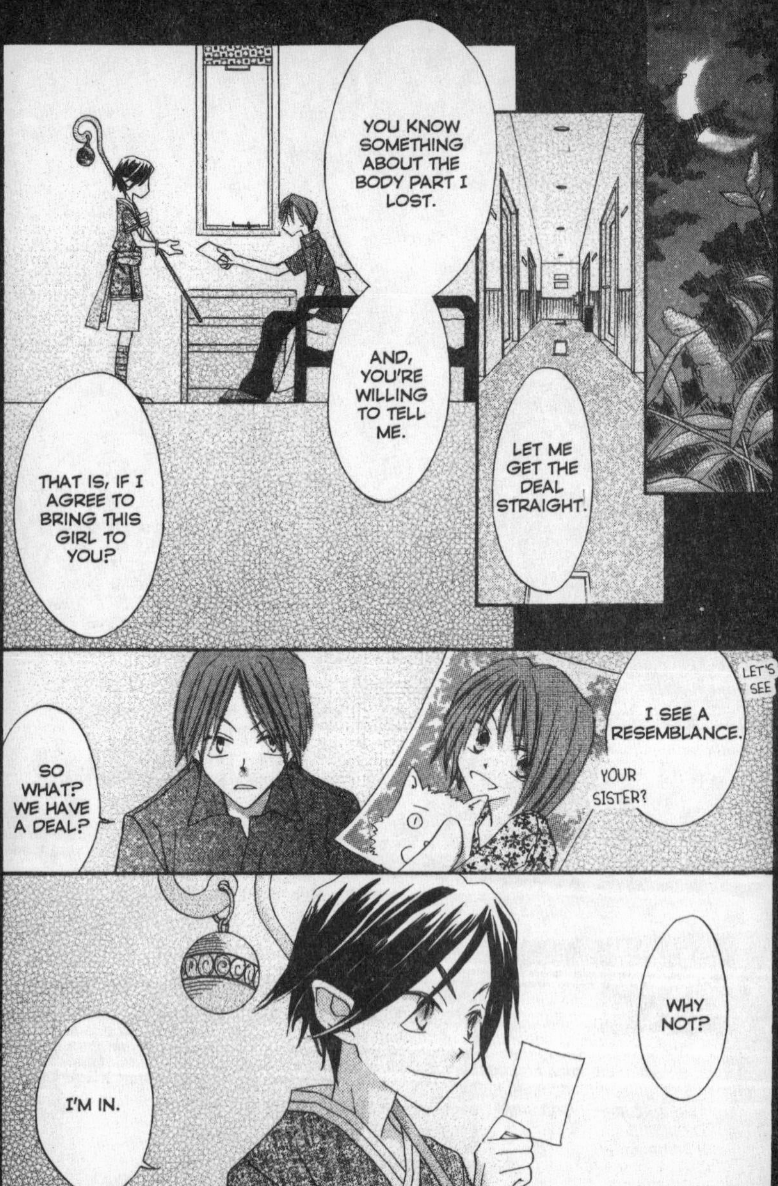
LET ME GET THE DEAL STRAIGHT.
YOU KNOW SOMETHING ABOUT THE BODY PART I LOST.
AND, YOU'RE WILLING TO TELL ME.
THAT IS, IF I AGREE TO BRING THIS GIRL TO YOU?
LET'S SEE
I SEE A RESEMBLANCE.
YOUR SISTER?
SO WHAT? WE HAVE A DEAL?
WHY NOT?
I'M IN.

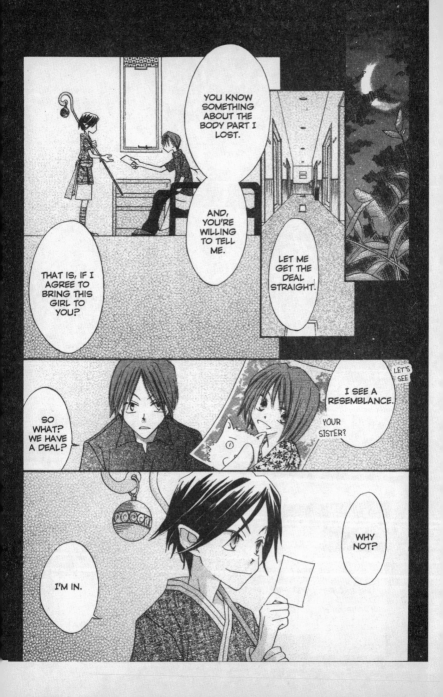

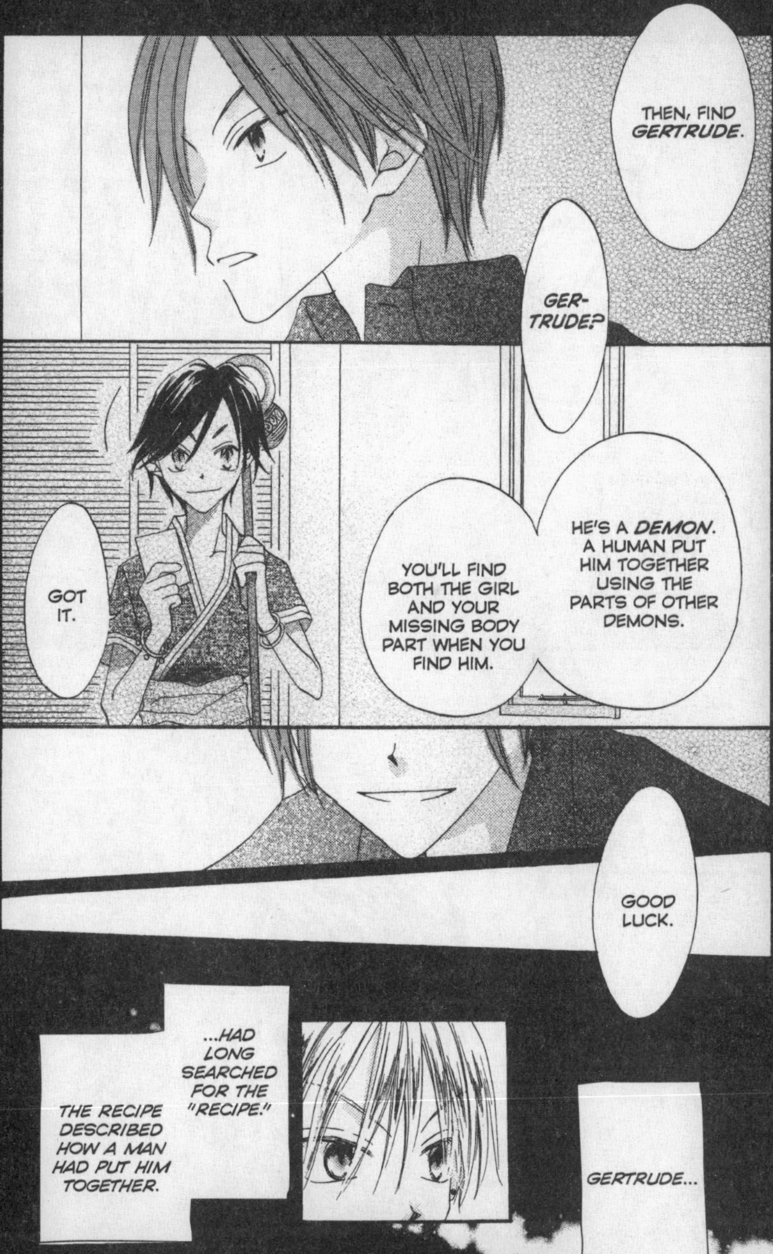
THEN, FIND *GERTRUDE*.
GER-TRUDE?
HE'S A *DEMON*. A HUMAN PUT HIM TOGETHER USING THE PARTS OF OTHER DEMONS.
YOU'LL FIND BOTH THE GIRL AND YOUR MISSING BODY PART WHEN YOU FIND HIM.
GOT IT.
GOOD LUCK.
GERTRUDE...
...HAD LONG SEARCHED FOR THE "RECIPE."
THE RECIPE DESCRIBED HOW A MAN HAD PUT HIM TOGETHER.

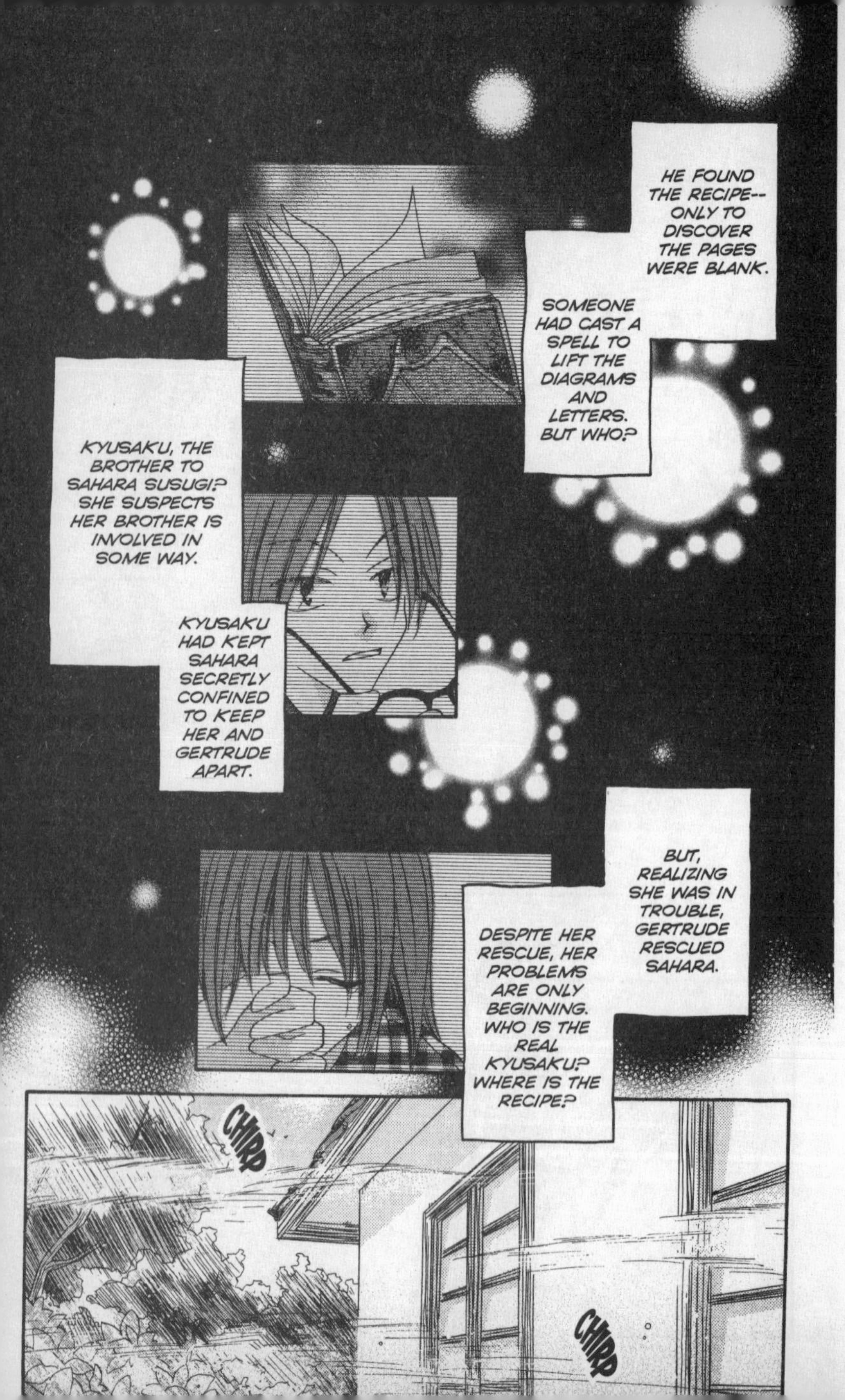
HE FOUND THE RECIPE-- ONLY TO DISCOVER THE PAGES WERE BLANK.
SOMEONE HAD CAST A SPELL TO LIFT THE DIAGRAMS AND LETTERS. BUT WHO?
KYUSAKU, THE BROTHER TO SAHARA SUSUGI? SHE SUSPECTS HER BROTHER IS INVOLVED IN SOME WAY.
KYUSAKU HAD KEPT SAHARA SECRETLY CONFINED TO KEEP HER AND GERTRUDE APART.
BUT, REALIZING SHE WAS IN TROUBLE, GERTRUDE RESCUED SAHARA.
DESPITE HER RESCUE, HER PROBLEMS ARE ONLY BEGINNING. WHO IS THE REAL KYUSAKU? WHERE IS THE RECIPE?
CHIRP
CHIRP

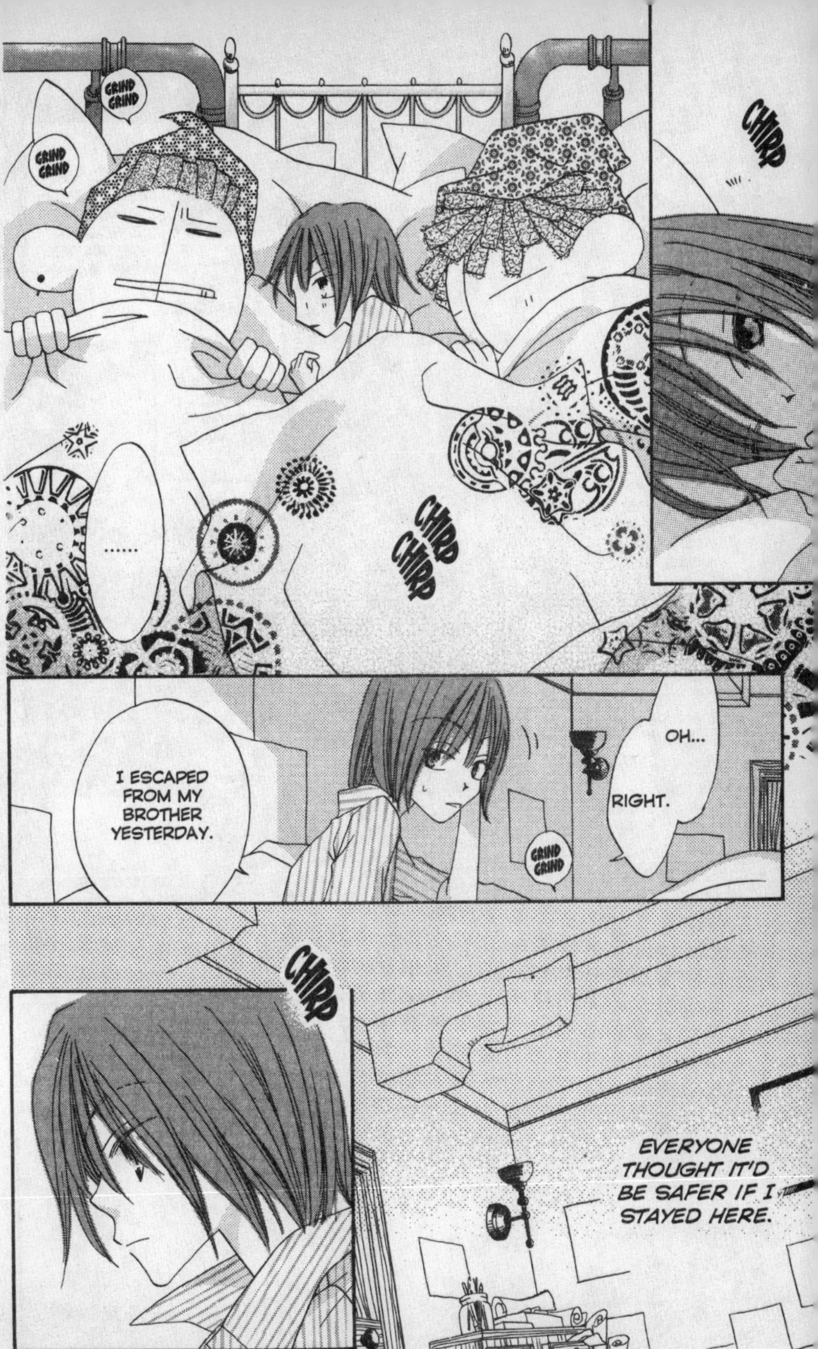
CHIRP
GRIND GRIND
GRIND GRIND
......
CHIRP CHIRP
OH... RIGHT.
I ESCAPED FROM MY BROTHER YESTERDAY.
GRIND GRIND
EVERYONE THOUGHT IT'D BE SAFER IF I STAYED HERE.
CHIRP

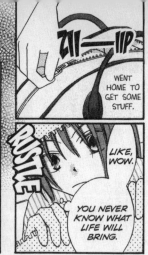

WENT HOME TO GET SOME STUFF.

RUSTLE

LIKE, WOW.

YOU NEVER KNOW WHAT LIFE WILL BRING.

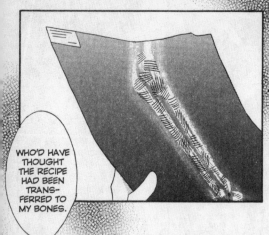

WHO'D HAVE THOUGHT THE RECIPE HAD BEEN TRANSFERRED TO MY BONES.

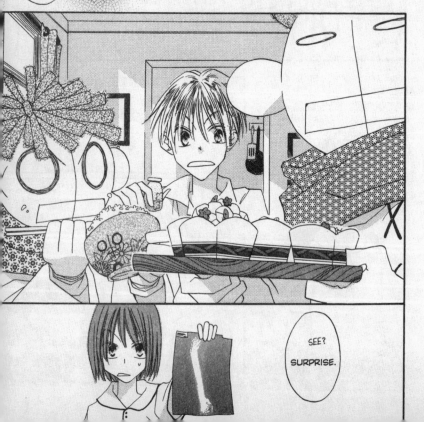

SEE?

SURPRISE.

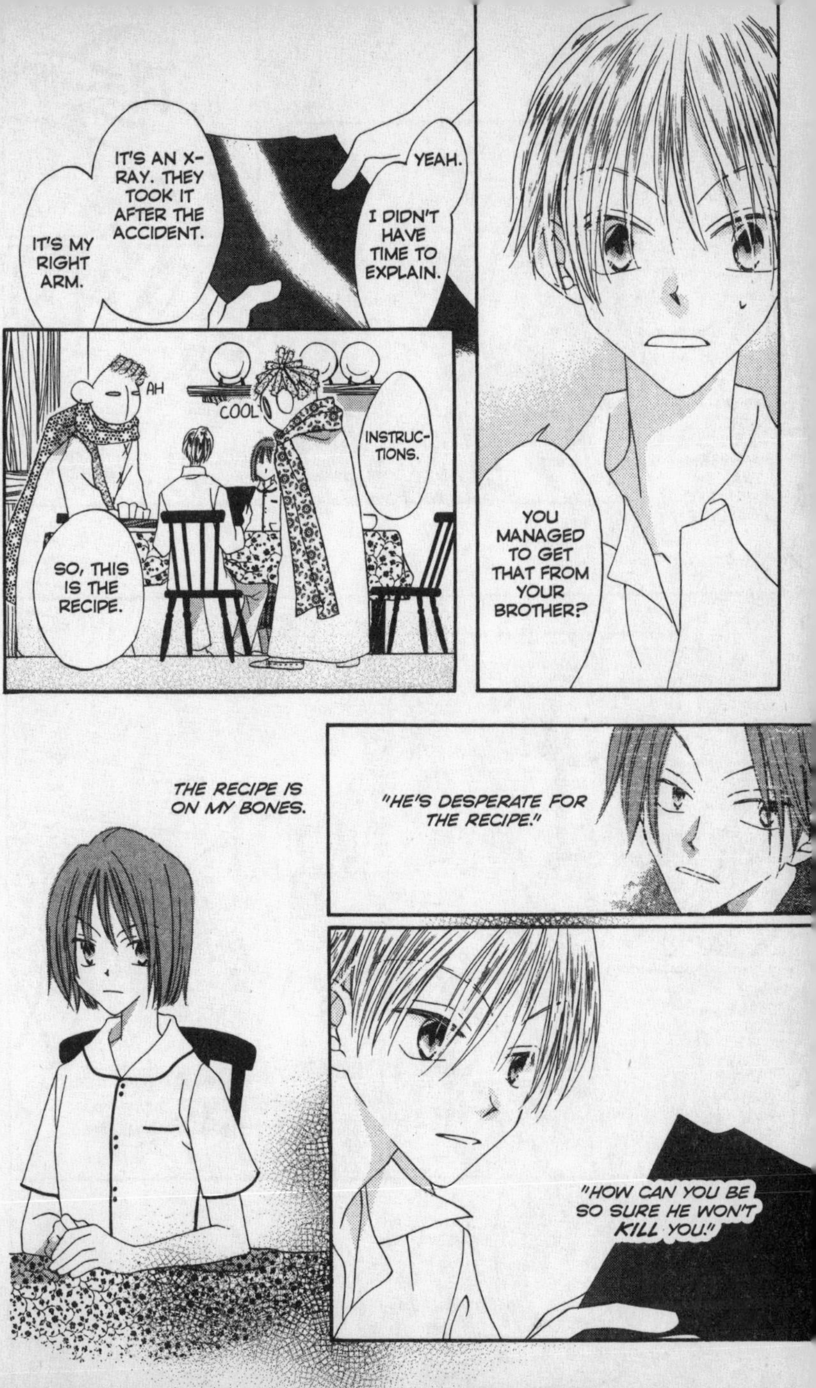
YOU MANAGED TO GET THAT FROM YOUR BROTHER?
YEAH.
I DIDN'T HAVE TIME TO EXPLAIN.
IT'S AN X-RAY. THEY TOOK IT AFTER THE ACCIDENT.
IT'S MY RIGHT ARM.
INSTRUCTIONS.
COOL
AH
SO, THIS IS THE RECIPE.
"HE'S DESPERATE FOR THE RECIPE."
"HOW CAN YOU BE SO SURE HE WON'T KILL YOU!"
THE RECIPE IS ON MY BONES.

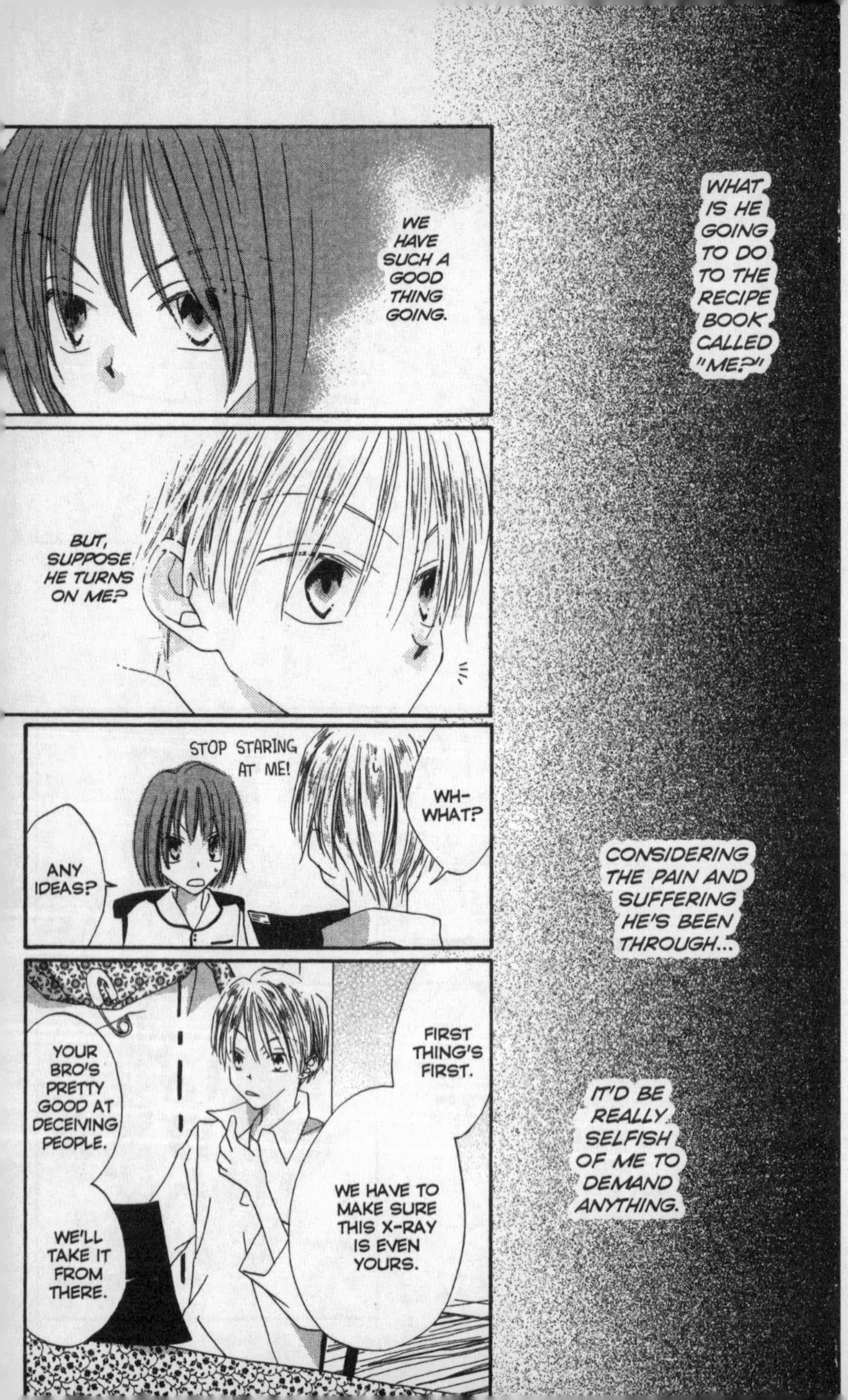
WHAT IS HE GOING TO DO TO THE RECIPE BOOK CALLED "ME?"
CONSIDERING THE PAIN AND SUFFERING HE'S BEEN THROUGH...
IT'D BE REALLY SELFISH OF ME TO DEMAND ANYTHING.
WE HAVE SUCH A GOOD THING GOING.
BUT, SUPPOSE HE TURNS ON ME?
STOP STARING AT ME!
WH-WHAT?
ANY IDEAS?
FIRST THING'S FIRST.
WE HAVE TO MAKE SURE THIS X-RAY IS EVEN YOURS.
YOUR BRO'S PRETTY GOOD AT DECEIVING PEOPLE.
WE'LL TAKE IT FROM THERE.

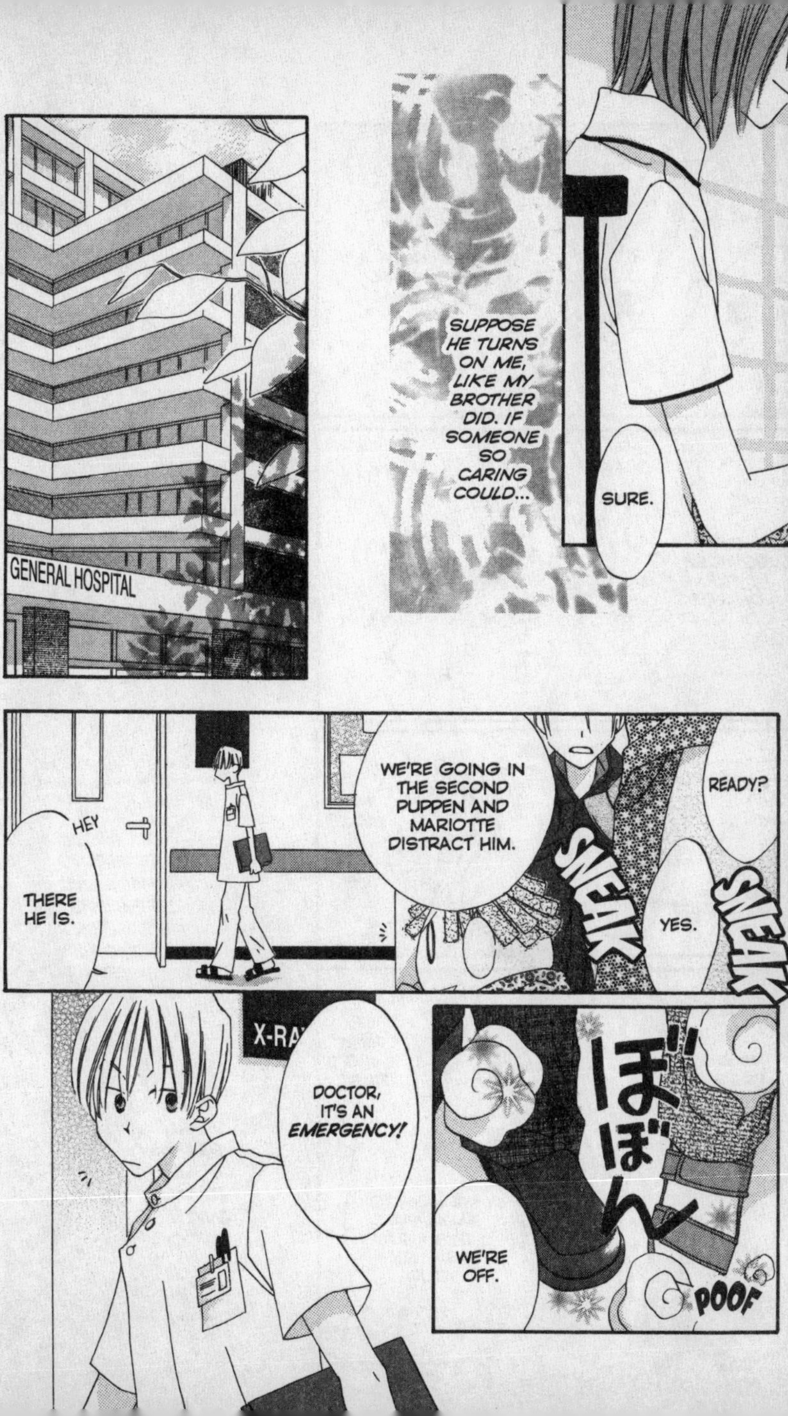
SURE.
SUPPOSE HE TURNS ON ME, LIKE MY BROTHER DID. IF SOMEONE SO CARING COULD...
GENERAL HOSPITAL
READY?
YES.
SNEAK
SNEAK
WE'RE GOING IN THE SECOND PUPPEN AND MARIOTTE DISTRACT HIM.
HEY
THERE HE IS.
ぼぼん
WE'RE OFF.
POOF
X-RA
DOCTOR, IT'S AN *EMERGENCY!*

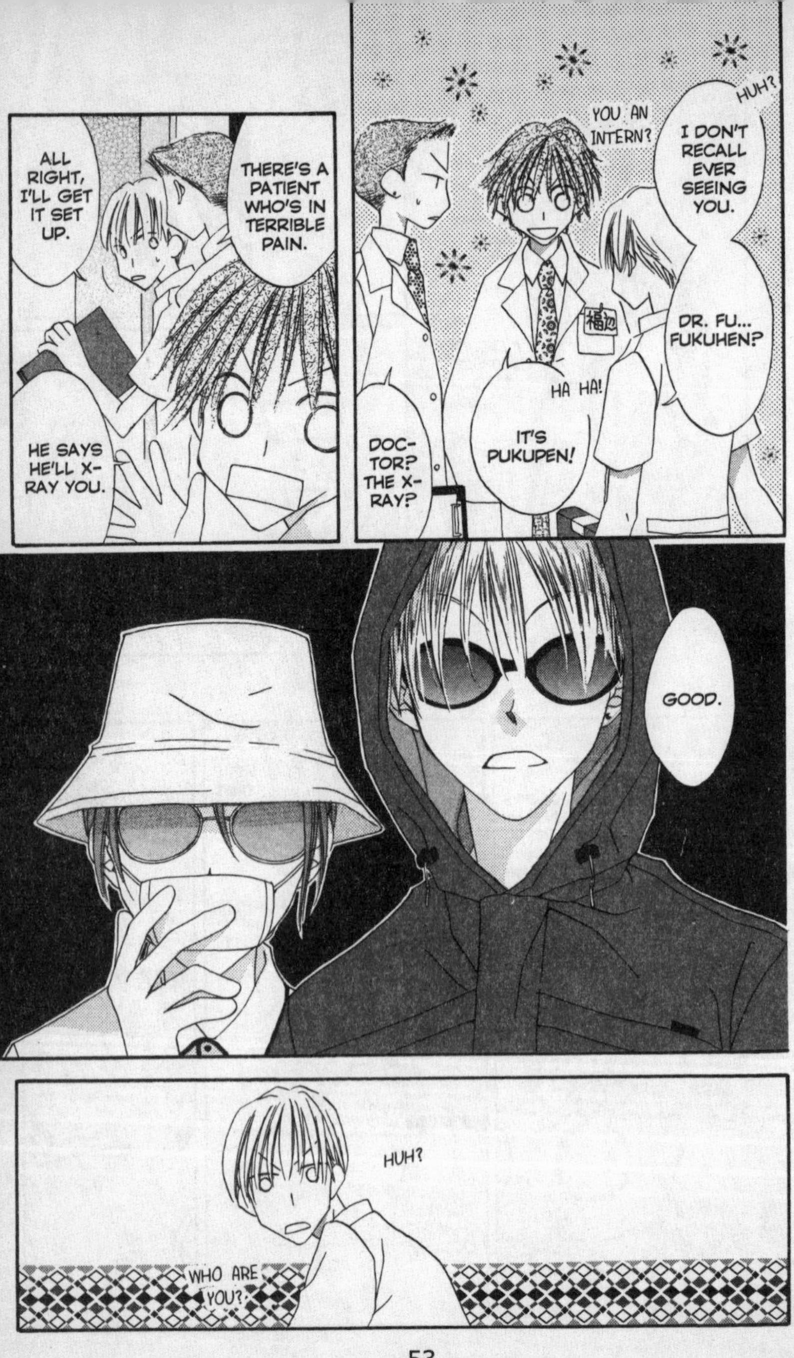
HUH?
I DON'T RECALL EVER SEEING YOU.
YOU AN INTERN?
DR. FU... FUKUHEN?
HA HA!
IT'S PUKUPEN!
DOCTOR? THE X-RAY?
THERE'S A PATIENT WHO'S IN TERRIBLE PAIN.
ALL RIGHT, I'LL GET IT SET UP.
HE SAYS HE'LL X-RAY YOU.
GOOD.
HUH?
WHO ARE YOU?

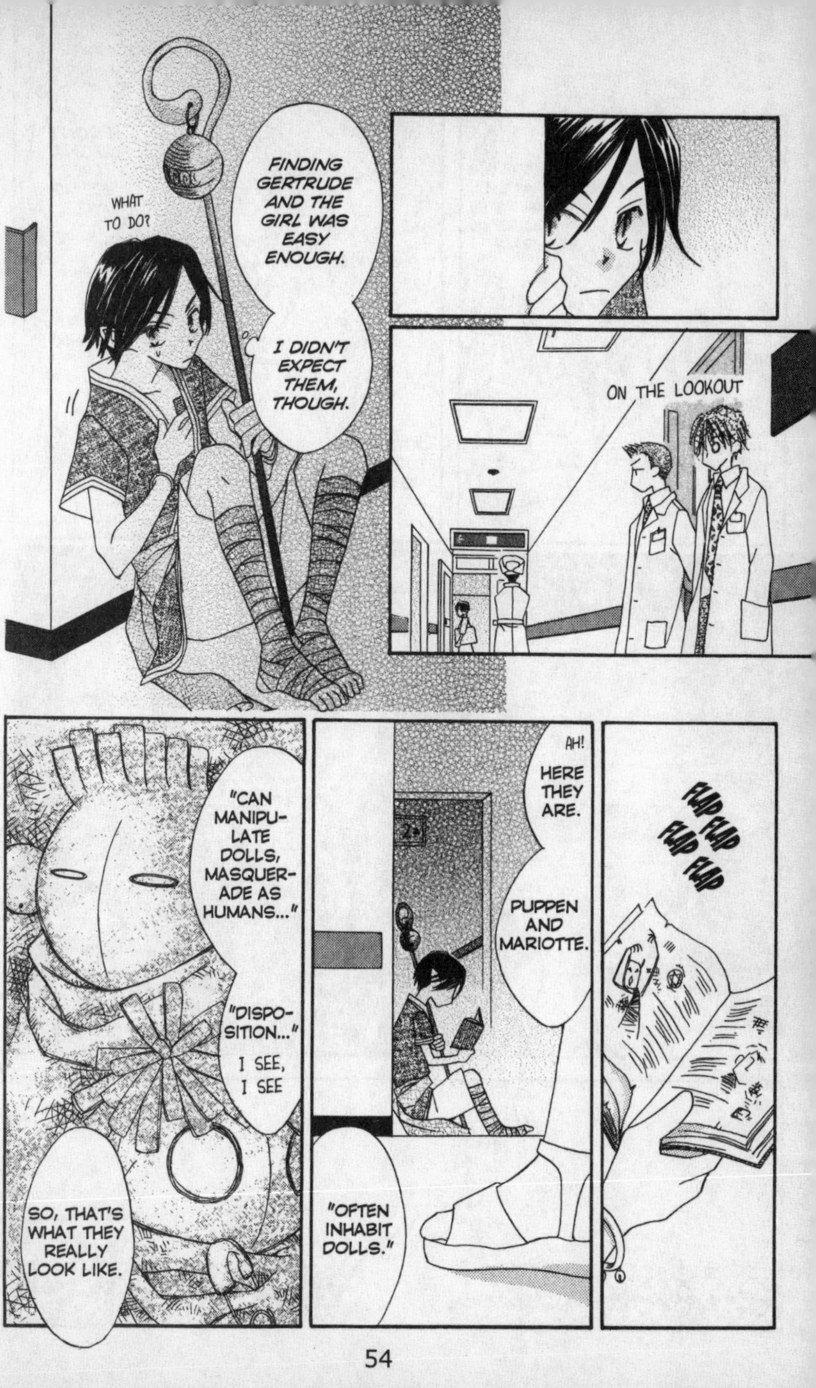
ON THE LOOKOUT
FINDING GERTRUDE AND THE GIRL WAS EASY ENOUGH.
WHAT TO DO?
I DIDN'T EXPECT THEM, THOUGH.
FLAP FLAP FLAP FLAP
AH!
HERE THEY ARE.
PUPPEN AND MARIOTTE.
"OFTEN INHABIT DOLLS."
"CAN MANIPULATE DOLLS, MASQUERADE AS HUMANS..."
"DISPOSITION..."
I SEE, I SEE
SO, THAT'S WHAT THEY REALLY LOOK LIKE.

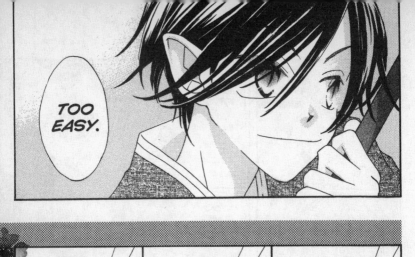

TOO EASY.

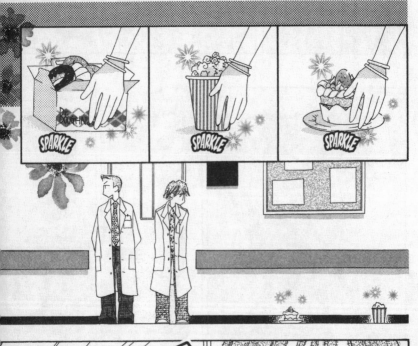

SPARKLE

SPARKLE

SPARKLE

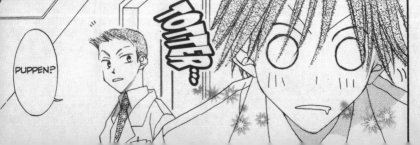

TOTTER...

PUPPEN?

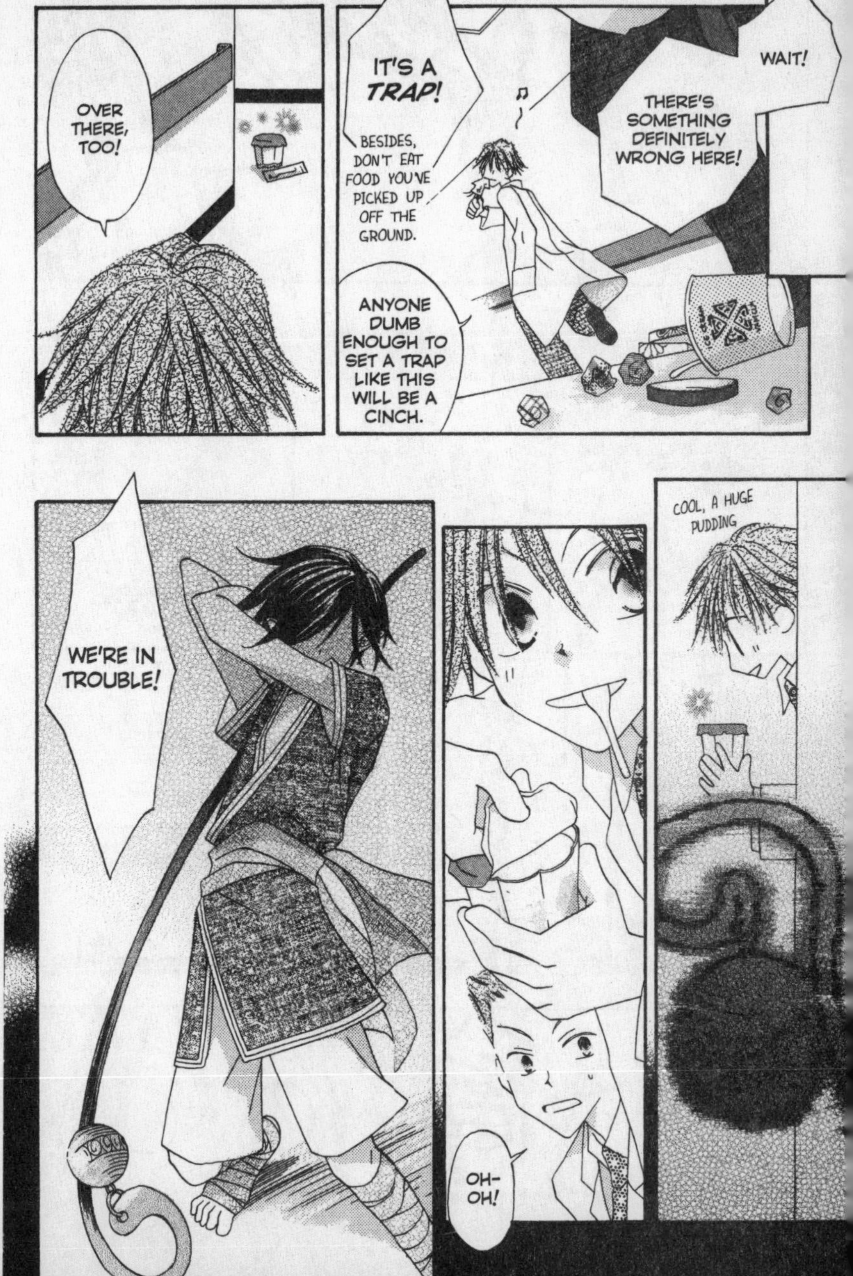

WAIT!
THERE'S SOMETHING DEFINITELY WRONG HERE!
IT'S A *TRAP!*
BESIDES, DON'T EAT FOOD YOU'VE PICKED UP OFF THE GROUND.
ANYONE DUMB ENOUGH TO SET A TRAP LIKE THIS WILL BE A CINCH.
OVER THERE, TOO!
COOL, A HUGE PUDDING
OH-OH!
WE'RE IN TROUBLE!

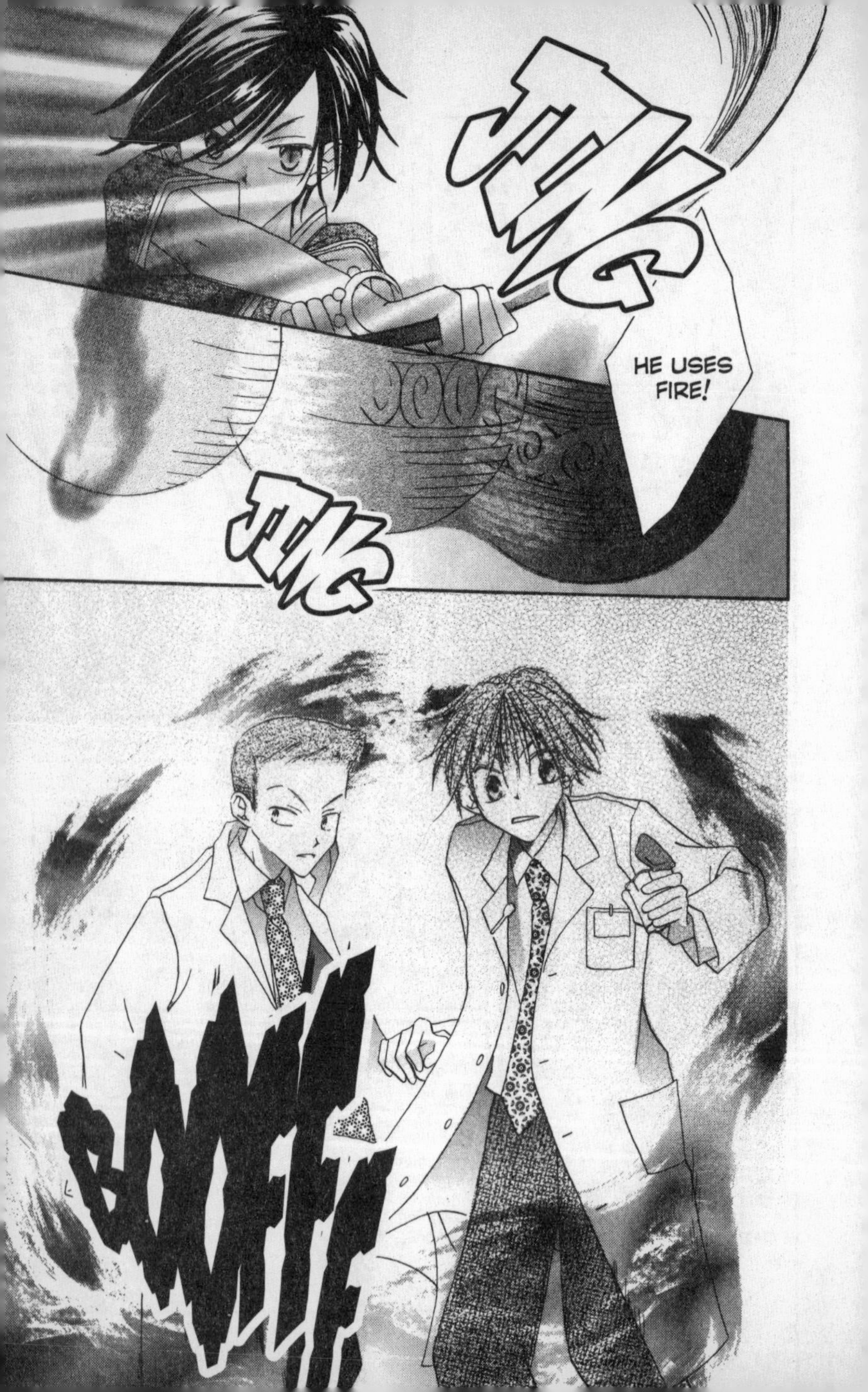
JING
HE USES FIRE!
JING

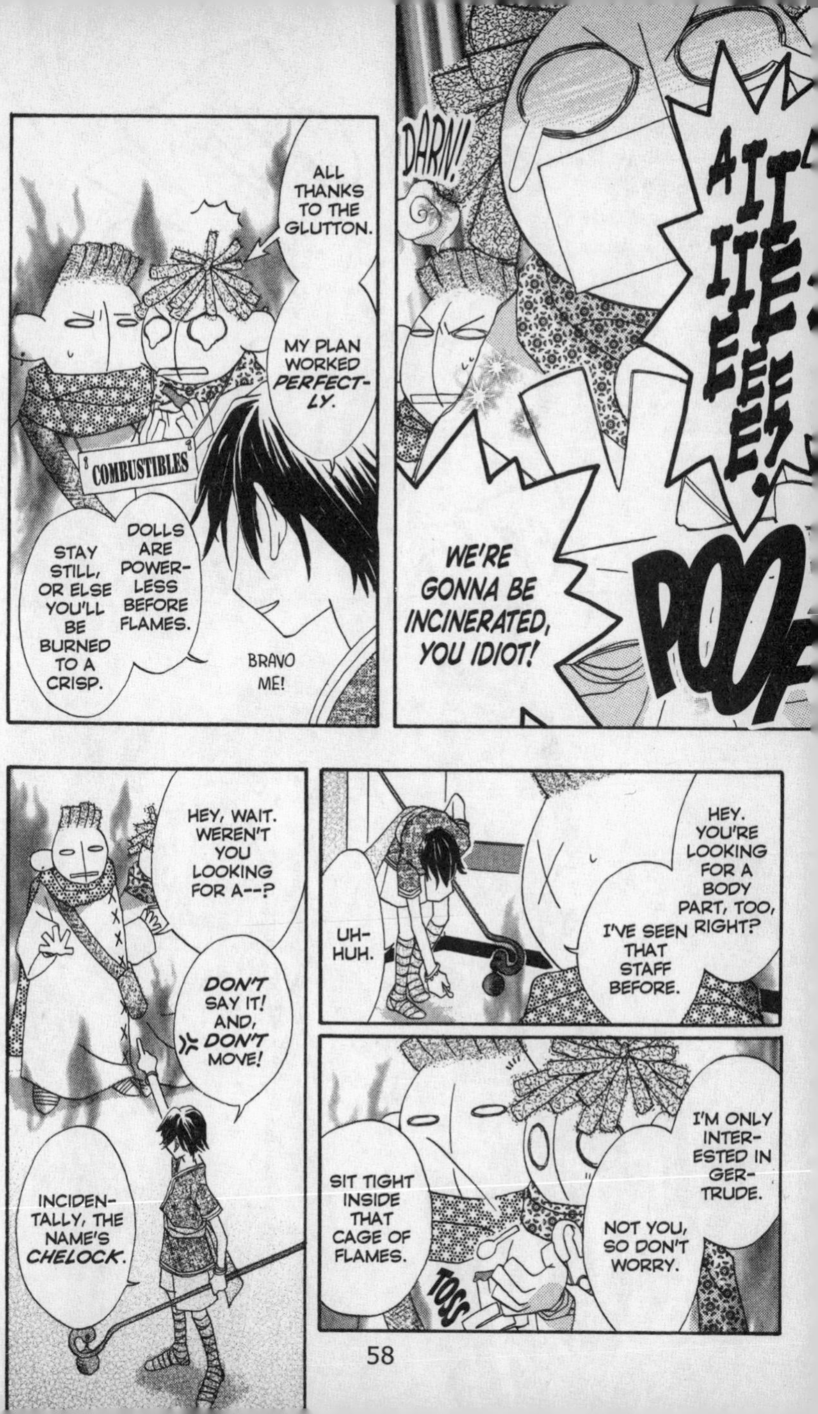
AIIIEEEE!
POO
DARN!
WE'RE GONNA BE INCINERATED, YOU IDIOT!
ALL THANKS TO THE GLUTTON.
MY PLAN WORKED PERFECTLY.
COMBUSTIBLES
DOLLS ARE POWERLESS BEFORE FLAMES.
STAY STILL, OR ELSE YOU'LL BE BURNED TO A CRISP.
BRAVO ME!
HEY. YOU'RE LOOKING FOR A BODY PART, TOO, RIGHT?
I'VE SEEN THAT STAFF BEFORE.
UH-HUH.
I'M ONLY INTERESTED IN GERTRUDE.
NOT YOU, SO DON'T WORRY.
SIT TIGHT INSIDE THAT CAGE OF FLAMES.
TOSS
HEY, WAIT. WEREN'T YOU LOOKING FOR A--?
DON'T SAY IT! AND, DON'T MOVE!
INCIDENTALLY, THE NAME'S CHELOCK.

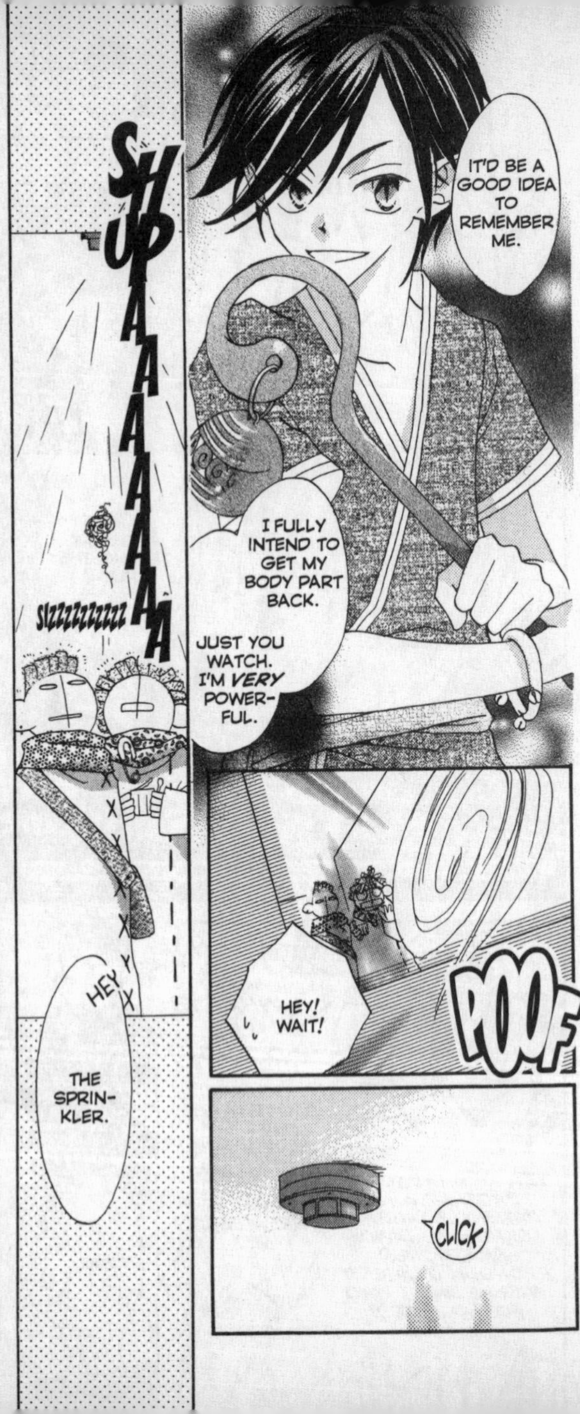
IT'D BE A GOOD IDEA TO REMEMBER ME.
I FULLY INTEND TO GET MY BODY PART BACK.
JUST YOU WATCH. I'M *VERY* POWERFUL.
POOF
HEY! WAIT!
CLICK
SHUPAAAAAAA
SIZZZZZZZZZZ
HEY
THE SPRINKLER.

02

I get a lot of letters containing questions specifically about me. Like my age (the horror!). Let's put it this way, when I was a preschooler Bunbun the fox was one of the characters on the "With Mom" show. I'm a Sagittarius whose blood type is B, and I like to daydream a lot. I'm told my self-portraits are not very accurate, but I really think I look that way.

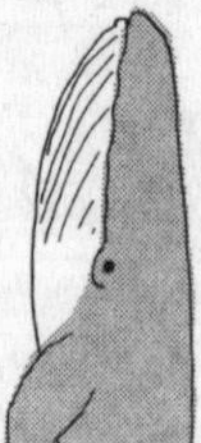

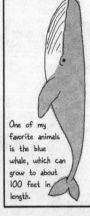

One of my favorite animals is the blue whale, which can grow to about 100 feet in length.

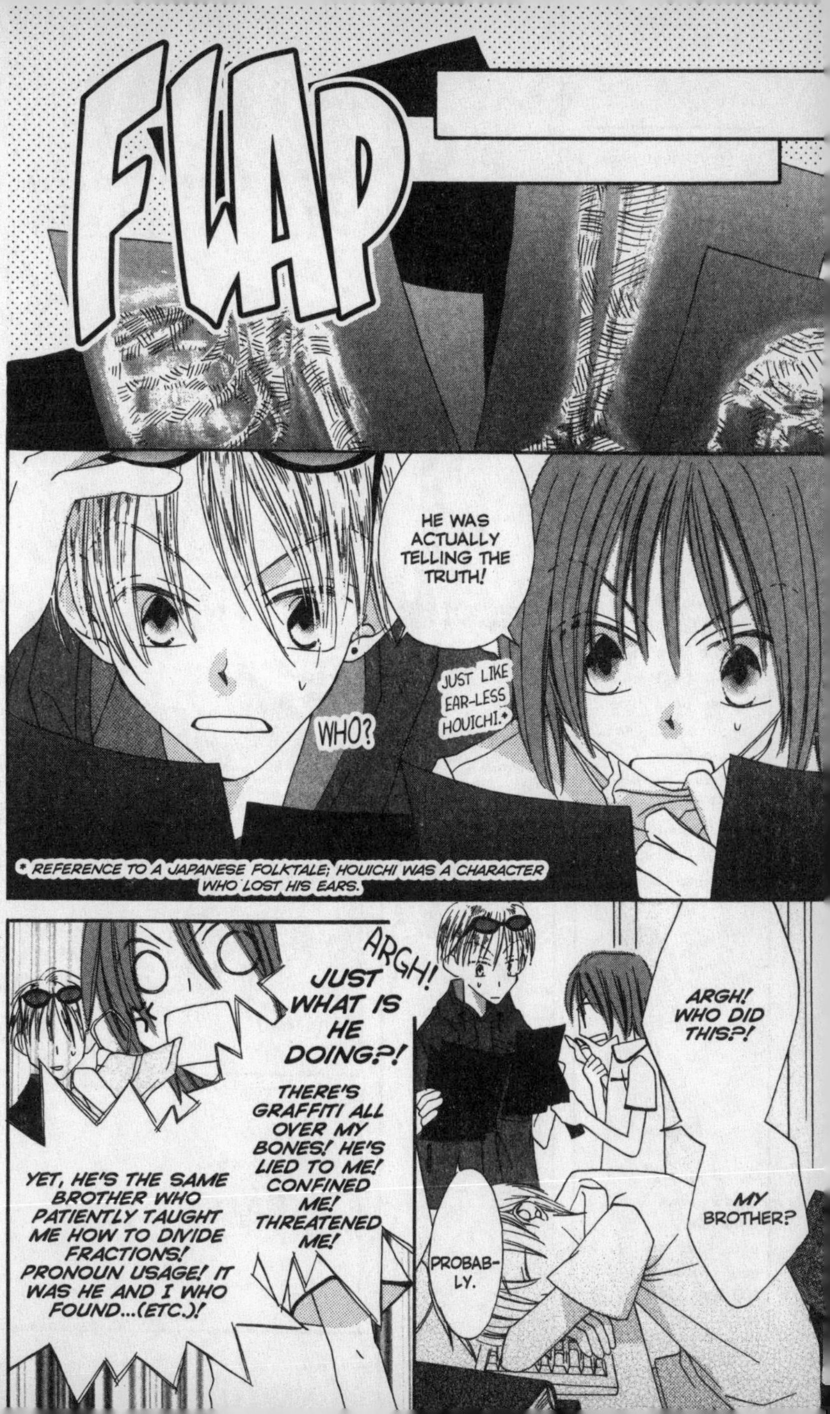
FLAP
HE WAS ACTUALLY TELLING THE TRUTH!
JUST LIKE EAR-LESS HOUICHI.*
WHO?
* REFERENCE TO A JAPANESE FOLKTALE; HOUICHI WAS A CHARACTER WHO LOST HIS EARS.
ARGH! WHO DID THIS?!
MY BROTHER?
PROBAB-LY.
ARGH!
JUST WHAT IS HE DOING?!
THERE'S GRAFFITI ALL OVER MY BONES! HE'S LIED TO ME! CONFINED ME! THREATENED ME!
YET, HE'S THE SAME BROTHER WHO PATIENTLY TAUGHT ME HOW TO DIVIDE FRACTIONS! PRONOUN USAGE! IT WAS HE AND I WHO FOUND...(ETC.)!

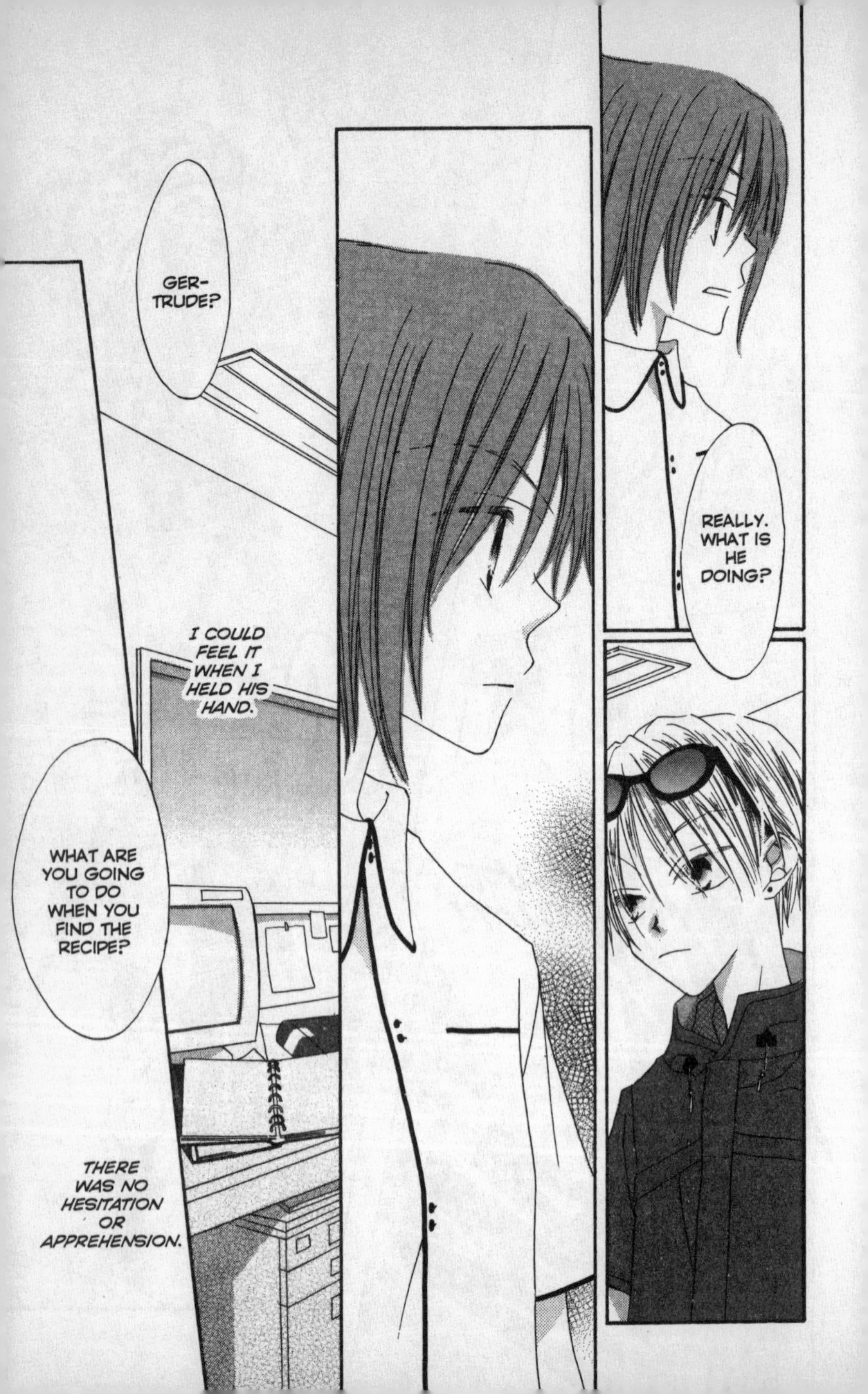
REALLY. WHAT IS HE DOING?
GER-TRUDE?
I COULD FEEL IT WHEN I HELD HIS HAND.
WHAT ARE YOU GOING TO DO WHEN YOU FIND THE RECIPE?
THERE WAS NO HESITATION OR APPREHENSION.

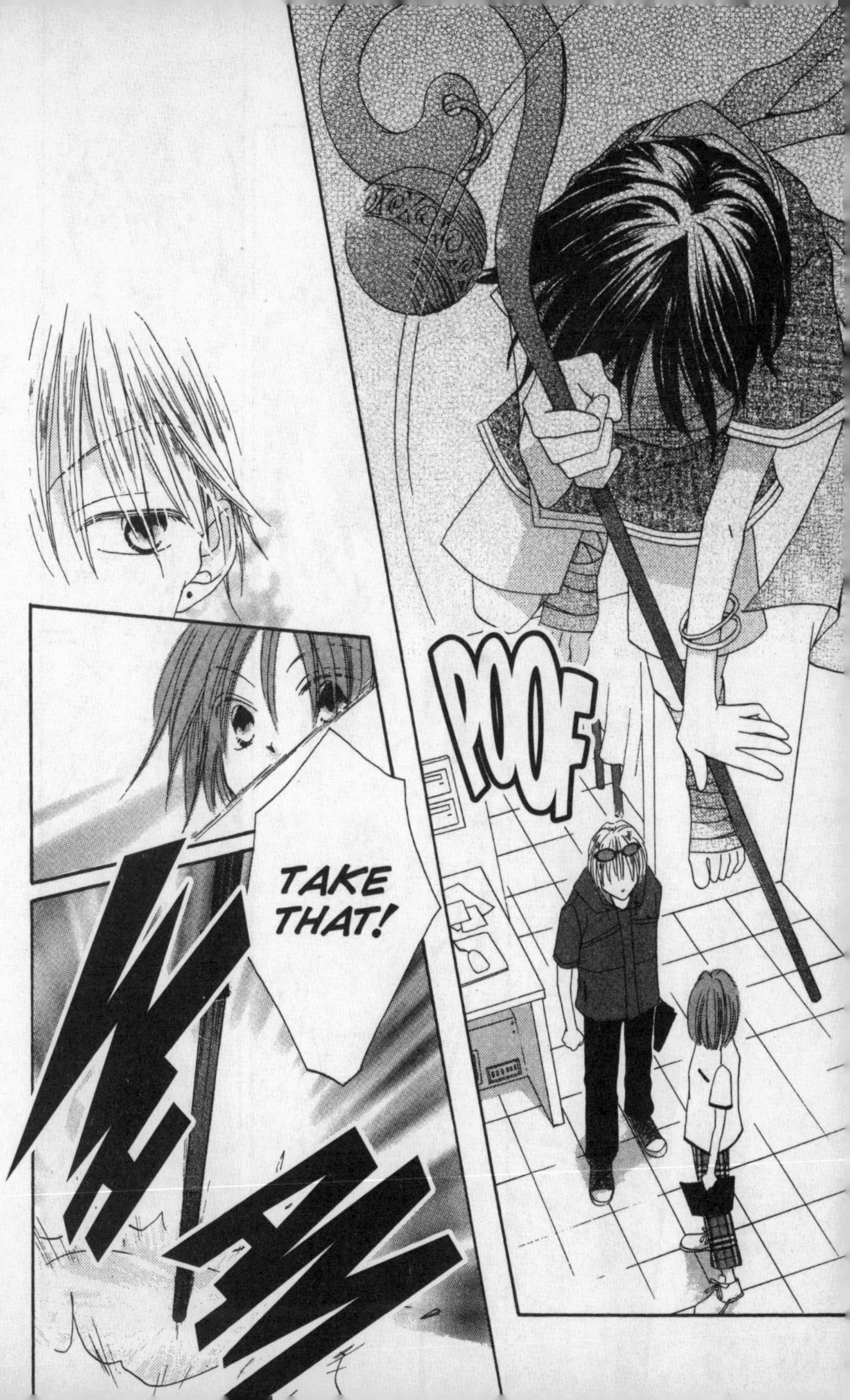
POOF
TAKE THAT!
WHAM

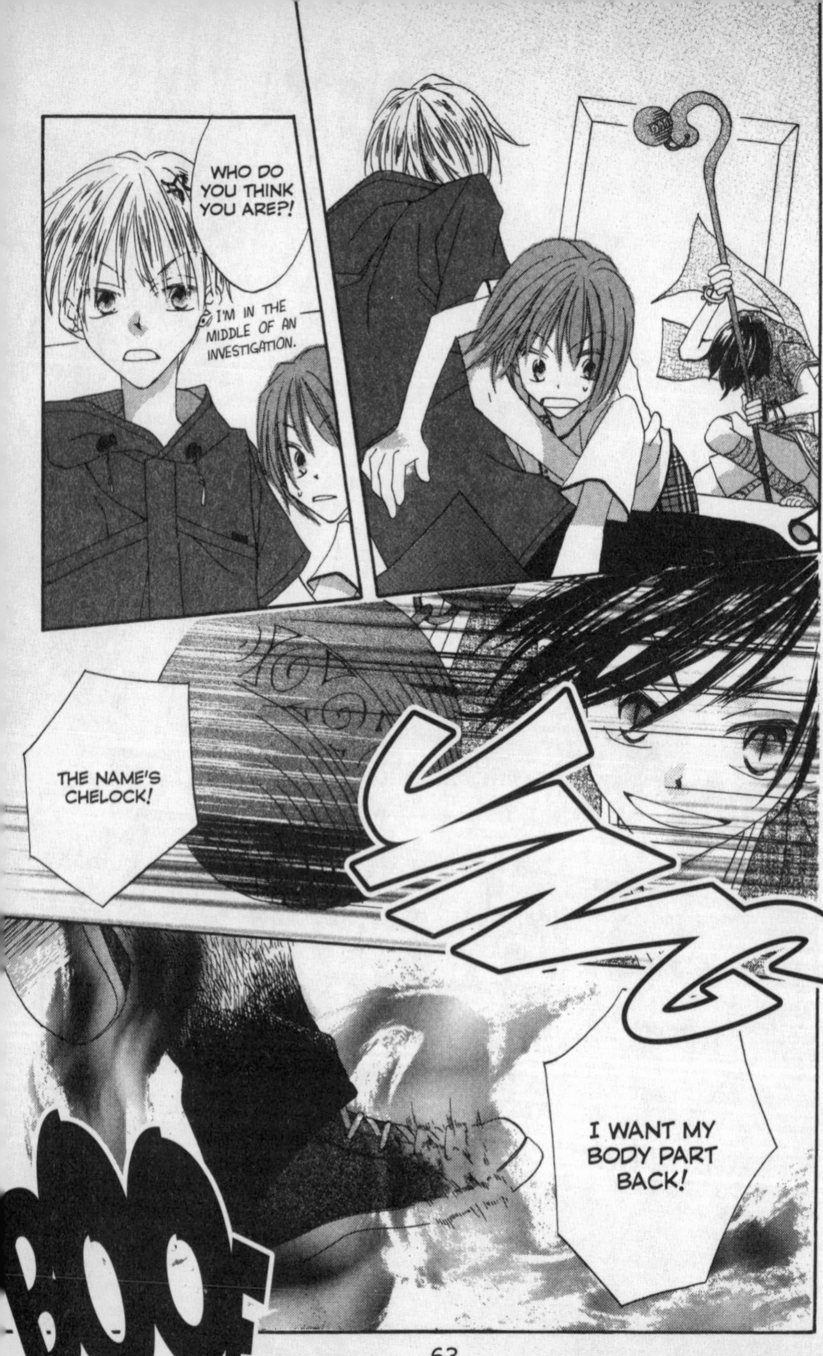
WHO DO YOU THINK YOU ARE?!
I'M IN THE MIDDLE OF AN INVESTIGATION.
ZING
THE NAME'S CHELOCK!
I WANT MY BODY PART BACK!
BOOF

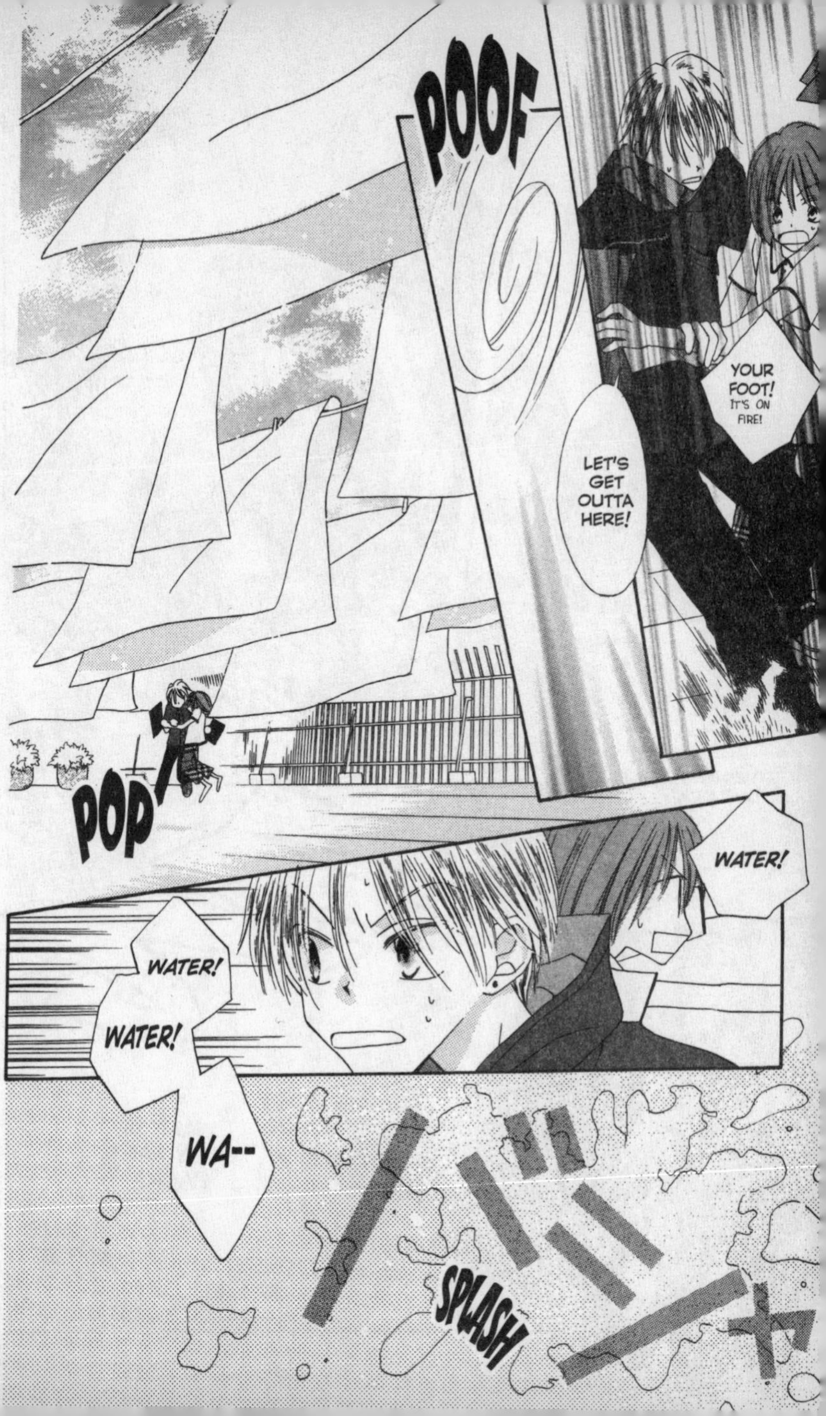
POOF
YOUR FOOT! IT'S ON FIRE!
LET'S GET OUTTA HERE!
POP
WATER!
WATER!
WATER!
WA--
SPLASH

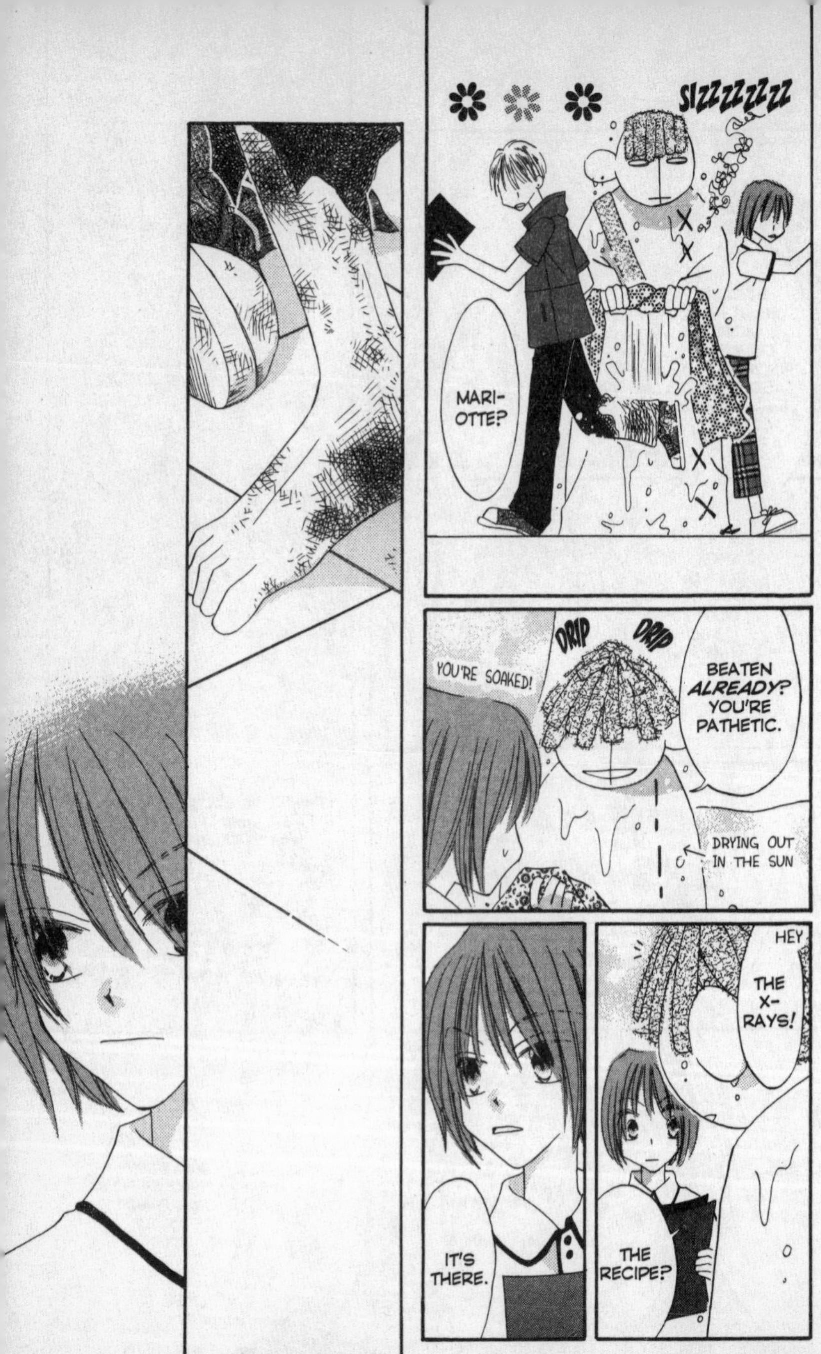
SIZZZZZZZZ
MARI-OTTE?
DRIP
DRIP
BEATEN *ALREADY?* YOU'RE PATHETIC.
YOU'RE SOAKED!
DRYING OUT IN THE SUN
HEY
THE X-RAYS!
THE RECIPE?
IT'S THERE.

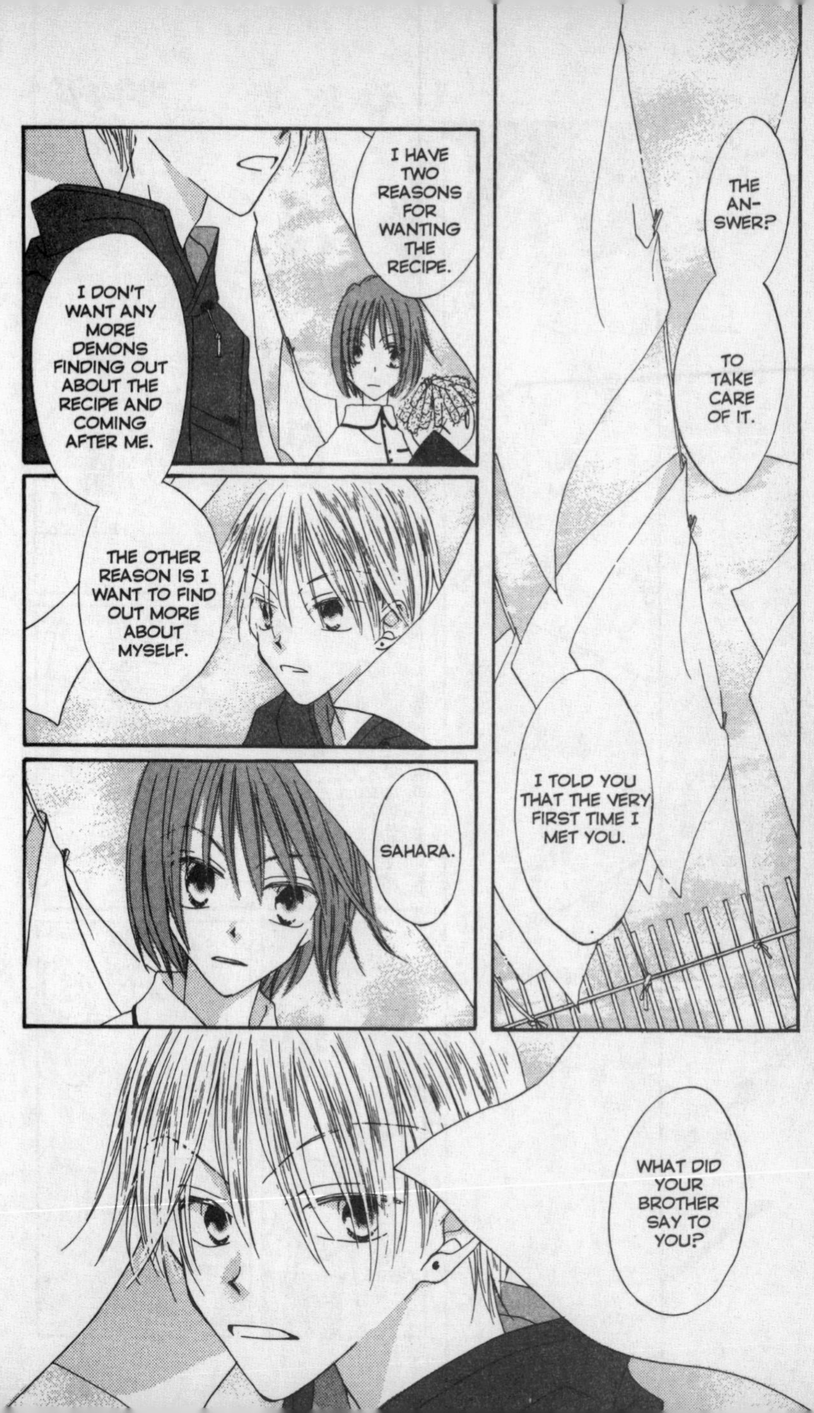
THE AN-SWER?
TO TAKE CARE OF IT.
I TOLD YOU THAT THE VERY FIRST TIME I MET YOU.
I HAVE TWO REASONS FOR WANTING THE RECIPE.
I DON'T WANT ANY MORE DEMONS FINDING OUT ABOUT THE RECIPE AND COMING AFTER ME.
THE OTHER REASON IS I WANT TO FIND OUT MORE ABOUT MYSELF.
SAHARA.
WHAT DID YOUR BROTHER SAY TO YOU?

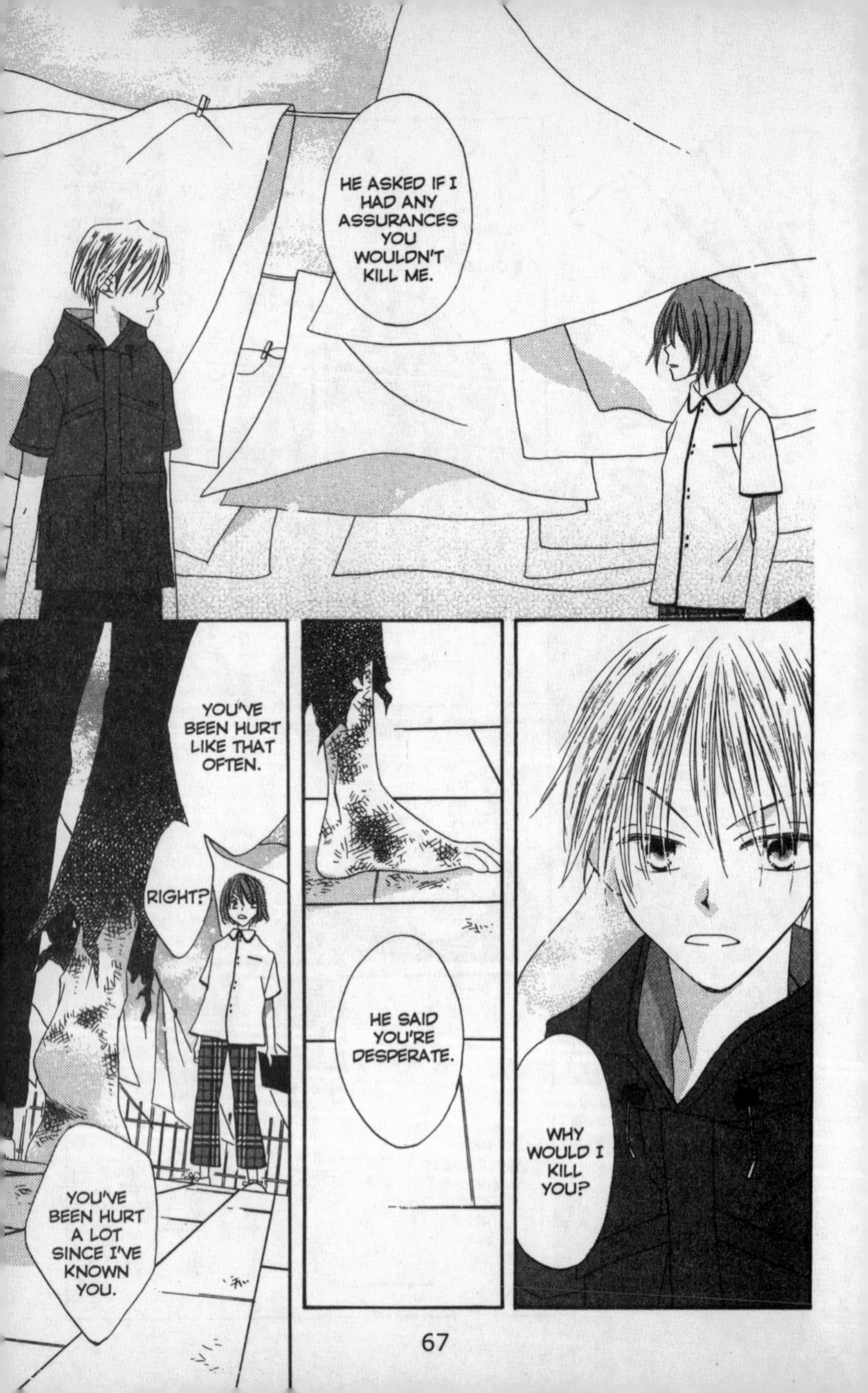
HE ASKED IF I HAD ANY ASSURANCES YOU WOULDN'T KILL ME.
WHY WOULD I KILL YOU?
HE SAID YOU'RE DESPERATE.
YOU'VE BEEN HURT LIKE THAT OFTEN.
RIGHT?
YOU'VE BEEN HURT A LOT SINCE I'VE KNOWN YOU.

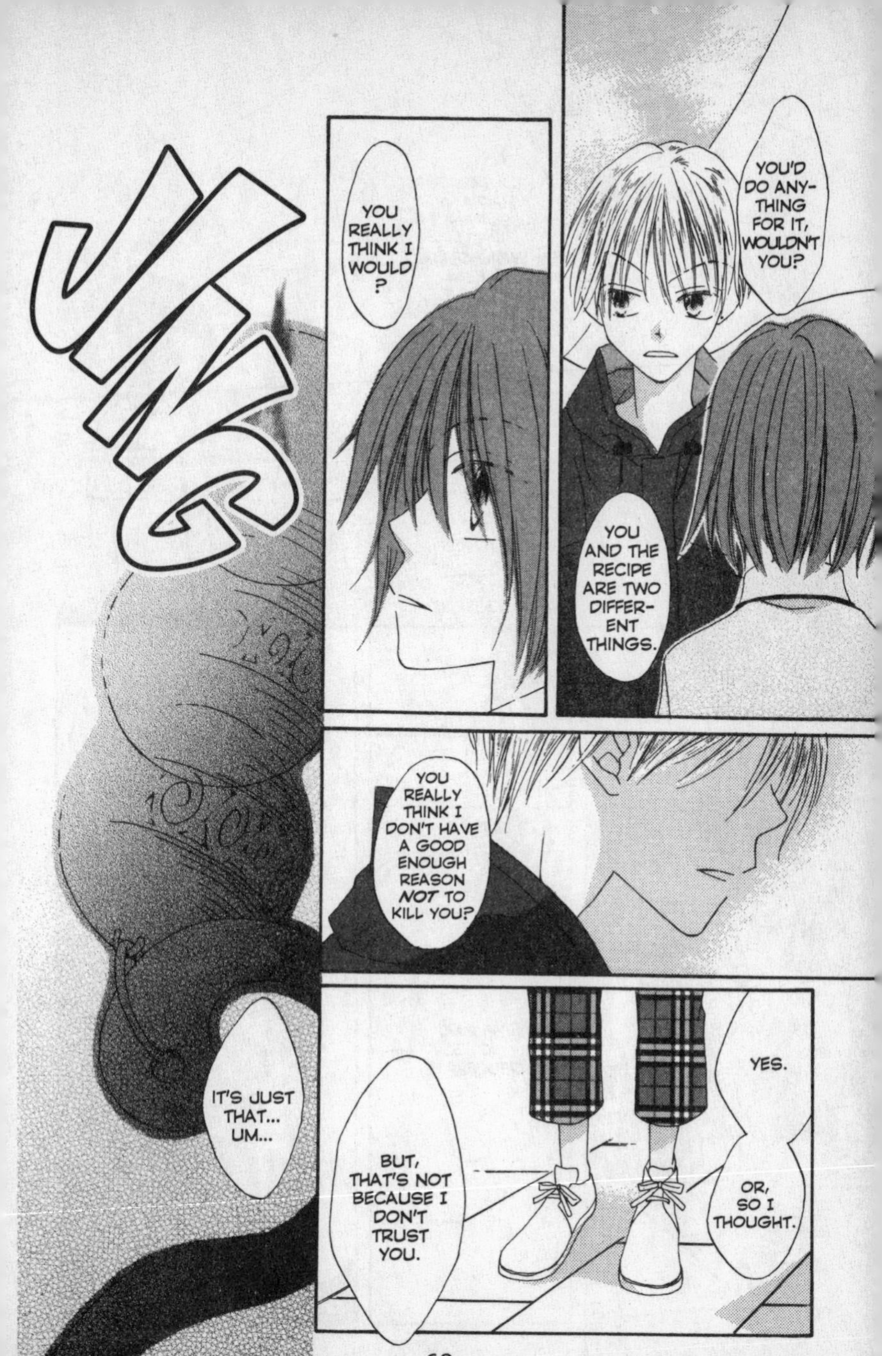
YOU'D DO ANY-THING FOR IT, WOULDN'T YOU?
YOU AND THE RECIPE ARE TWO DIFFER-ENT THINGS.
YOU REALLY THINK I WOULD?
YOU REALLY THINK I DON'T HAVE A GOOD ENOUGH REASON *NOT* TO KILL YOU?
YES.
OR, SO I THOUGHT.
BUT, THAT'S NOT BECAUSE I DON'T TRUST YOU.
JING
IT'S JUST THAT... UM...

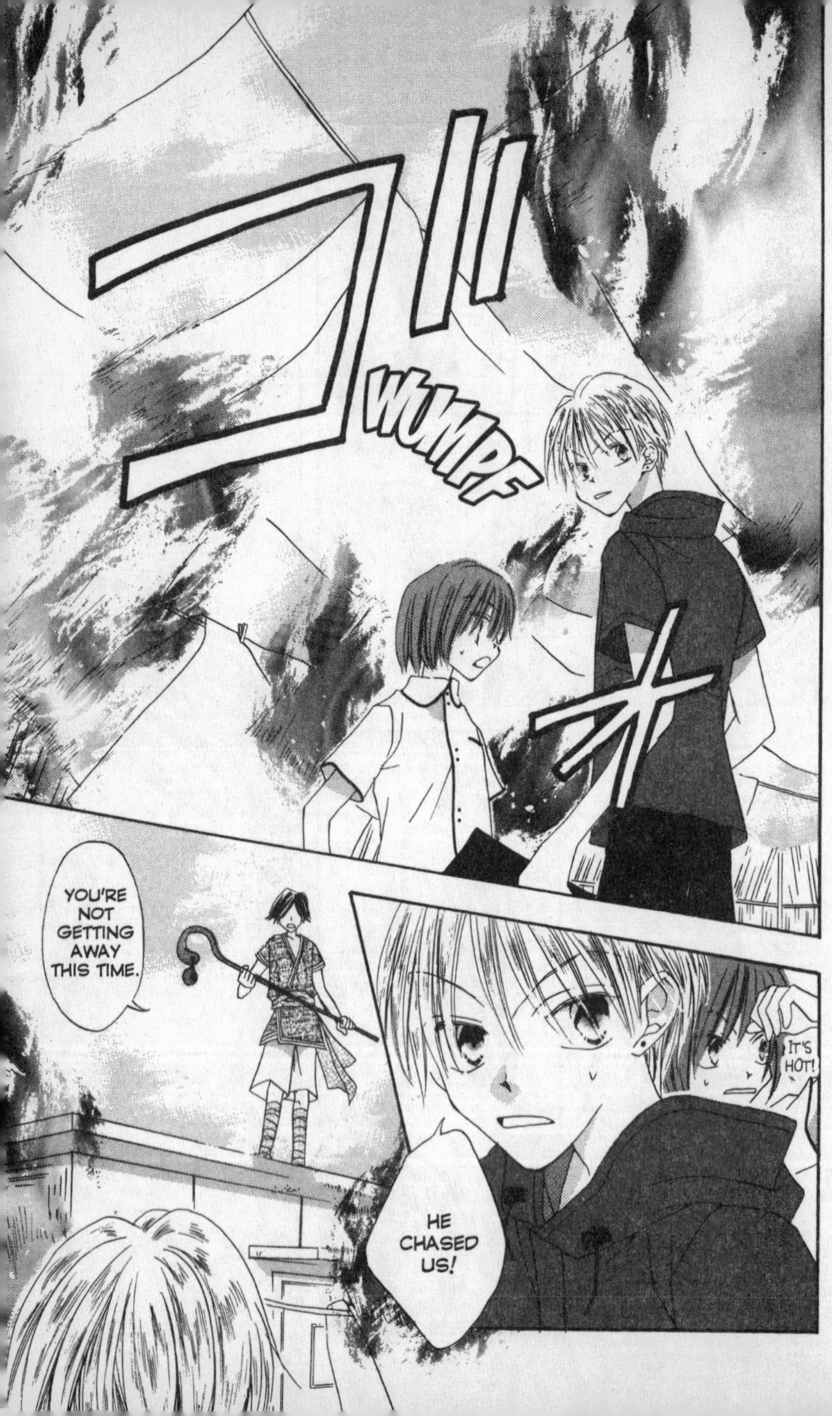
WUMPF
IT'S HOT!
HE CHASED US!
YOU'RE NOT GETTING AWAY THIS TIME.

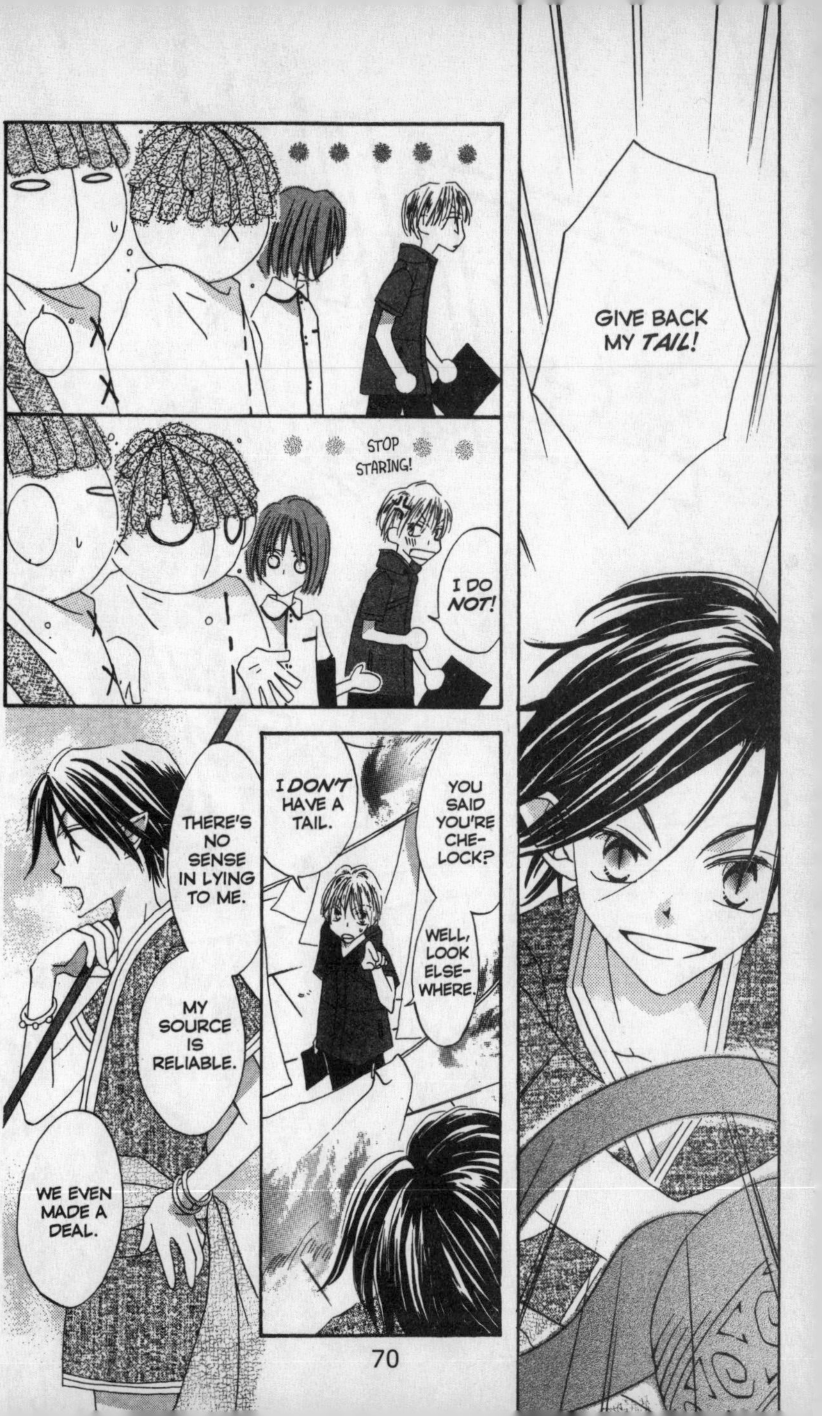
GIVE BACK MY *TAIL!*
STOP STARING!
I DO *NOT!*
YOU SAID YOU'RE CHE-LOCK?
I *DON'T* HAVE A TAIL.
WELL, LOOK ELSEWHERE.
THERE'S NO SENSE IN LYING TO ME.
MY SOURCE IS RELIABLE.
WE EVEN MADE A DEAL.

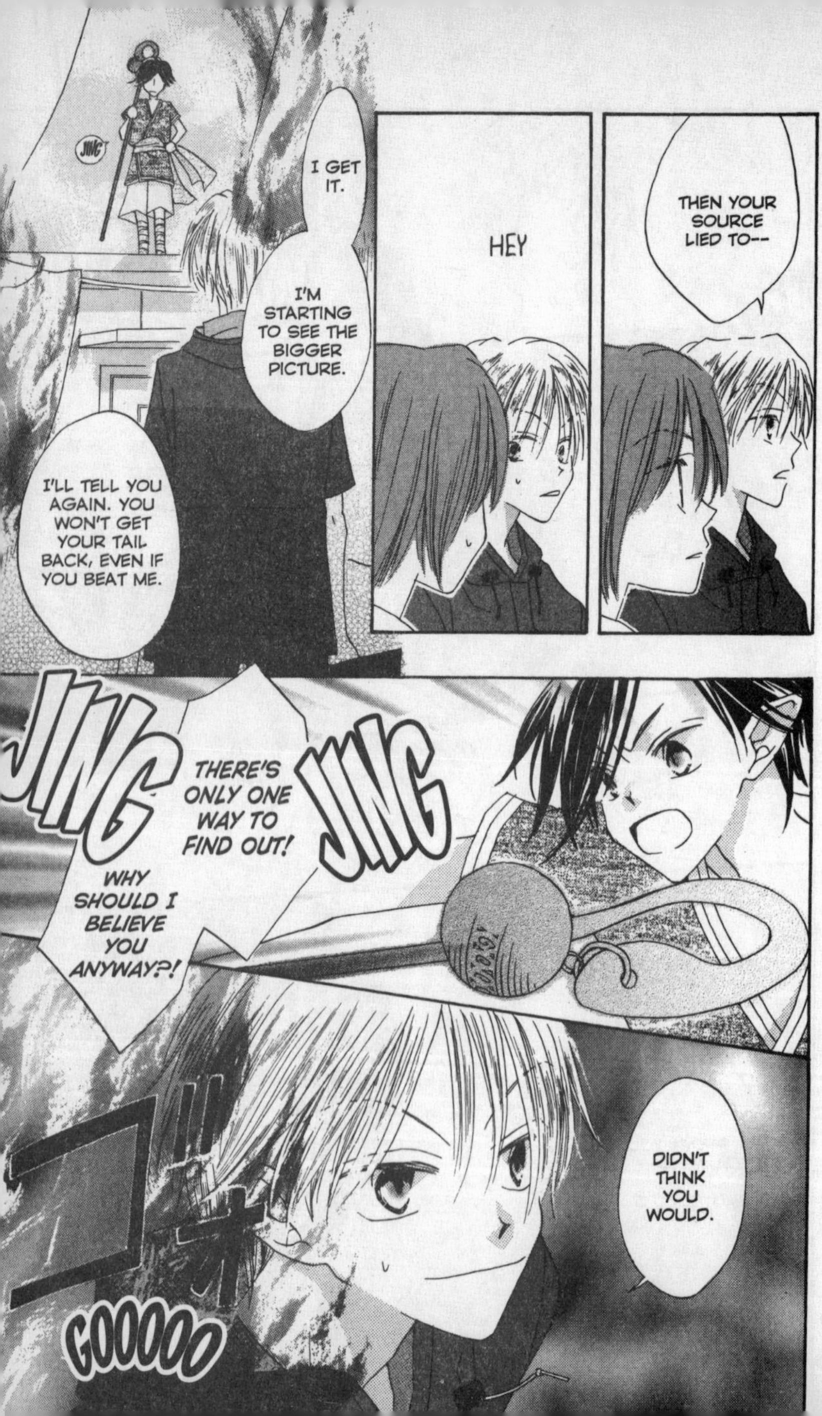

THEN YOUR SOURCE LIED TO--
HEY
I GET IT.
I'M STARTING TO SEE THE BIGGER PICTURE.
JING
I'LL TELL YOU AGAIN. YOU WON'T GET YOUR TAIL BACK, EVEN IF YOU BEAT ME.
JING
THERE'S ONLY ONE WAY TO FIND OUT!
JING
WHY SHOULD I BELIEVE YOU ANYWAY?!
DIDN'T THINK YOU WOULD.
GOOOOO

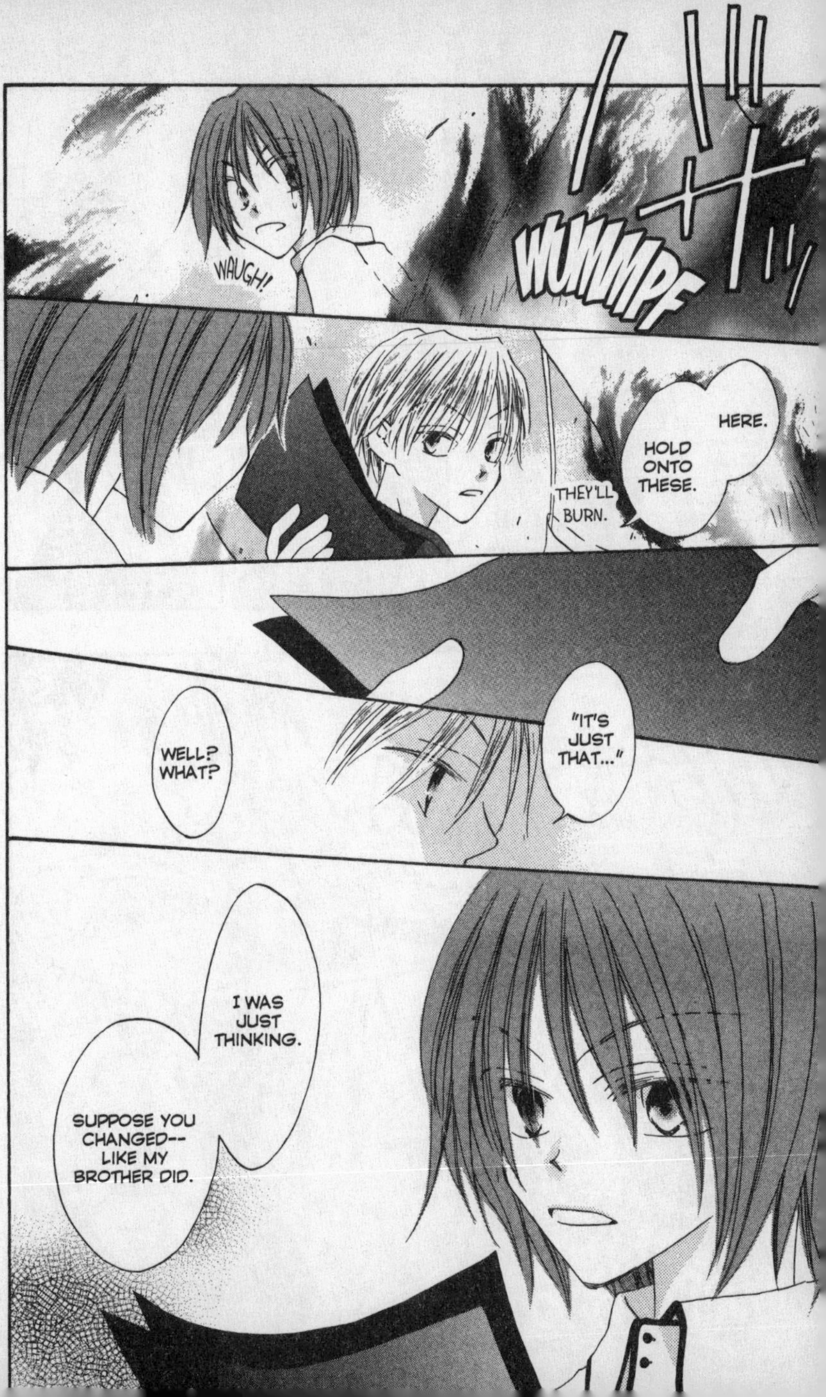
WUMMPF
WAUGH!
HERE.
HOLD ONTO THESE.
THEY'LL BURN.
"IT'S JUST THAT..."
WELL? WHAT?
I WAS JUST THINKING.
SUPPOSE YOU CHANGED--LIKE MY BROTHER DID.

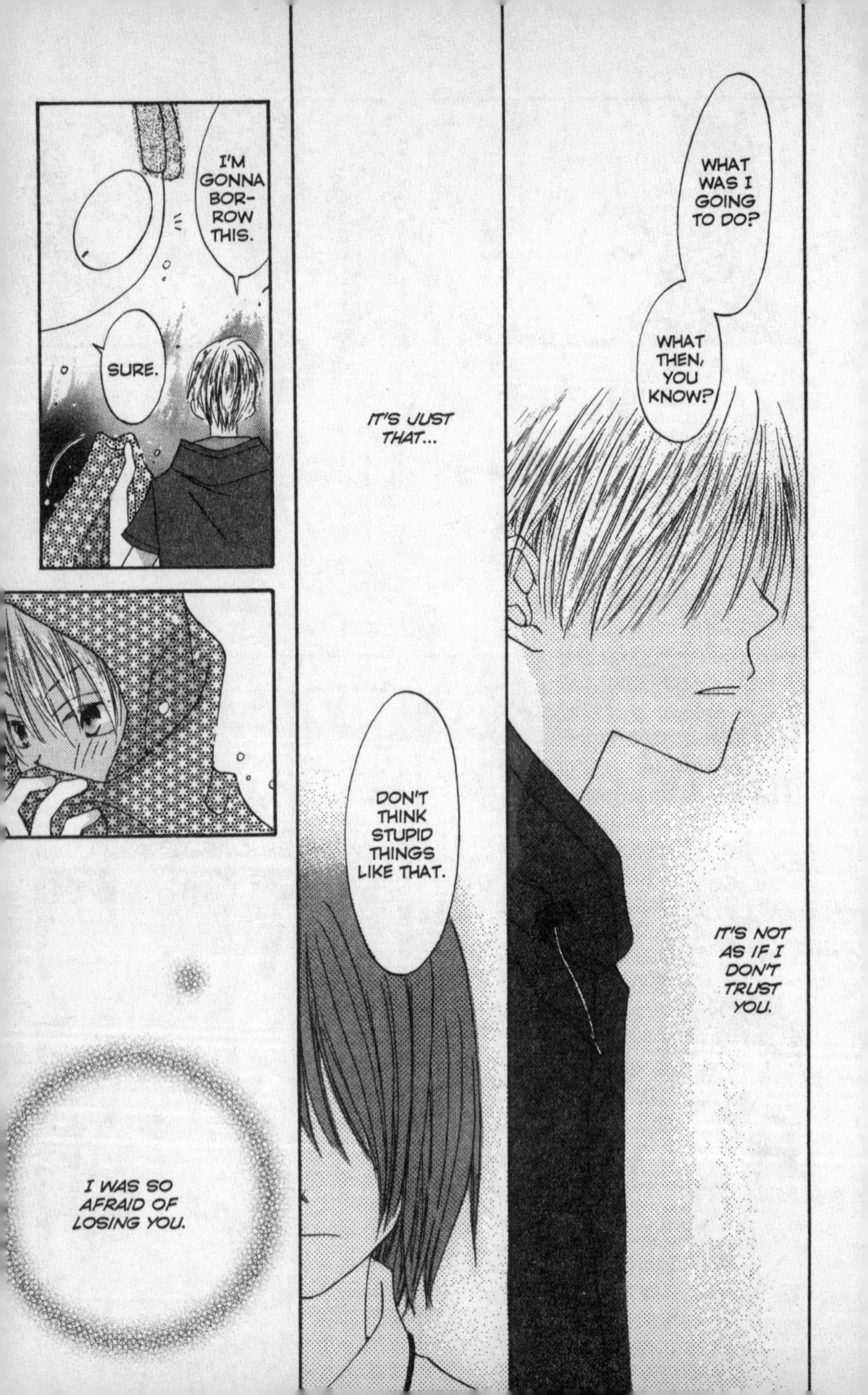
WHAT WAS I GOING TO DO?
WHAT THEN, YOU KNOW?
IT'S NOT AS IF I DON'T TRUST YOU.
IT'S JUST THAT...
DON'T THINK STUPID THINGS LIKE THAT.
I'M GONNA BOR-ROW THIS.
SURE.
I WAS SO AFRAID OF LOSING YOU.

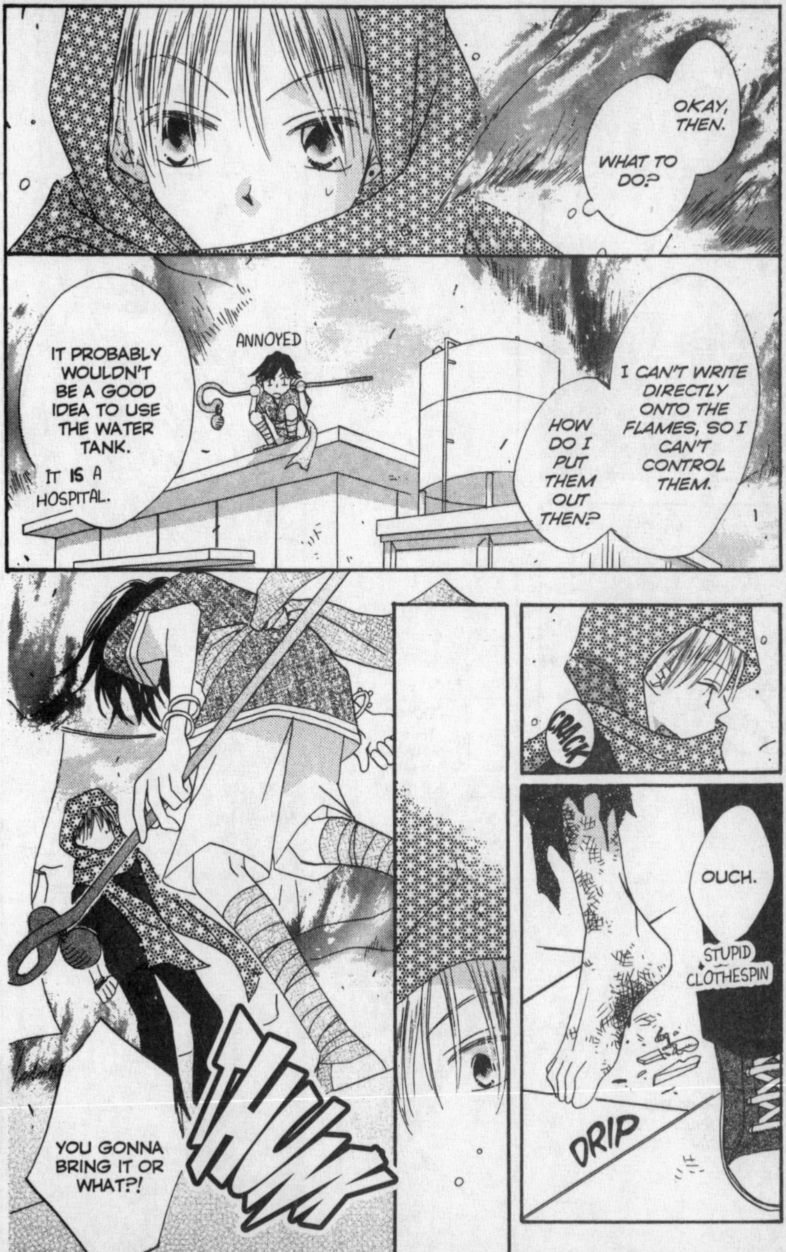
OKAY, THEN.
WHAT TO DO?
I CAN'T WRITE DIRECTLY ONTO THE FLAMES, SO I CAN'T CONTROL THEM.
HOW DO I PUT THEM OUT THEN?
ANNOYED
IT PROBABLY WOULDN'T BE A GOOD IDEA TO USE THE WATER TANK.
IT IS A HOSPITAL.
CRACK
OUCH.
STUPID CLOTHESPIN
DRIP
THUNK
YOU GONNA BRING IT OR WHAT?!

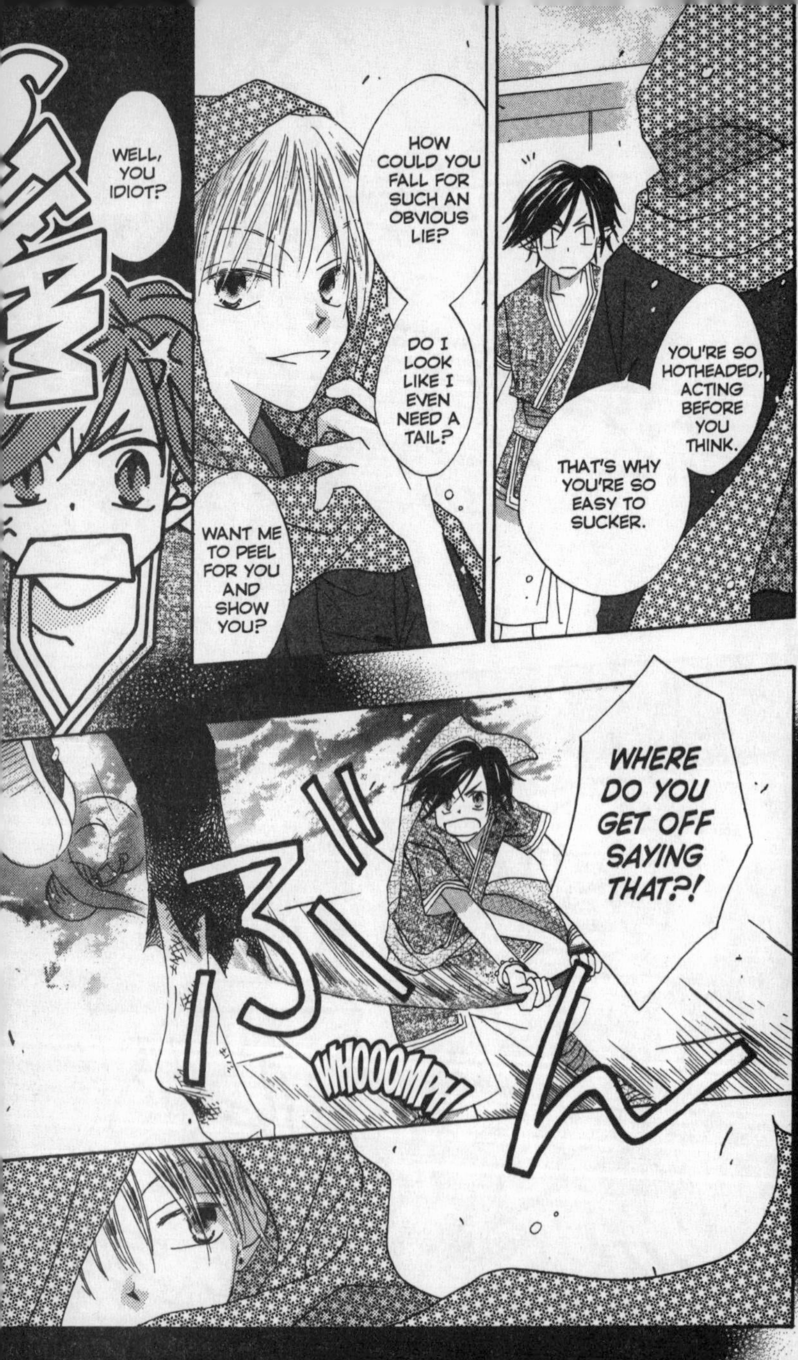
YOU'RE SO HOTHEADED, ACTING BEFORE YOU THINK.
THAT'S WHY YOU'RE SO EASY TO SUCKER.
HOW COULD YOU FALL FOR SUCH AN OBVIOUS LIE?
DO I LOOK LIKE I EVEN NEED A TAIL?
WANT ME TO PEEL FOR YOU AND SHOW YOU?
WELL, YOU IDIOT?
WHERE DO YOU GET OFF SAYING THAT?!
WHOOOMPH

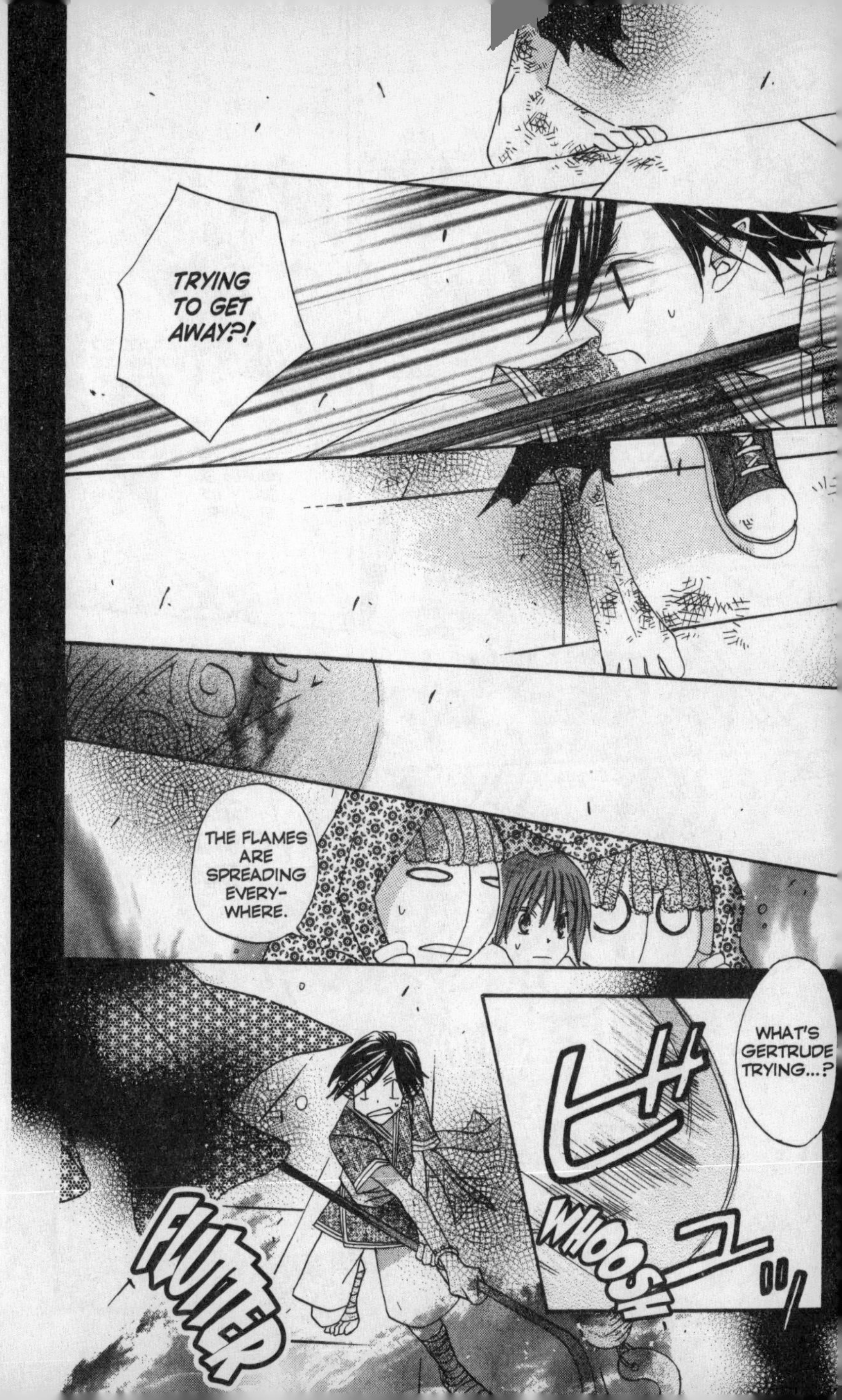
TRYING TO GET AWAY?!
THE FLAMES ARE SPREADING EVERY-WHERE.
WHAT'S GERTRUDE TRYING...?
WHOOSH
FLUTTER

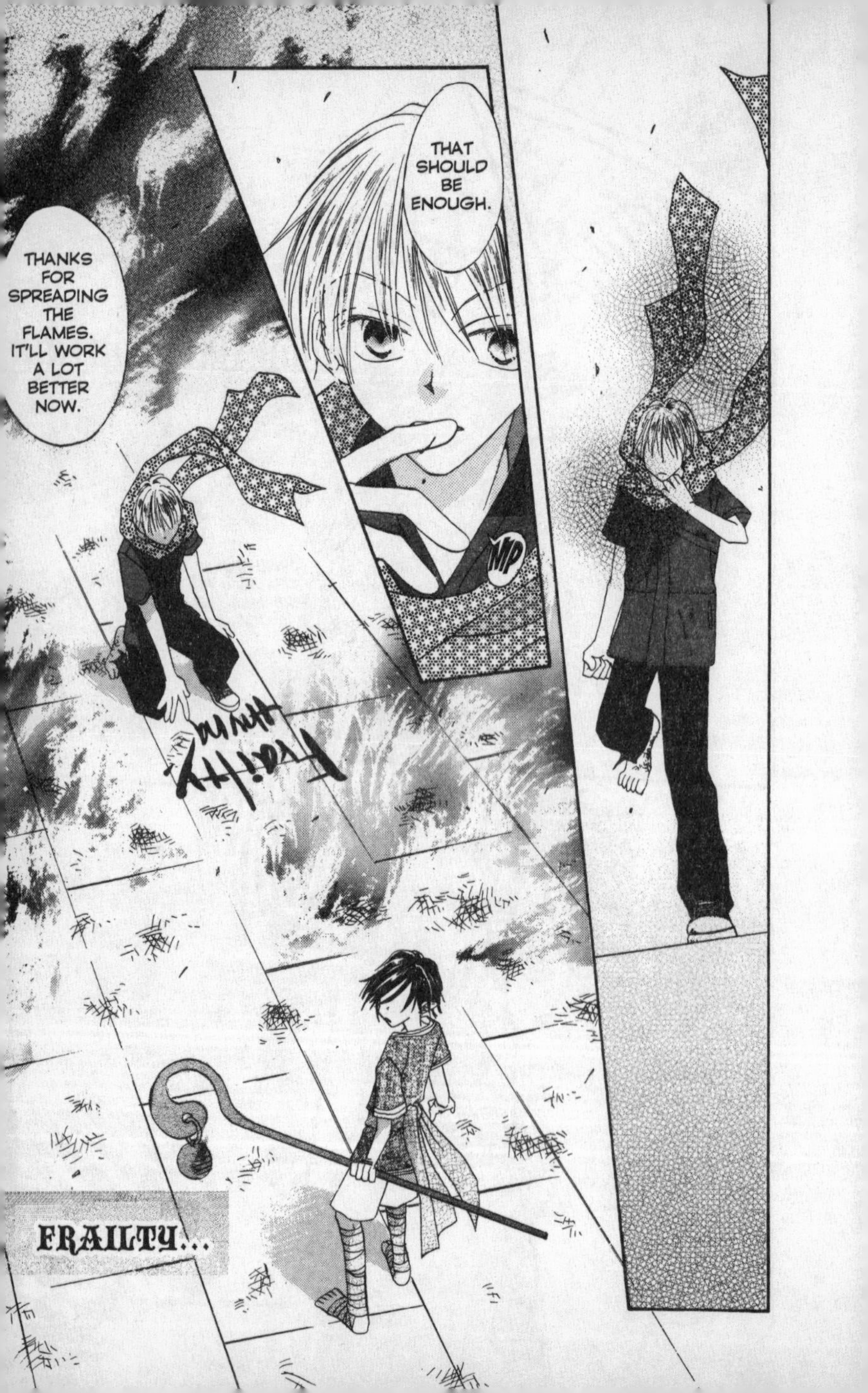
THAT SHOULD BE ENOUGH.
THANKS FOR SPREADING THE FLAMES. IT'LL WORK A LOT BETTER NOW.
FRAILTY...

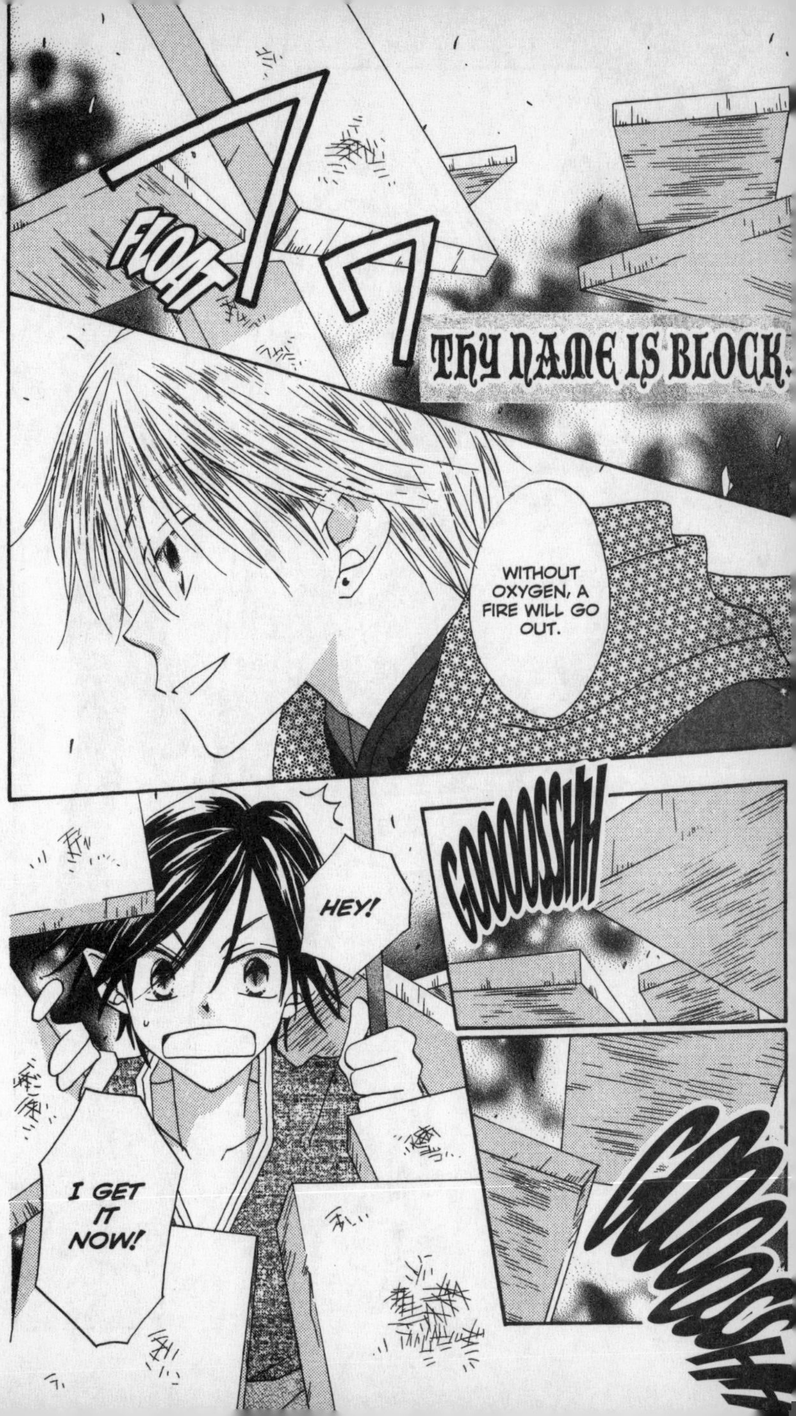
FLOAT
THY NAME IS BLOCK.
WITHOUT OXYGEN, A FIRE WILL GO OUT.
GOOOOSSHH
HEY!
I GET IT NOW!

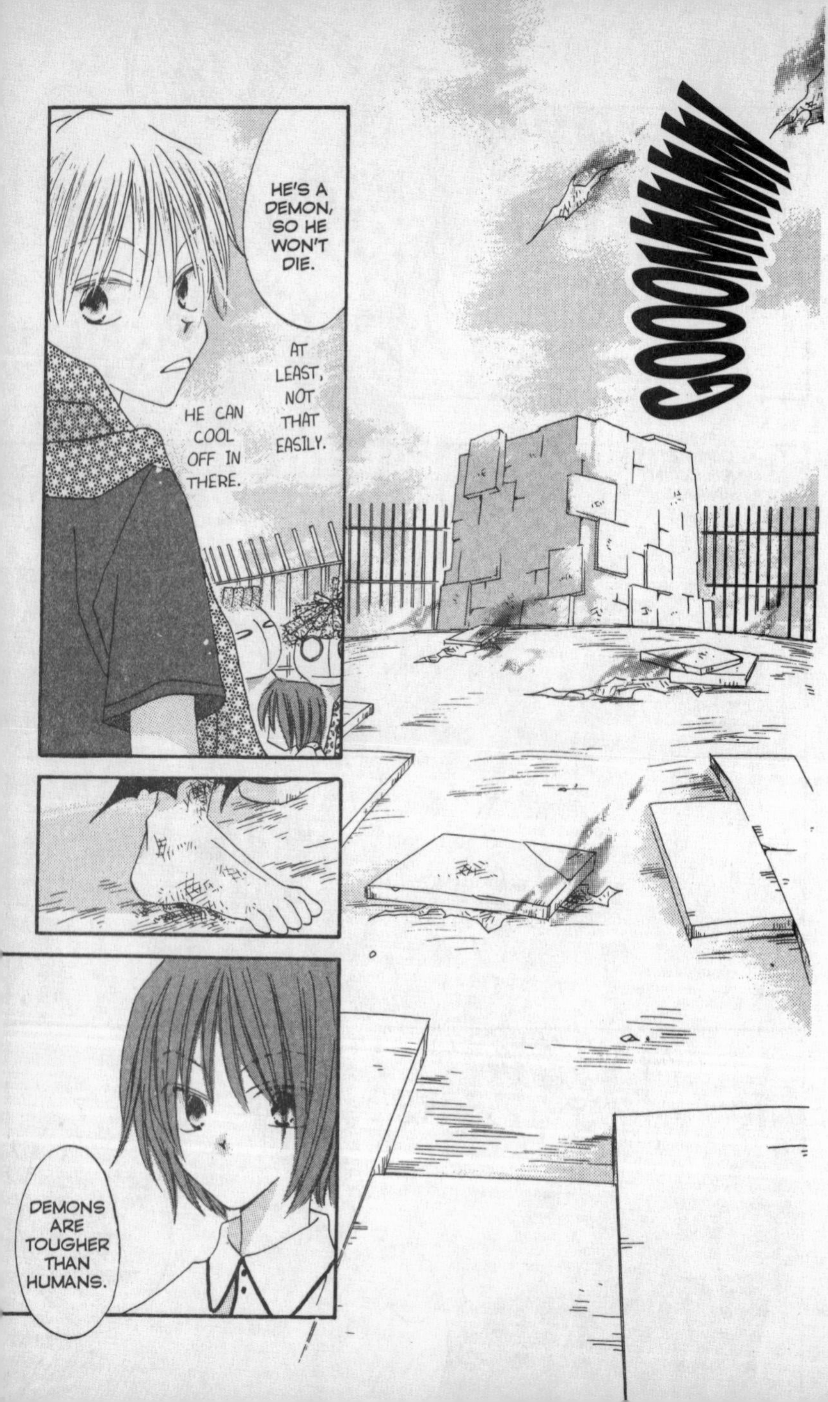
GOOOMMM
HE'S A DEMON, SO HE WON'T DIE.
AT LEAST, NOT THAT EASILY.
HE CAN COOL OFF IN THERE.
DEMONS ARE TOUGHER THAN HUMANS.

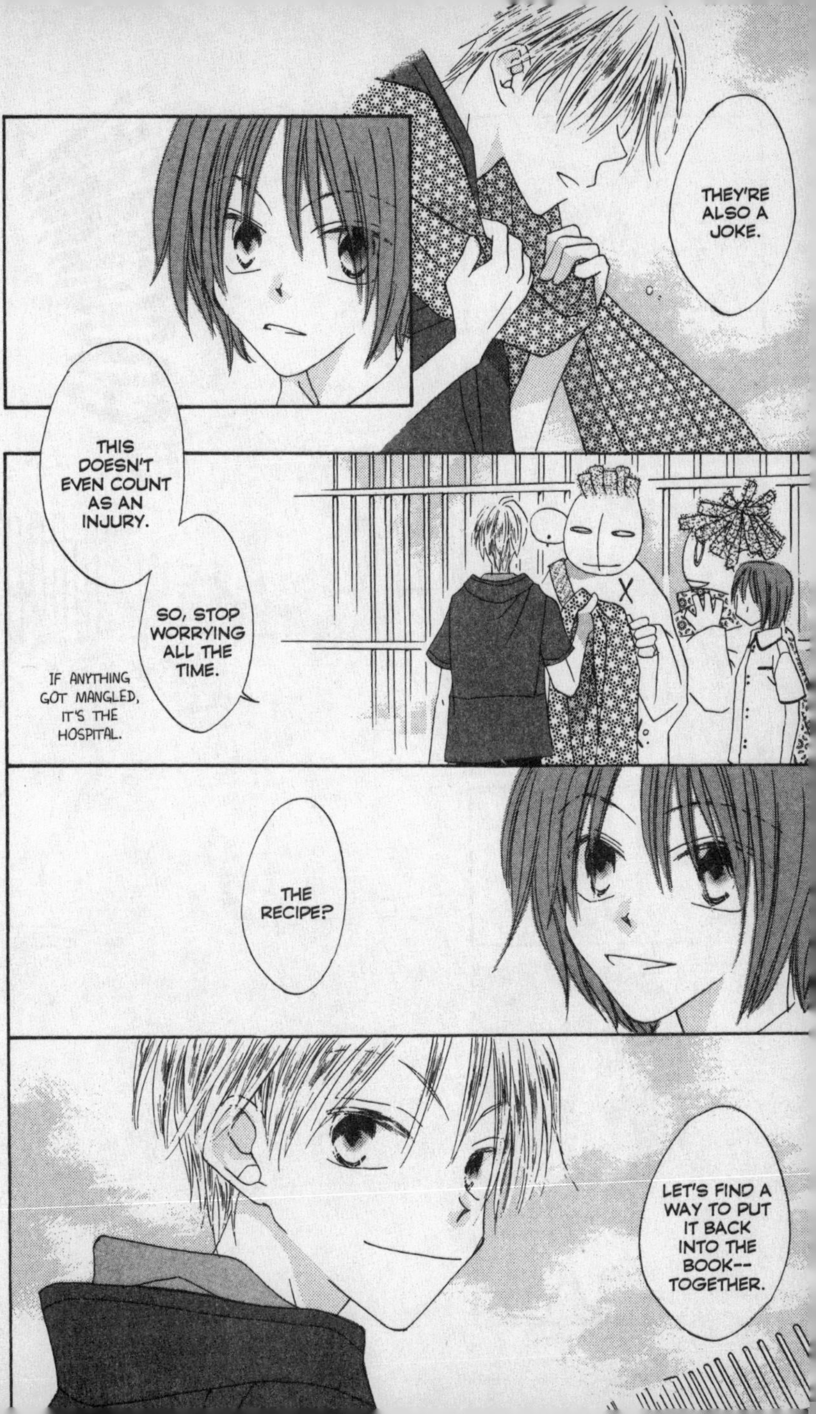
THEY'RE ALSO A JOKE.
THIS DOESN'T EVEN COUNT AS AN INJURY.
SO, STOP WORRYING ALL THE TIME.
IF ANYTHING GOT MANGLED, IT'S THE HOSPITAL.
THE RECIPE?
LET'S FIND A WAY TO PUT IT BACK INTO THE BOOK--TOGETHER.

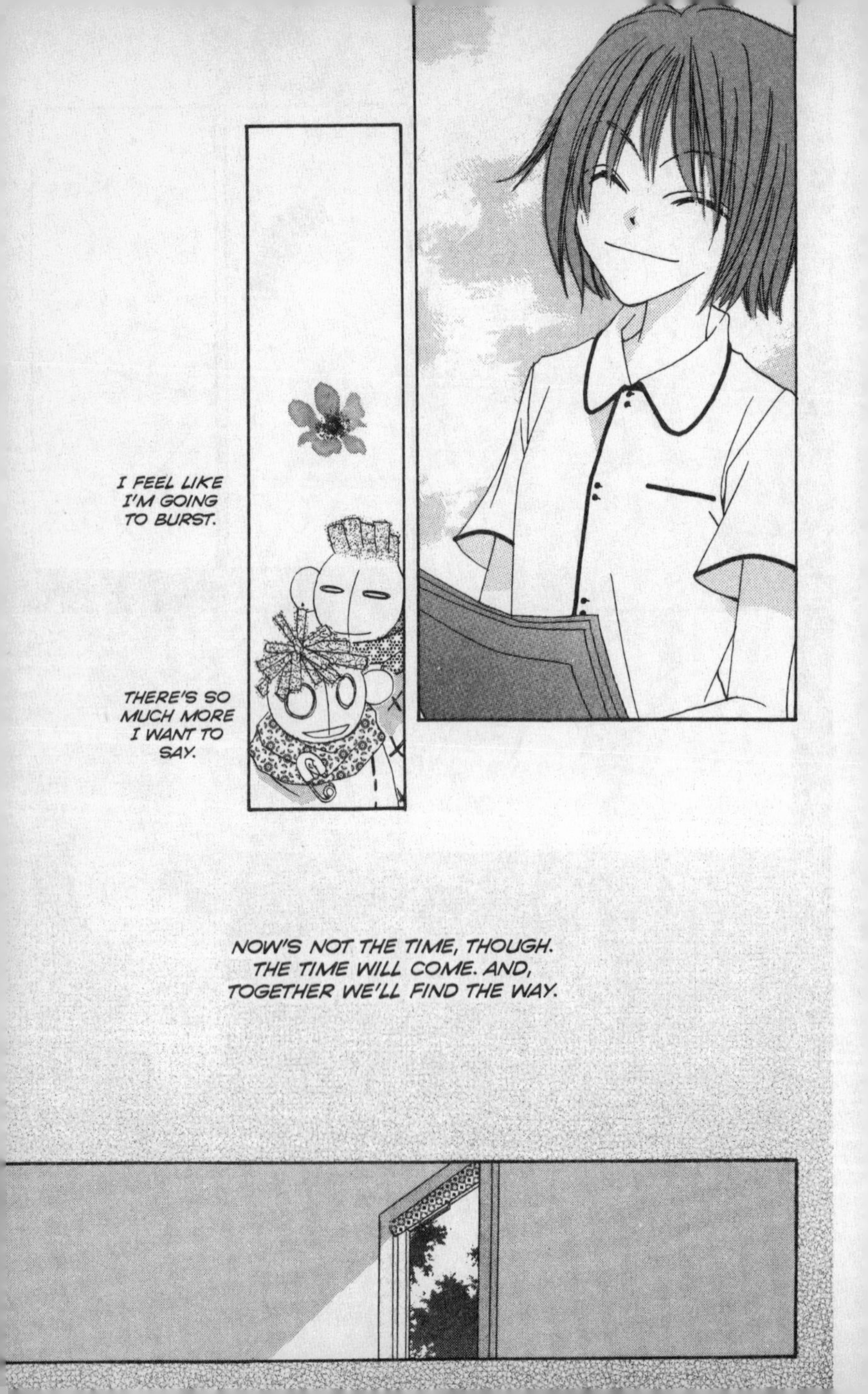
I FEEL LIKE I'M GOING TO BURST.
THERE'S SO MUCH MORE I WANT TO SAY.
NOW'S NOT THE TIME, THOUGH. THE TIME WILL COME. AND, TOGETHER WE'LL FIND THE WAY.

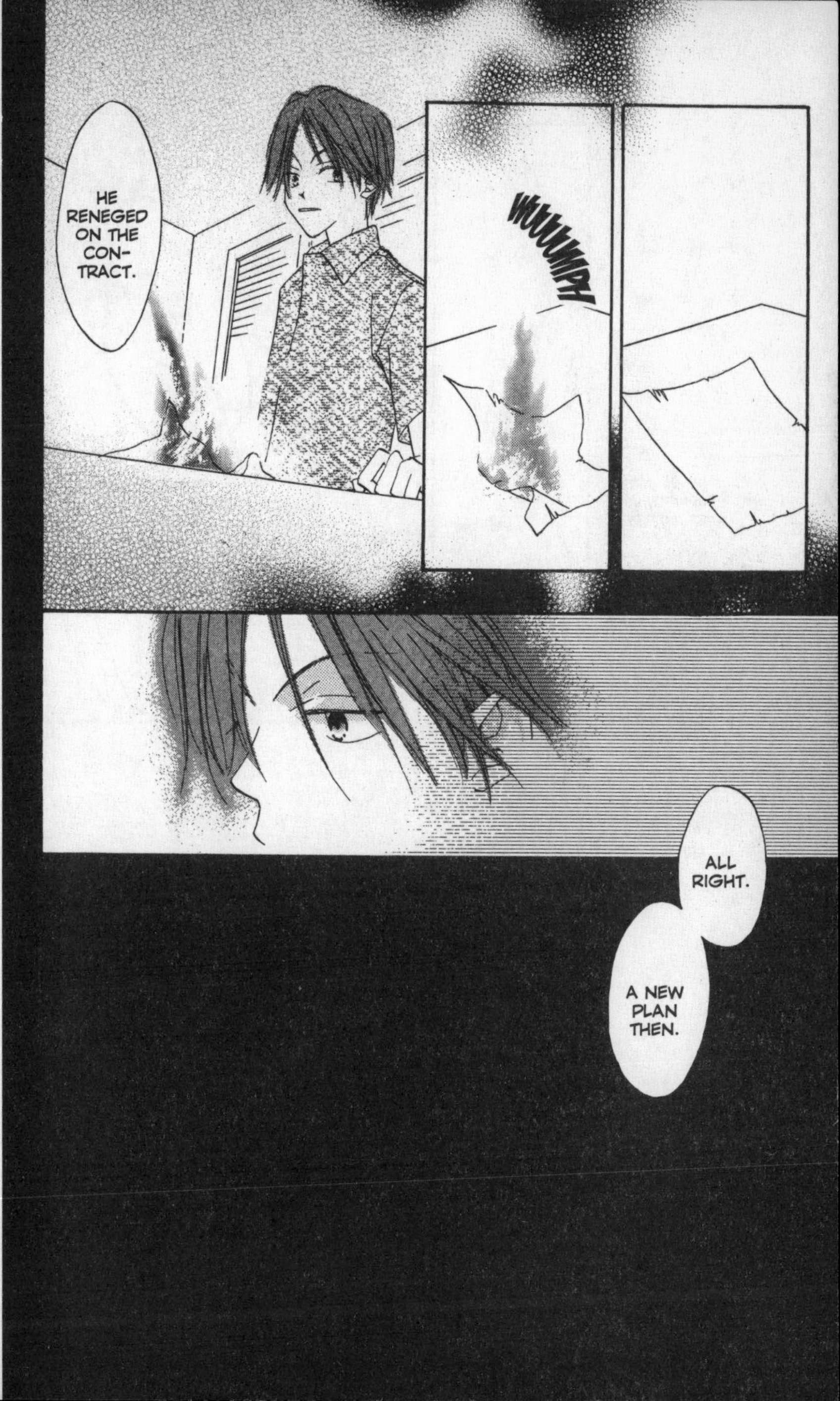
WUUUMPH
HE RENEGED ON THE CON-TRACT.
ALL RIGHT.
A NEW PLAN THEN.

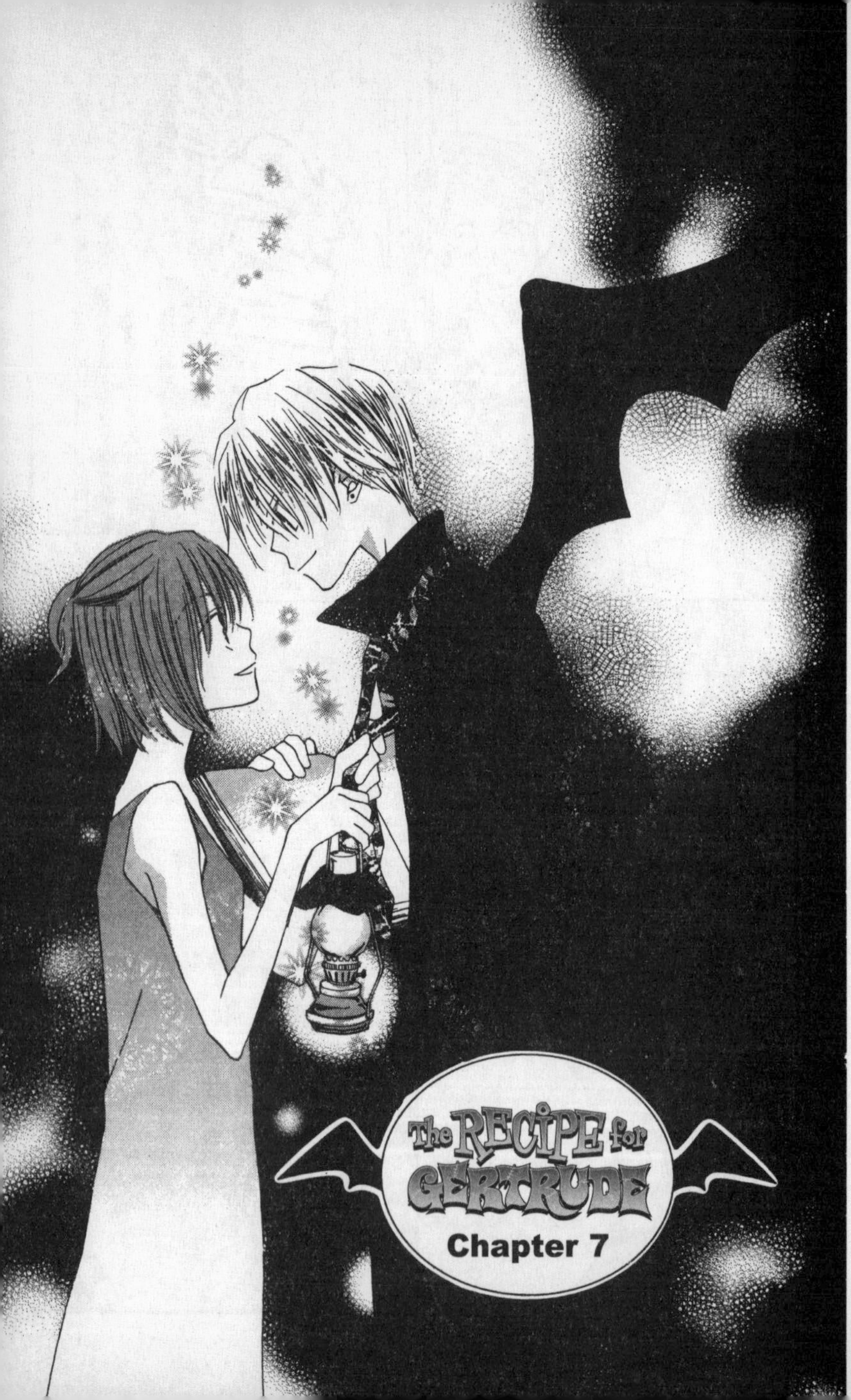
The RECIPE for GERTRUDE
Chapter 7

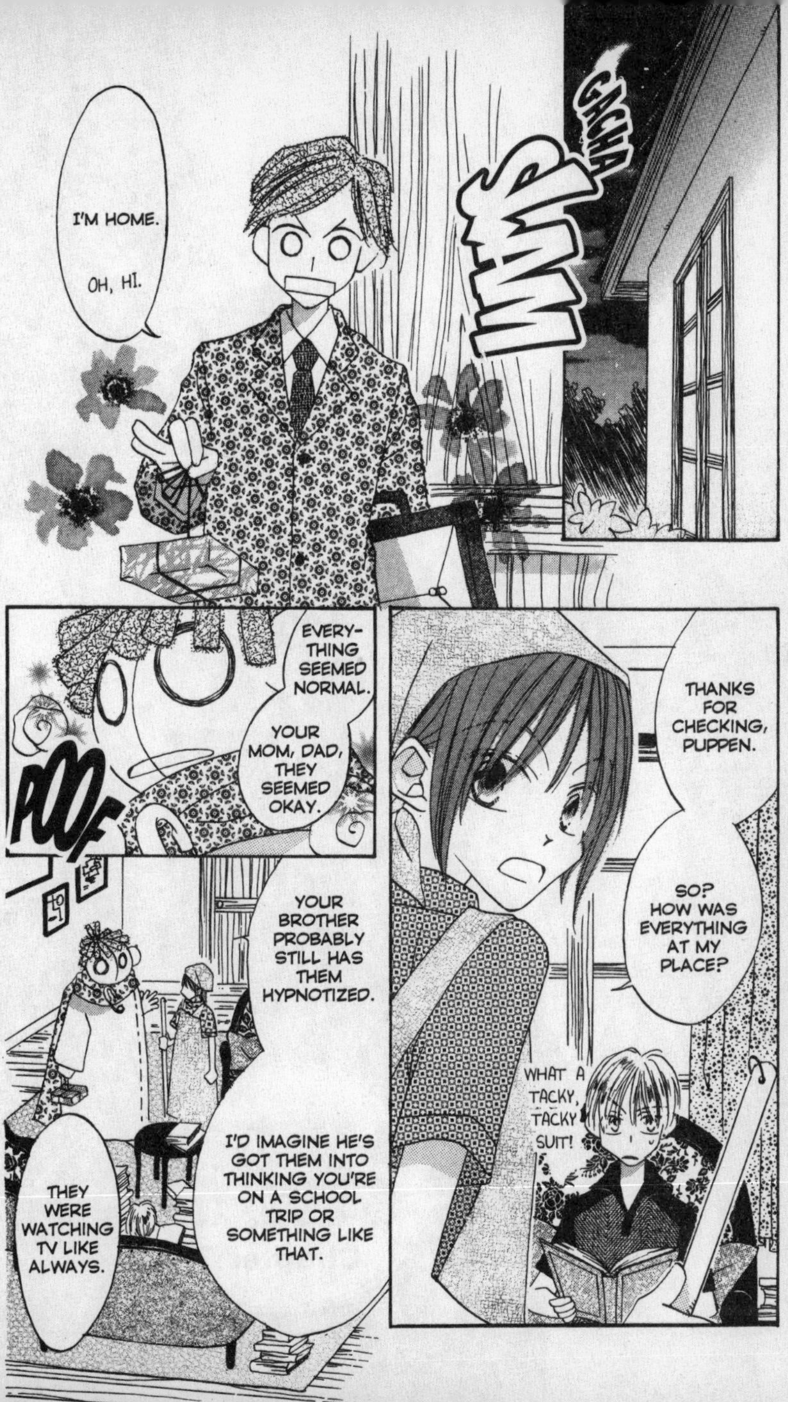
GACHA
I'M HOME.
OH, HI.
THANKS FOR CHECKING, PUPPEN.
SO? HOW WAS EVERYTHING AT MY PLACE?
WHAT A TACKY, TACKY SUIT!
EVERYTHING SEEMED NORMAL.
YOUR MOM, DAD, THEY SEEMED OKAY.
POOF
YOUR BROTHER PROBABLY STILL HAS THEM HYPNOTIZED.
I'D IMAGINE HE'S GOT THEM INTO THINKING YOU'RE ON A SCHOOL TRIP OR SOMETHING LIKE THAT.
THEY WERE WATCHING TV LIKE ALWAYS.

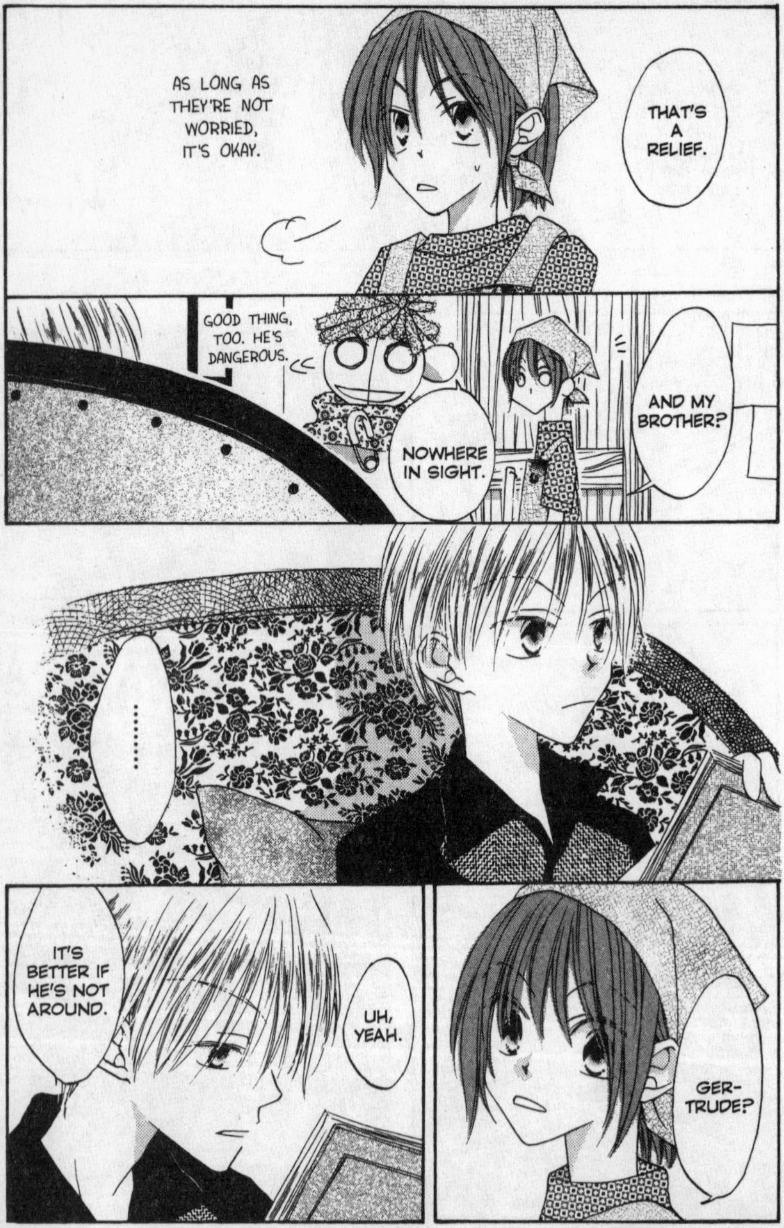
THAT'S A RELIEF.
AS LONG AS THEY'RE NOT WORRIED, IT'S OKAY.
AND MY BROTHER?
NOWHERE IN SIGHT.
GOOD THING, TOO. HE'S DANGEROUS.
......
GER-TRUDE?
UH, YEAH.
IT'S BETTER IF HE'S NOT AROUND.

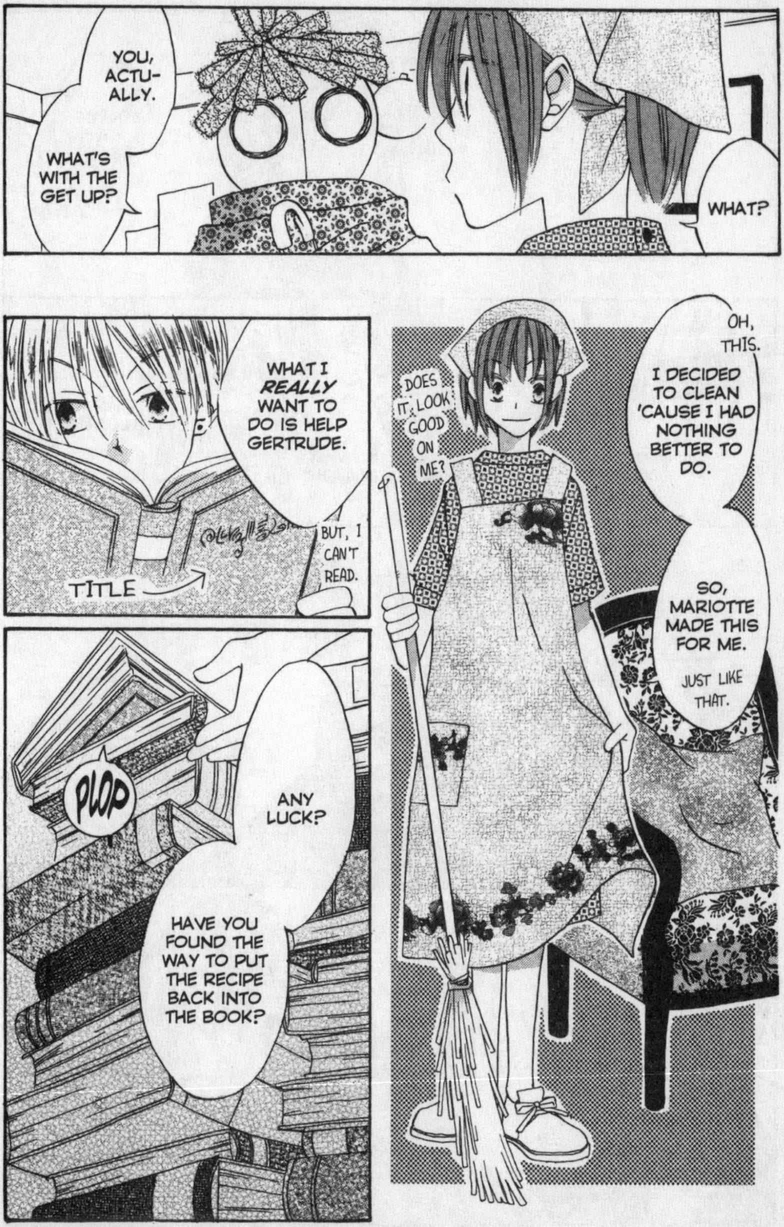
WHAT'S WITH THE GET UP?
WHAT?
YOU, ACTUALLY.
OH, THIS. I DECIDED TO CLEAN 'CAUSE I HAD NOTHING BETTER TO DO.
SO, MARIOTTE MADE THIS FOR ME.
JUST LIKE THAT.
DOES IT LOOK GOOD ON ME?
WHAT I *REALLY* WANT TO DO IS HELP GERTRUDE.
BUT, I CAN'T READ.
TITLE
PLOP
ANY LUCK?
HAVE YOU FOUND THE WAY TO PUT THE RECIPE BACK INTO THE BOOK?

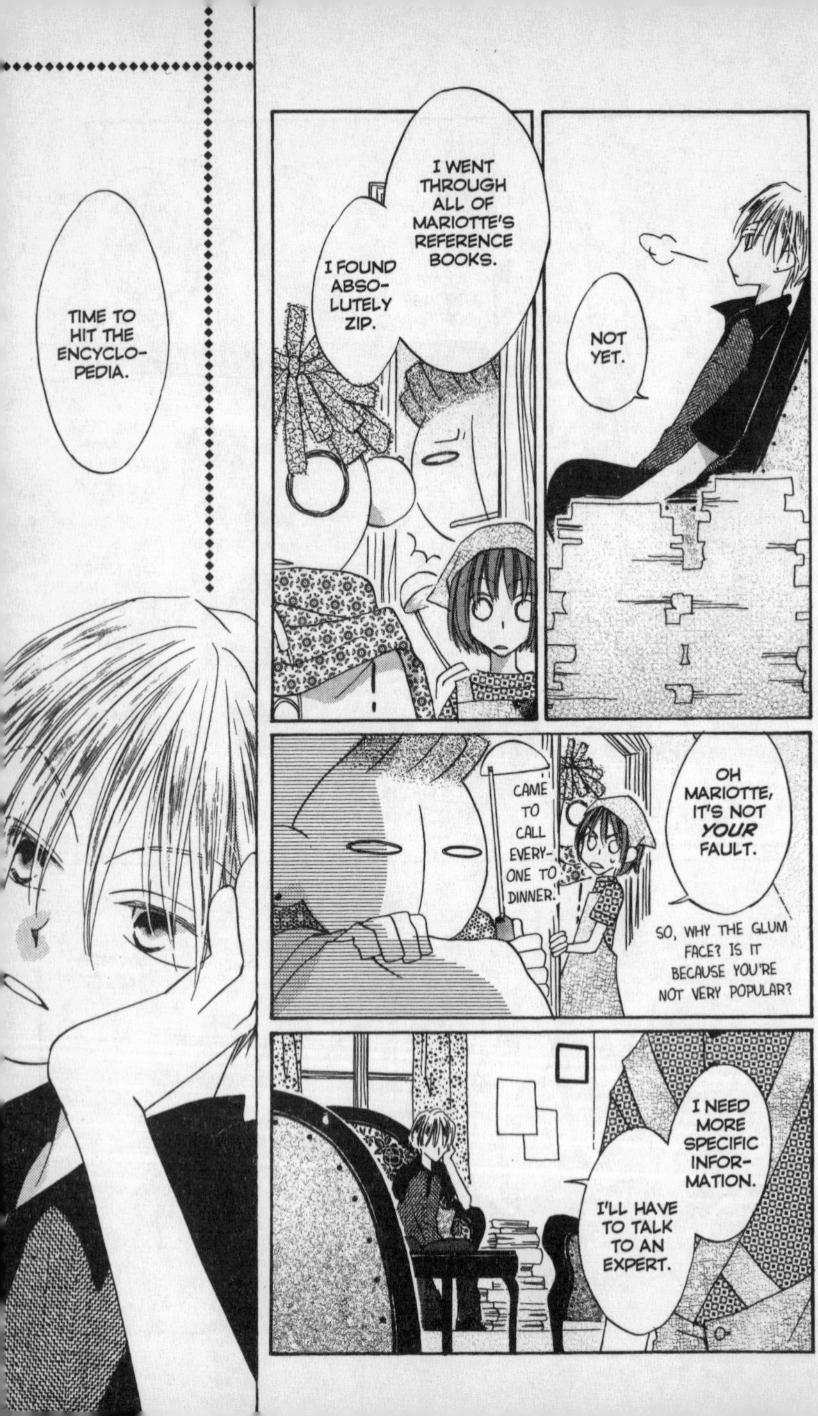
NOT YET.
I WENT THROUGH ALL OF MARIOTTE'S REFERENCE BOOKS.
I FOUND ABSO-LUTELY ZIP.
OH MARIOTTE, IT'S NOT *YOUR* FAULT.
SO, WHY THE GLUM FACE? IS IT BECAUSE YOU'RE NOT VERY POPULAR?
CAME TO CALL EVERY-ONE TO DINNER.
I NEED MORE SPECIFIC INFOR-MATION.
I'LL HAVE TO TALK TO AN EXPERT.
TIME TO HIT THE ENCYCLO-PEDIA.

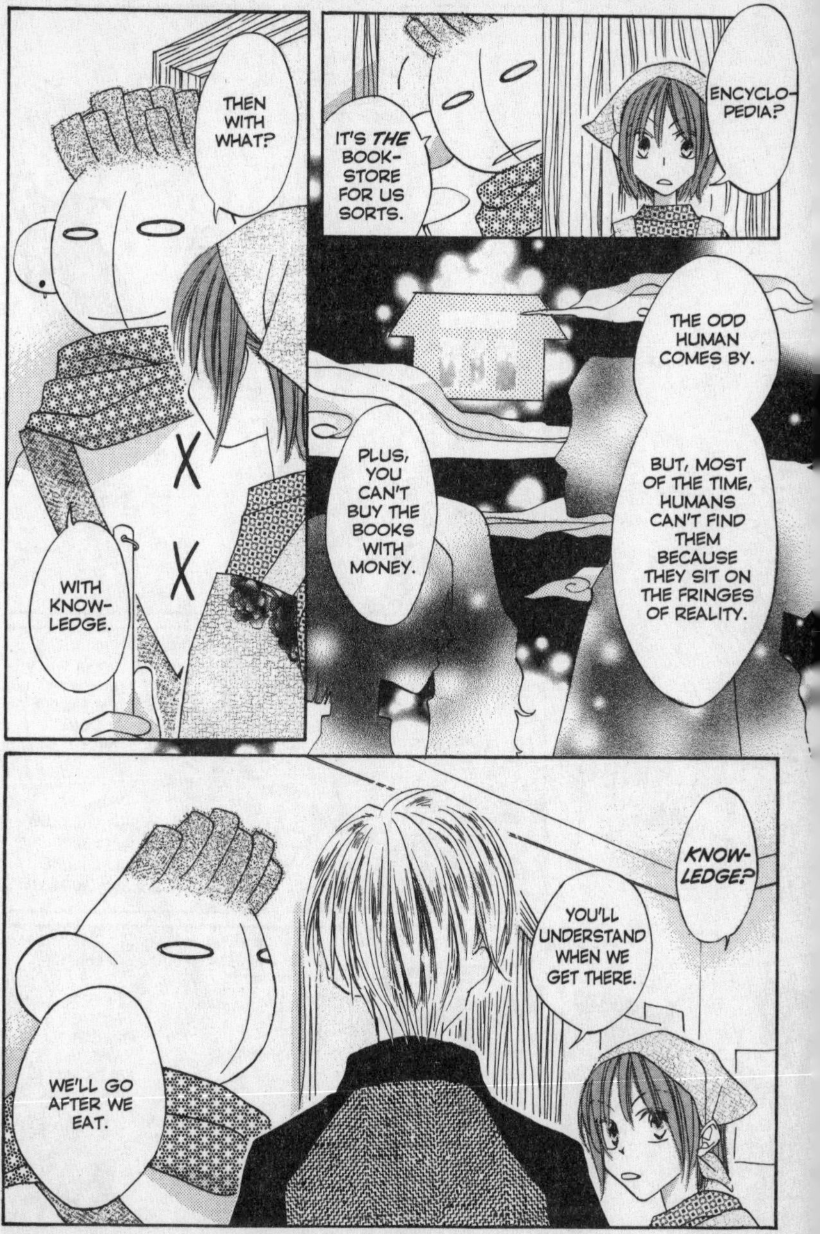
ENCYCLOPEDIA?
IT'S THE BOOKSTORE FOR US SORTS.
THE ODD HUMAN COMES BY.
BUT, MOST OF THE TIME, HUMANS CAN'T FIND THEM BECAUSE THEY SIT ON THE FRINGES OF REALITY.
PLUS, YOU CAN'T BUY THE BOOKS WITH MONEY.
THEN WITH WHAT?
WITH KNOWLEDGE.
KNOWLEDGE?
YOU'LL UNDERSTAND WHEN WE GET THERE.
WE'LL GO AFTER WE EAT.

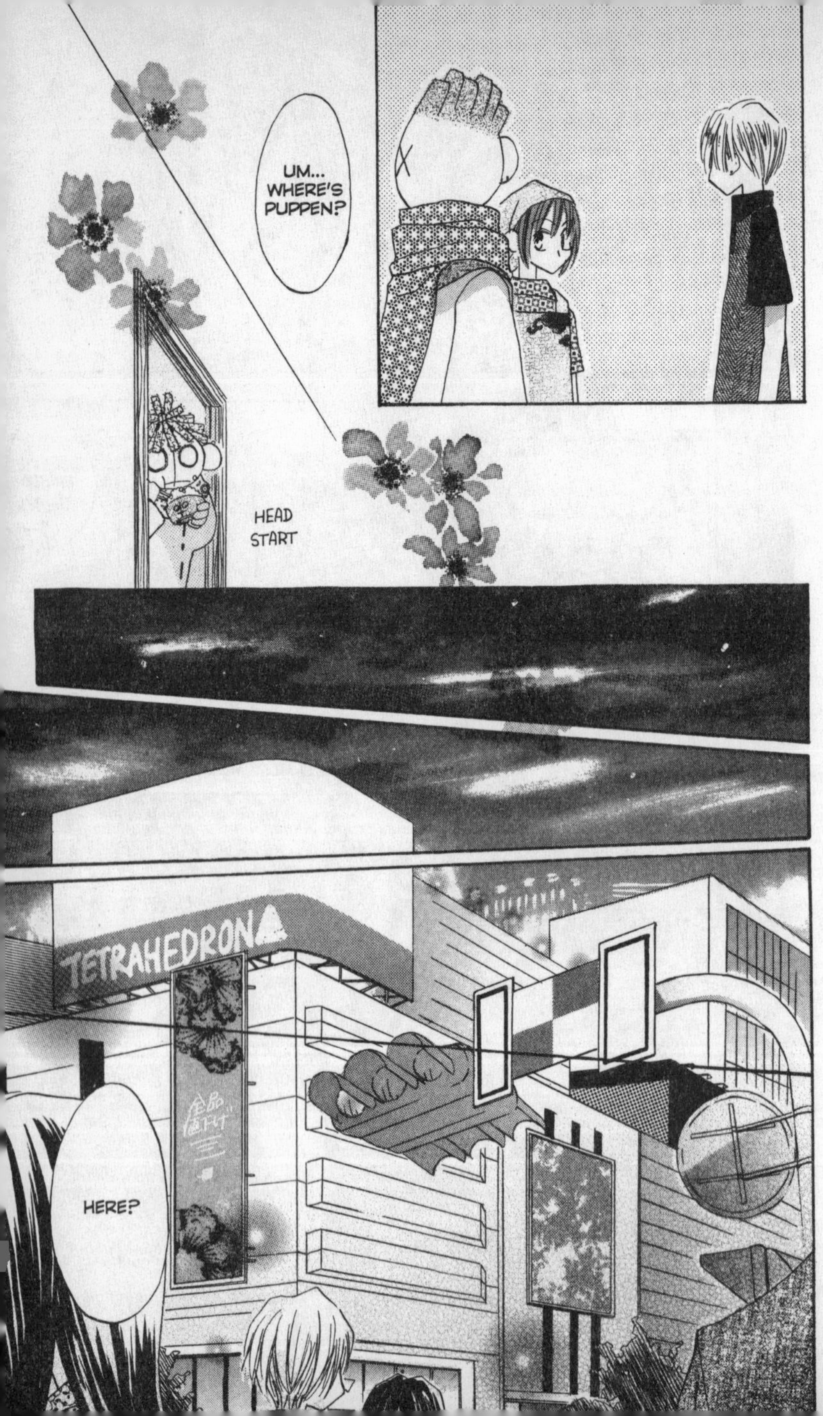
UM... WHERE'S PUPPEN?
HEAD START
TETRAHEDRON
全品値下げ
HERE?

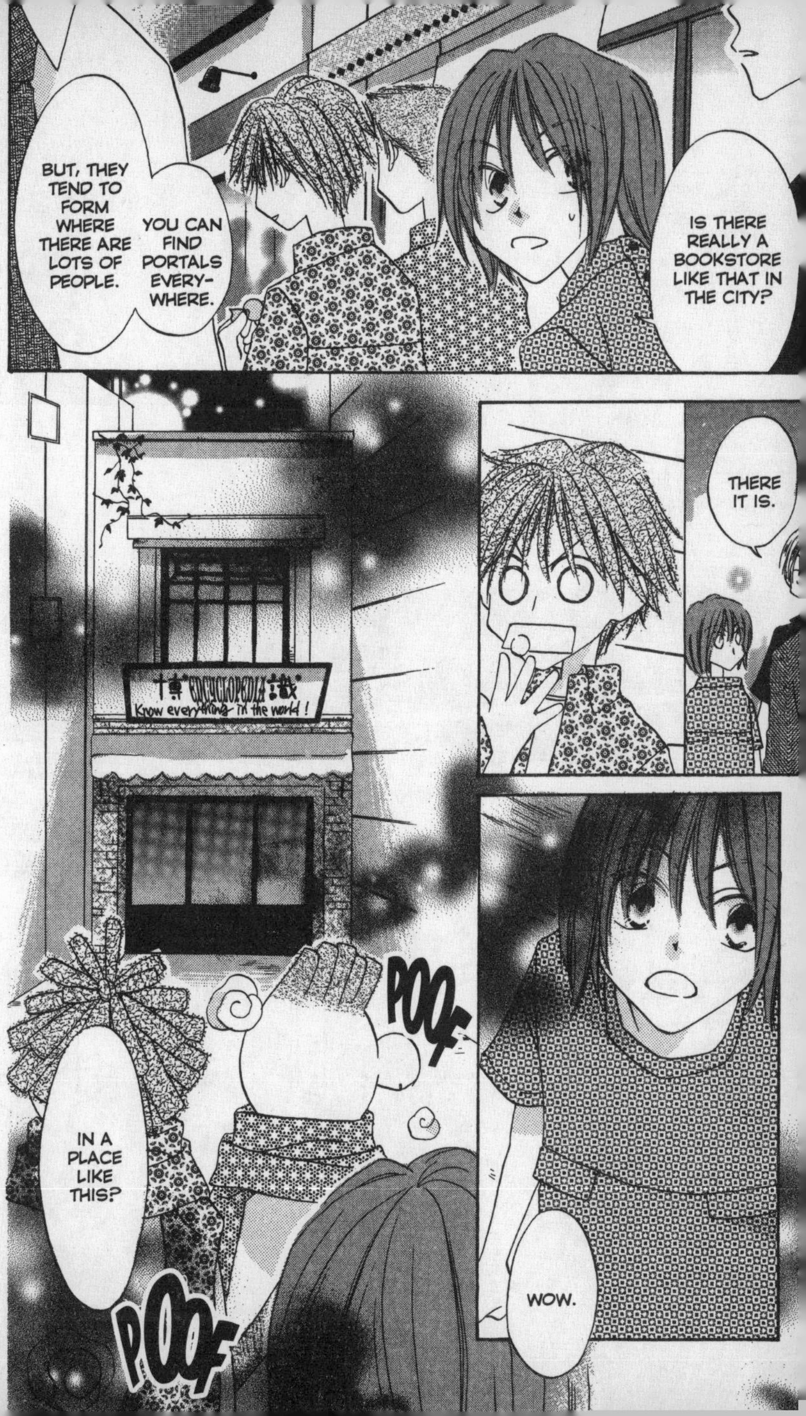
IS THERE REALLY A BOOKSTORE LIKE THAT IN THE CITY?
YOU CAN FIND PORTALS EVERY-WHERE.
BUT, THEY TEND TO FORM WHERE THERE ARE LOTS OF PEOPLE.
THERE IT IS.
WOW.
"ENCYCLOPEDIA"
Know everything in the world!
POOF
IN A PLACE LIKE THIS?
POOF

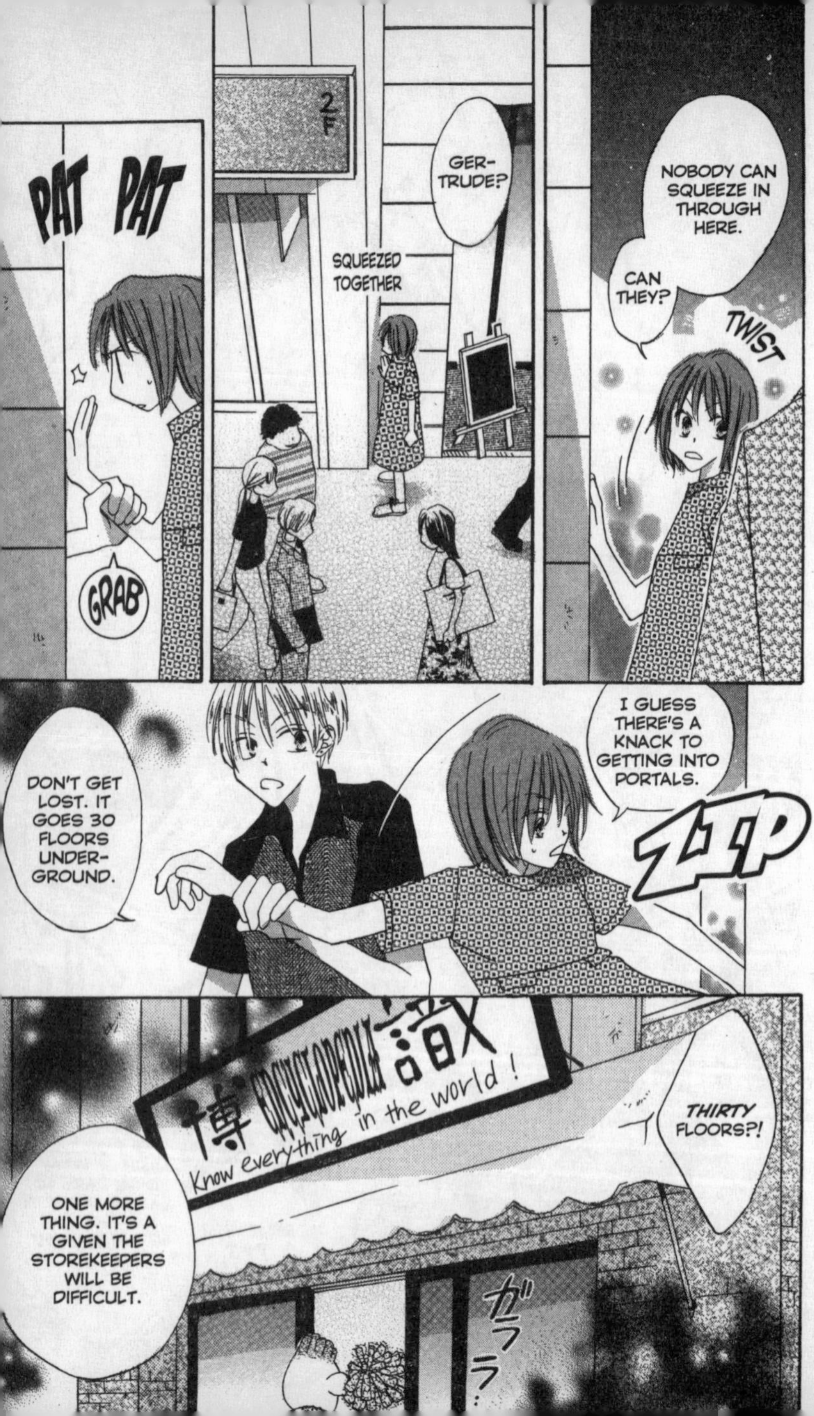
NOBODY CAN SQUEEZE IN THROUGH HERE.
CAN THEY?
TWIST
GER-TRUDE?
SQUEEZED TOGETHER
PAT PAT
GRAB
I GUESS THERE'S A KNACK TO GETTING INTO PORTALS.
ZIP
DON'T GET LOST. IT GOES 30 FLOORS UNDER-GROUND.
THIRTY FLOORS?!
博 ENCYCLOPEDIA 識
Know everything in the world!
ONE MORE THING. IT'S A GIVEN THE STOREKEEPERS WILL BE DIFFICULT.
ガララ

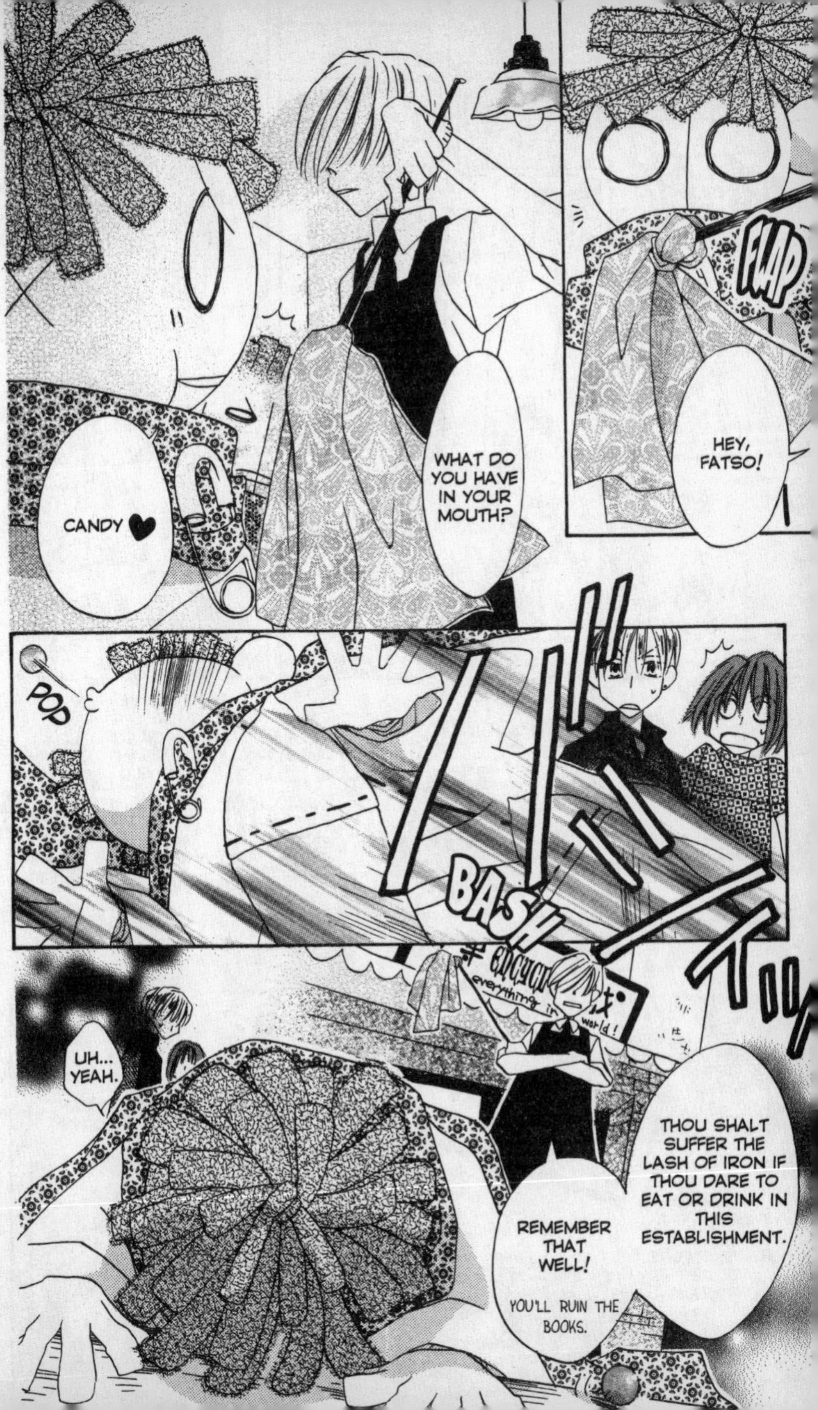
FLAP
HEY, FATSO!
WHAT DO YOU HAVE IN YOUR MOUTH?
CANDY ♥
BASH
POP
THOU SHALT SUFFER THE LASH OF IRON IF THOU DARE TO EAT OR DRINK IN THIS ESTABLISHMENT.
REMEMBER THAT WELL!
YOU'LL RUIN THE BOOKS.
UH... YEAH.

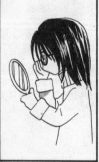

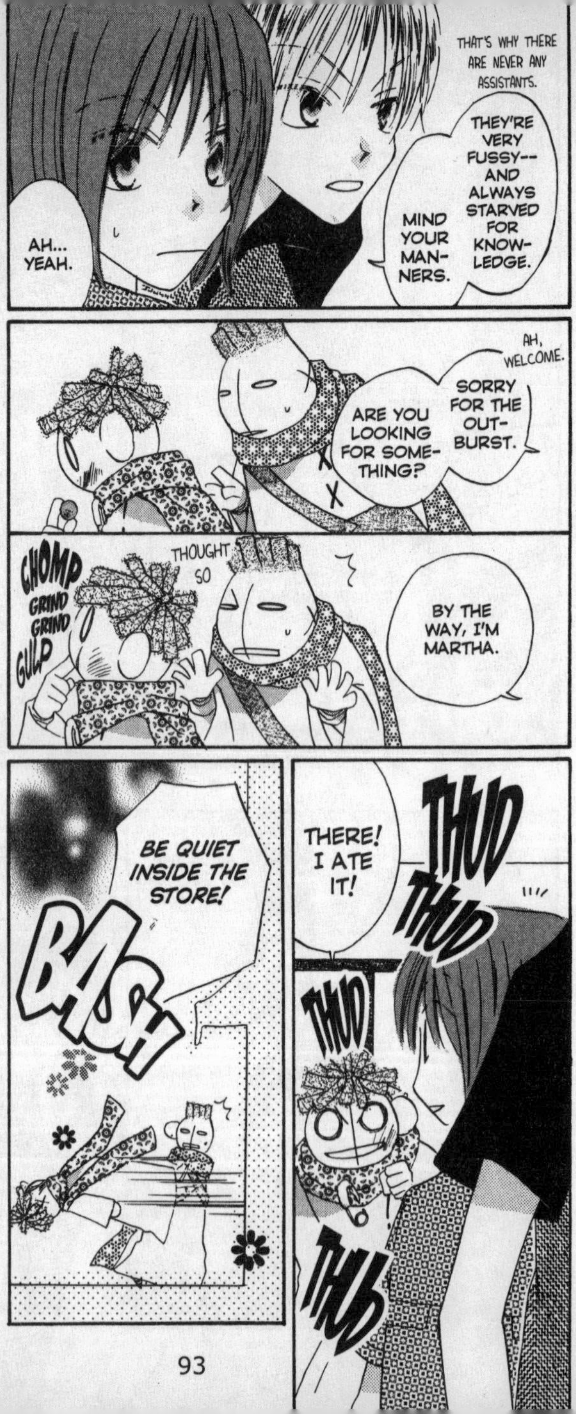
THAT'S WHY THERE ARE NEVER ANY ASSISTANTS.
THEY'RE VERY FUSSY--AND ALWAYS STARVED FOR KNOW-LEDGE.
MIND YOUR MAN-NERS.
AH... YEAH.
AH, WELCOME.
SORRY FOR THE OUT-BURST.
ARE YOU LOOKING FOR SOME-THING?
BY THE WAY, I'M MARTHA.
THOUGHT SO
CHOMP GRIND GRIND GULP
THERE! I ATE IT!
THUD THUD
THUD
THUD
BE QUIET INSIDE THE STORE!
BASH

03

It's been pointed out to me that many of my characters wear glasses. I admit it. I like glasses. More specifically, they're something I've always wanted. My eyesight has always been good (although it might've gone down a shade recently), so I never got the chance to wear them. They don't suit me whenever I do try on a pair. Actually, they **do** suit me, but in a bad sort of way. Either way, it looks really weird when I put them on, so I don't even put on those fashion pairs that don't actually have corrective lenses.

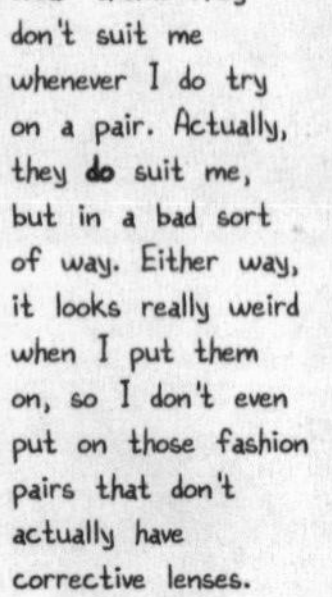

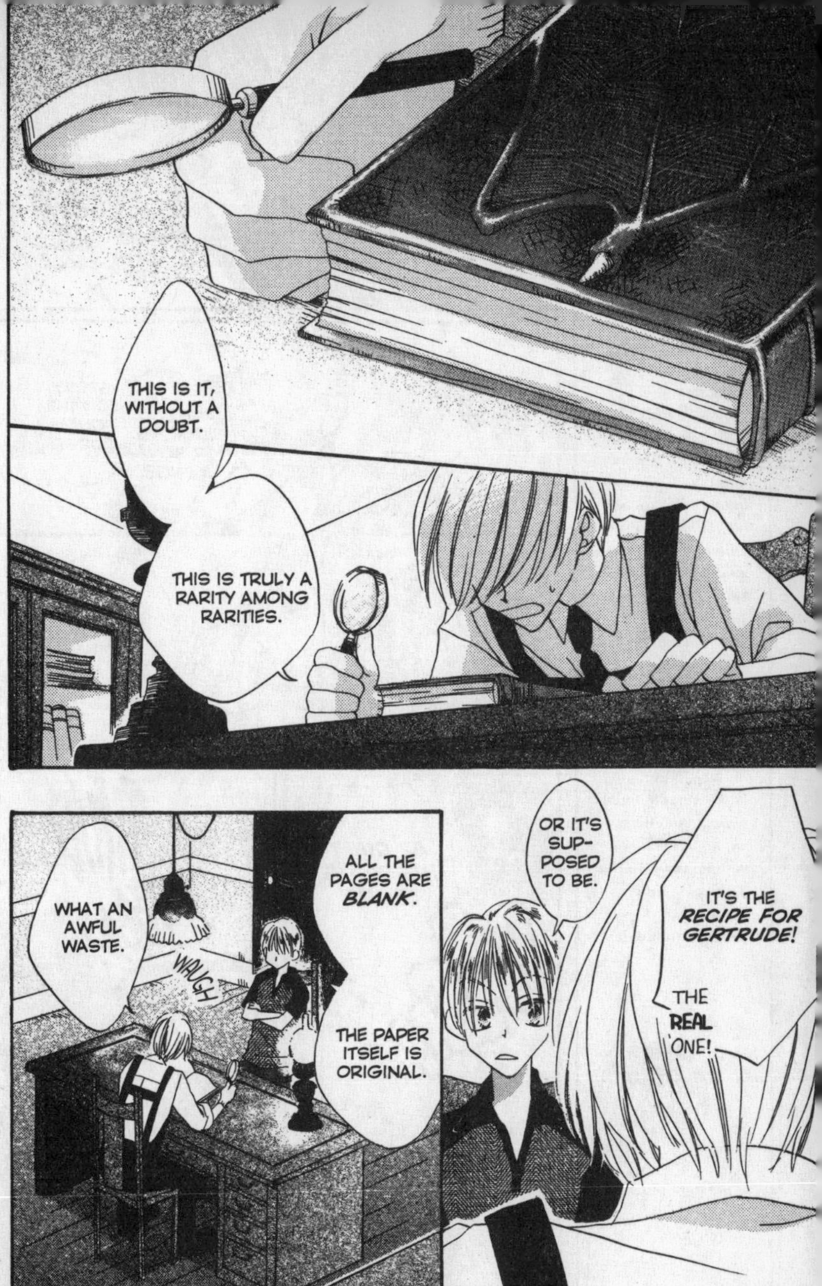
THIS IS IT, WITHOUT A DOUBT.
THIS IS TRULY A RARITY AMONG RARITIES.
IT'S THE *RECIPE FOR GERTRUDE!*
THE **REAL** ONE!
OR IT'S SUP-POSED TO BE.
ALL THE PAGES ARE *BLANK*.
THE PAPER ITSELF IS ORIGINAL.
WAUGH
WHAT AN AWFUL WASTE.

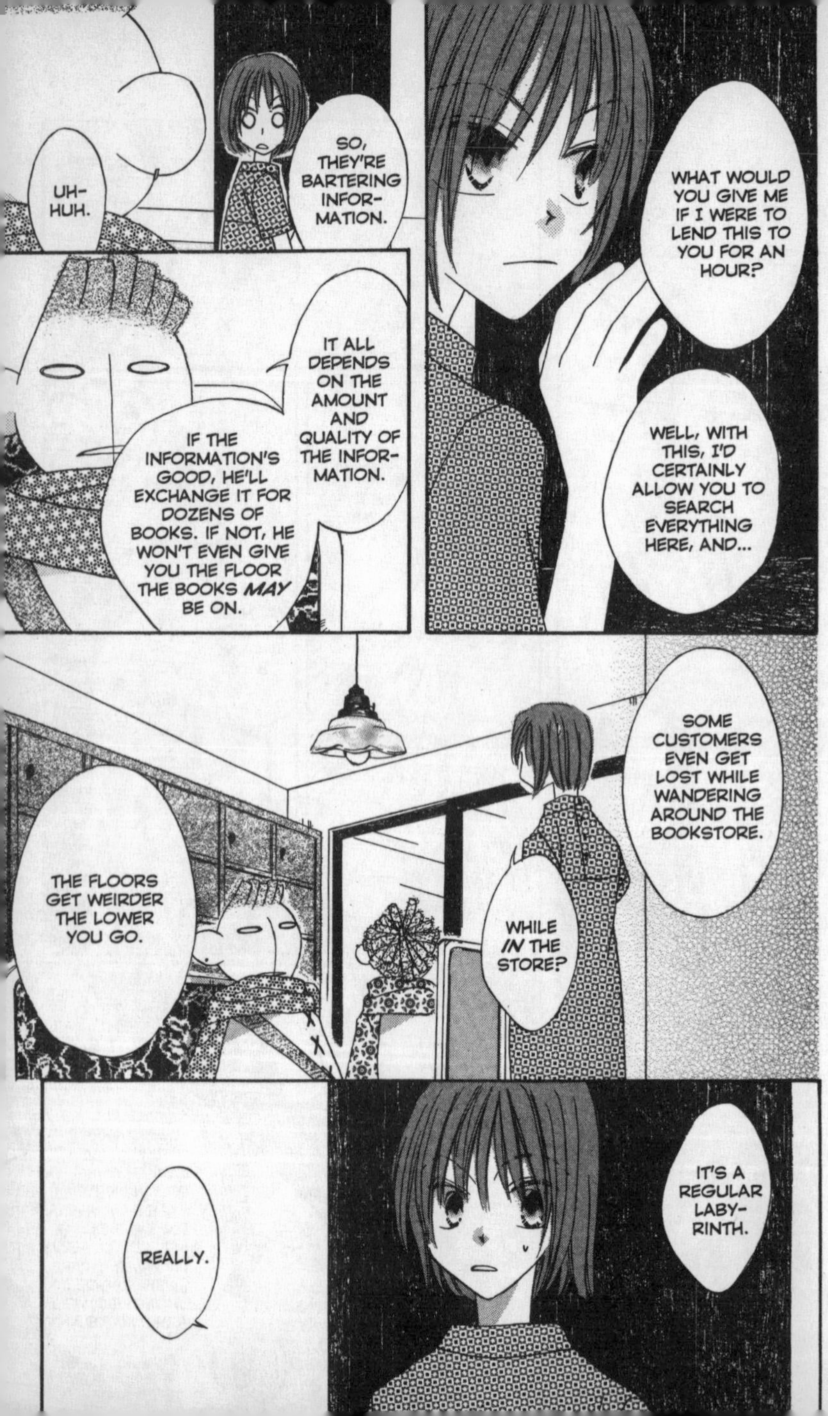
WHAT WOULD YOU GIVE ME IF I WERE TO LEND THIS TO YOU FOR AN HOUR?
WELL, WITH THIS, I'D CERTAINLY ALLOW YOU TO SEARCH EVERYTHING HERE, AND...
SO, THEY'RE BARTERING INFORMATION.
UH-HUH.
IT ALL DEPENDS ON THE AMOUNT AND QUALITY OF THE INFORMATION.
IF THE INFORMATION'S GOOD, HE'LL EXCHANGE IT FOR DOZENS OF BOOKS. IF NOT, HE WON'T EVEN GIVE YOU THE FLOOR THE BOOKS *MAY* BE ON.
SOME CUSTOMERS EVEN GET LOST WHILE WANDERING AROUND THE BOOKSTORE.
WHILE *IN* THE STORE?
THE FLOORS GET WEIRDER THE LOWER YOU GO.
IT'S A REGULAR LABYRINTH.
REALLY.

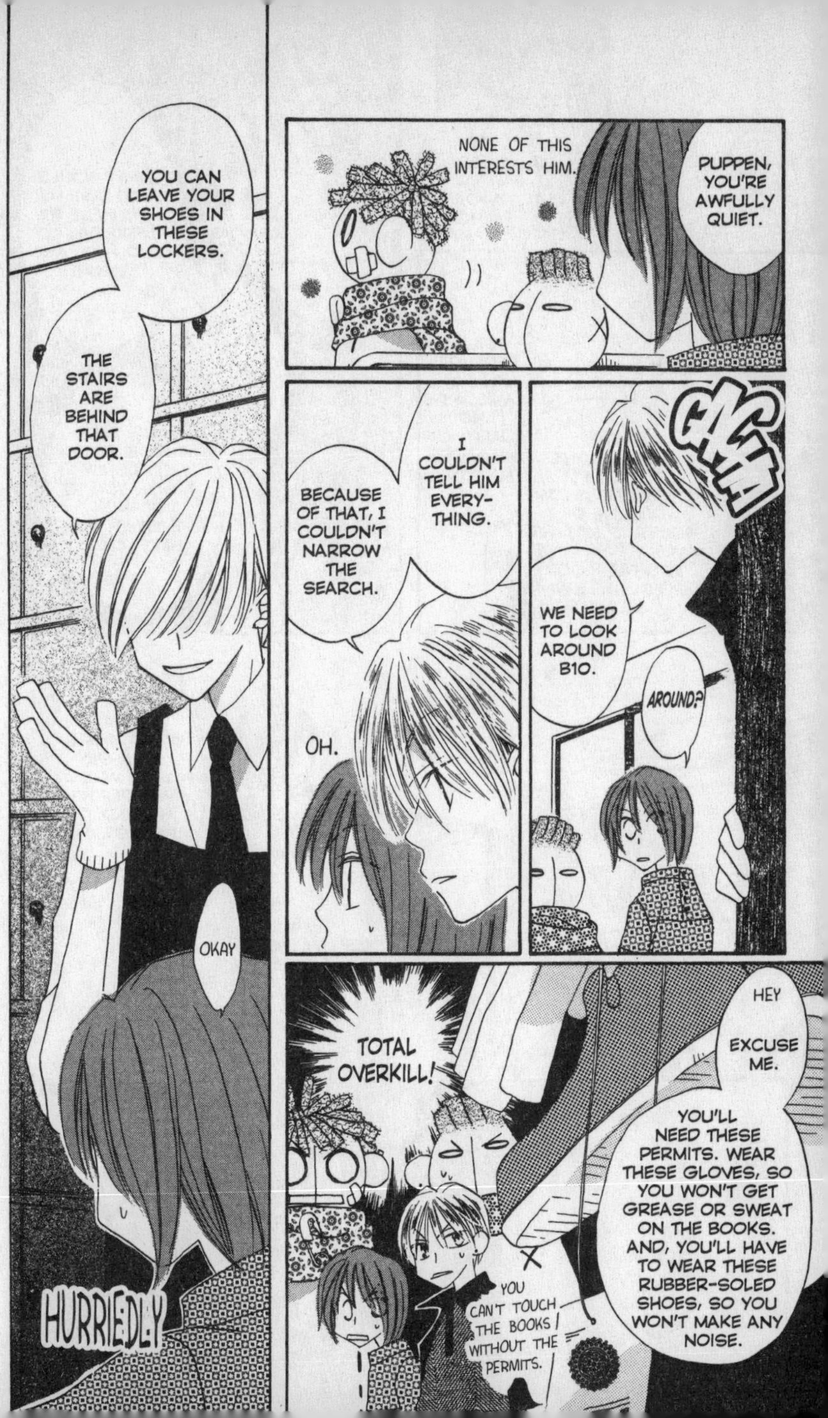
PUPPEN, YOU'RE AWFULLY QUIET.
NONE OF THIS INTERESTS HIM.
GACHA
WE NEED TO LOOK AROUND B10.
AROUND?
I COULDN'T TELL HIM EVERYTHING.
BECAUSE OF THAT, I COULDN'T NARROW THE SEARCH.
OH.
HEY
EXCUSE ME.
YOU'LL NEED THESE PERMITS. WEAR THESE GLOVES, SO YOU WON'T GET GREASE OR SWEAT ON THE BOOKS. AND, YOU'LL HAVE TO WEAR THESE RUBBER-SOLED SHOES, SO YOU WON'T MAKE ANY NOISE.
YOU CAN'T TOUCH THE BOOKS WITHOUT THE PERMITS.
TOTAL OVERKILL!
YOU CAN LEAVE YOUR SHOES IN THESE LOCKERS.
THE STAIRS ARE BEHIND THAT DOOR.
OKAY
HURRIEDLY

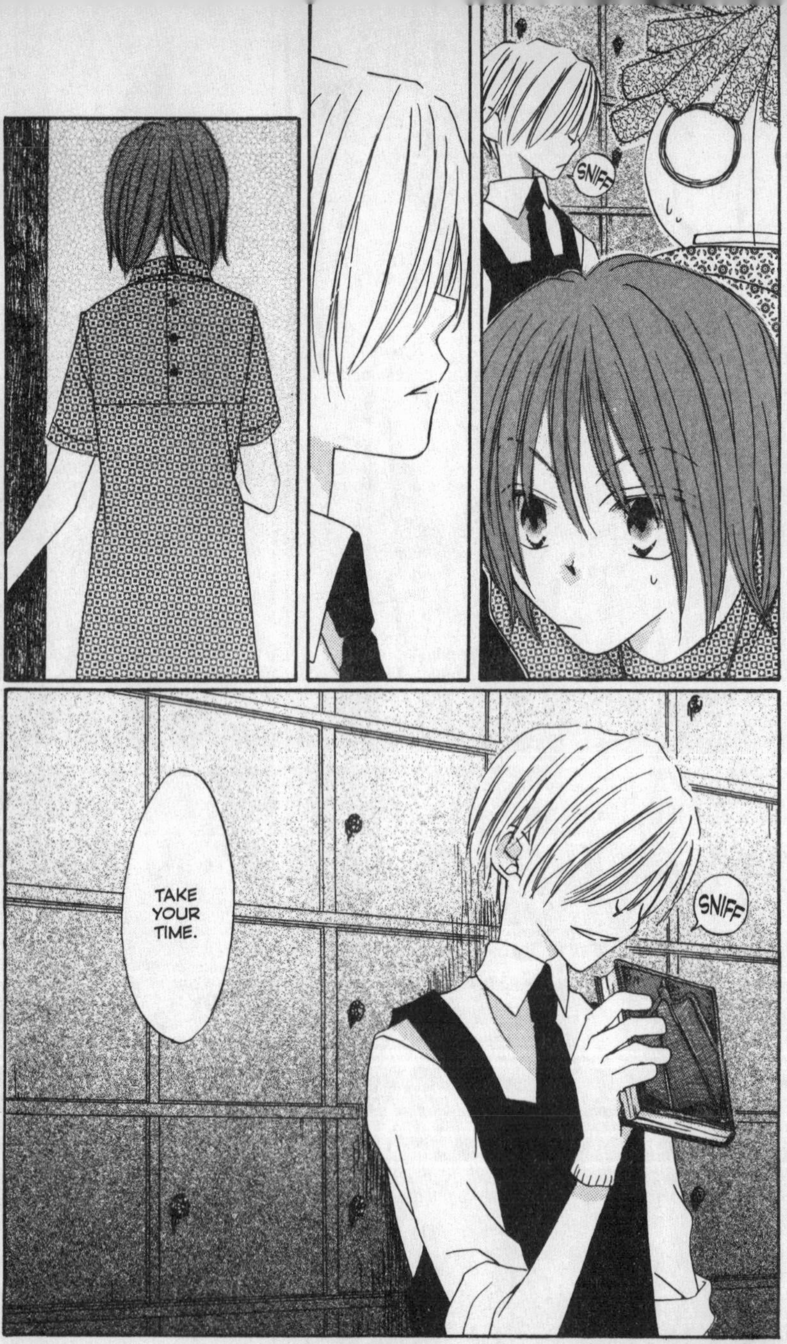
SNIFF
SNIFF
TAKE YOUR TIME.

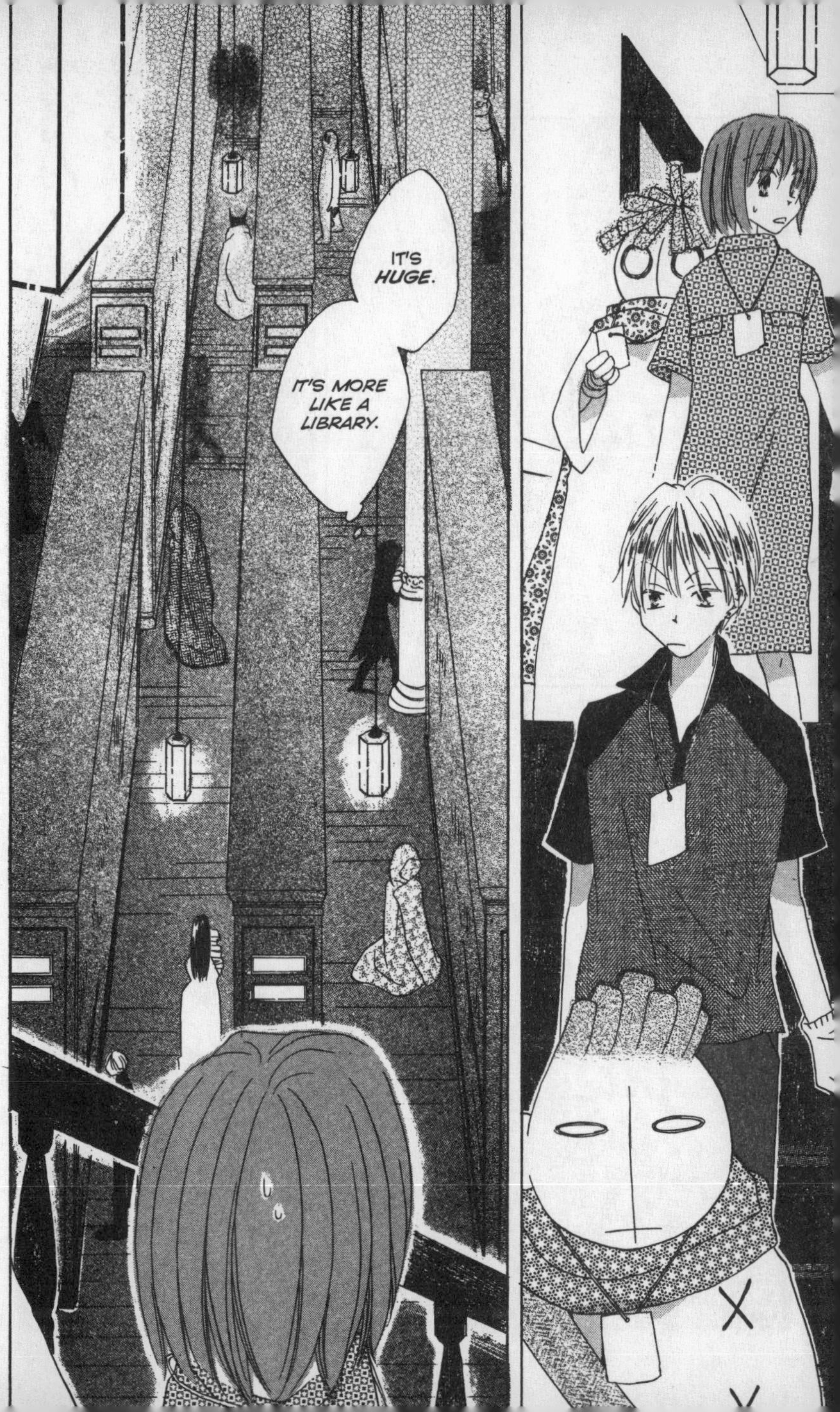
IT'S *HUGE.*
IT'S MORE LIKE A LIBRARY.

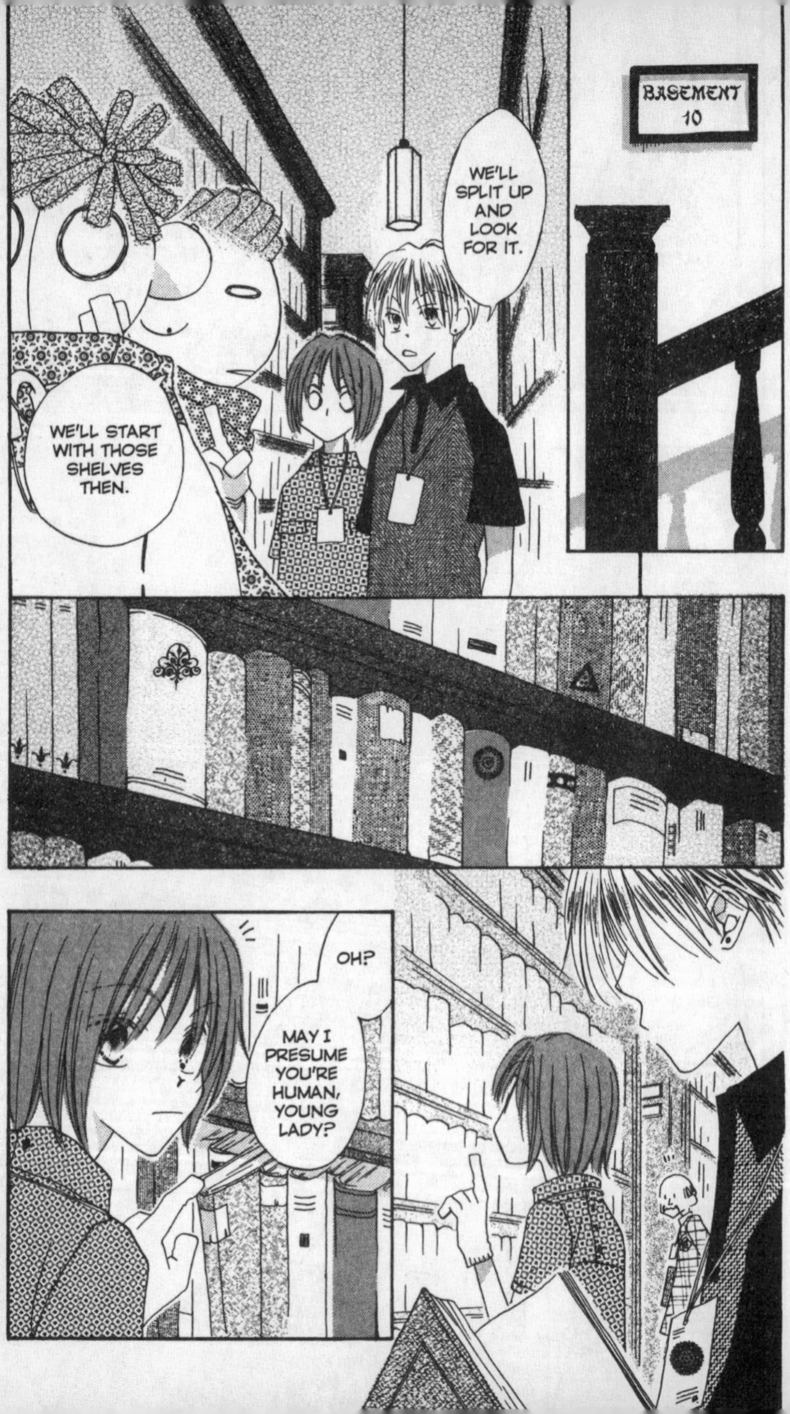
BASEMENT 10
WE'LL SPLIT UP AND LOOK FOR IT.
WE'LL START WITH THOSE SHELVES THEN.
OH?
MAY I PRESUME YOU'RE HUMAN, YOUNG LADY?

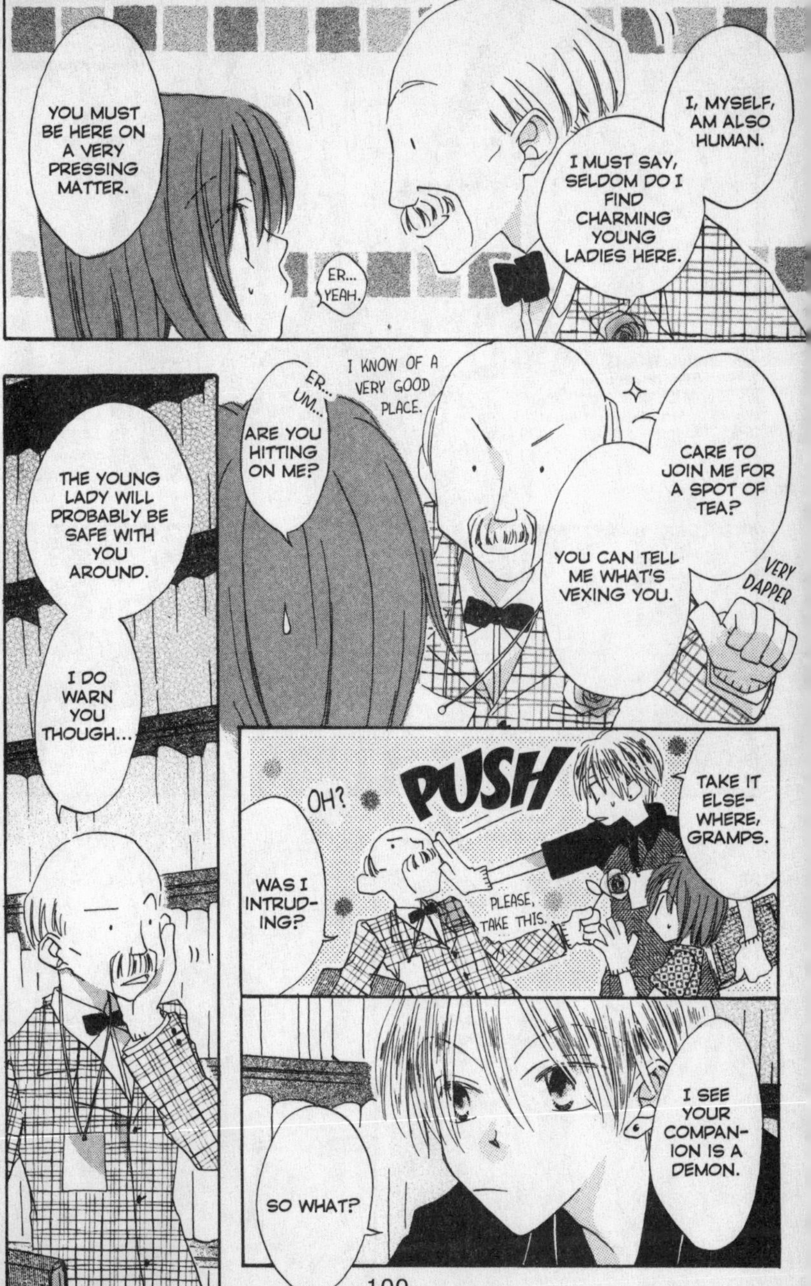
I, MYSELF, AM ALSO HUMAN.
I MUST SAY, SELDOM DO I FIND CHARMING YOUNG LADIES HERE.
ER... YEAH.
YOU MUST BE HERE ON A VERY PRESSING MATTER.
CARE TO JOIN ME FOR A SPOT OF TEA?
YOU CAN TELL ME WHAT'S VEXING YOU.
VERY DAPPER
I KNOW OF A VERY GOOD PLACE.
ER... UM...
ARE YOU HITTING ON ME?
TAKE IT ELSE-WHERE, GRAMPS.
PUSH
PLEASE, TAKE THIS.
OH?
WAS I INTRUD-ING?
I SEE YOUR COMPAN-ION IS A DEMON.
SO WHAT?
THE YOUNG LADY WILL PROBABLY BE SAFE WITH YOU AROUND.
I DO WARN YOU THOUGH...

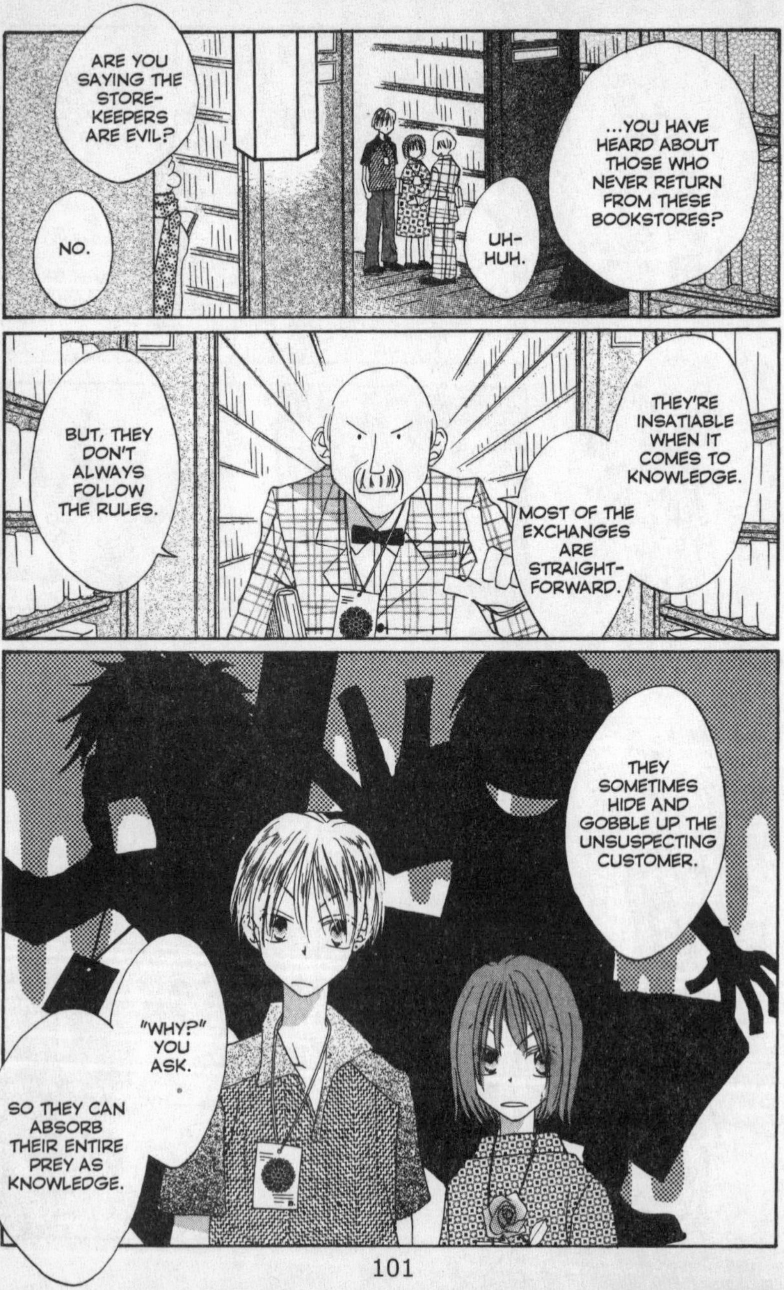
...YOU HAVE HEARD ABOUT THOSE WHO NEVER RETURN FROM THESE BOOKSTORES?
UH-HUH.
ARE YOU SAYING THE STORE-KEEPERS ARE EVIL?
NO.
THEY'RE INSATIABLE WHEN IT COMES TO KNOWLEDGE.
MOST OF THE EXCHANGES ARE STRAIGHT-FORWARD.
BUT, THEY DON'T ALWAYS FOLLOW THE RULES.
THEY SOMETIMES HIDE AND GOBBLE UP THE UNSUSPECTING CUSTOMER.
"WHY?" YOU ASK.
SO THEY CAN ABSORB THEIR ENTIRE PREY AS KNOWLEDGE.

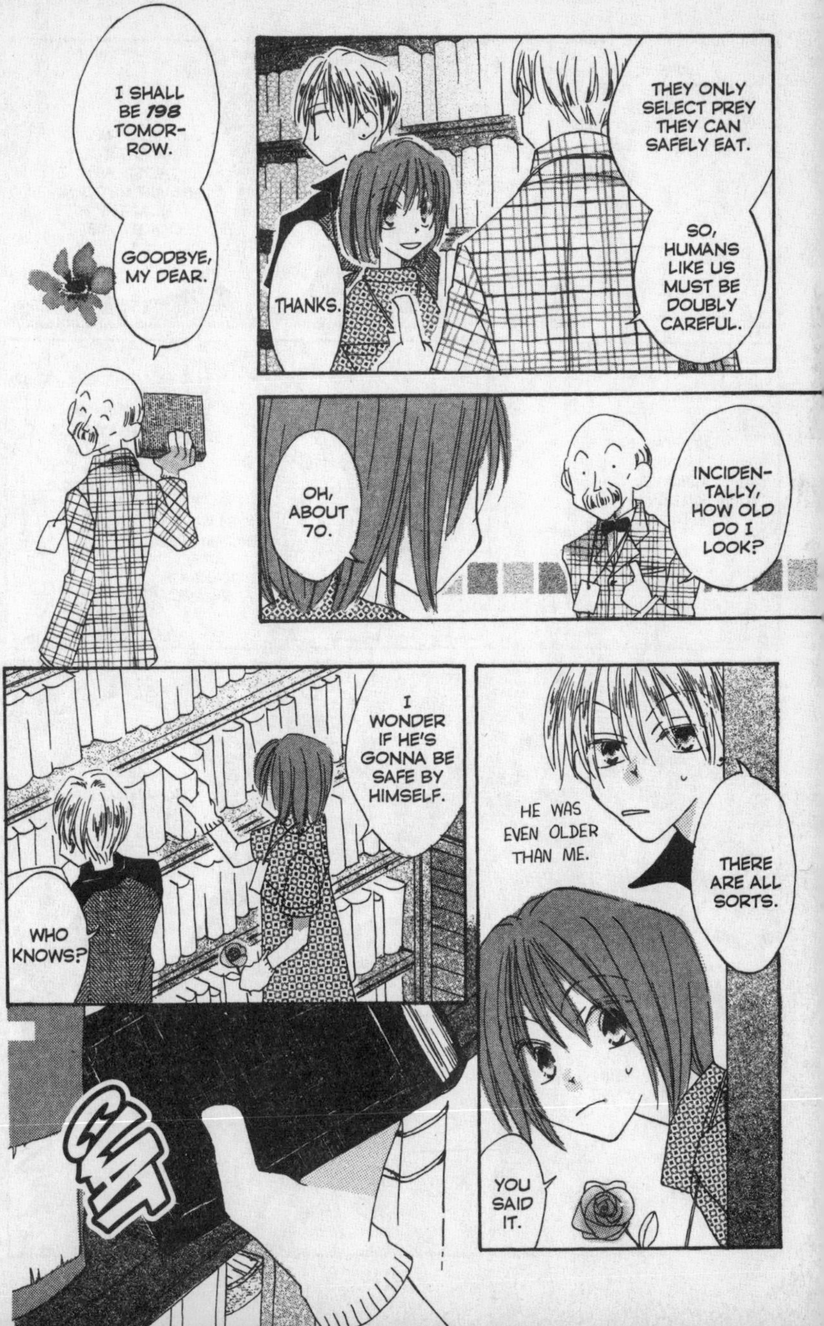
THEY ONLY SELECT PREY THEY CAN SAFELY EAT.
SO, HUMANS LIKE US MUST BE DOUBLY CAREFUL.
THANKS.
INCIDENTALLY, HOW OLD DO I LOOK?
OH, ABOUT 70.
I SHALL BE 798 TOMORROW.
GOODBYE, MY DEAR.
THERE ARE ALL SORTS.
HE WAS EVEN OLDER THAN ME.
YOU SAID IT.
I WONDER IF HE'S GONNA BE SAFE BY HIMSELF.
WHO KNOWS?
CLAT

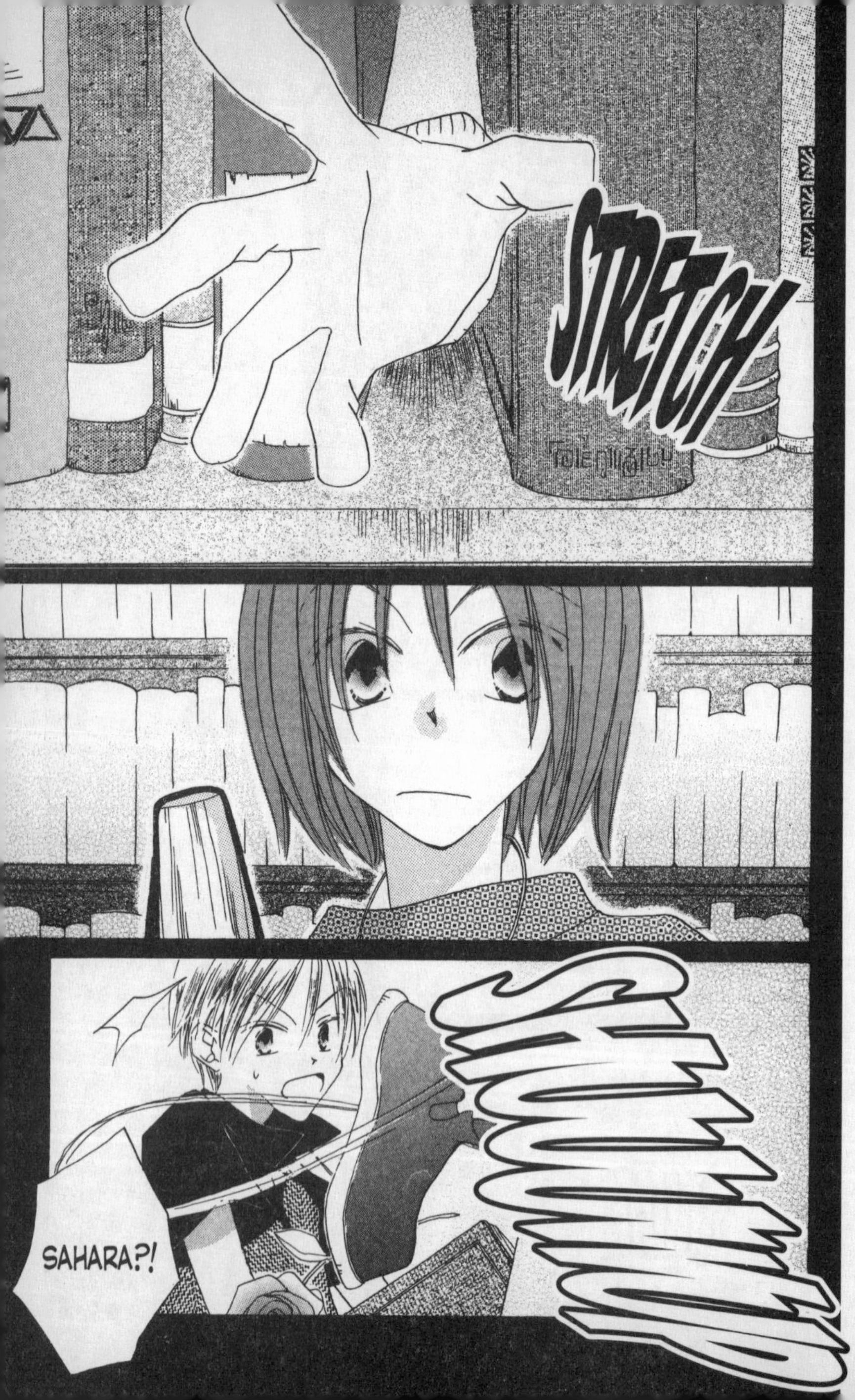
STRETCH
SHOOMP
SAHARA?!

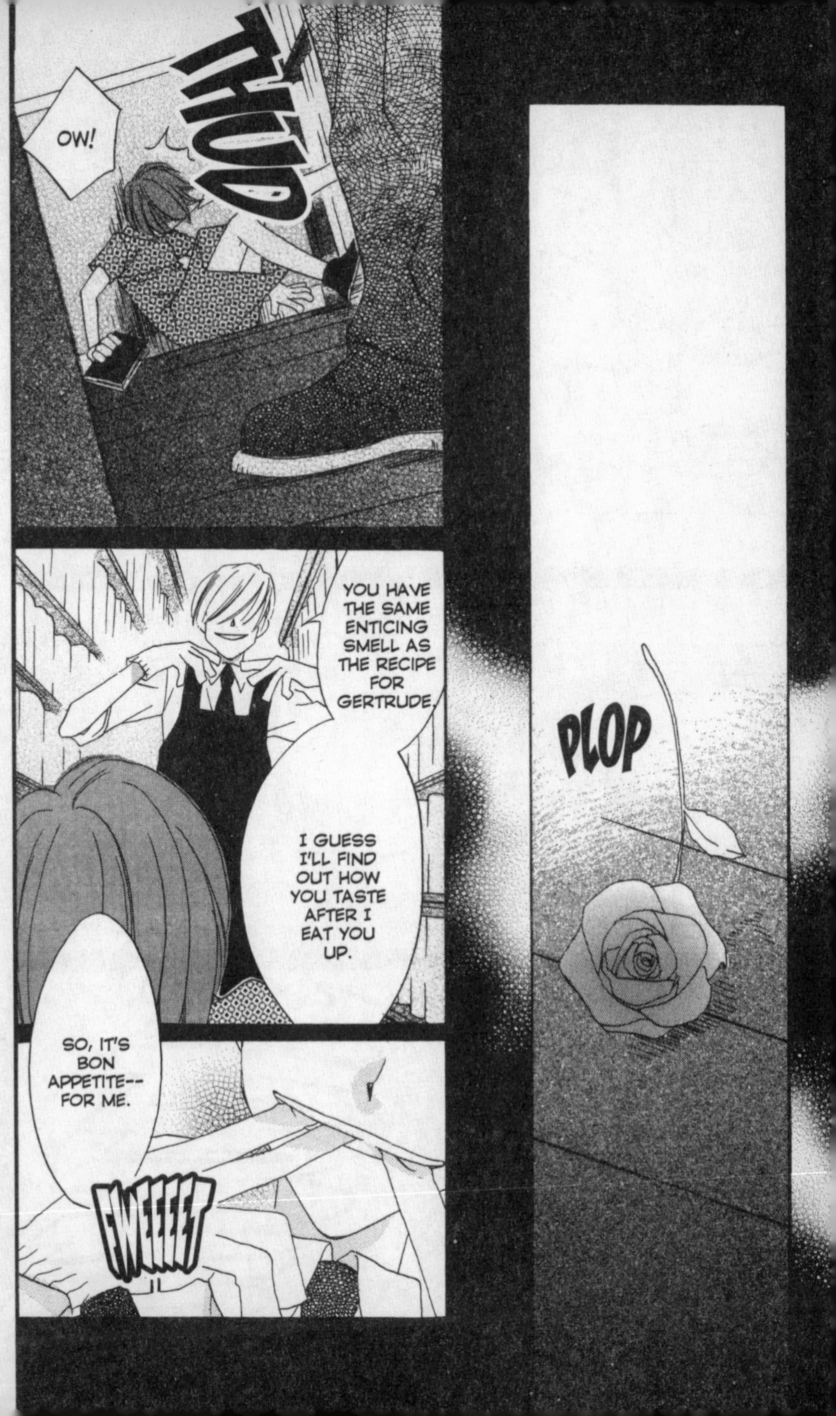
PLOP
OW!
THUD
YOU HAVE THE SAME ENTICING SMELL AS THE RECIPE FOR GERTRUDE.
I GUESS I'LL FIND OUT HOW YOU TASTE AFTER I EAT YOU UP.
SO, IT'S BON APPETITE-- FOR ME.
SWEEEET

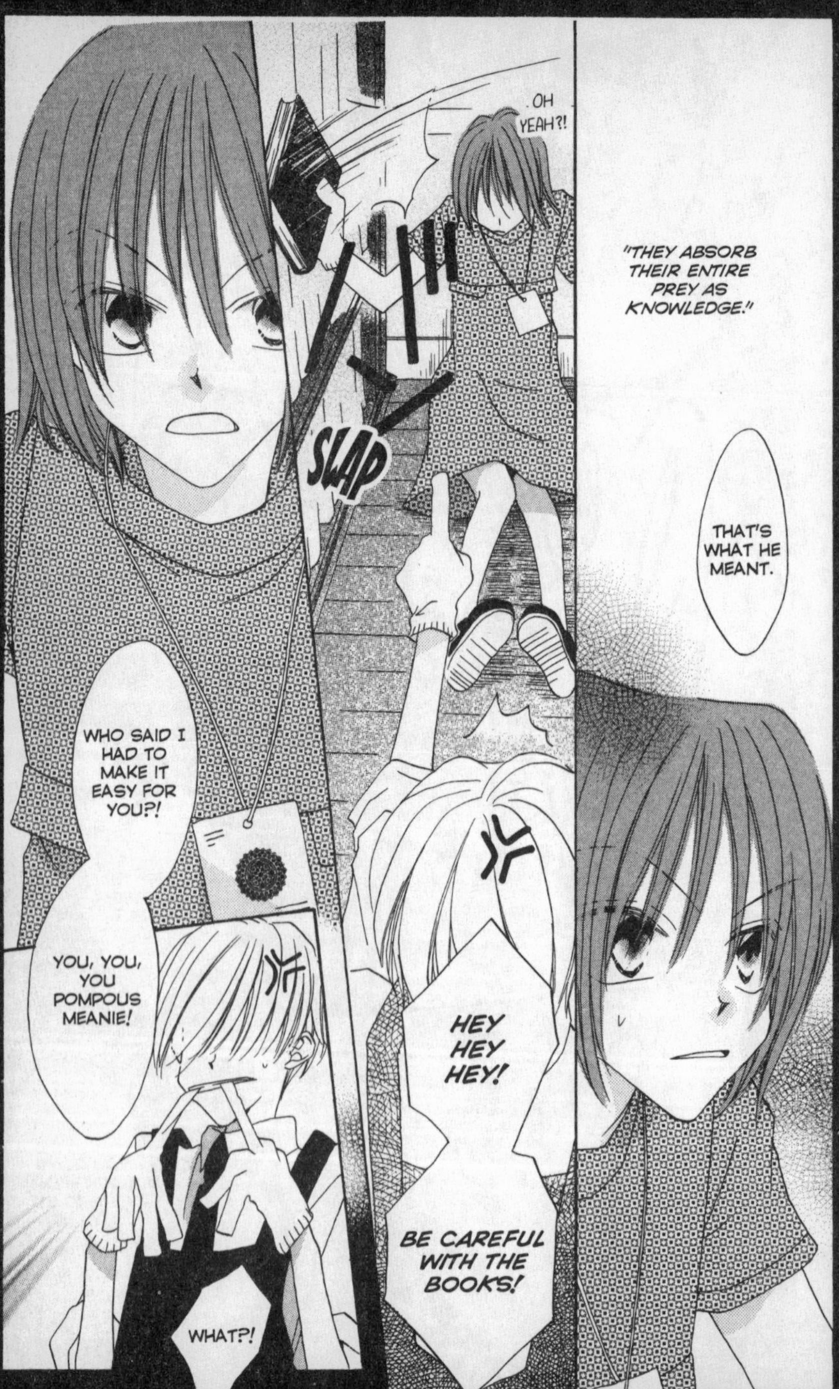
"THEY ABSORB THEIR ENTIRE PREY AS KNOWLEDGE."
THAT'S WHAT HE MEANT.
.OH YEAH?!
SLAP
WHO SAID I HAD TO MAKE IT EASY FOR YOU?!
HEY HEY HEY!
BE CAREFUL WITH THE BOOKS!
YOU, YOU, YOU POMPOUS MEANIE!
WHAT?!

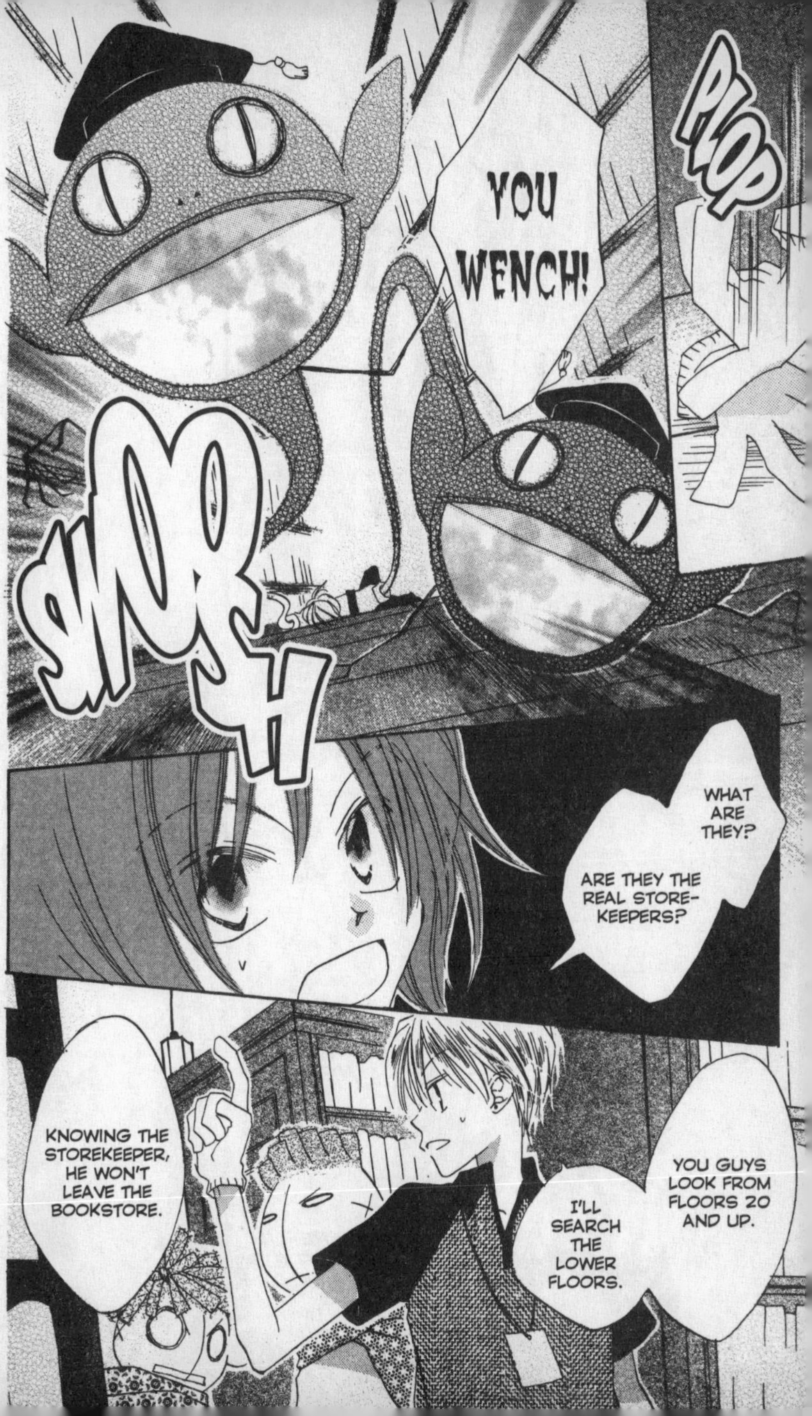
PLOP
YOU WENCH!
SWOOSH
WHAT ARE THEY?
ARE THEY THE REAL STORE-KEEPERS?
YOU GUYS LOOK FROM FLOORS 20 AND UP.
I'LL SEARCH THE LOWER FLOORS.
KNOWING THE STOREKEEPER, HE WON'T LEAVE THE BOOKSTORE.

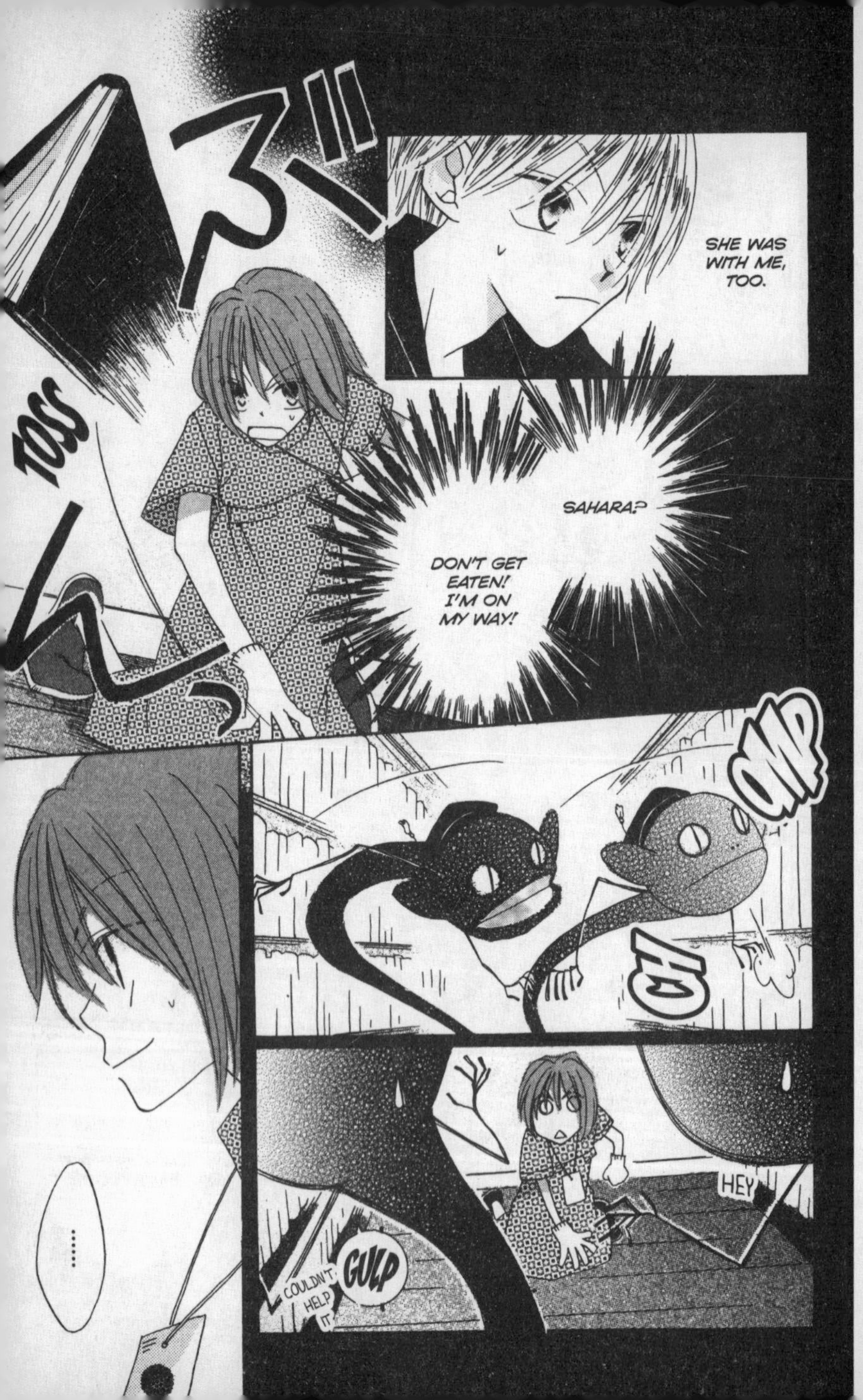
SHE WAS WITH ME, TOO.
TOSS
SAHARA?
DON'T GET EATEN! I'M ON MY WAY!
CHOMP
HEY
GULP
COULDN'T HELP IT
......

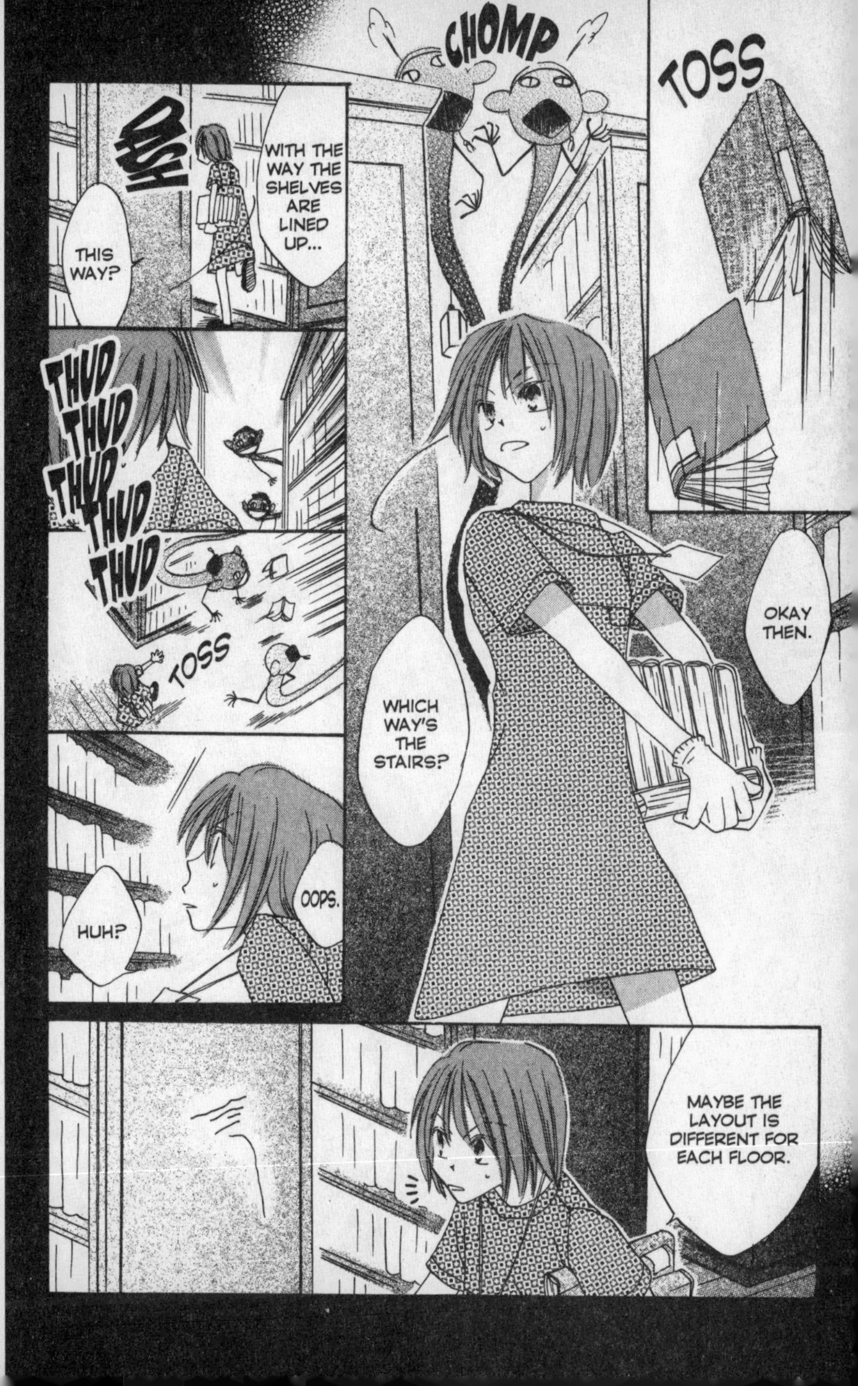
TOSS
OKAY THEN.
CHOMP
WHICH WAY'S THE STAIRS?
WITH THE WAY THE SHELVES ARE LINED UP...
DASH
THIS WAY?
THUD THUD THUD THUD THUD
TOSS
OOPS.
HUH?
MAYBE THE LAYOUT IS DIFFERENT FOR EACH FLOOR.

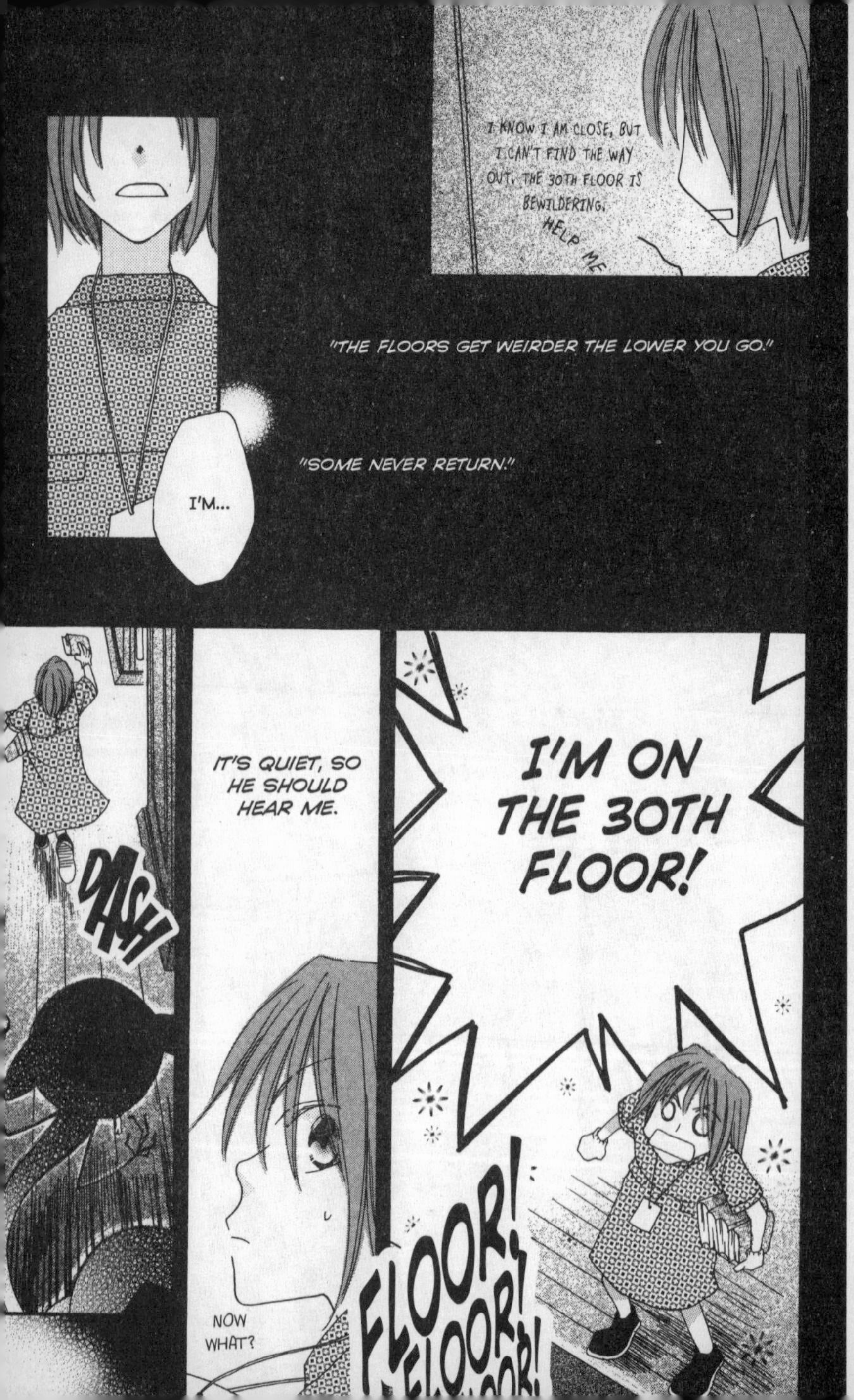
I KNOW I AM CLOSE, BUT I CAN'T FIND THE WAY OUT. THE 30TH FLOOR IS BEWILDERING.
HELP ME
"THE FLOORS GET WEIRDER THE LOWER YOU GO."
"SOME NEVER RETURN."
I'M...
I'M ON THE 30TH FLOOR!
FLOOR, FLOOR! FLOOR!
IT'S QUIET, SO HE SHOULD HEAR ME.
NOW WHAT?
DASH

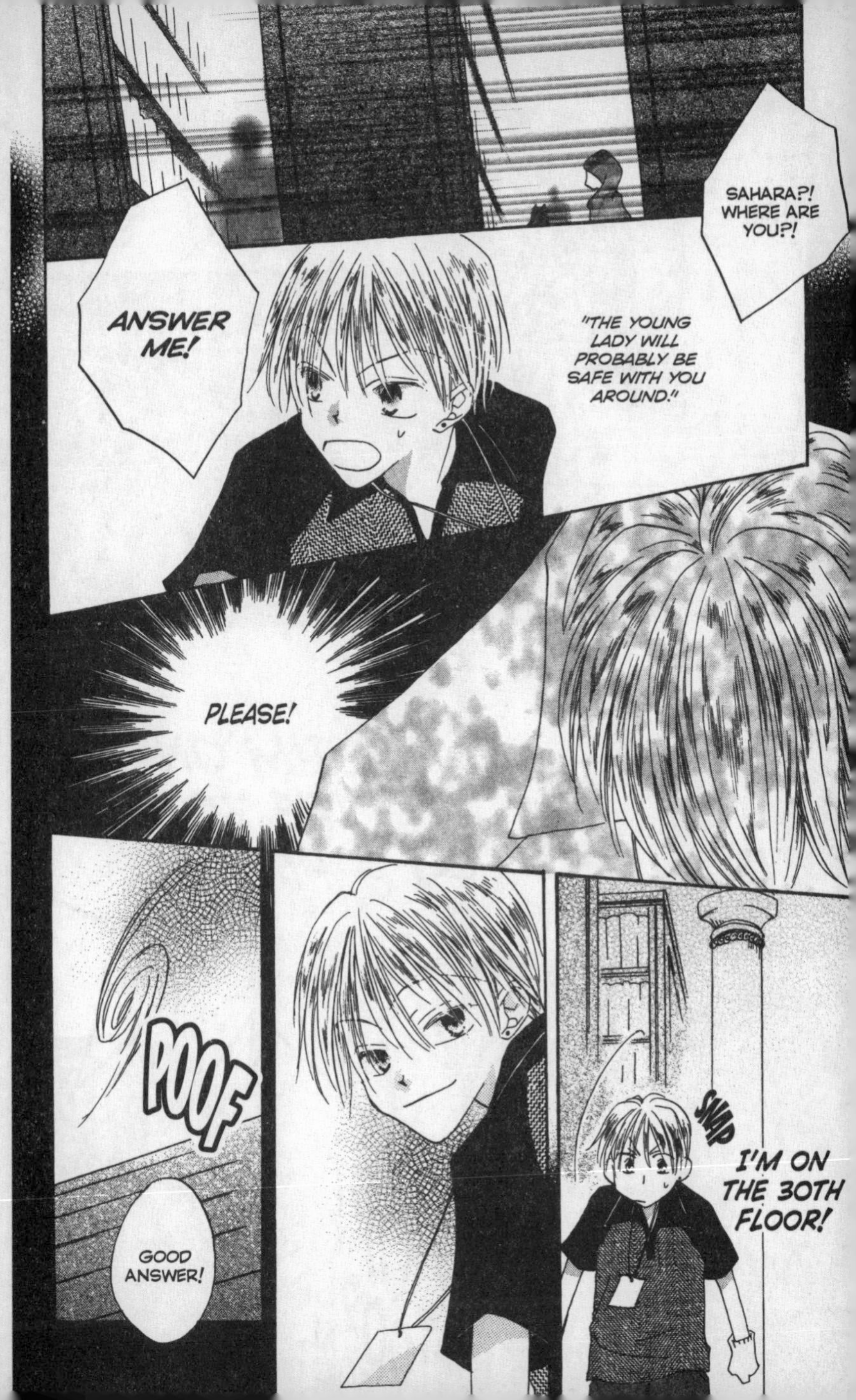
SAHARA?! WHERE ARE YOU?!
"THE YOUNG LADY WILL PROBABLY BE SAFE WITH YOU AROUND."
ANSWER ME!
PLEASE!
SNAP
I'M ON THE 30TH FLOOR!
POOF
GOOD ANSWER!

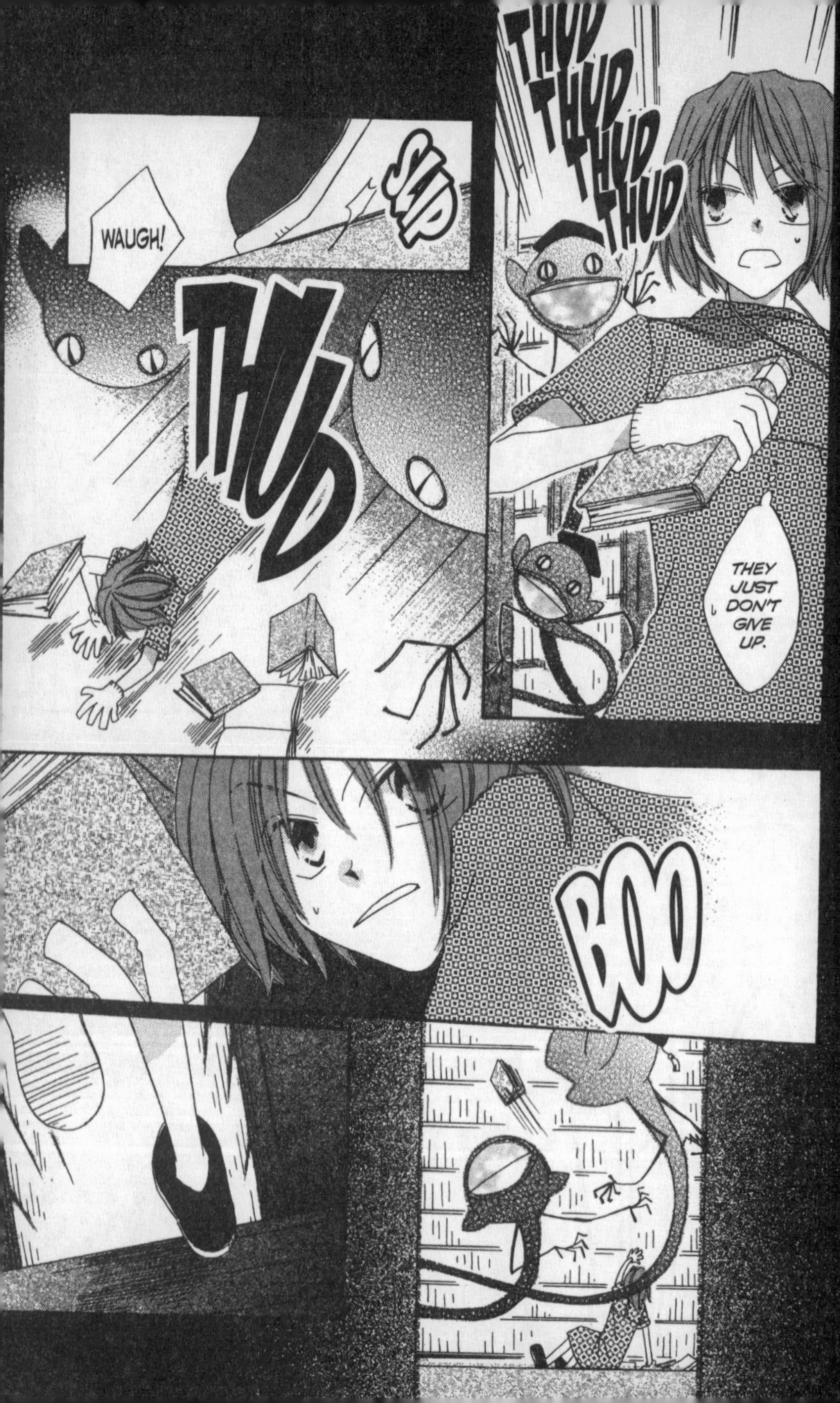
THUD THUD THUD THUD
THEY JUST DON'T GIVE UP.
SKIP
WAUGH!
THUD
BOO

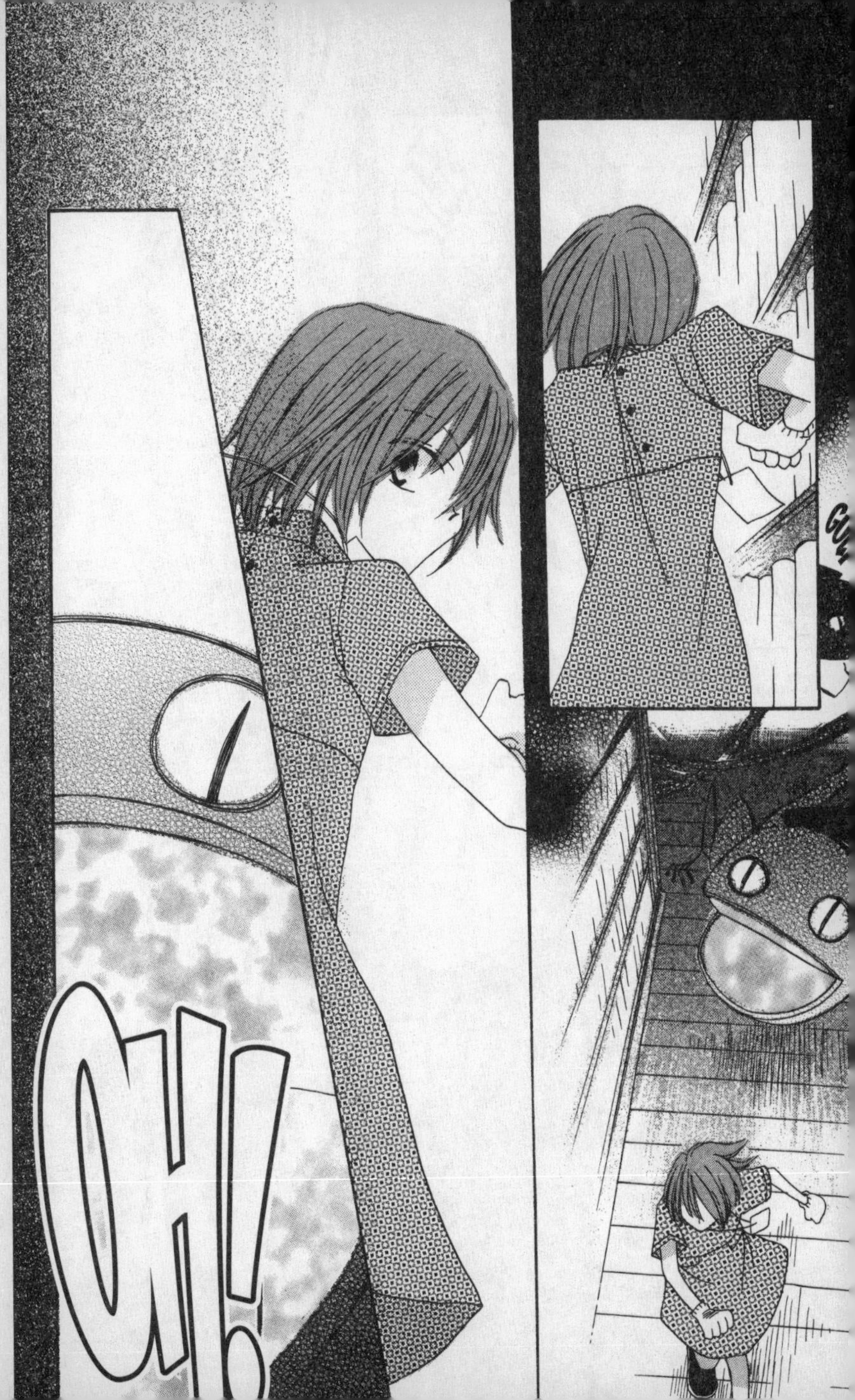
GU
CH!

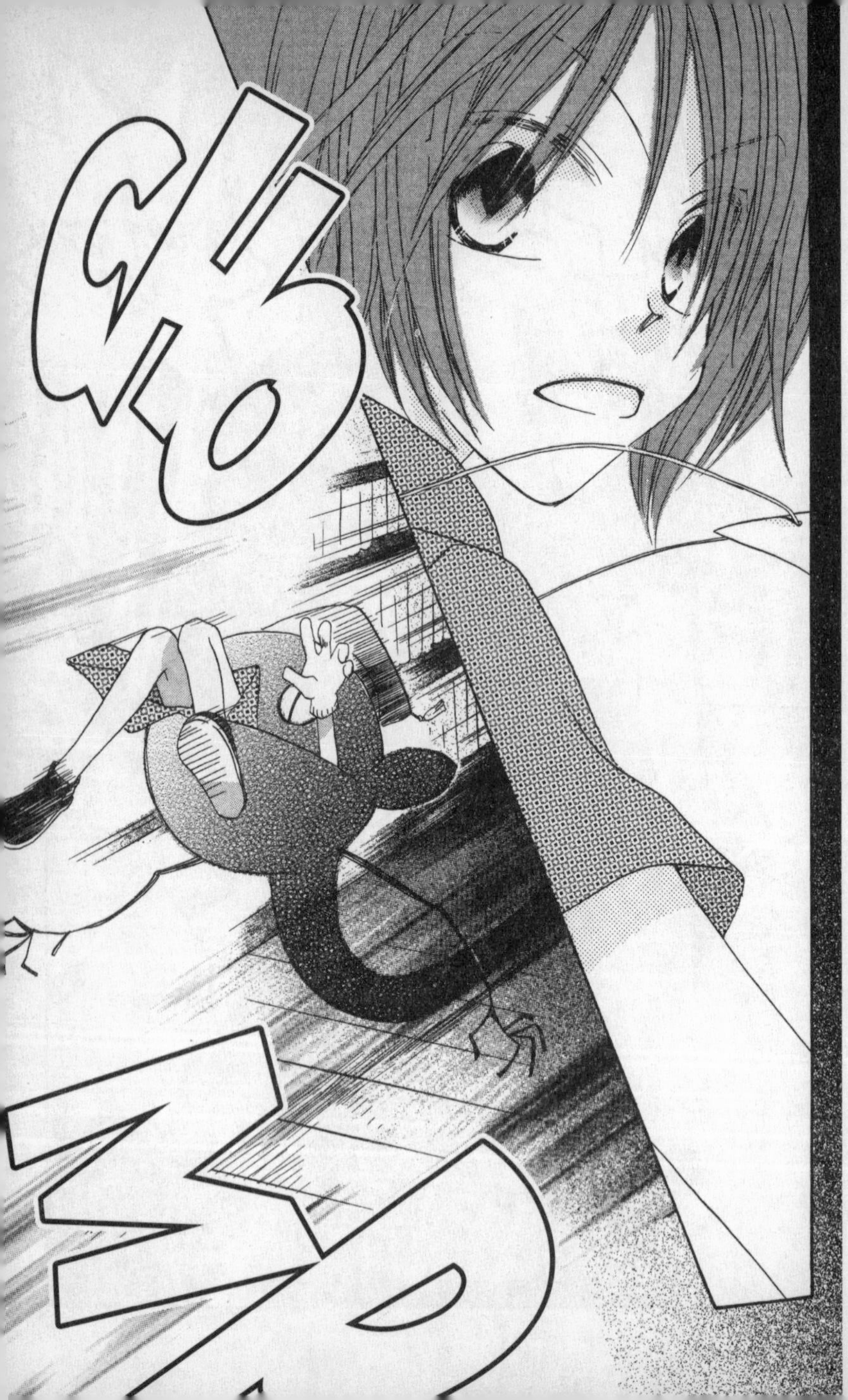

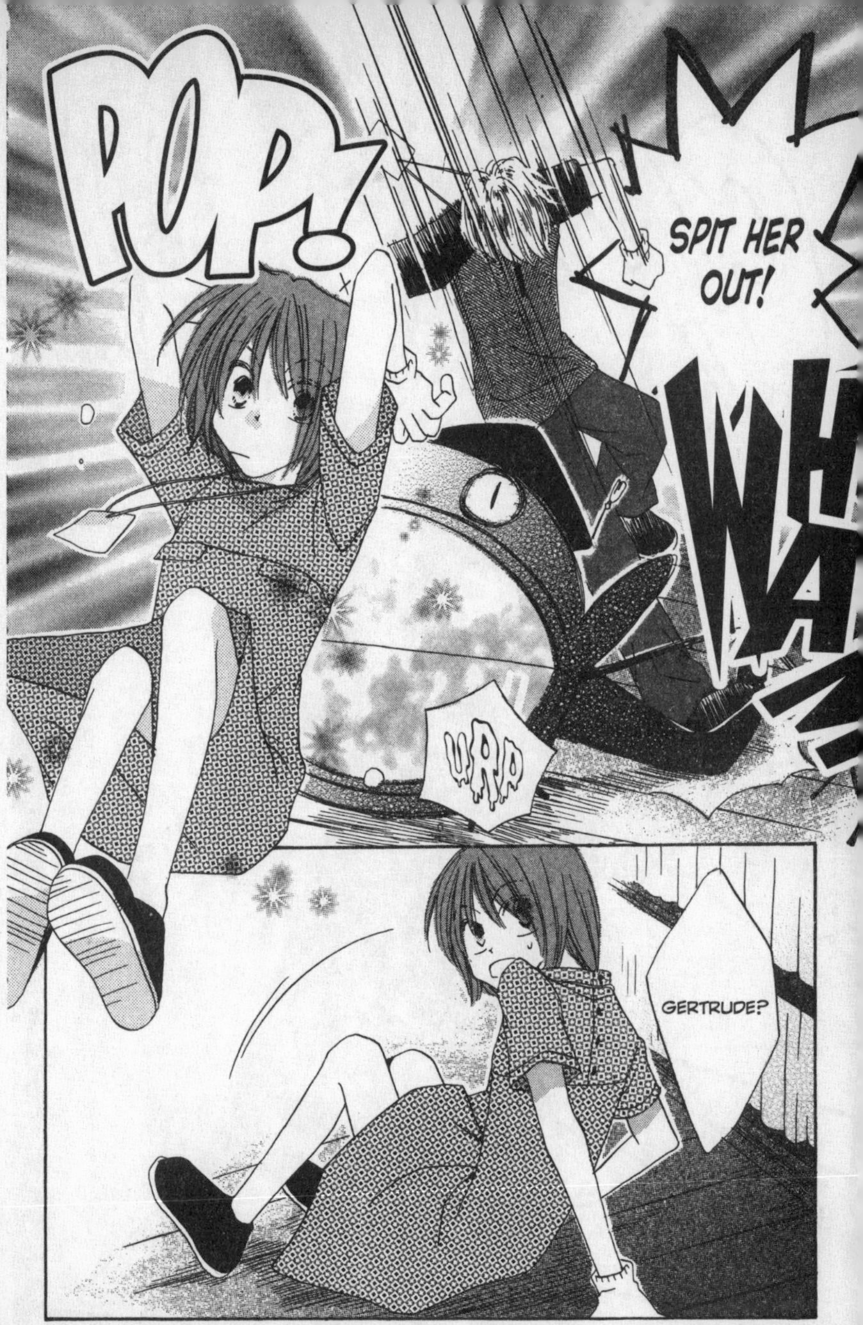
SPIT HER OUT!
POP!
URP
GERTRUDE?

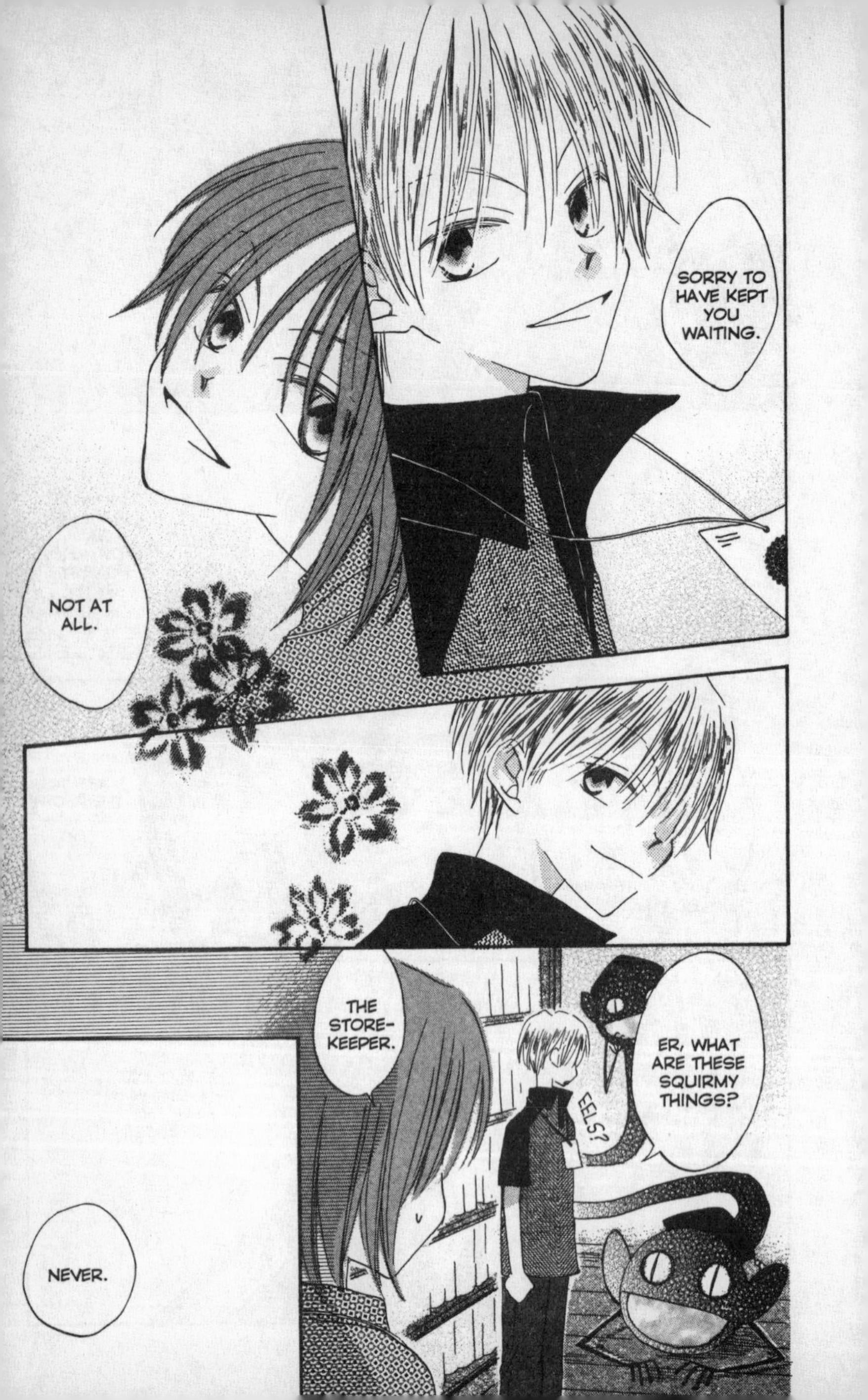
SORRY TO HAVE KEPT YOU WAITING.
NOT AT ALL.
ER, WHAT ARE THESE SQUIRMY THINGS?
EELS?
THE STORE-KEEPER.
NEVER.

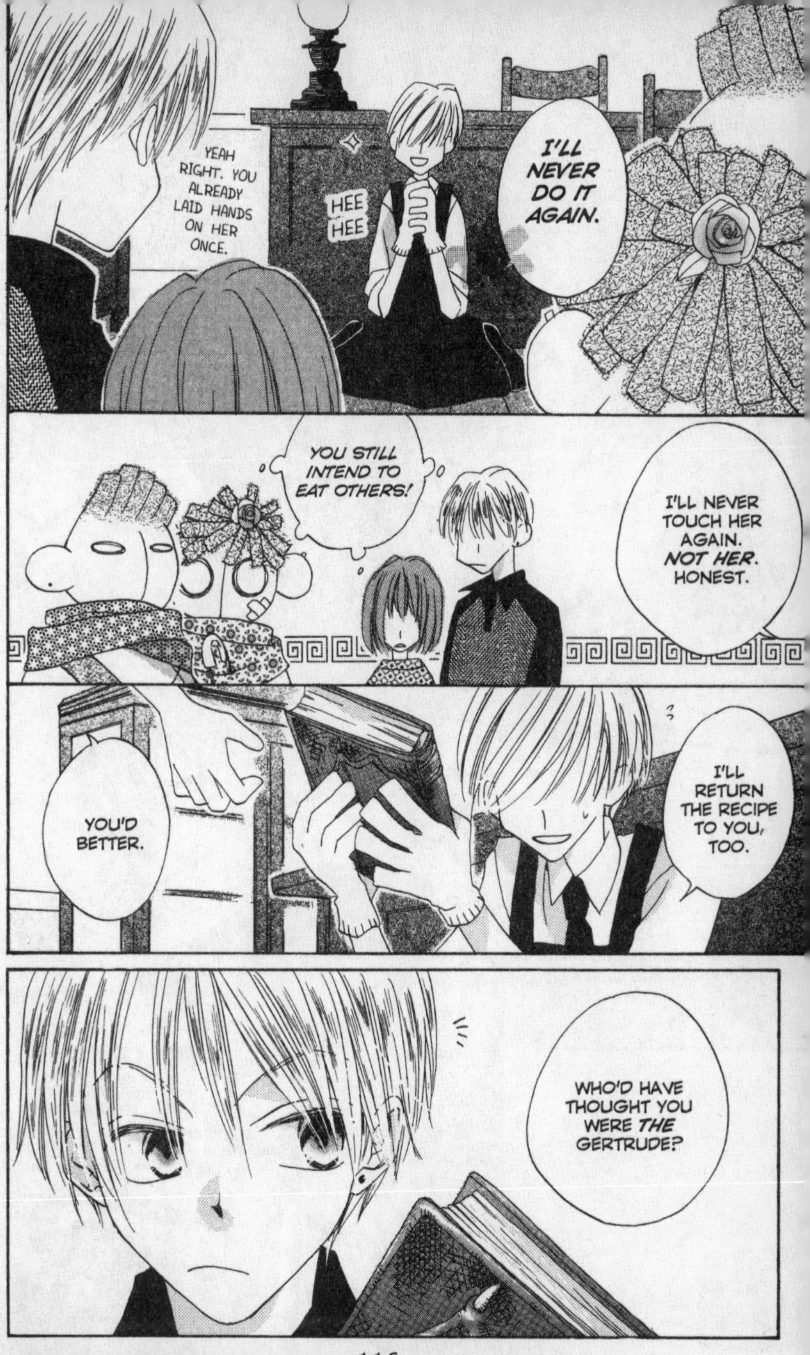
I'LL NEVER DO IT AGAIN.
HEE HEE
YEAH RIGHT. YOU ALREADY LAID HANDS ON HER ONCE.
I'LL NEVER TOUCH HER AGAIN. *NOT HER*. HONEST.
YOU STILL INTEND TO EAT OTHERS!
I'LL RETURN THE RECIPE TO YOU, TOO.
YOU'D BETTER.
WHO'D HAVE THOUGHT YOU WERE *THE* GERTRUDE?

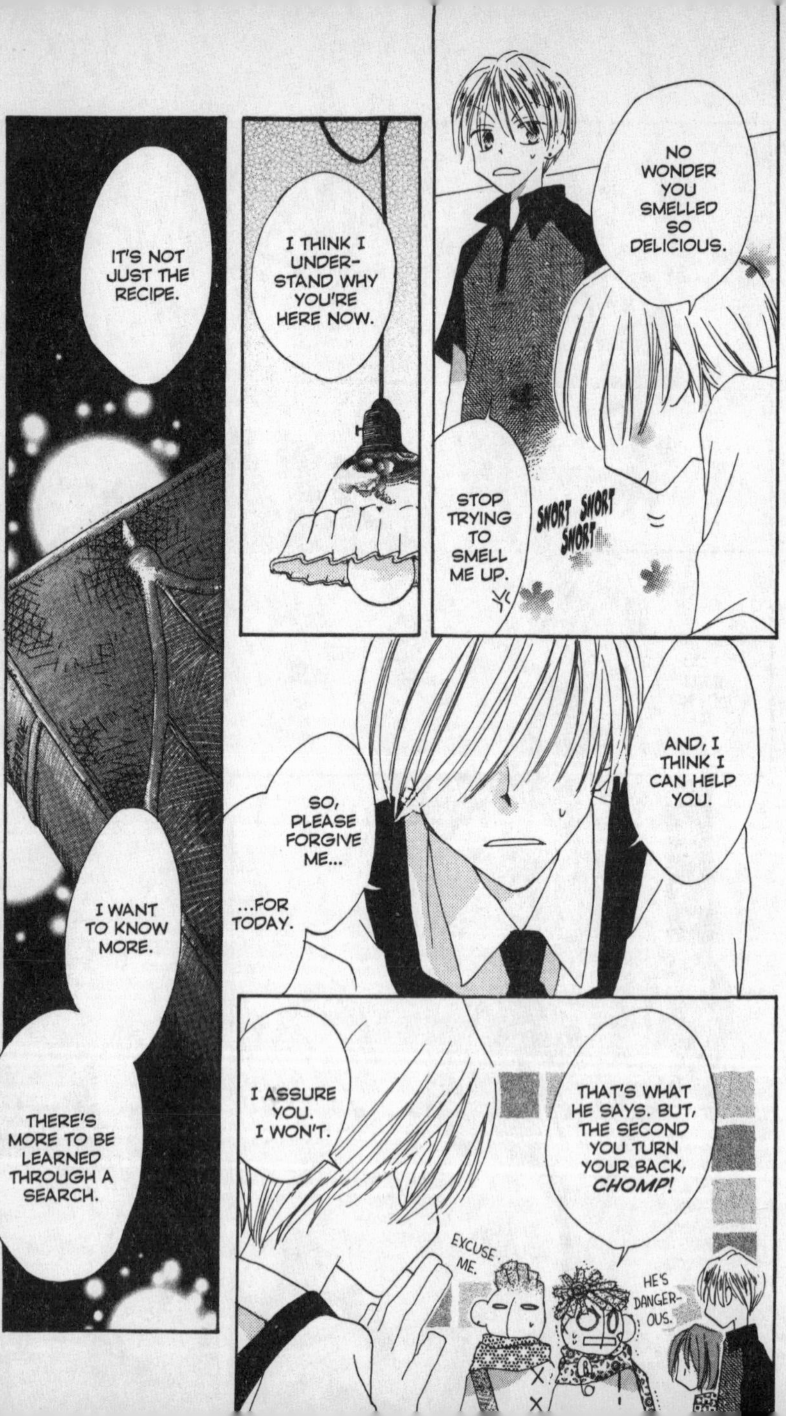
NO WONDER YOU SMELLED SO DELICIOUS.
SNORT SNORT SNORT
STOP TRYING TO SMELL ME UP.
I THINK I UNDER-STAND WHY YOU'RE HERE NOW.
AND, I THINK I CAN HELP YOU.
SO, PLEASE FORGIVE ME...
...FOR TODAY.
THAT'S WHAT HE SAYS. BUT, THE SECOND YOU TURN YOUR BACK, *CHOMP!*
I ASSURE YOU. I WON'T.
HE'S DANGER-OUS.
EXCUSE ME.
IT'S NOT JUST THE RECIPE.
I WANT TO KNOW MORE.
THERE'S MORE TO BE LEARNED THROUGH A SEARCH.

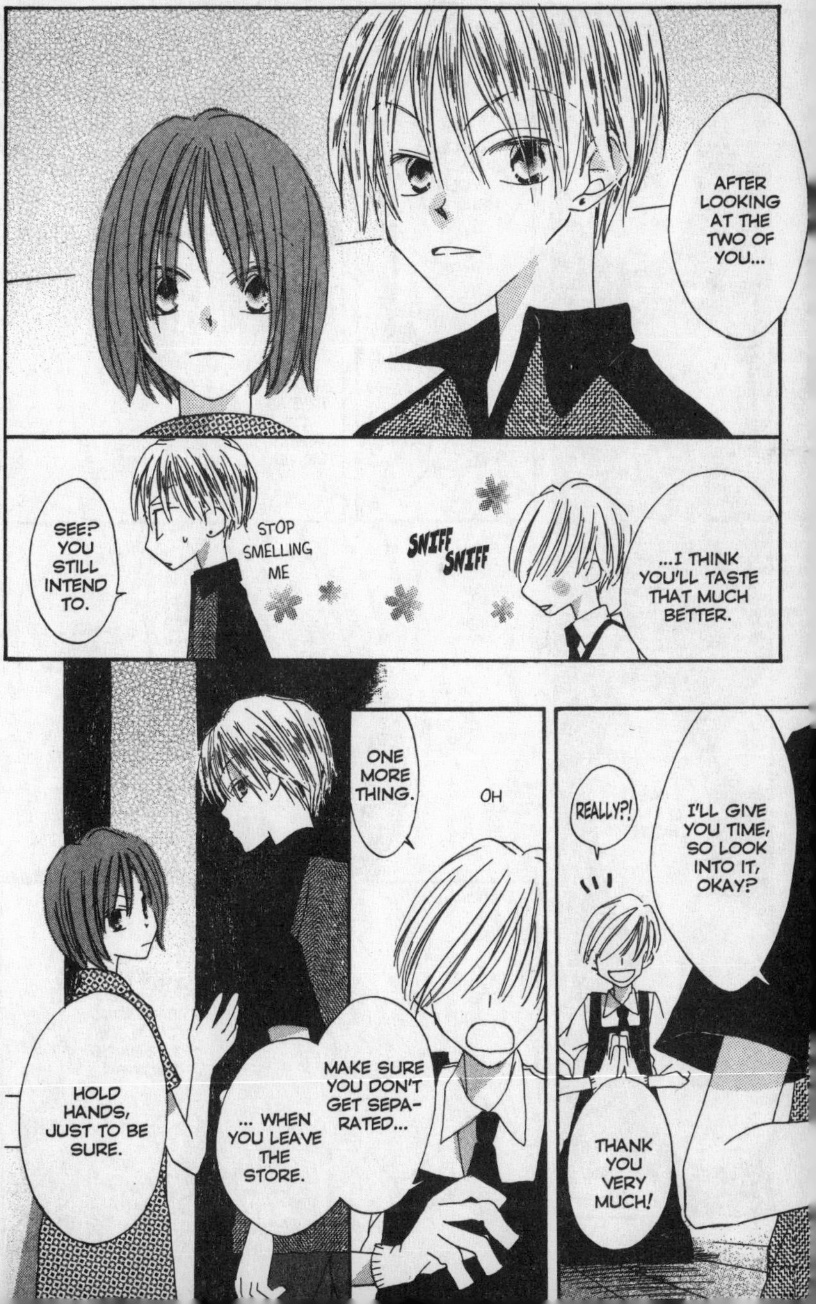
AFTER LOOKING AT THE TWO OF YOU...
...I THINK YOU'LL TASTE THAT MUCH BETTER.
SNIFF SNIFF
STOP SMELLING ME
SEE? YOU STILL INTEND TO.
I'LL GIVE YOU TIME, SO LOOK INTO IT, OKAY?
REALLY?!
THANK YOU VERY MUCH!
OH
ONE MORE THING.
MAKE SURE YOU DON'T GET SEPA- RATED...
... WHEN YOU LEAVE THE STORE.
HOLD HANDS, JUST TO BE SURE.

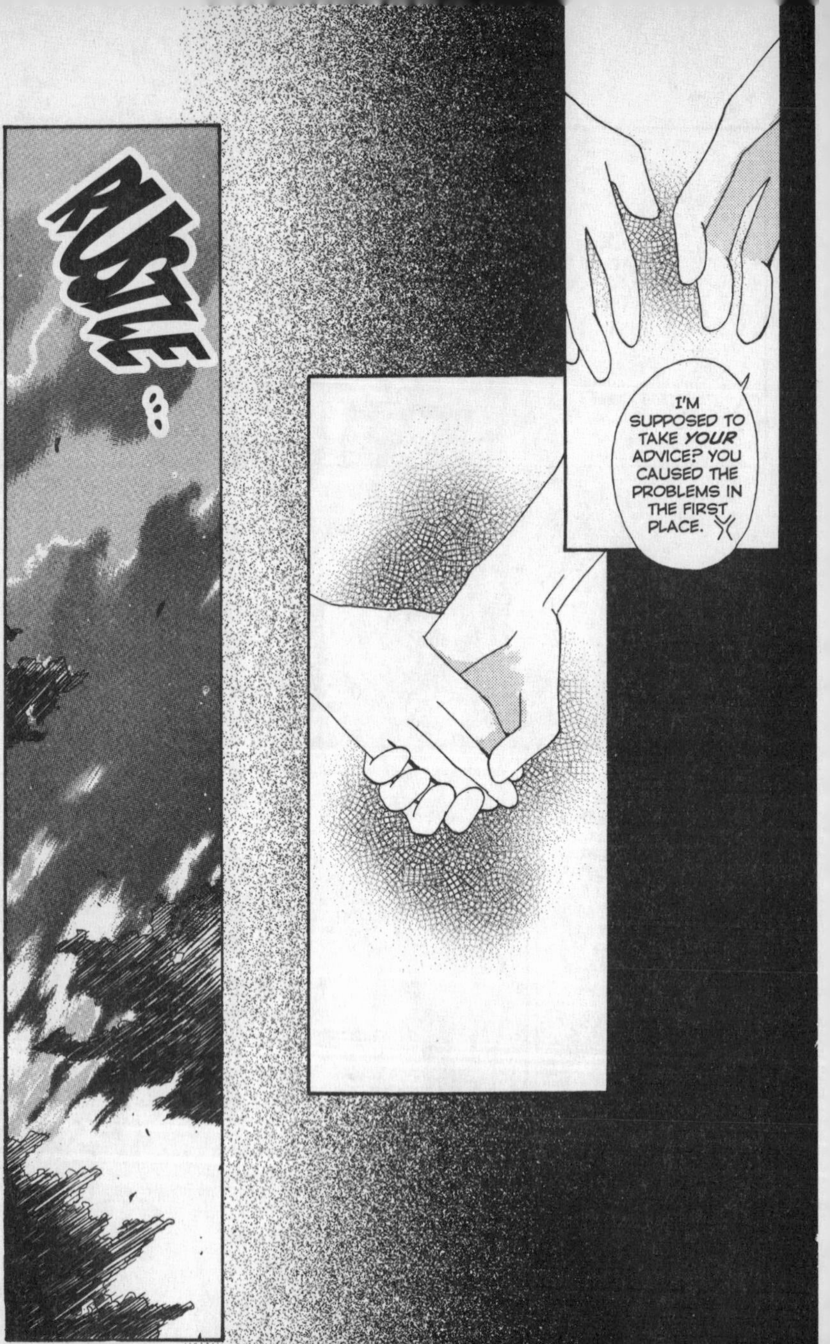
I'M SUPPOSED TO TAKE *YOUR* ADVICE? YOU CAUSED THE PROBLEMS IN THE FIRST PLACE.
RUSTLE

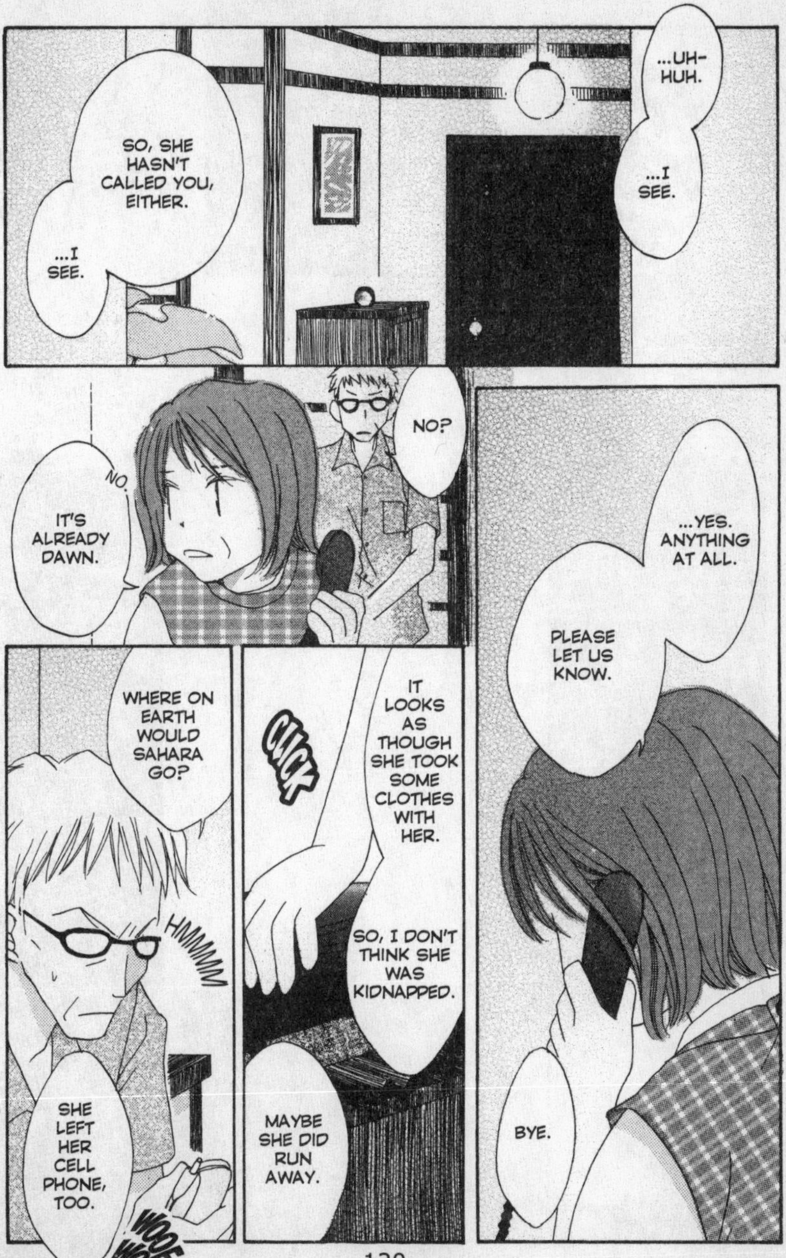
...UH-HUH.
...I SEE.
SO, SHE HASN'T CALLED YOU, EITHER.
...I SEE.
...YES. ANYTHING AT ALL.
PLEASE LET US KNOW.
BYE.
NO?
NO.
IT'S ALREADY DAWN.
IT LOOKS AS THOUGH SHE TOOK SOME CLOTHES WITH HER.
CLICK
SO, I DON'T THINK SHE WAS KIDNAPPED.
MAYBE SHE DID RUN AWAY.
WHERE ON EARTH WOULD SAHARA GO?
HMMMM
SHE LEFT HER CELL PHONE, TOO.
WOOF WOOF

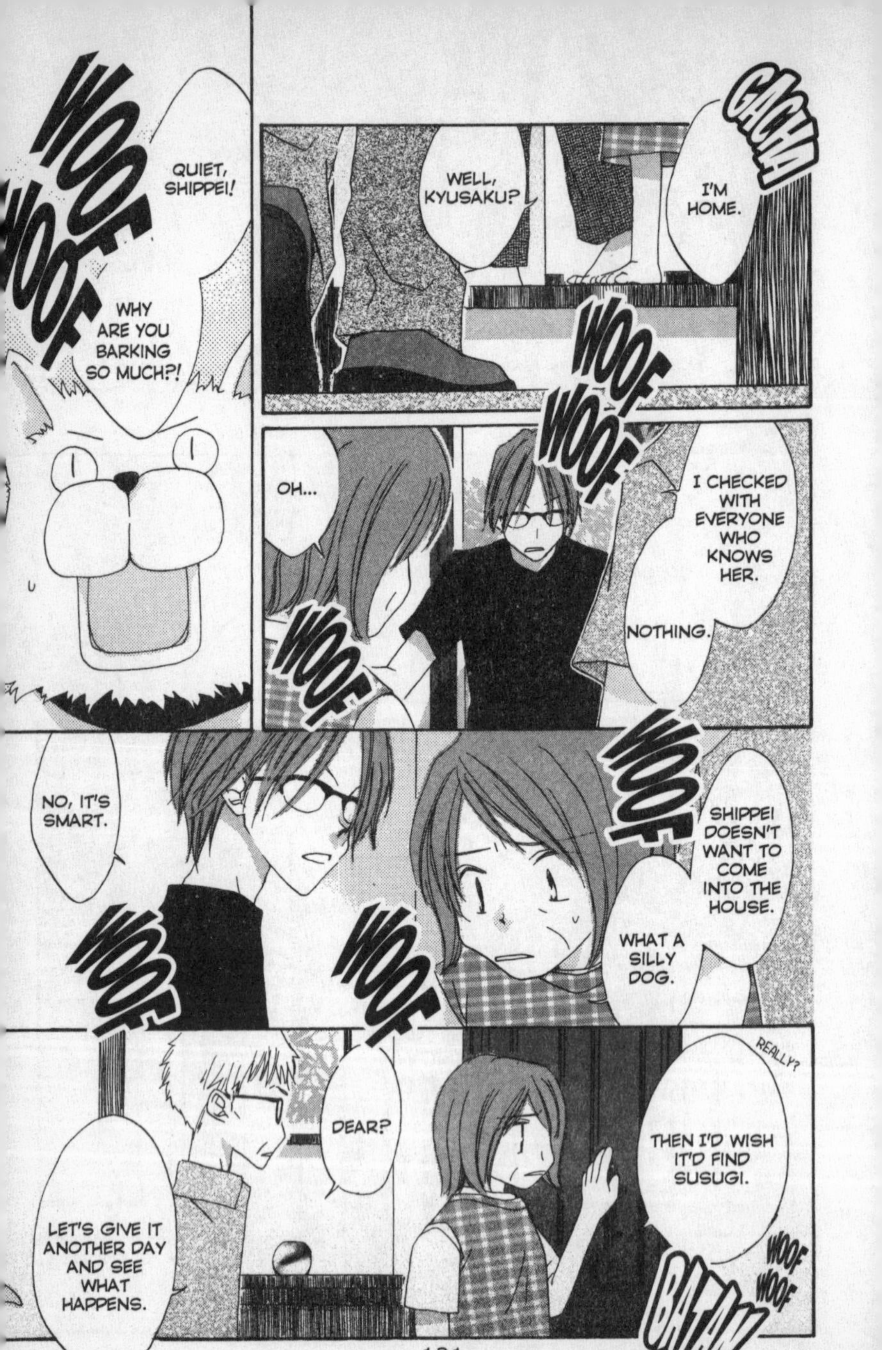
GACHA
I'M HOME.
WELL, KYUSAKU?
WOOF WOOF
I CHECKED WITH EVERYONE WHO KNOWS HER.
NOTHING.
OH...
WOOF
WOOF WOOF
QUIET, SHIPPEI!
WHY ARE YOU BARKING SO MUCH?!
WOOF
SHIPPEI DOESN'T WANT TO COME INTO THE HOUSE.
WHAT A SILLY DOG.
WOOF
NO, IT'S SMART.
WOOF
REALLY?
THEN I'D WISH IT'D FIND SUSUGI.
WOOF WOOF
BATAN
DEAR?
LET'S GIVE IT ANOTHER DAY AND SEE WHAT HAPPENS.

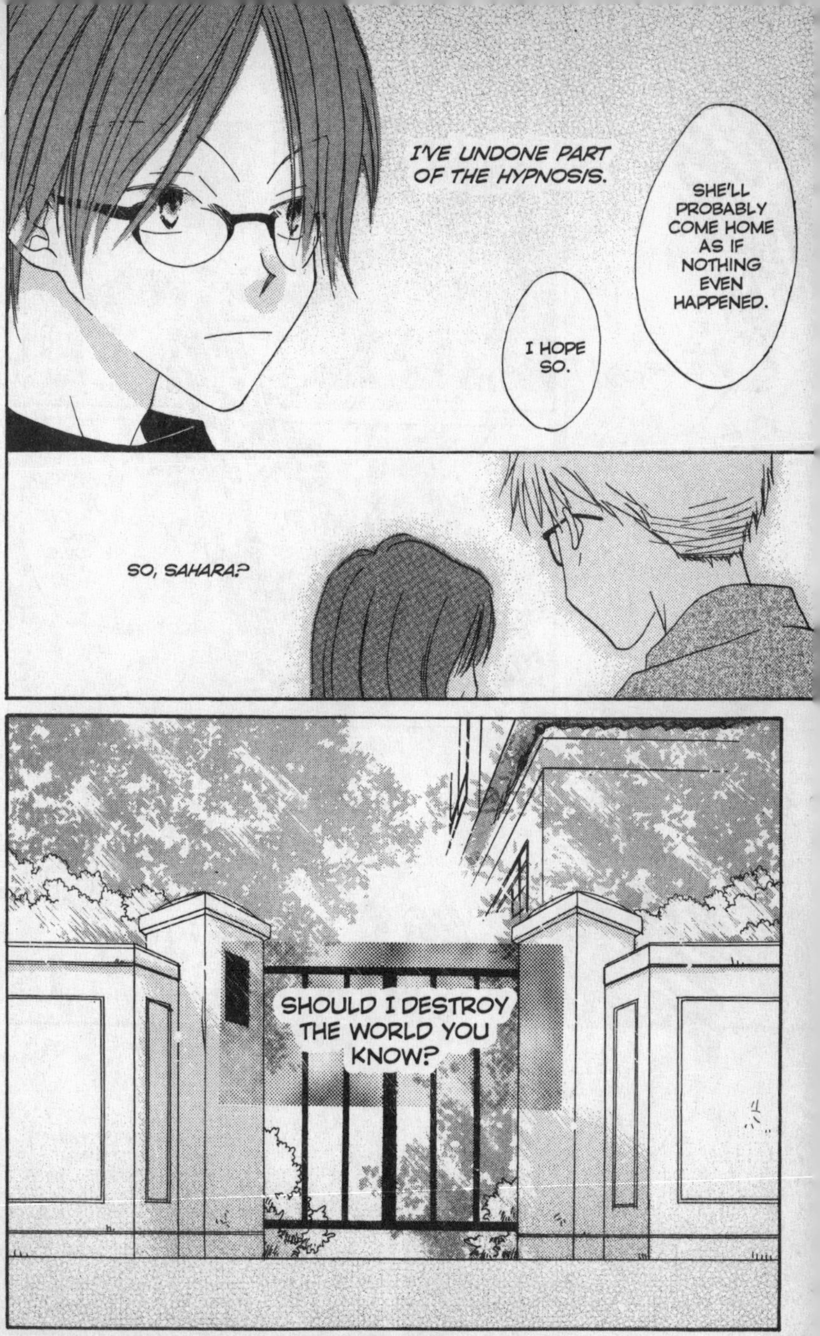
SHE'LL PROBABLY COME HOME AS IF NOTHING EVEN HAPPENED.
I HOPE SO.
I'VE UNDONE PART OF THE HYPNOSIS.
SO, SAHARA?
SHOULD I DESTROY THE WORLD YOU KNOW?

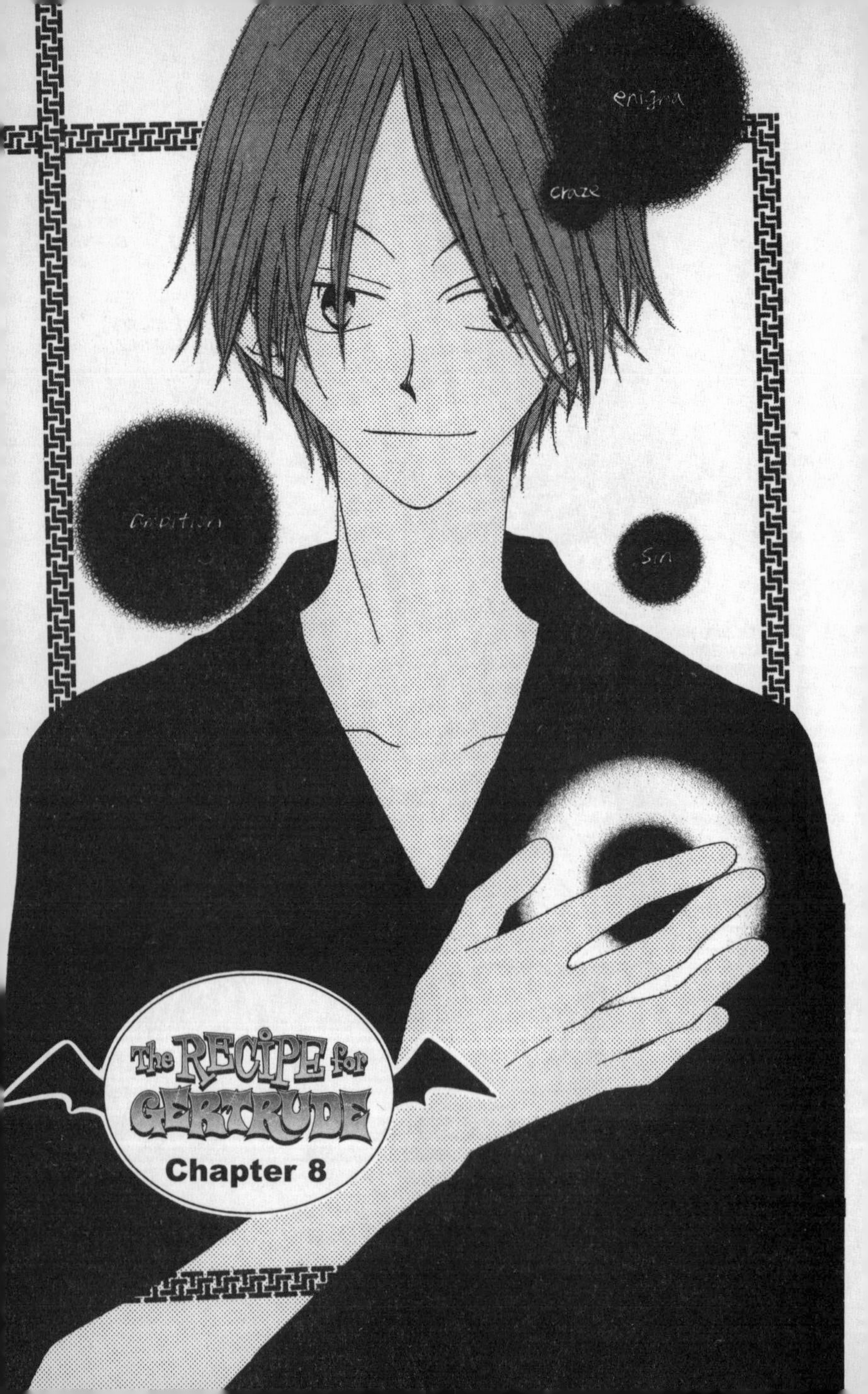
enigma
craze
ambition
sin
The RECIPE for GERTRUDE
Chapter 8

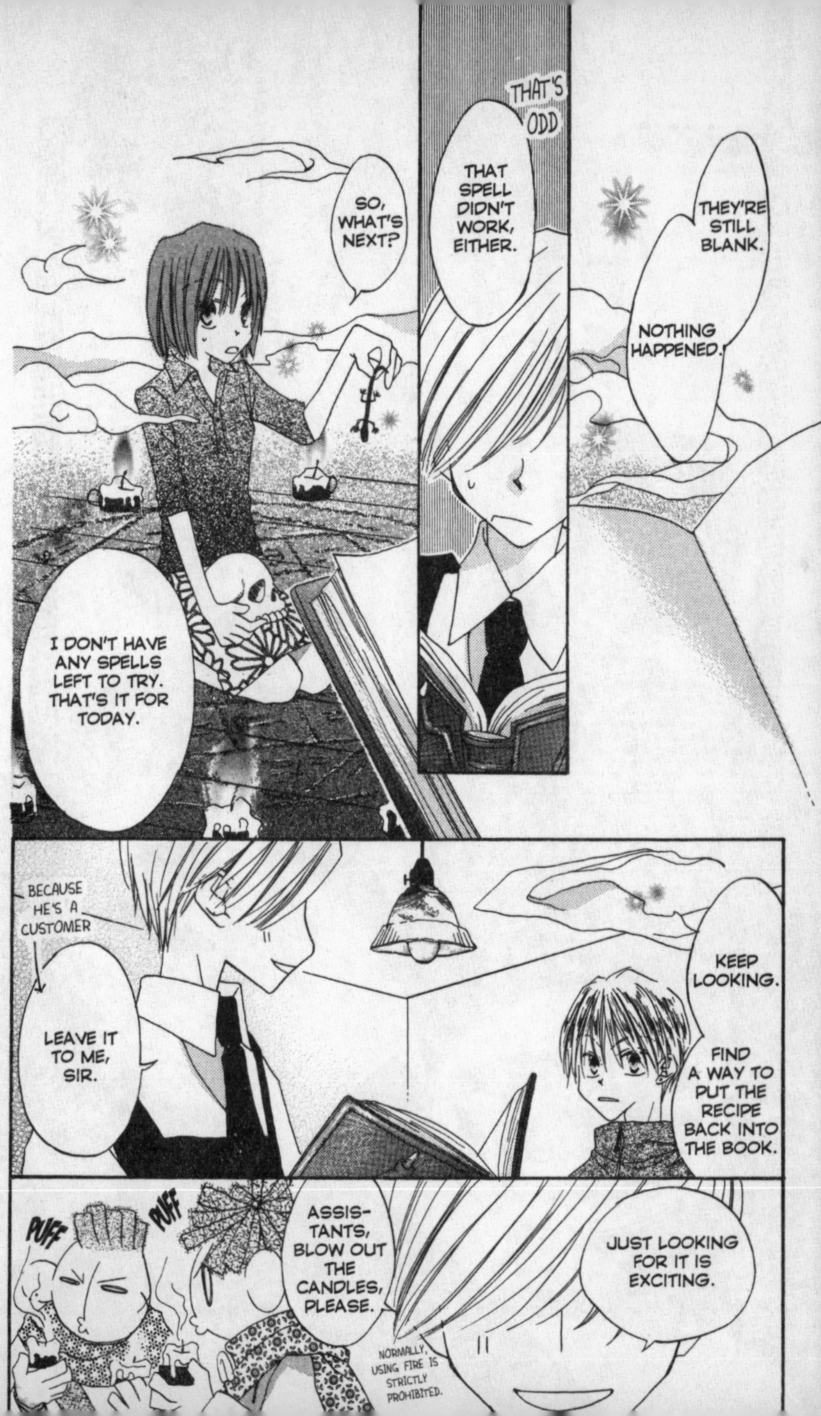
THEY'RE STILL BLANK.
NOTHING HAPPENED.
THAT'S ODD
THAT SPELL DIDN'T WORK, EITHER.
SO, WHAT'S NEXT?
I DON'T HAVE ANY SPELLS LEFT TO TRY. THAT'S IT FOR TODAY.
KEEP LOOKING.
FIND A WAY TO PUT THE RECIPE BACK INTO THE BOOK.
BECAUSE HE'S A CUSTOMER
LEAVE IT TO ME, SIR.
JUST LOOKING FOR IT IS EXCITING.
ASSIS-TANTS, BLOW OUT THE CANDLES, PLEASE.
NORMALLY, USING FIRE IS STRICTLY PROHIBITED.
PUFF
PUFF

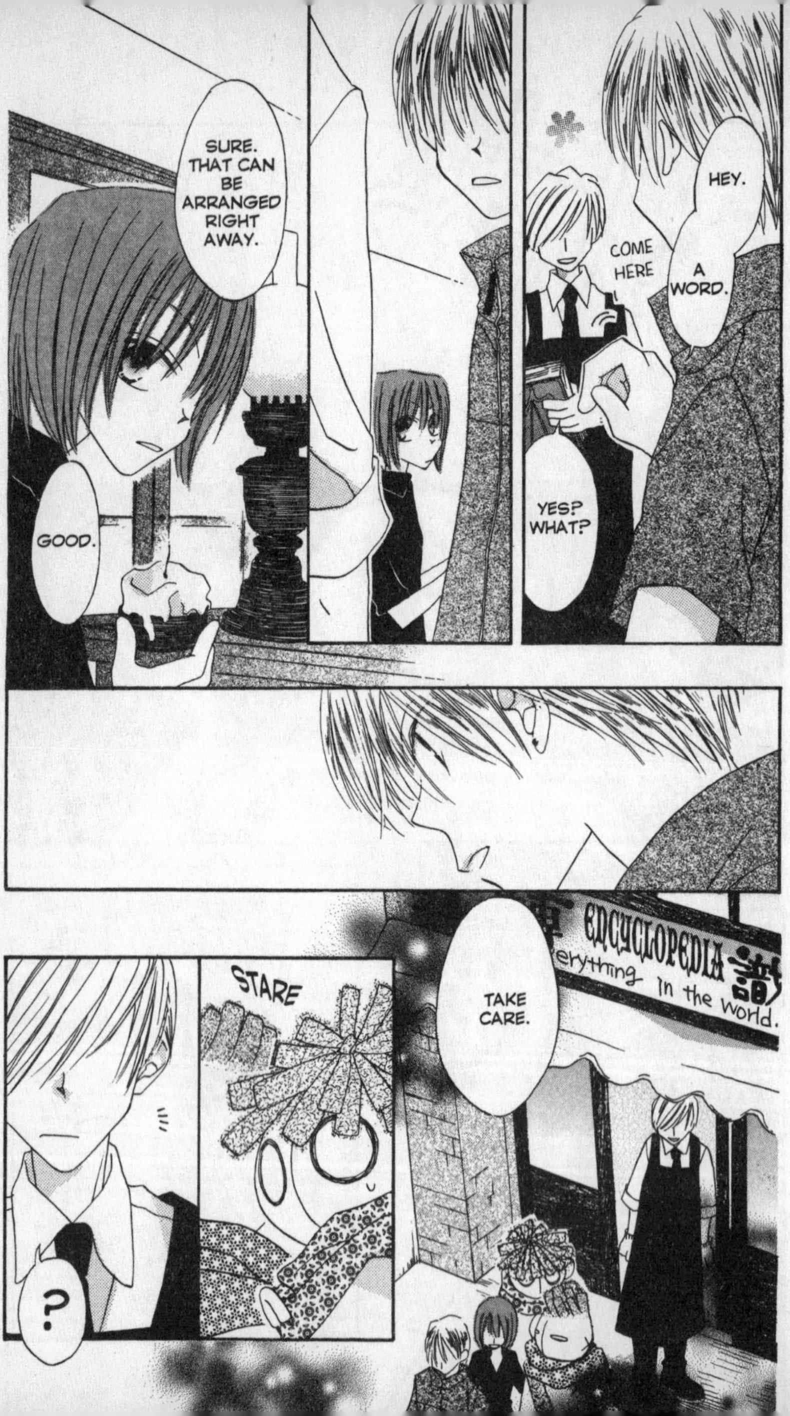
HEY.
A WORD.
COME HERE
YES? WHAT?
SURE. THAT CAN BE ARRANGED RIGHT AWAY.
GOOD.
ENCYCLOPEDIA
erything in the world.
TAKE CARE.
STARE
?

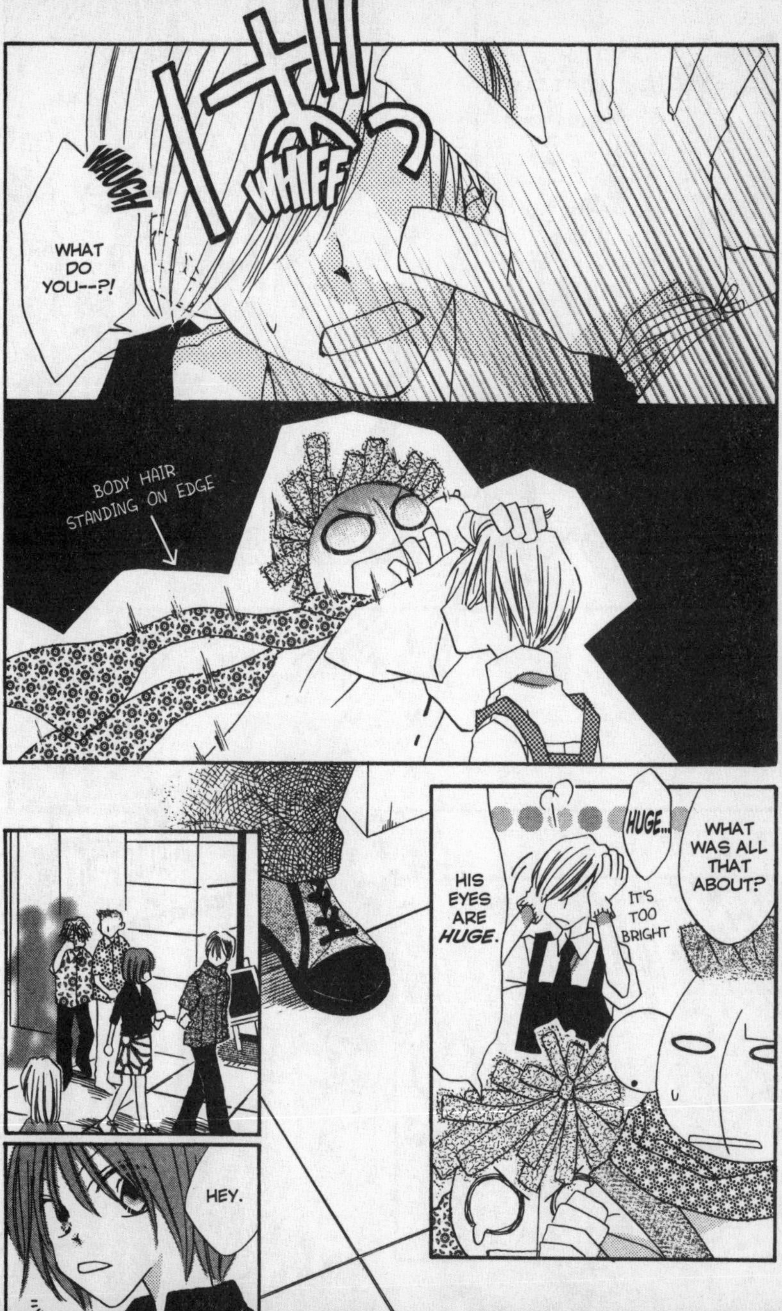
WHIFF
WAUGH
WHAT DO YOU--?!
BODY HAIR STANDING ON EDGE
WHAT WAS ALL THAT ABOUT?
HUGE...
IT'S TOO BRIGHT
HIS EYES ARE ***HUGE***.
HEY.

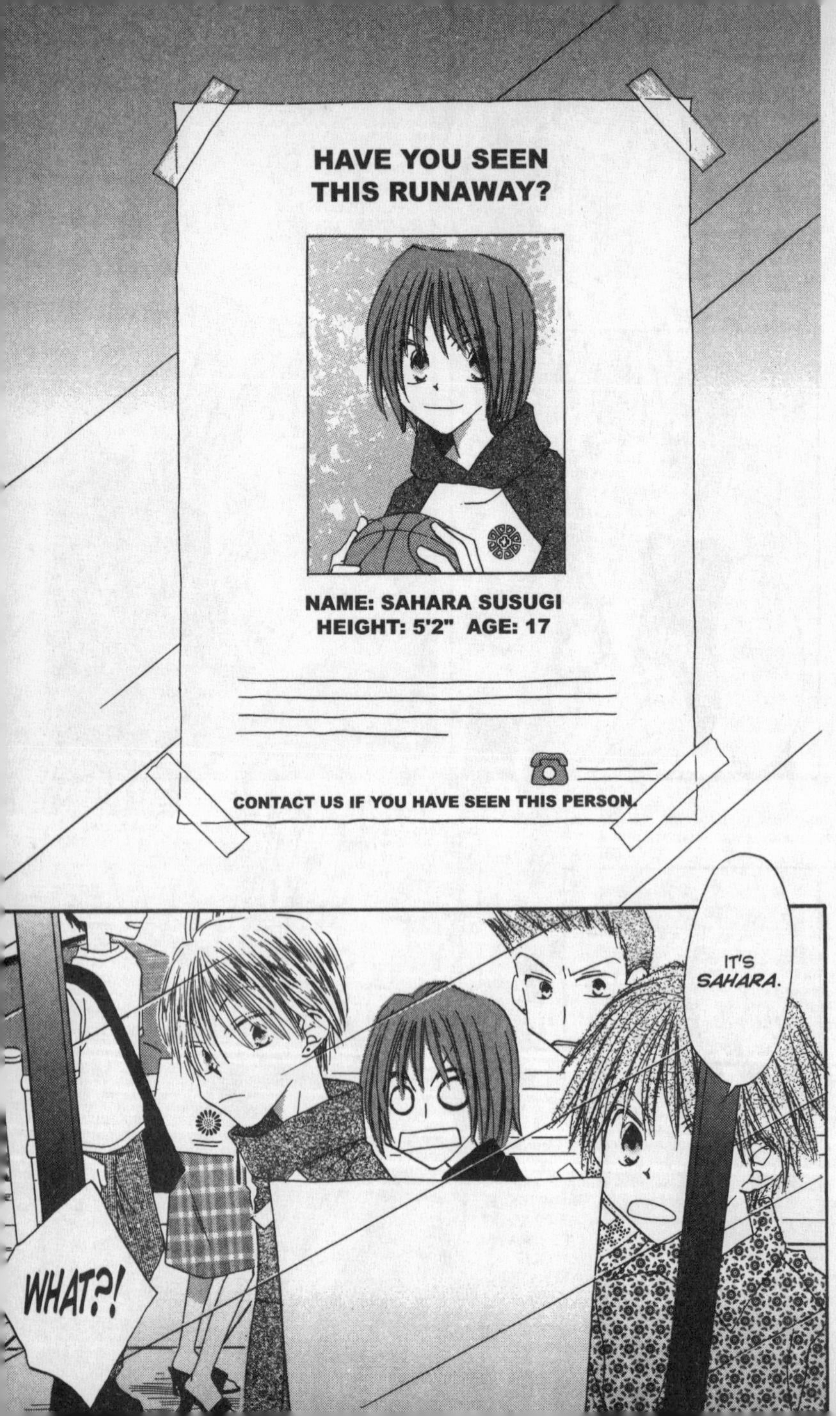
HAVE YOU SEEN THIS RUNAWAY?
NAME: SAHARA SUSUGI
HEIGHT: 5'2" AGE: 17
CONTACT US IF YOU HAVE SEEN THIS PERSON.
IT'S SAHARA.
WHAT?!

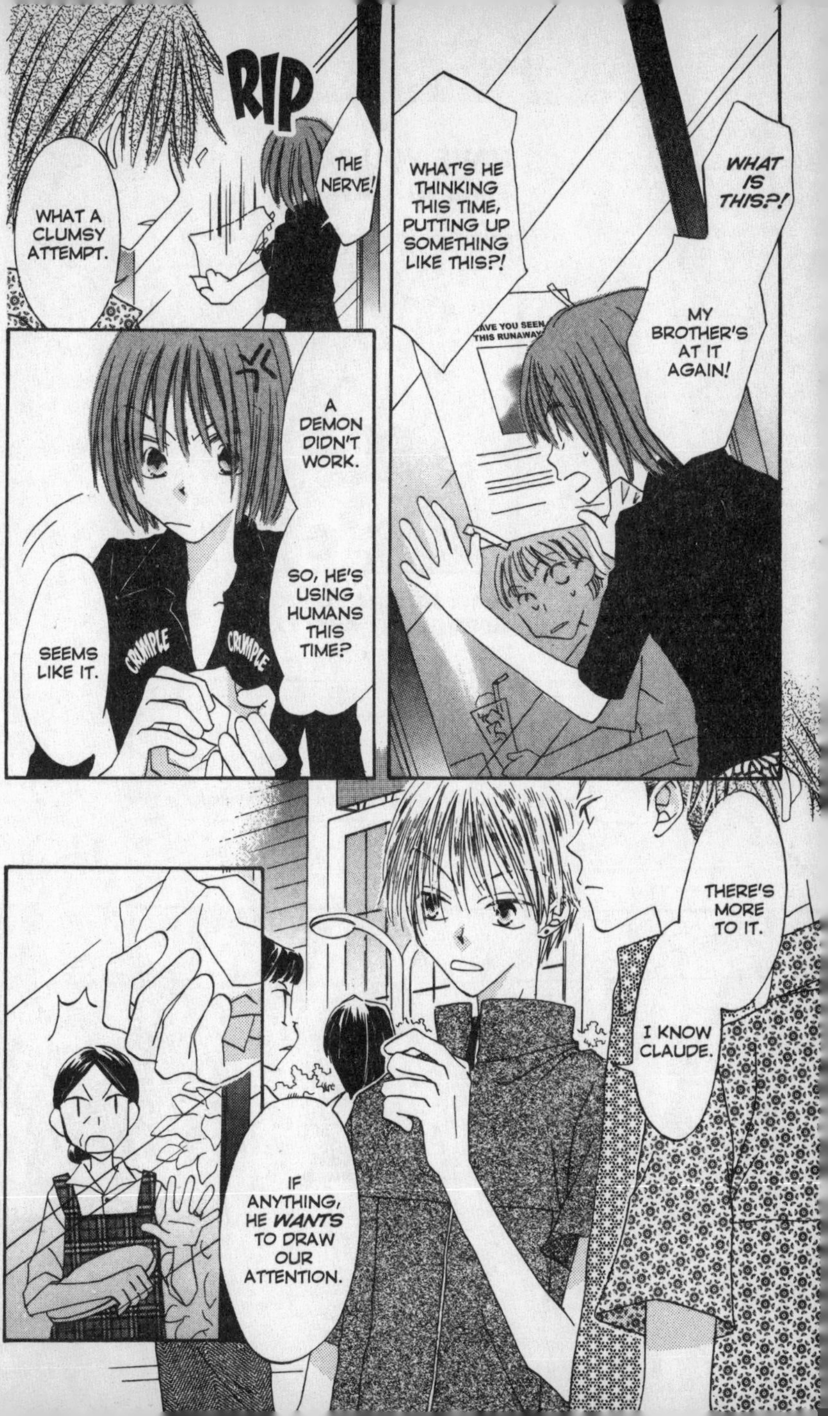
WHAT IS THIS?!
WHAT'S HE THINKING THIS TIME, PUTTING UP SOMETHING LIKE THIS?!
AVE YOU SEEN THIS RUNAWAY
MY BROTHER'S AT IT AGAIN!
RIP
THE NERVE!
WHAT A CLUMSY ATTEMPT.
A DEMON DIDN'T WORK.
SO, HE'S USING HUMANS THIS TIME?
CRUMPLE
CRUMPLE
SEEMS LIKE IT.
THERE'S MORE TO IT.
I KNOW CLAUDE.
IF ANYTHING, HE WANTS TO DRAW OUR ATTENTION.

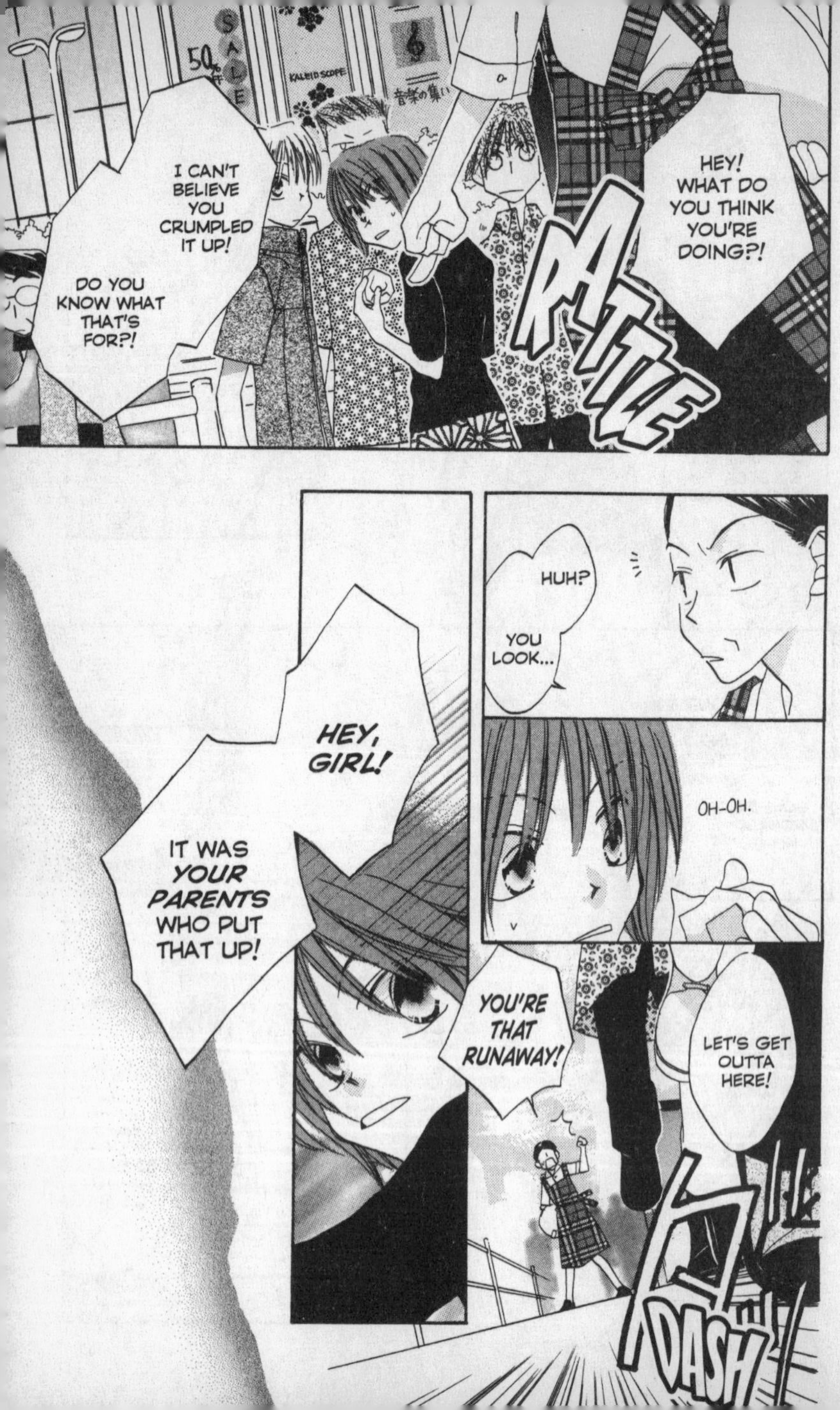
SALE
KALEIDSCOPE
音楽の集い
HEY! WHAT DO YOU THINK YOU'RE DOING?!
I CAN'T BELIEVE YOU CRUMPLED IT UP!
DO YOU KNOW WHAT THAT'S FOR?!
HUH?
YOU LOOK...
OH-OH.
LET'S GET OUTTA HERE!
YOU'RE THAT RUNAWAY!
DASH
HEY, GIRL!
IT WAS YOUR PARENTS WHO PUT THAT UP!

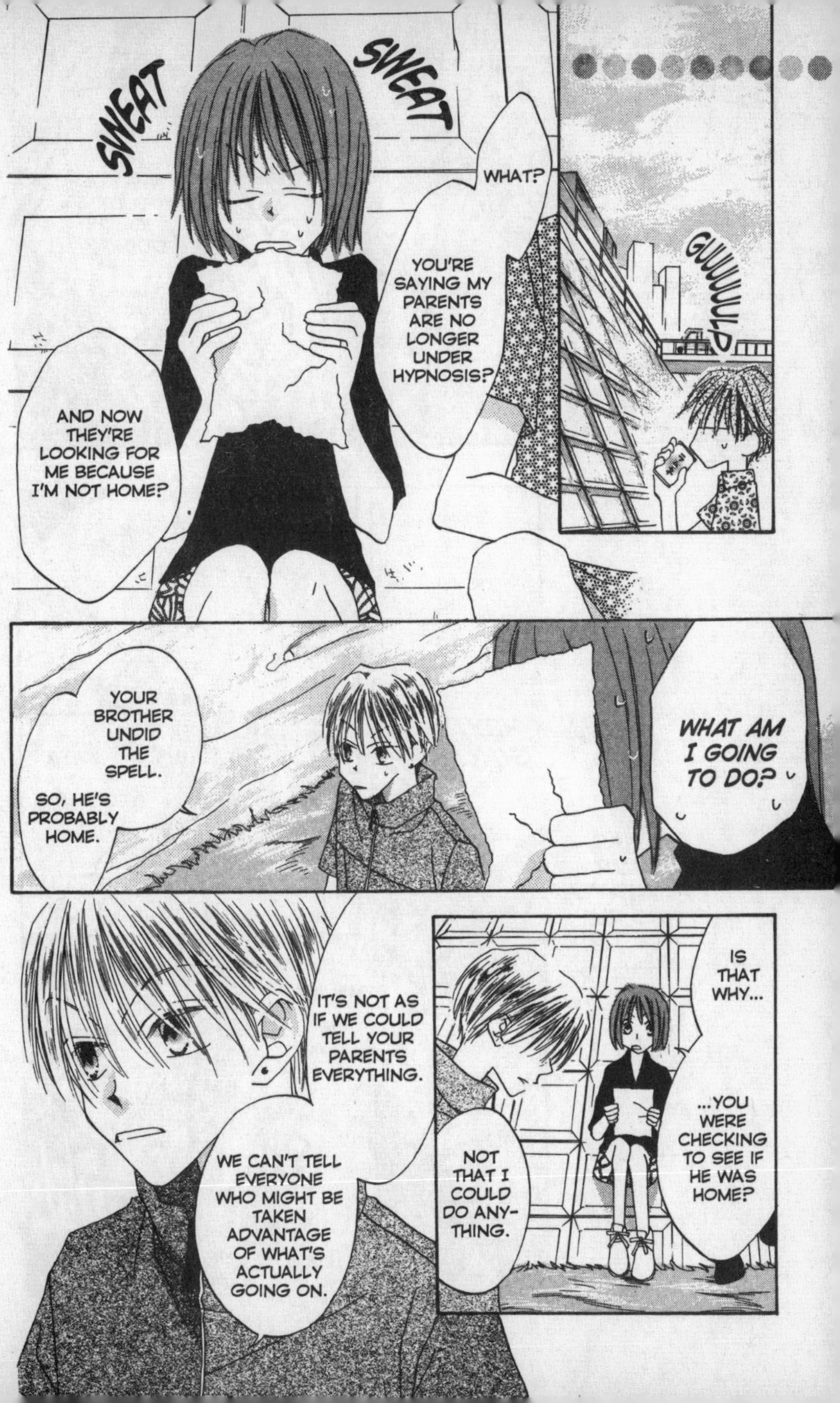
GUUUUULP
SWEAT
SWEAT
WHAT?
YOU'RE SAYING MY PARENTS ARE NO LONGER UNDER HYPNOSIS?
AND NOW THEY'RE LOOKING FOR ME BECAUSE I'M NOT HOME?
WHAT AM I GOING TO DO?
YOUR BROTHER UNDID THE SPELL.
SO, HE'S PROBABLY HOME.
IS THAT WHY...
...YOU WERE CHECKING TO SEE IF HE WAS HOME?
NOT THAT I COULD DO ANY-THING.
IT'S NOT AS IF WE COULD TELL YOUR PARENTS EVERYTHING.
WE CAN'T TELL EVERYONE WHO MIGHT BE TAKEN ADVANTAGE OF WHAT'S ACTUALLY GOING ON.

04

Some people wanted to know what supplies I use. Here are the main ones.

- o Zebra ballpoint pens ands filler
- o Pilot art ink
- o IC manga paper (300 lb.)
- o Screen tone cutter (replacement blades: 30°)
- o Dr. Martin's White (Bleed Proof White)
- o Screen tone, pens, etc.
- o Coloring, on illustration boards. Mainly Copic and sometimes Dr. Martin colored ink.

Someone once told me the ink goes on easier if you heat the pen tips. Since then, I've gotten good at using a lighter--even though I don't smoke.

See you at the end of the book.

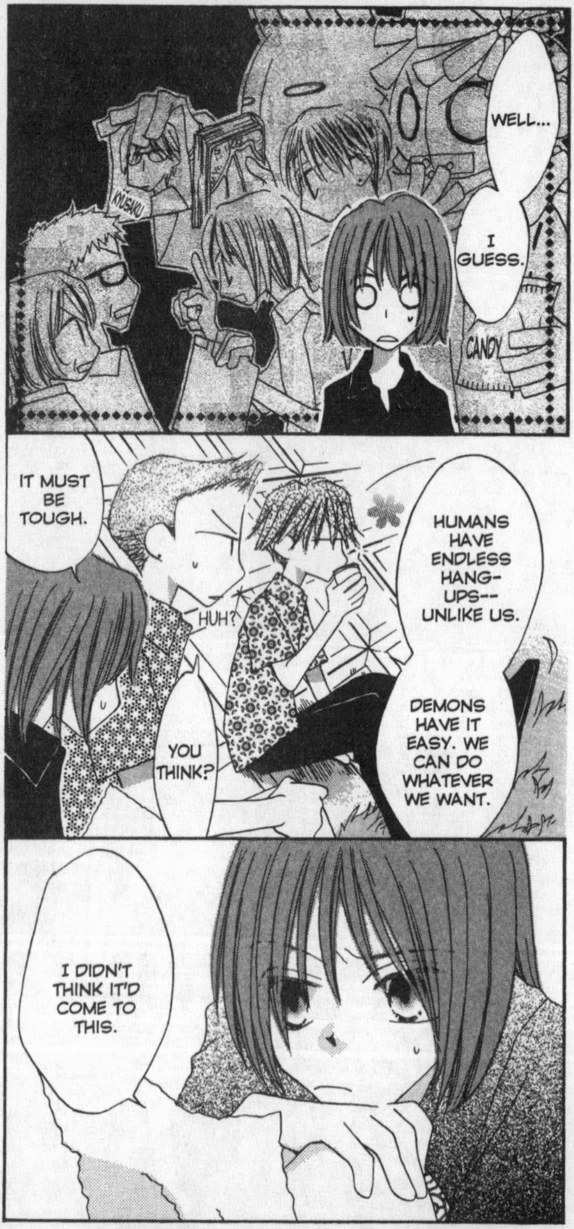
WELL...
I GUESS.
KYUSAKU
CANDY
HUMANS HAVE ENDLESS HANG-UPS--UNLIKE US.
IT MUST BE TOUGH.
HUH?
DEMONS HAVE IT EASY. WE CAN DO WHATEVER WE WANT.
YOU THINK?
I DIDN'T THINK IT'D COME TO THIS.

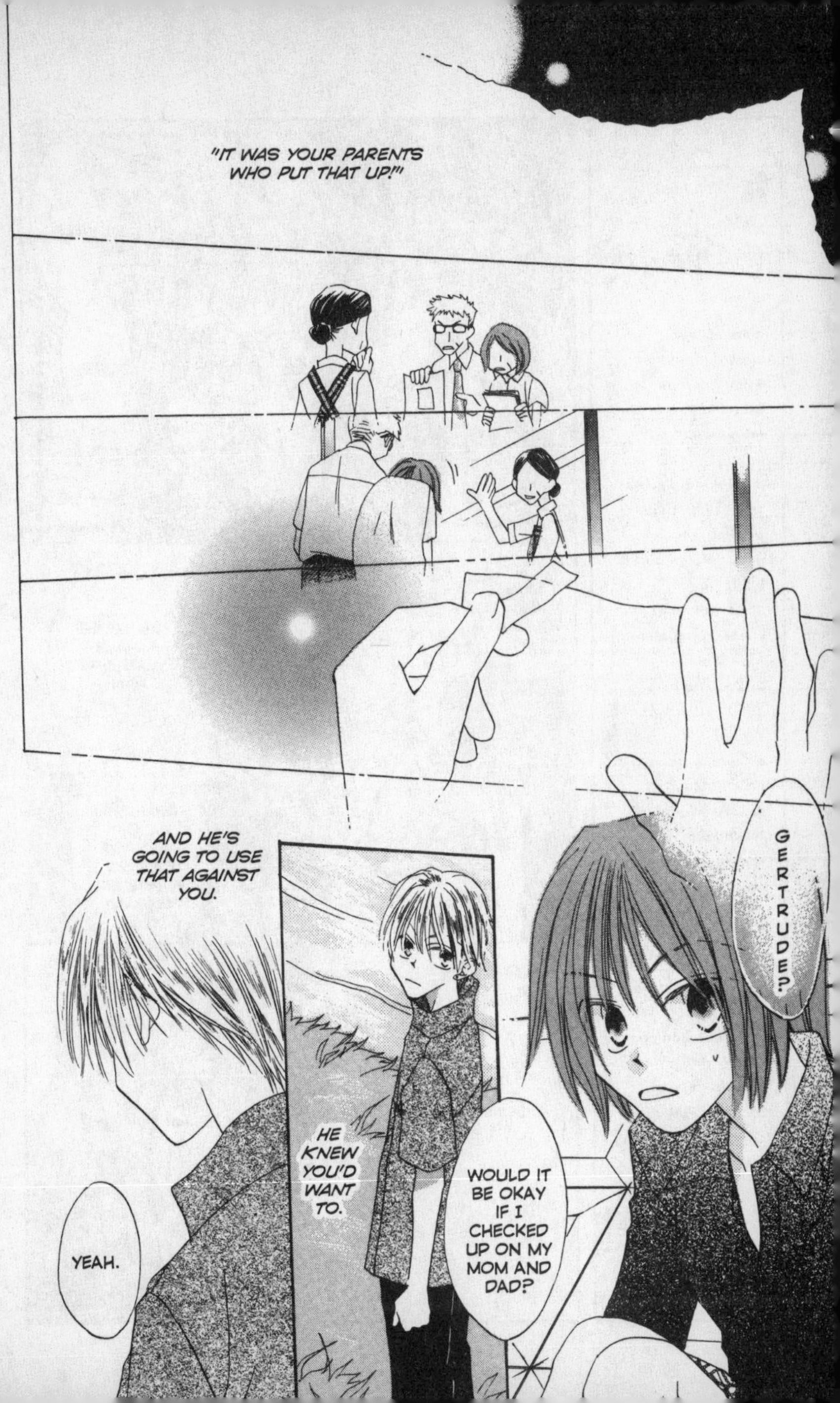
"IT WAS YOUR PARENTS WHO PUT THAT UP!"
GERTRUDE?
WOULD IT BE OKAY IF I CHECKED UP ON MY MOM AND DAD?
HE KNEW YOU'D WANT TO.
AND HE'S GOING TO USE THAT AGAINST YOU.
YEAH.

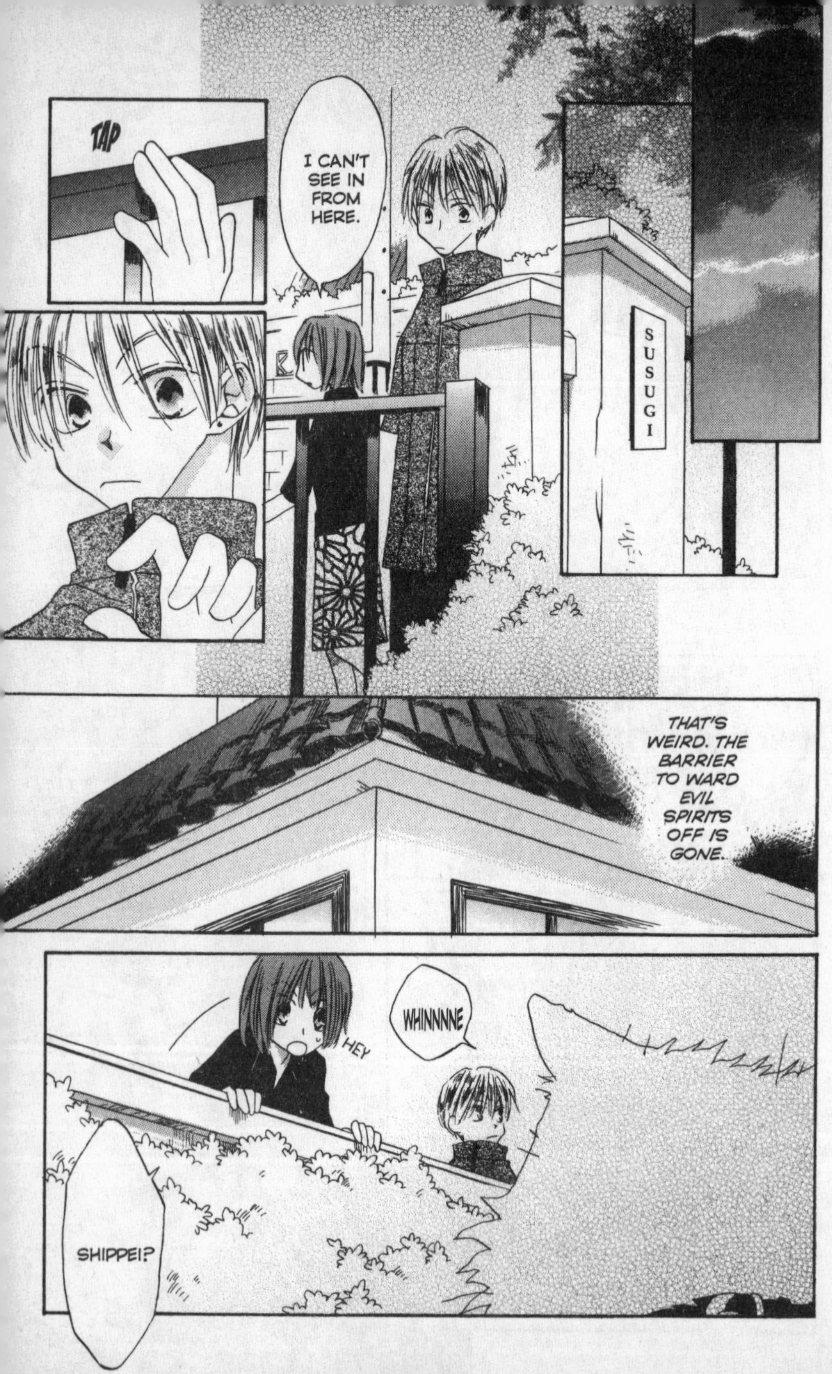
SUSUGI
I CAN'T SEE IN FROM HERE.
TAP
THAT'S WEIRD. THE BARRIER TO WARD EVIL SPIRITS OFF IS GONE.
WHINNNNE
HEY
SHIPPEI?

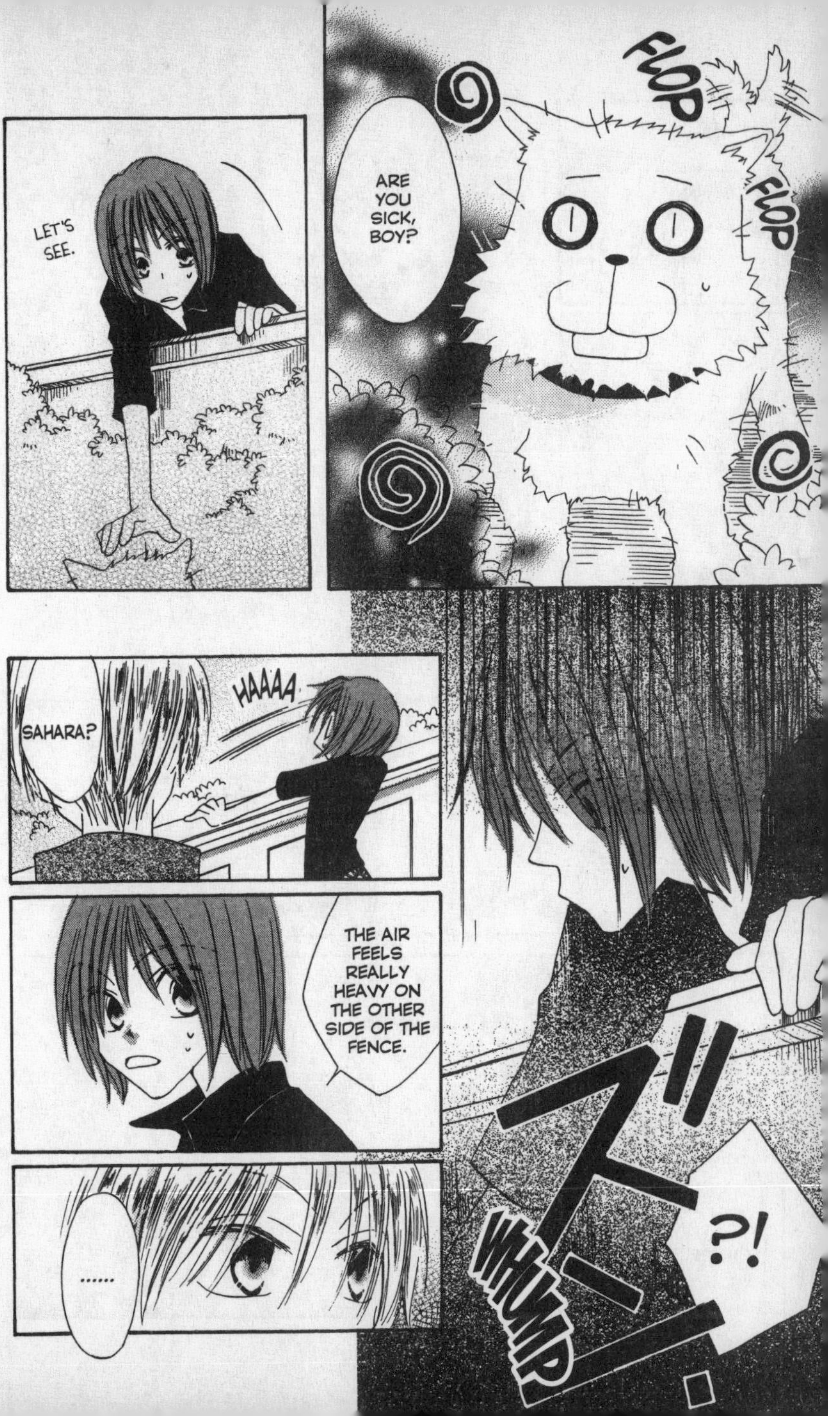
FLOP
FLOP
ARE YOU SICK, BOY?
LET'S SEE.
?!
WHUMP
HAAAA
SAHARA?
THE AIR FEELS REALLY HEAVY ON THE OTHER SIDE OF THE FENCE.
......

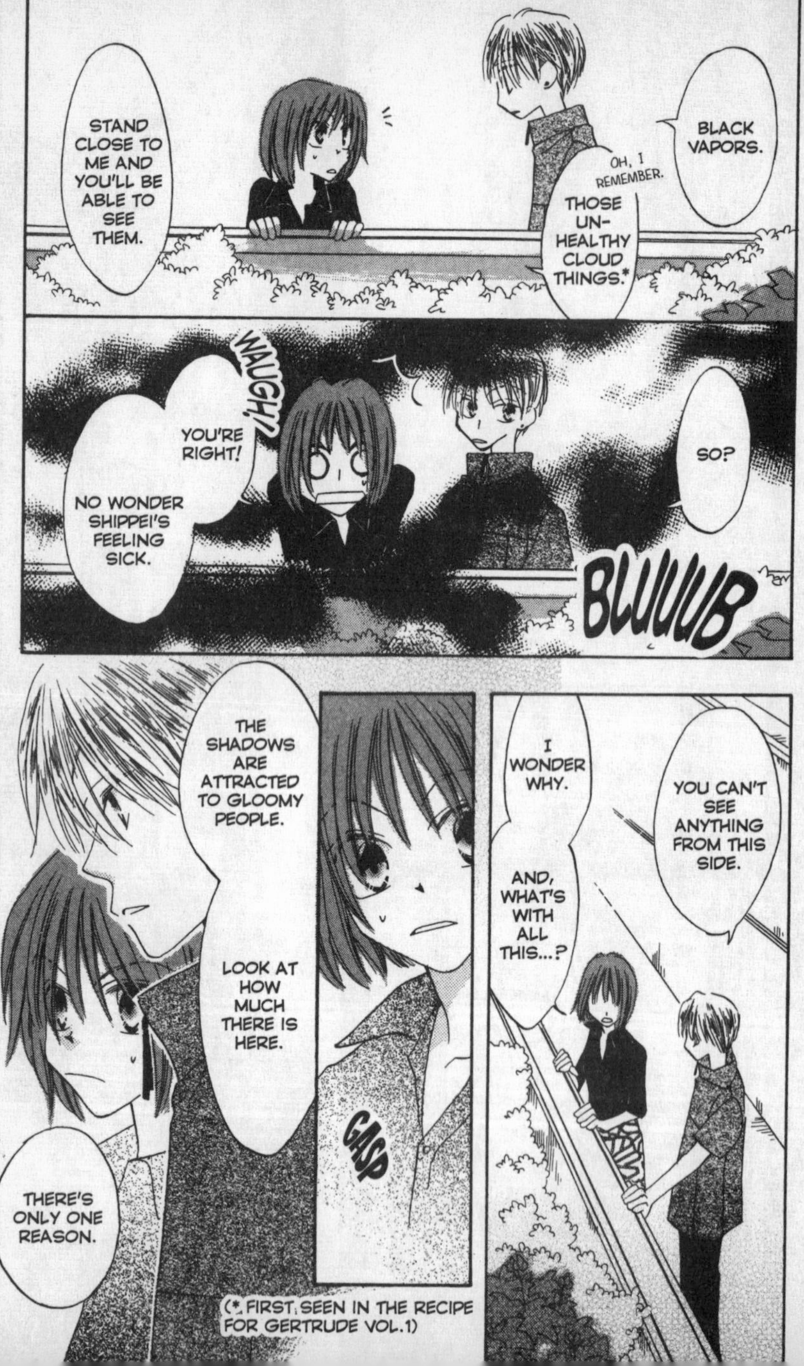
BLACK VAPORS.
OH, I REMEMBER.
THOSE UN-HEALTHY CLOUD THINGS.*
STAND CLOSE TO ME AND YOU'LL BE ABLE TO SEE THEM.
SO?
WAUGH!
YOU'RE RIGHT!
NO WONDER SHIPPEI'S FEELING SICK.
BLUUUB
YOU CAN'T SEE ANYTHING FROM THIS SIDE.
I WONDER WHY.
AND, WHAT'S WITH ALL THIS...?
THE SHADOWS ARE ATTRACTED TO GLOOMY PEOPLE.
LOOK AT HOW MUCH THERE IS HERE.
GASP
THERE'S ONLY ONE REASON.

(*: FIRST SEEN IN THE RECIPE FOR GERTRUDE VOL.1)

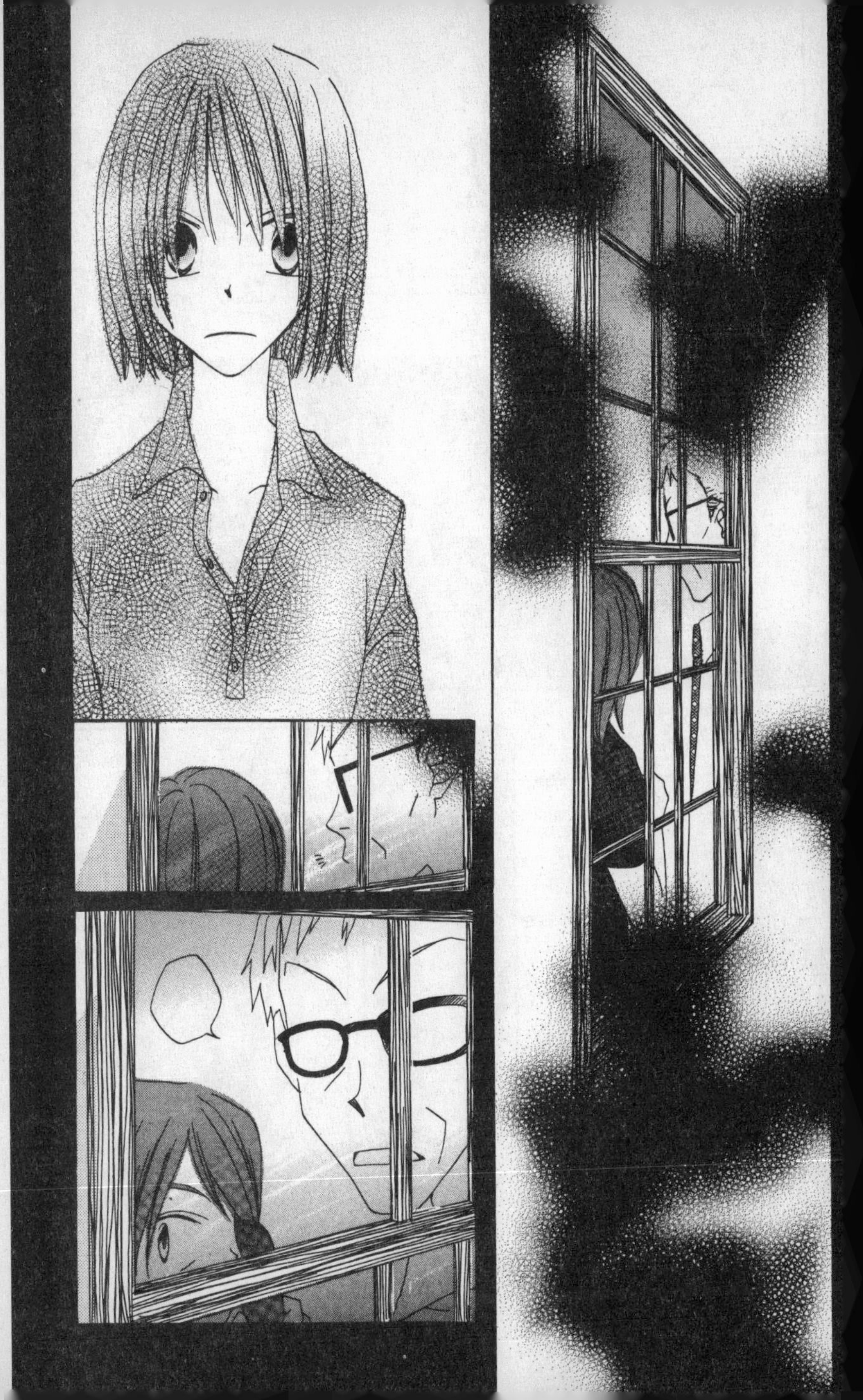

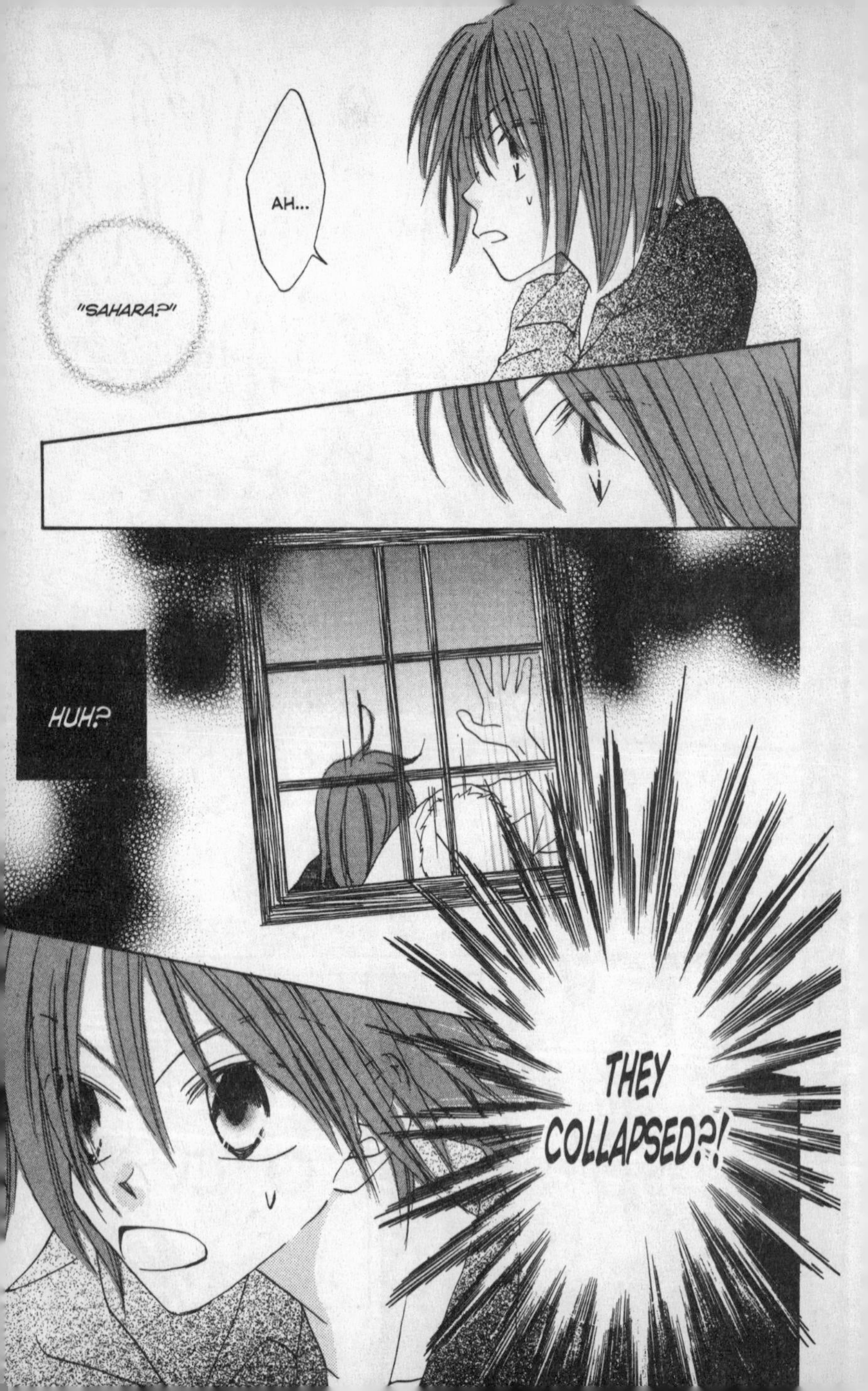
AH...
"SAHARA?"
HUH?
THEY COLLAPSED?!

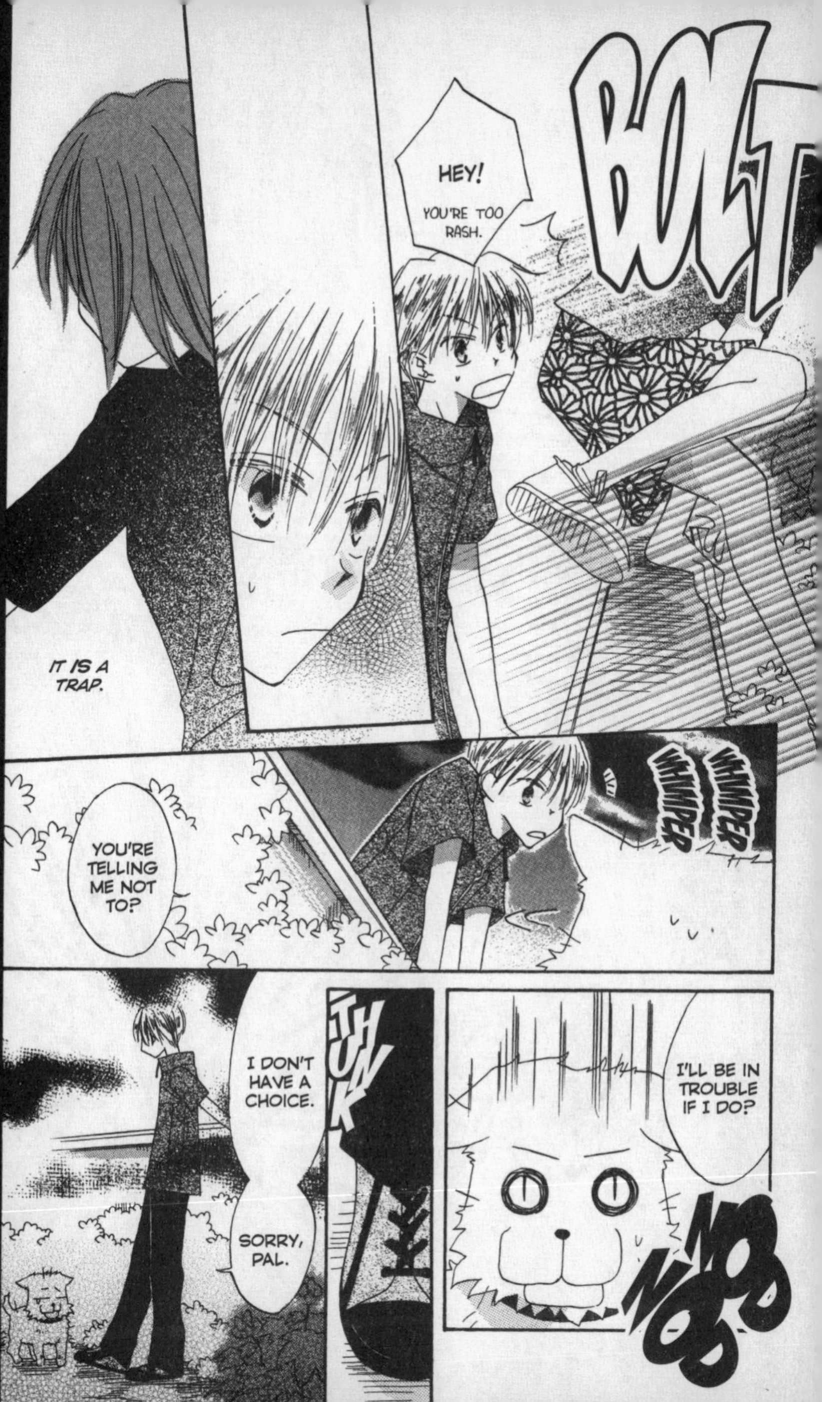
BOLT
HEY!
YOU'RE TOO RASH.
IT IS A TRAP.
WHIMPER WHIMPER
YOU'RE TELLING ME NOT TO?
I'LL BE IN TROUBLE IF I DO?
NOOOO
THUNK
I DON'T HAVE A CHOICE.
SORRY, PAL.

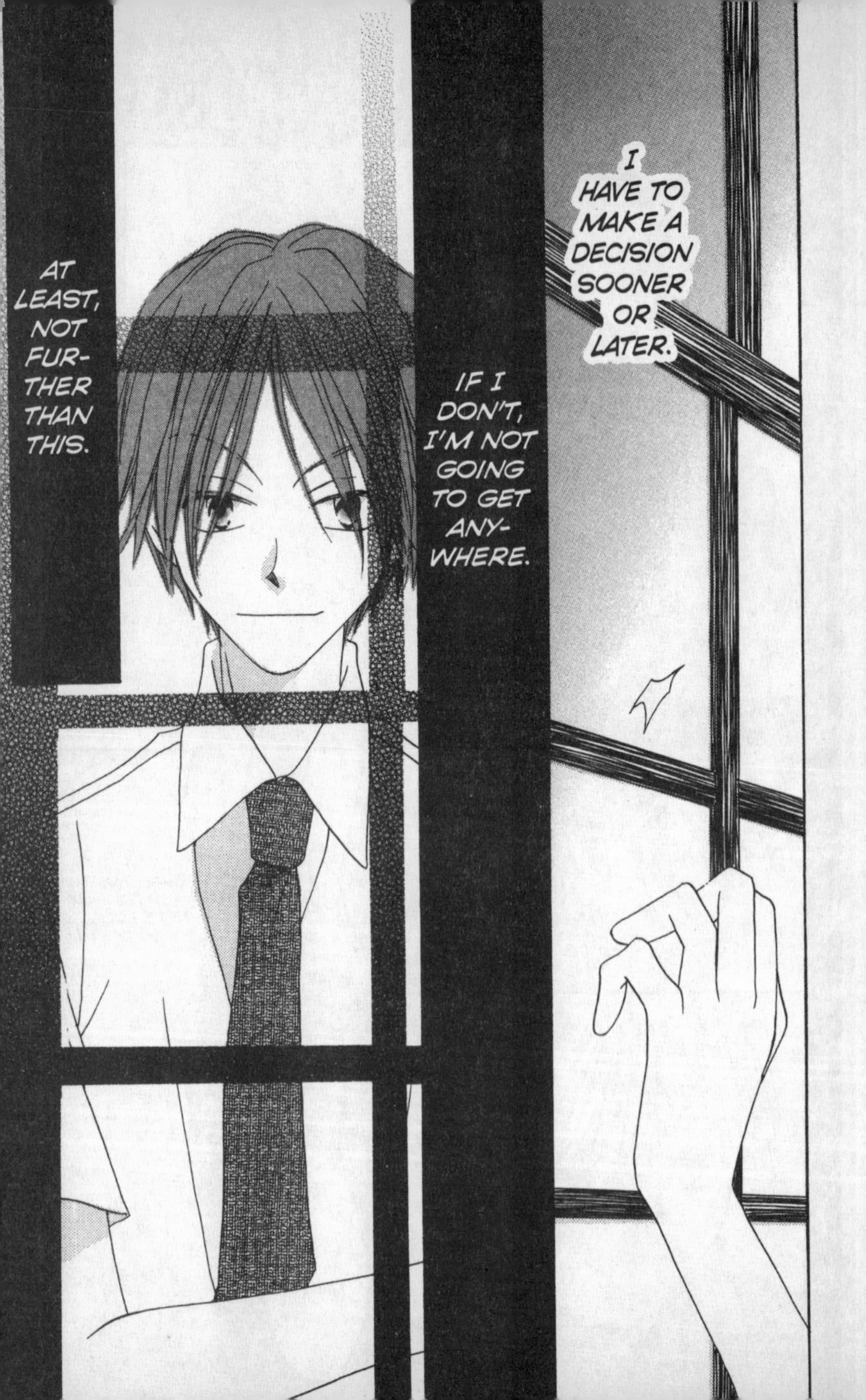
I HAVE TO MAKE A DECISION SOONER OR LATER.
IF I DON'T, I'M NOT GOING TO GET ANYWHERE.
AT LEAST, NOT FURTHER THAN THIS.

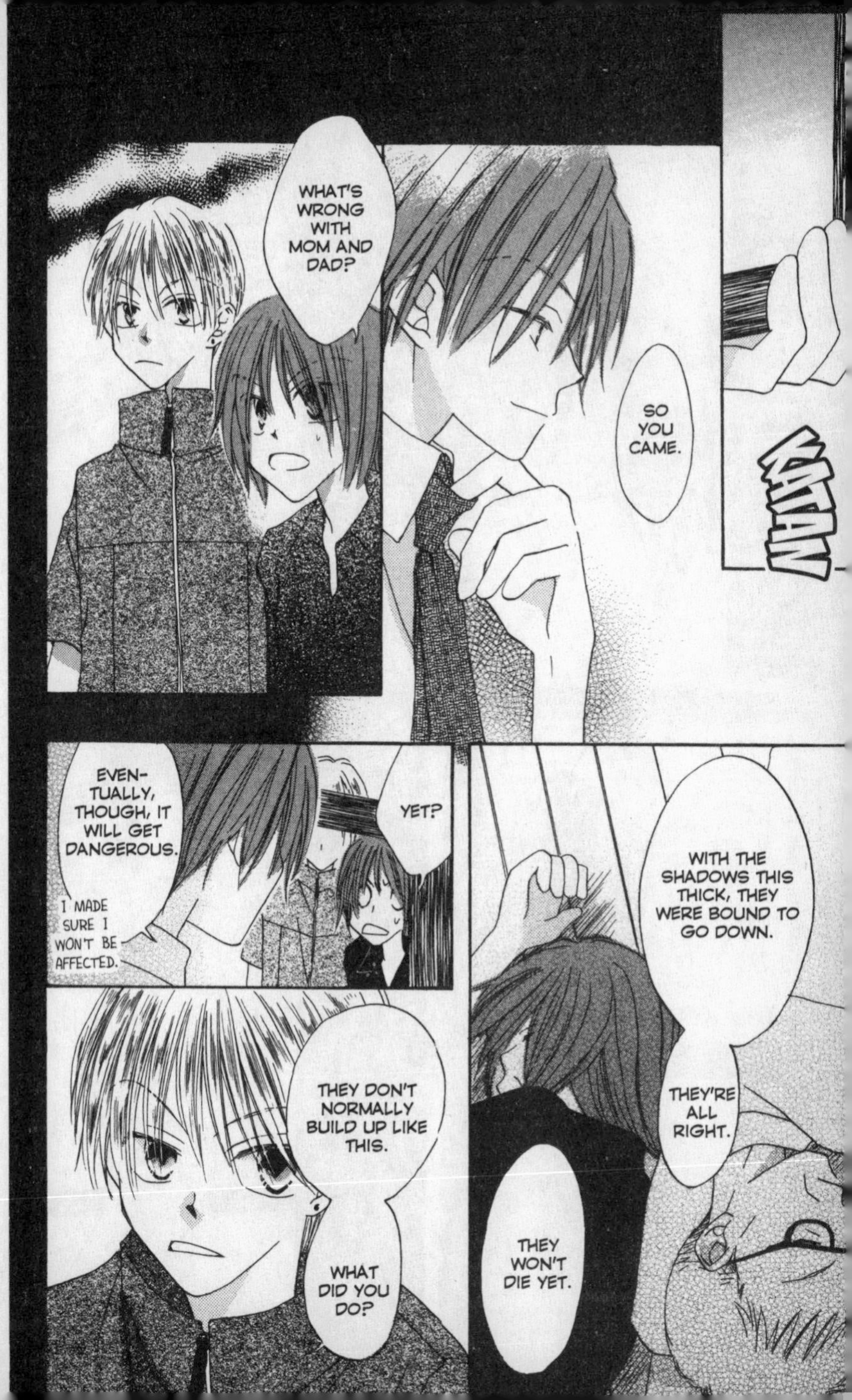
KATAN
SO YOU CAME.
WHAT'S WRONG WITH MOM AND DAD?
WITH THE SHADOWS THIS THICK, THEY WERE BOUND TO GO DOWN.
THEY'RE ALL RIGHT.
THEY WON'T DIE YET.
YET?
EVEN-TUALLY, THOUGH, IT WILL GET DANGEROUS.
I MADE SURE I WON'T BE AFFECTED.
THEY DON'T NORMALLY BUILD UP LIKE THIS.
WHAT DID YOU DO?

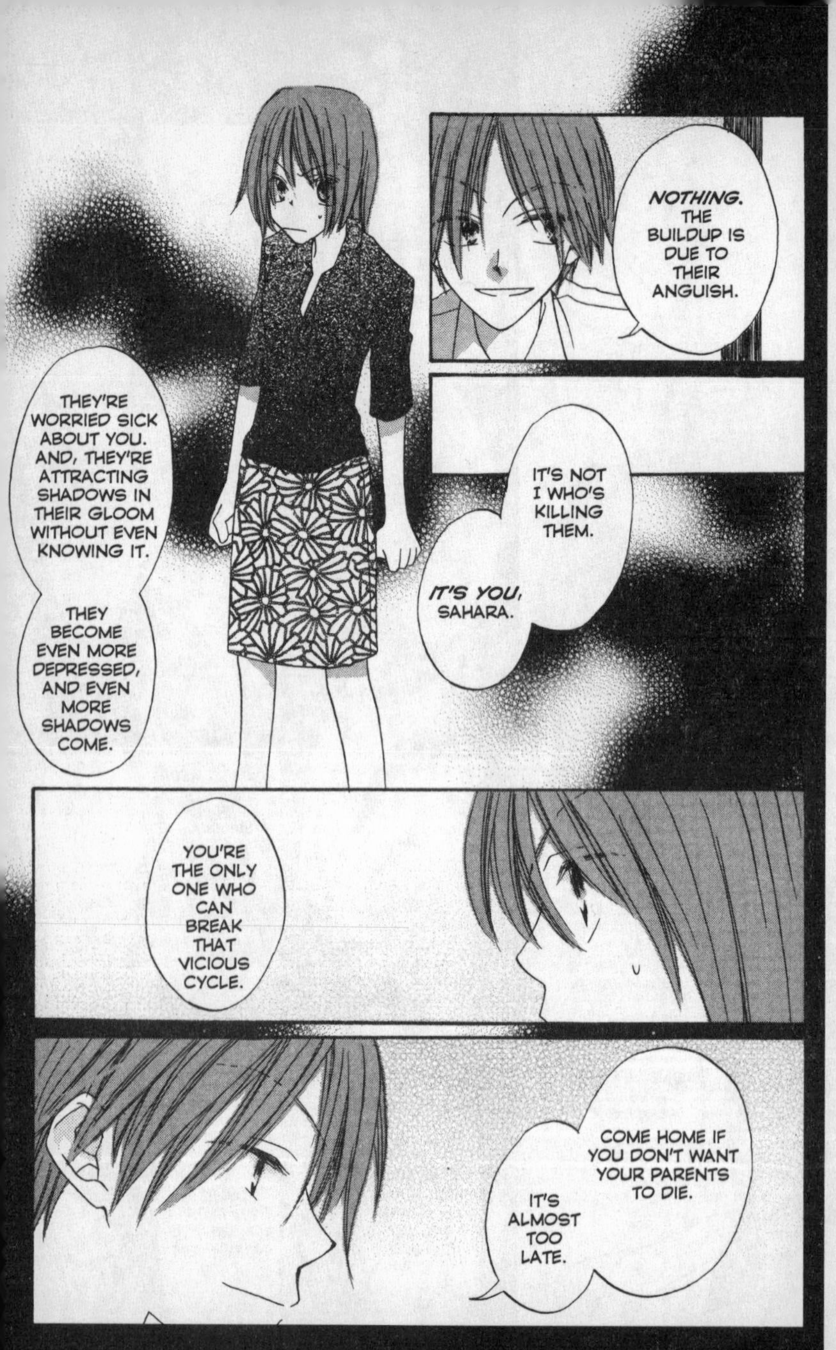

NOTHING. THE BUILDUP IS DUE TO THEIR ANGUISH.
THEY'RE WORRIED SICK ABOUT YOU. AND, THEY'RE ATTRACTING SHADOWS IN THEIR GLOOM WITHOUT EVEN KNOWING IT.
THEY BECOME EVEN MORE DEPRESSED, AND EVEN MORE SHADOWS COME.
IT'S NOT I WHO'S KILLING THEM.
IT'S YOU, SAHARA.
YOU'RE THE ONLY ONE WHO CAN BREAK THAT VICIOUS CYCLE.
COME HOME IF YOU DON'T WANT YOUR PARENTS TO DIE.
IT'S ALMOST TOO LATE.

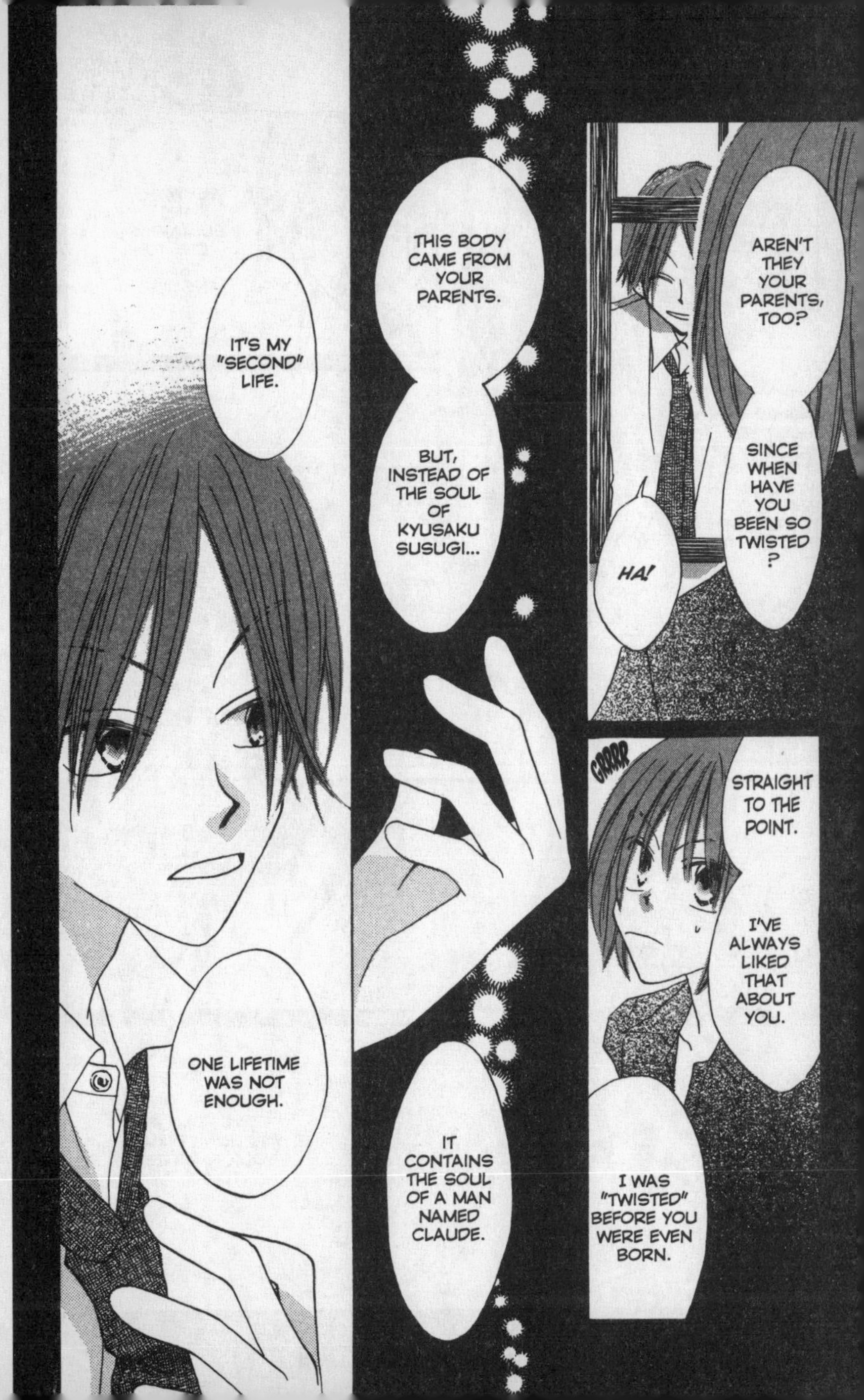
AREN'T THEY YOUR PARENTS, TOO?
SINCE WHEN HAVE YOU BEEN SO TWISTED?
HA!
GRRRR
STRAIGHT TO THE POINT.
I'VE ALWAYS LIKED THAT ABOUT YOU.
I WAS "TWISTED" BEFORE YOU WERE EVEN BORN.
THIS BODY CAME FROM YOUR PARENTS.
BUT, INSTEAD OF THE SOUL OF KYUSAKU SUSUGI...
IT CONTAINS THE SOUL OF A MAN NAMED CLAUDE.
IT'S MY "SECOND" LIFE.
ONE LIFETIME WAS NOT ENOUGH.

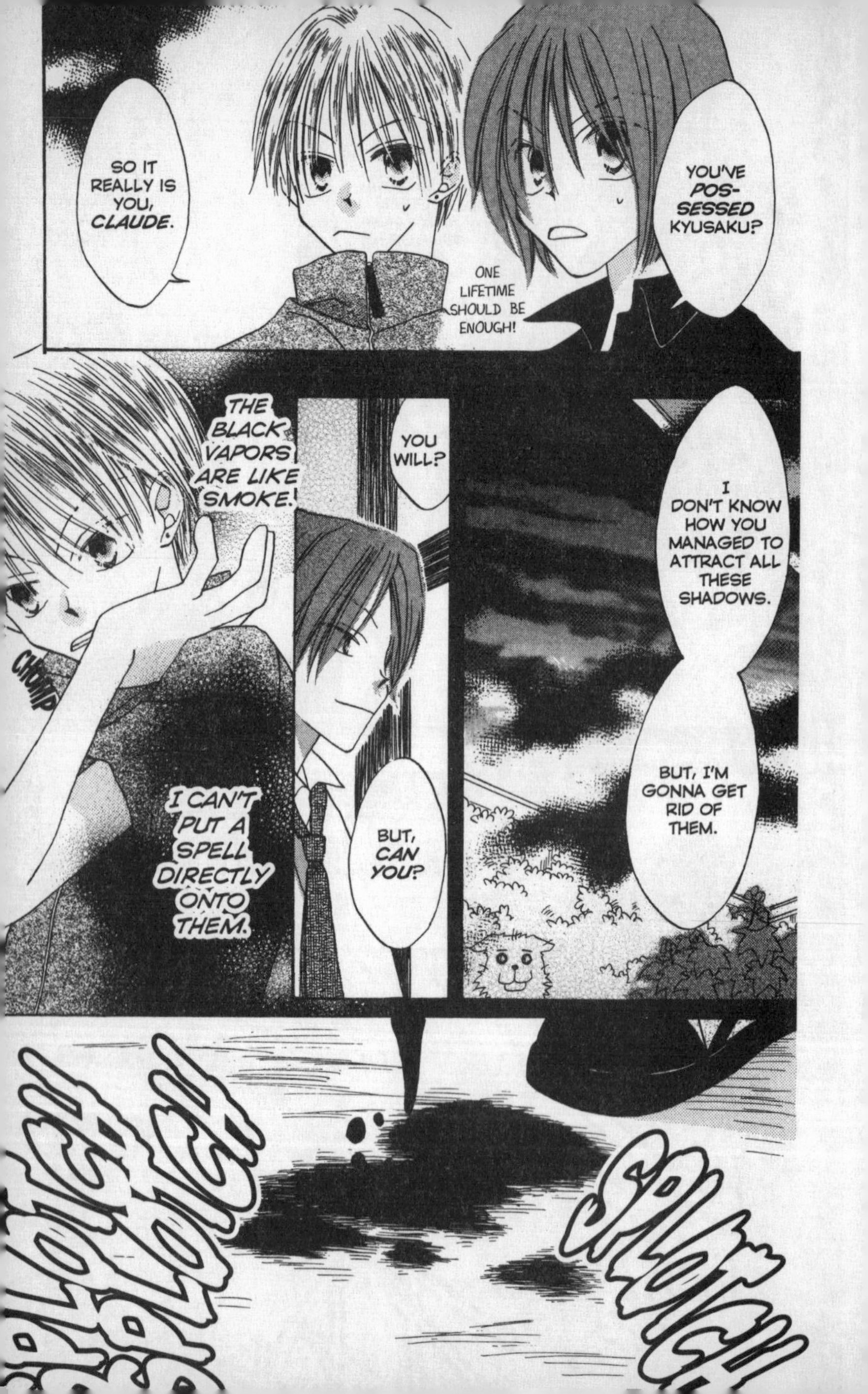

YOU'VE POSSESSED KYUSAKU?
SO IT REALLY IS YOU, CLAUDE.
ONE LIFETIME SHOULD BE ENOUGH!
I DON'T KNOW HOW YOU MANAGED TO ATTRACT ALL THESE SHADOWS.
BUT, I'M GONNA GET RID OF THEM.
YOU WILL?
BUT, CAN YOU?
THE BLACK VAPORS ARE LIKE SMOKE!
CHOMP
I CAN'T PUT A SPELL DIRECTLY ONTO THEM.
SPLOTCH
SPLOTCH SPLOTCH

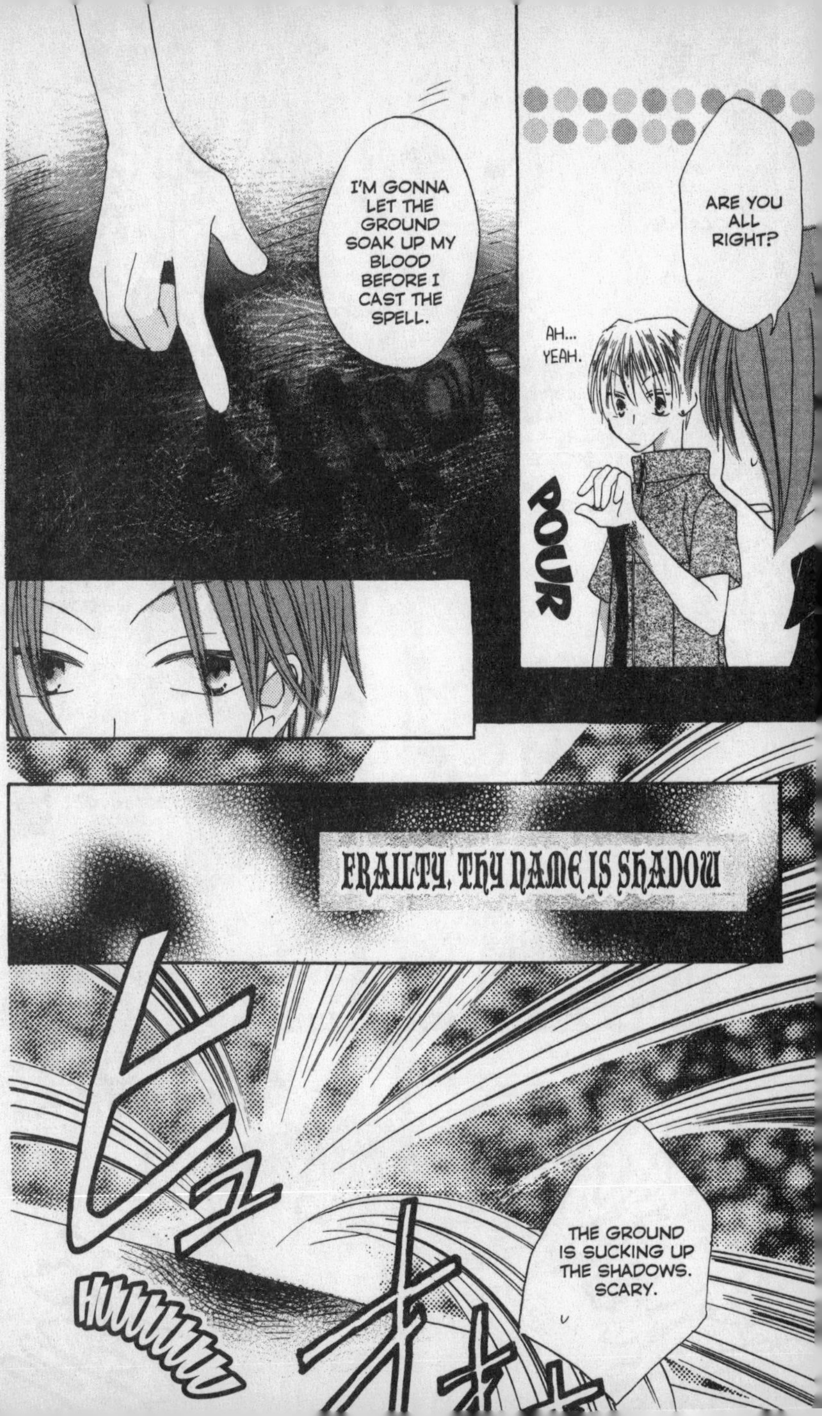
ARE YOU ALL RIGHT?
AH... YEAH.
POUR
I'M GONNA LET THE GROUND SOAK UP MY BLOOD BEFORE I CAST THE SPELL.
FRAILTY, THY NAME IS SHADOW
ヒュオォ
HUUUUWWW
THE GROUND IS SUCKING UP THE SHADOWS. SCARY.

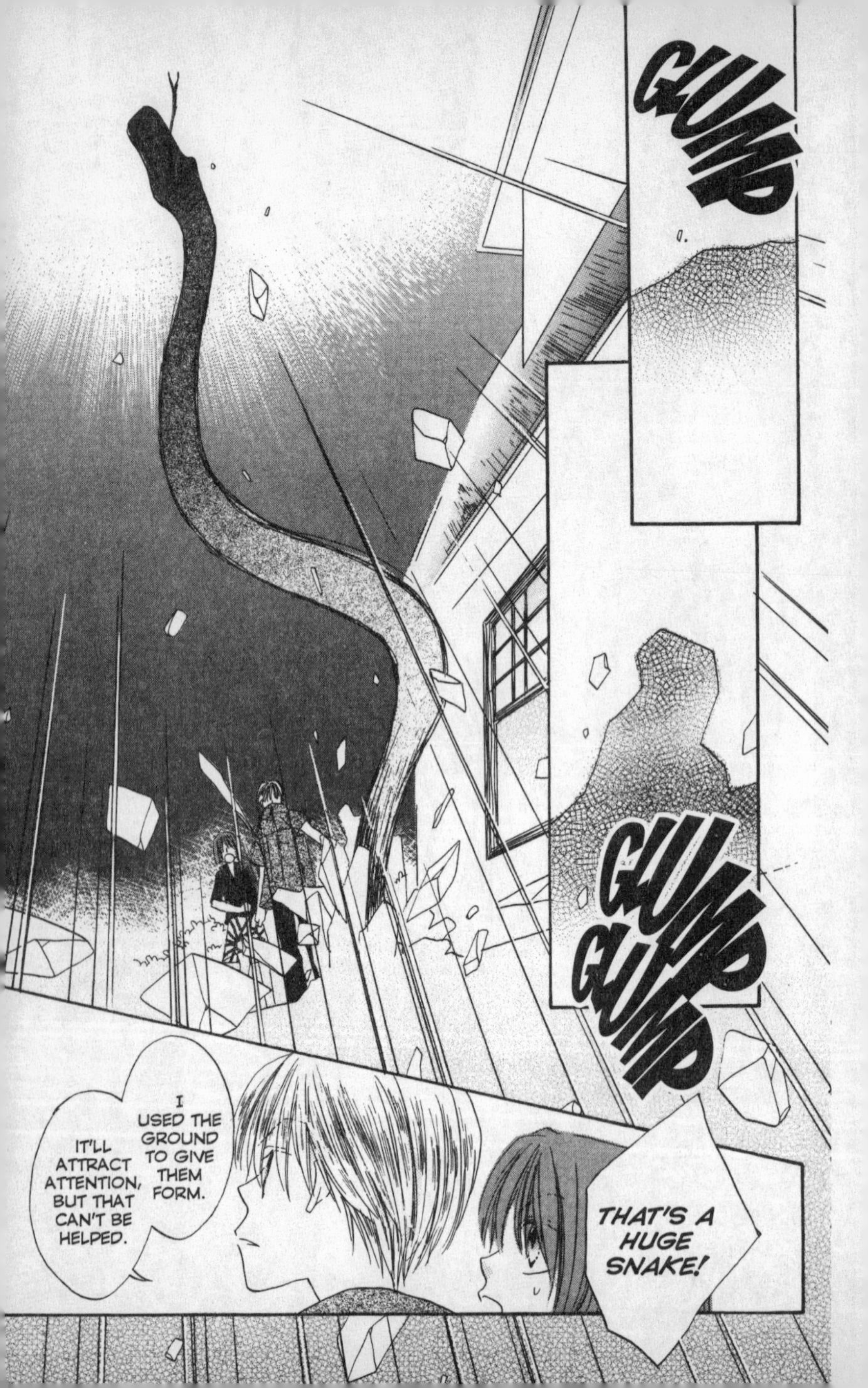
GUMP
GUMP GUMP
THAT'S A HUGE SNAKE!
I USED THE GROUND TO GIVE THEM FORM.
IT'LL ATTRACT ATTENTION, BUT THAT CAN'T BE HELPED.

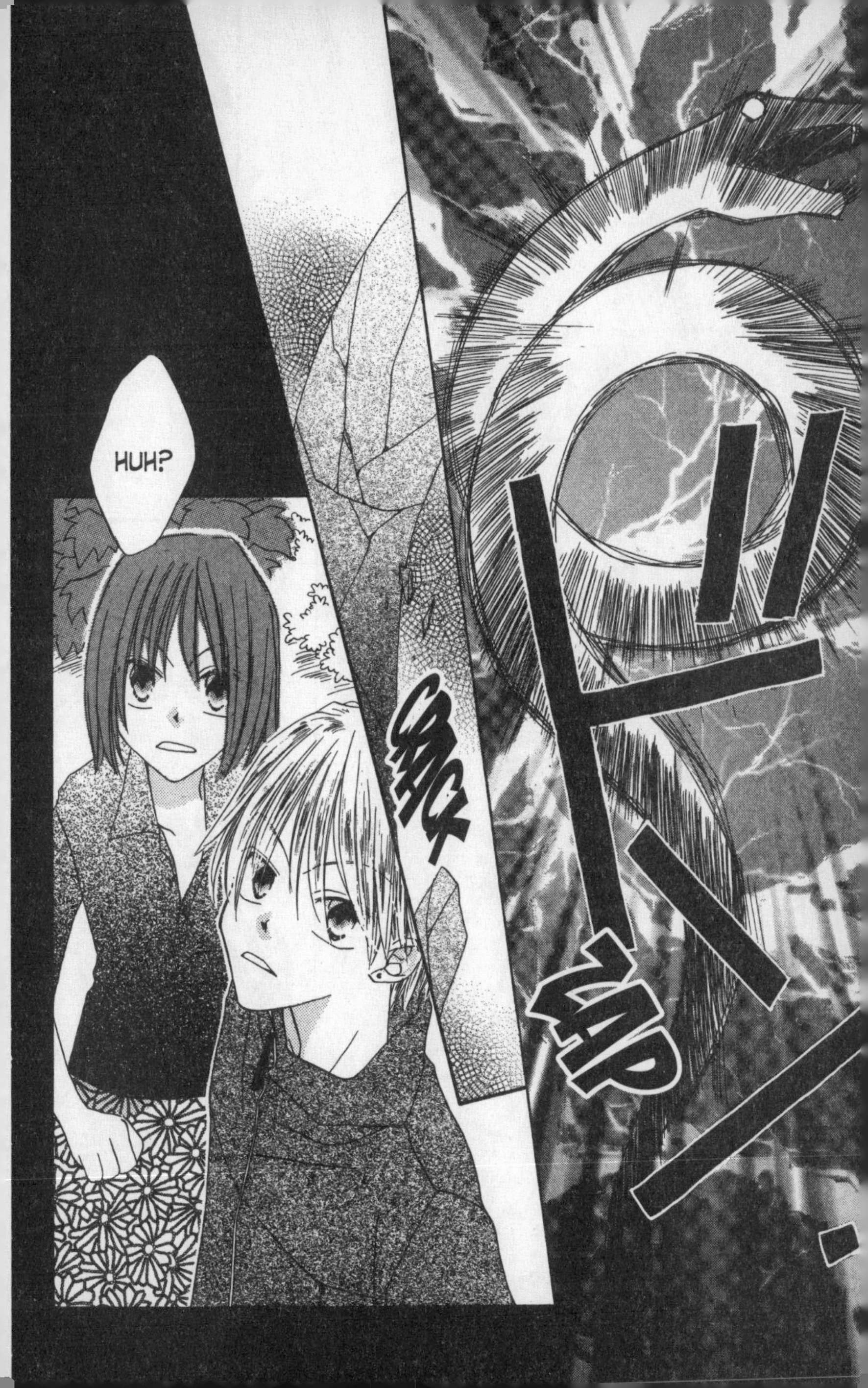
ZAP
CRACK
HUH?

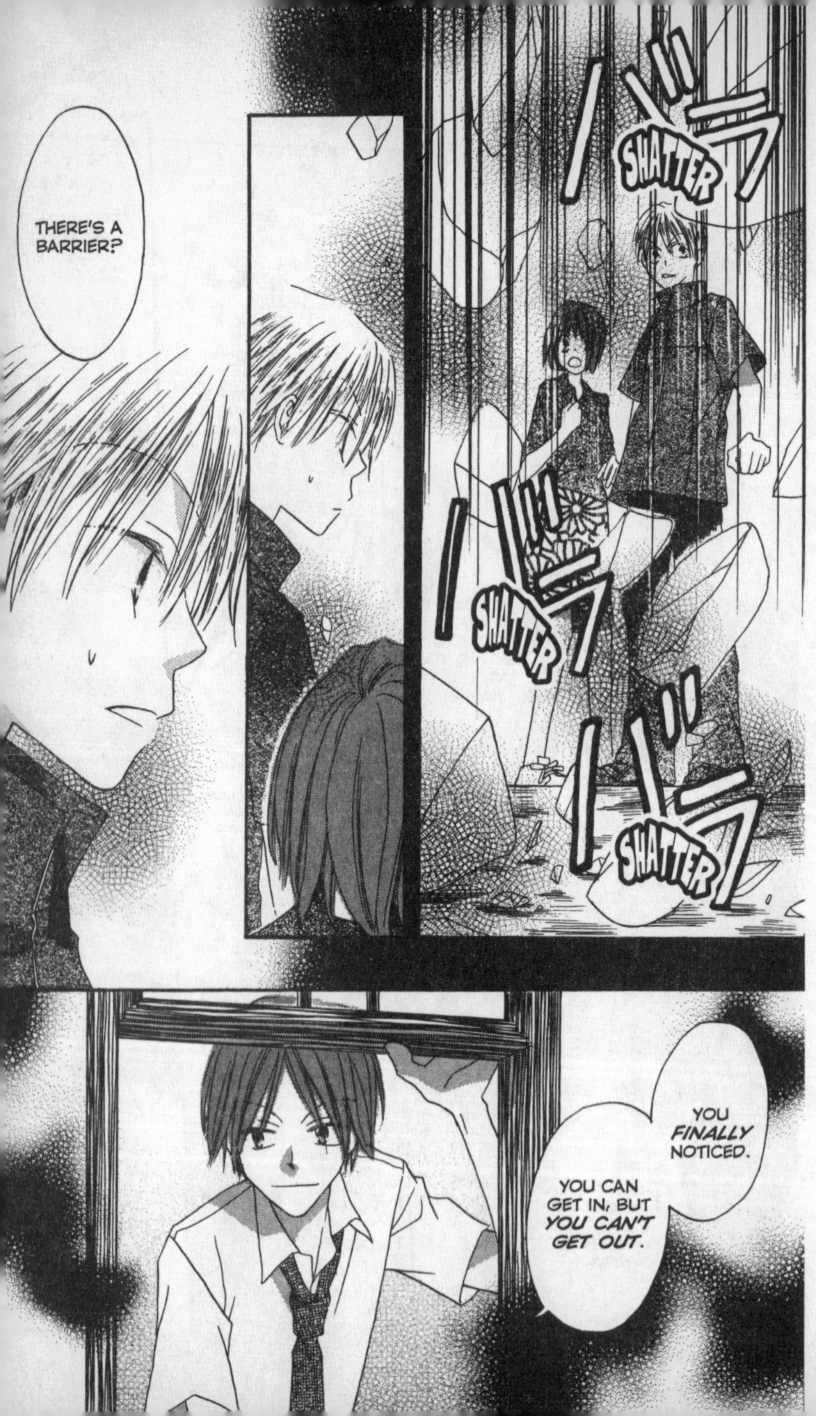
SHATTER
SHATTER
SHATTER
THERE'S A BARRIER?
YOU *FINALLY* NOTICED.
YOU CAN GET IN, BUT *YOU CAN'T GET OUT*.

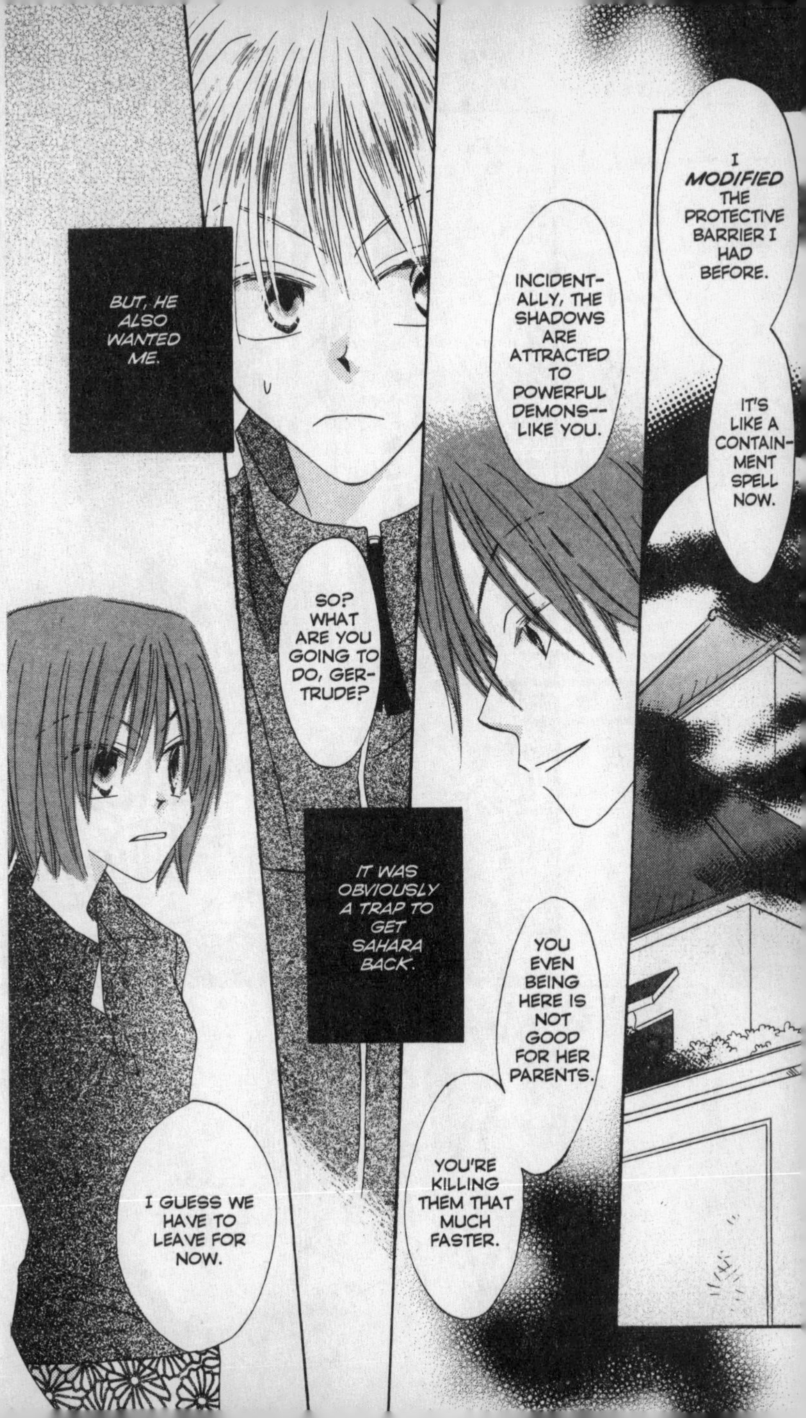
I *MODIFIED* THE PROTECTIVE BARRIER I HAD BEFORE.
IT'S LIKE A CONTAINMENT SPELL NOW.
INCIDENTALLY, THE SHADOWS ARE ATTRACTED TO POWERFUL DEMONS--LIKE YOU.
YOU EVEN BEING HERE IS NOT GOOD FOR HER PARENTS.
YOU'RE KILLING THEM THAT MUCH FASTER.
SO? WHAT ARE YOU GOING TO DO, GERTRUDE?
IT WAS OBVIOUSLY A TRAP TO GET SAHARA BACK.
BUT, HE ALSO WANTED ME.
I GUESS WE HAVE TO LEAVE FOR NOW.

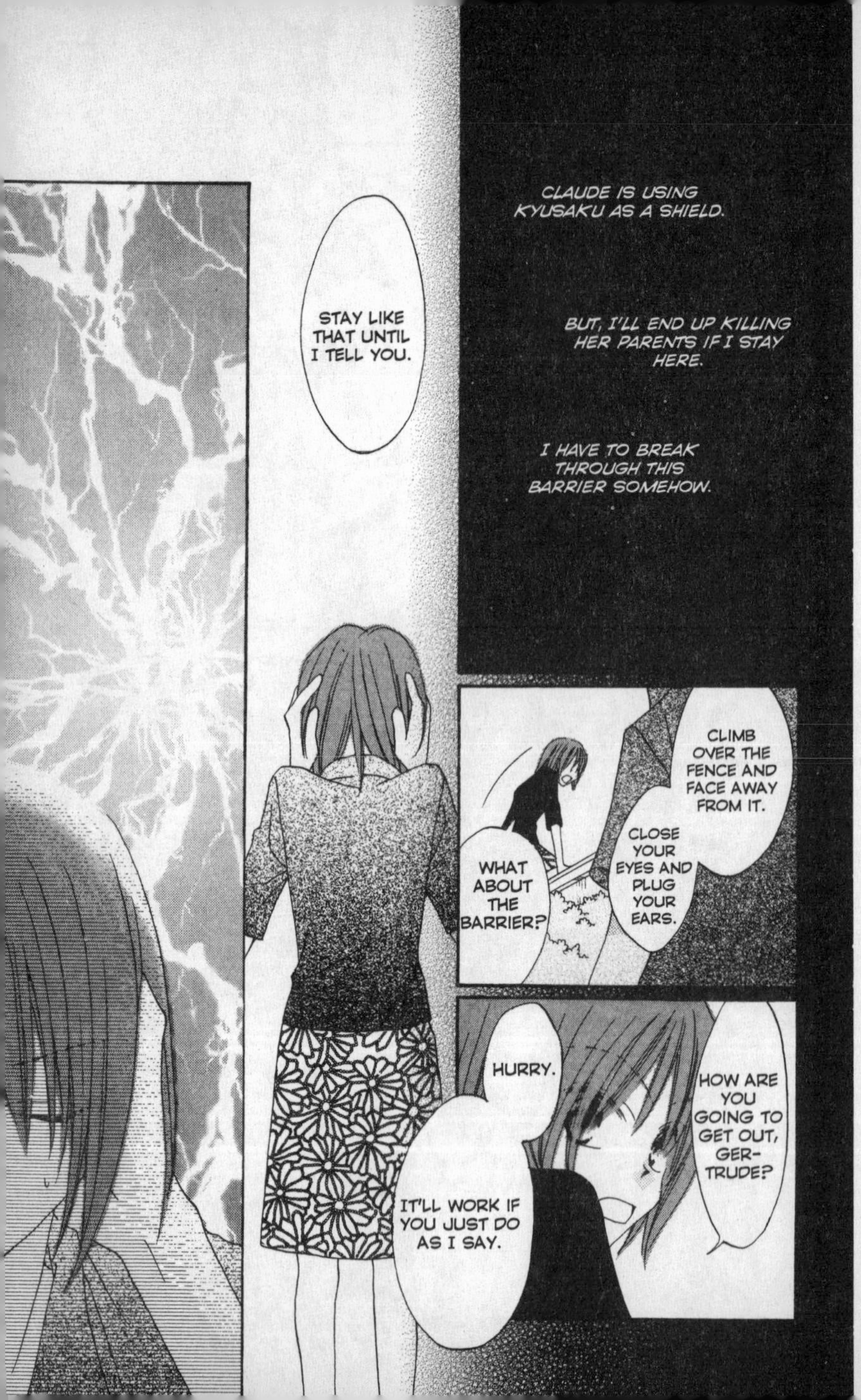
CLAUDE IS USING KYUSAKU AS A SHIELD.
BUT, I'LL END UP KILLING HER PARENTS IF I STAY HERE.
I HAVE TO BREAK THROUGH THIS BARRIER SOMEHOW.
STAY LIKE THAT UNTIL I TELL YOU.
CLIMB OVER THE FENCE AND FACE AWAY FROM IT.
CLOSE YOUR EYES AND PLUG YOUR EARS.
WHAT ABOUT THE BARRIER?
HOW ARE YOU GOING TO GET OUT, GER-TRUDE?
HURRY.
IT'LL WORK IF YOU JUST DO AS I SAY.

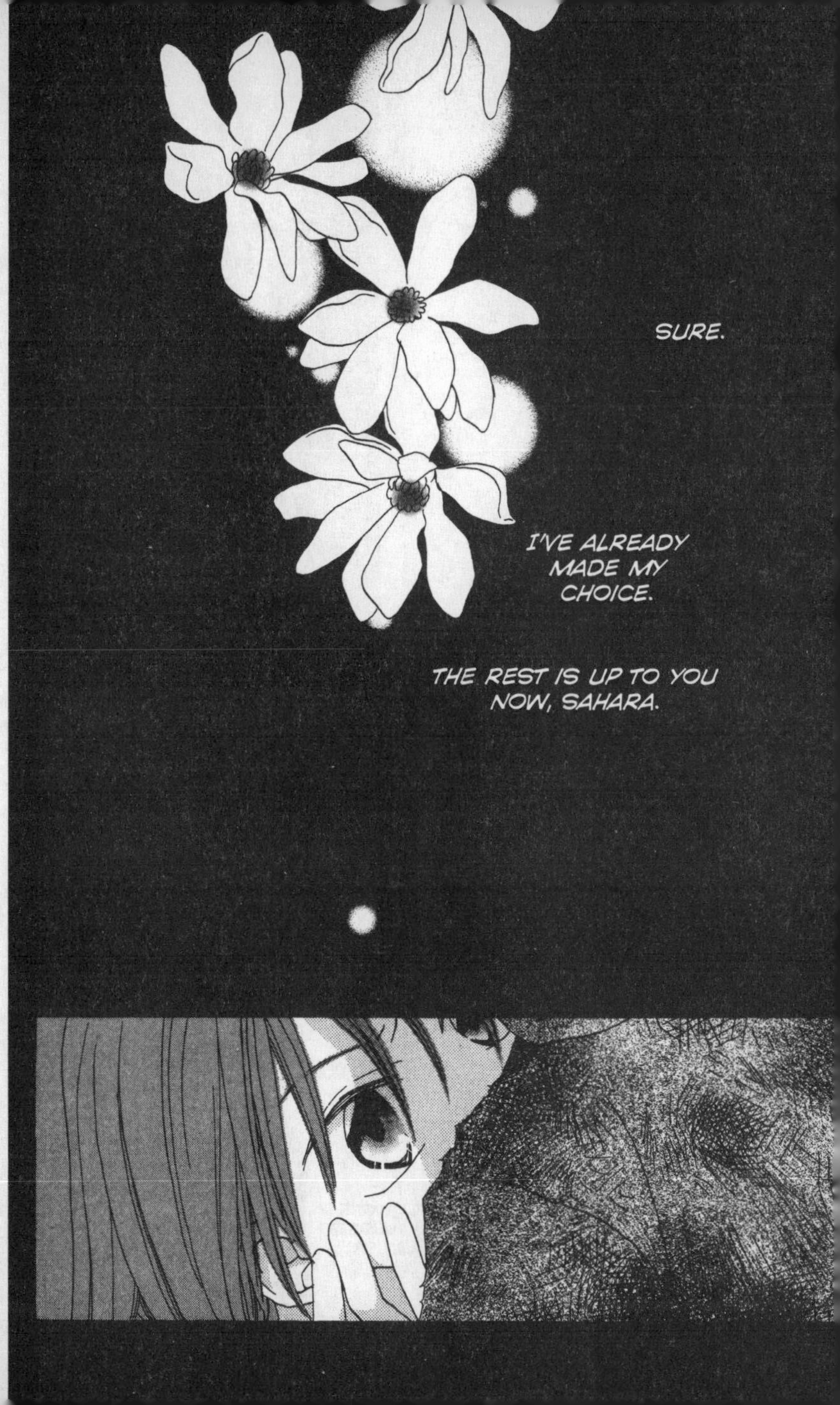
SURE.
I'VE ALREADY MADE MY CHOICE.
THE REST IS UP TO YOU NOW, SAHARA.

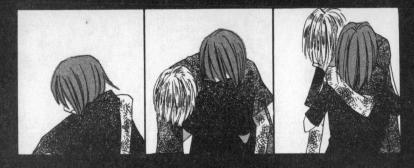

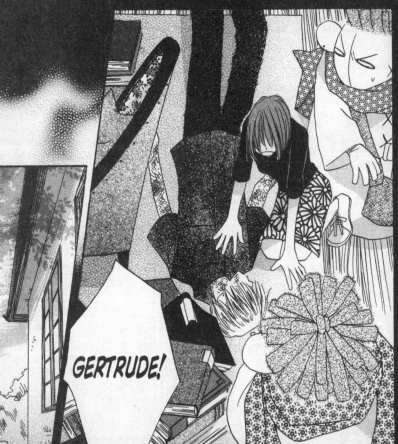

GERTRUDE!

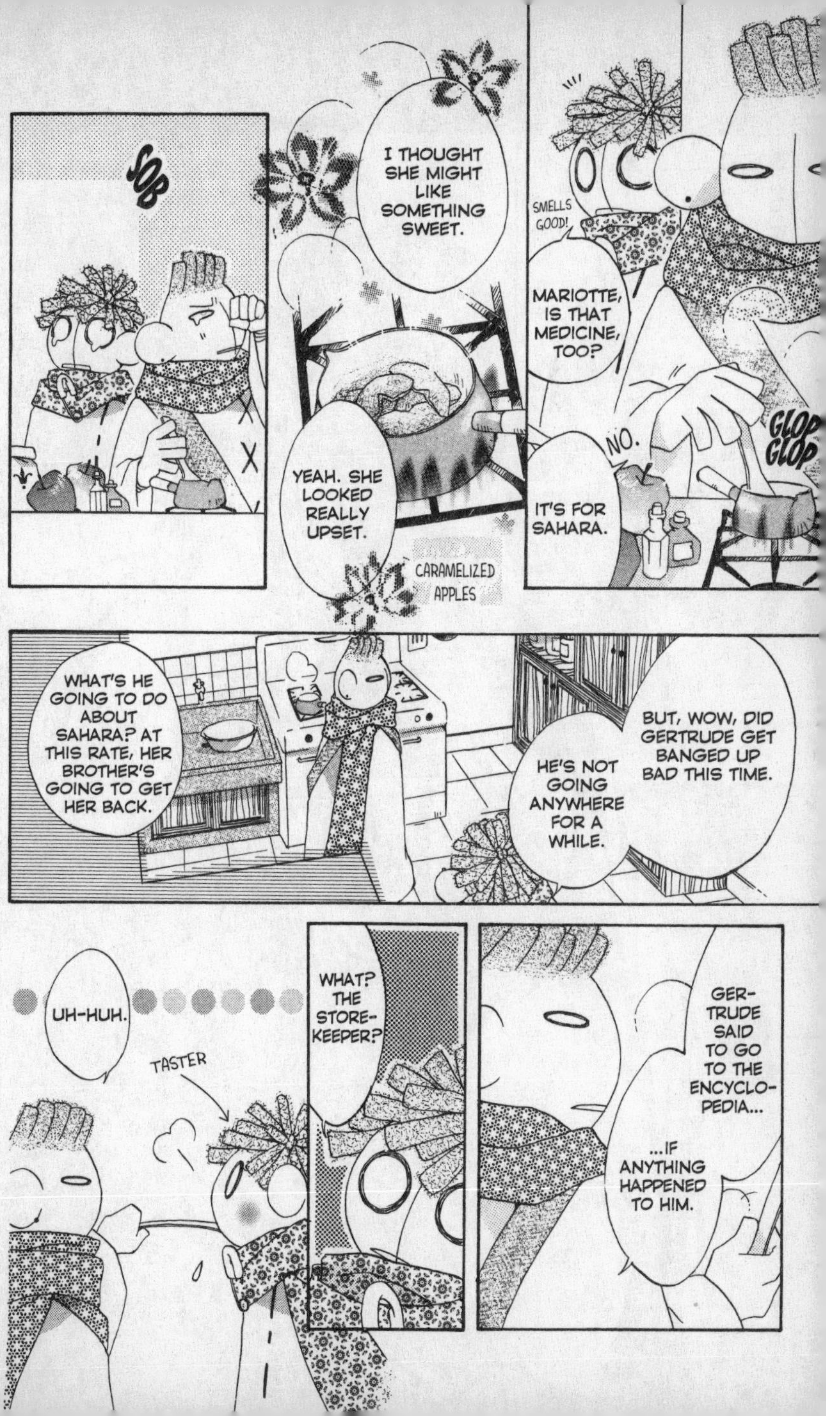
SMELLS GOOD!
MARIOTTE, IS THAT MEDICINE, TOO?
GLOP GLOP
NO.
IT'S FOR SAHARA.
I THOUGHT SHE MIGHT LIKE SOMETHING SWEET.
YEAH. SHE LOOKED REALLY UPSET.
CARAMELIZED APPLES
SOB
BUT, WOW, DID GERTRUDE GET BANGED UP BAD THIS TIME.
HE'S NOT GOING ANYWHERE FOR A WHILE.
WHAT'S HE GOING TO DO ABOUT SAHARA? AT THIS RATE, HER BROTHER'S GOING TO GET HER BACK.
GER-TRUDE SAID TO GO TO THE ENCYCLO-PEDIA...
...IF ANYTHING HAPPENED TO HIM.
WHAT? THE STORE-KEEPER?
UH-HUH.
TASTER

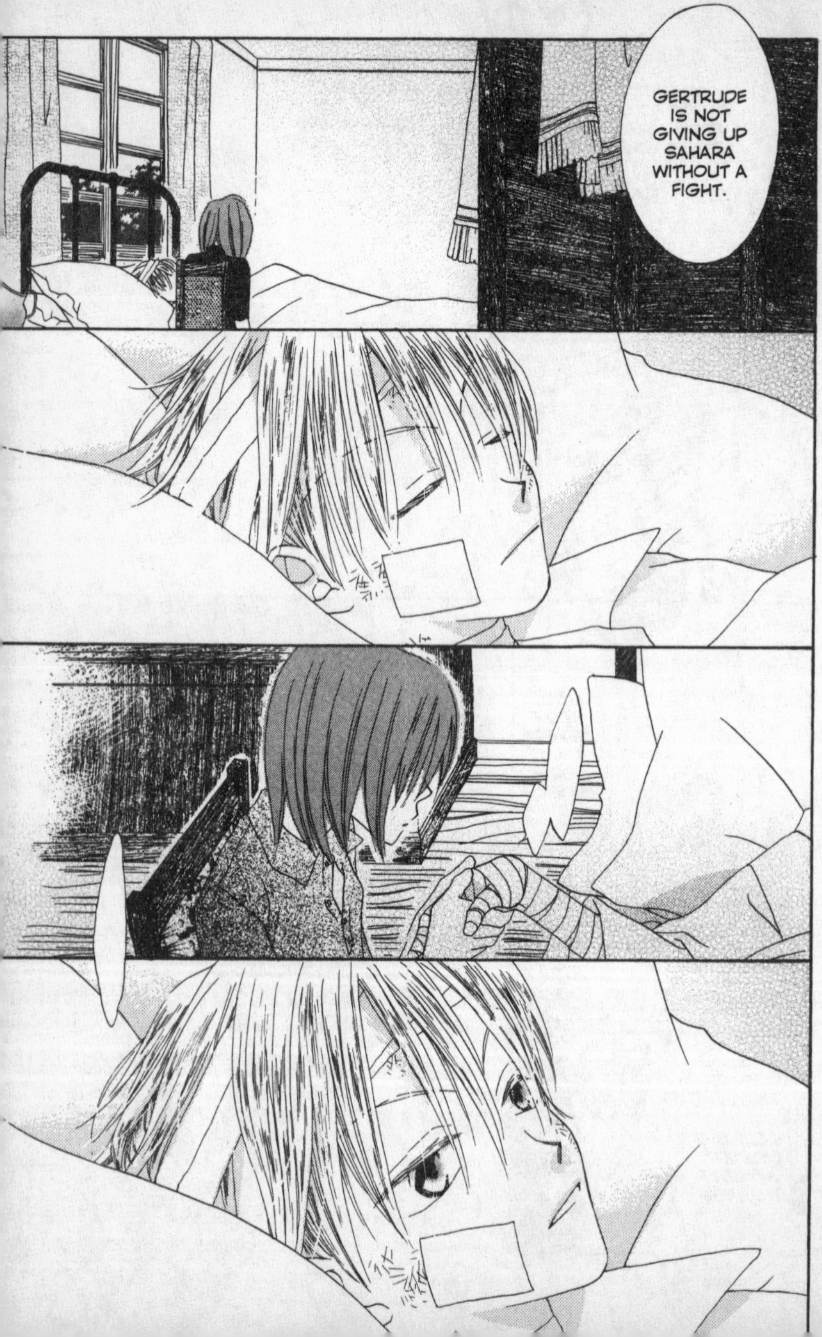
GERTRUDE IS NOT GIVING UP SAHARA WITHOUT A FIGHT.

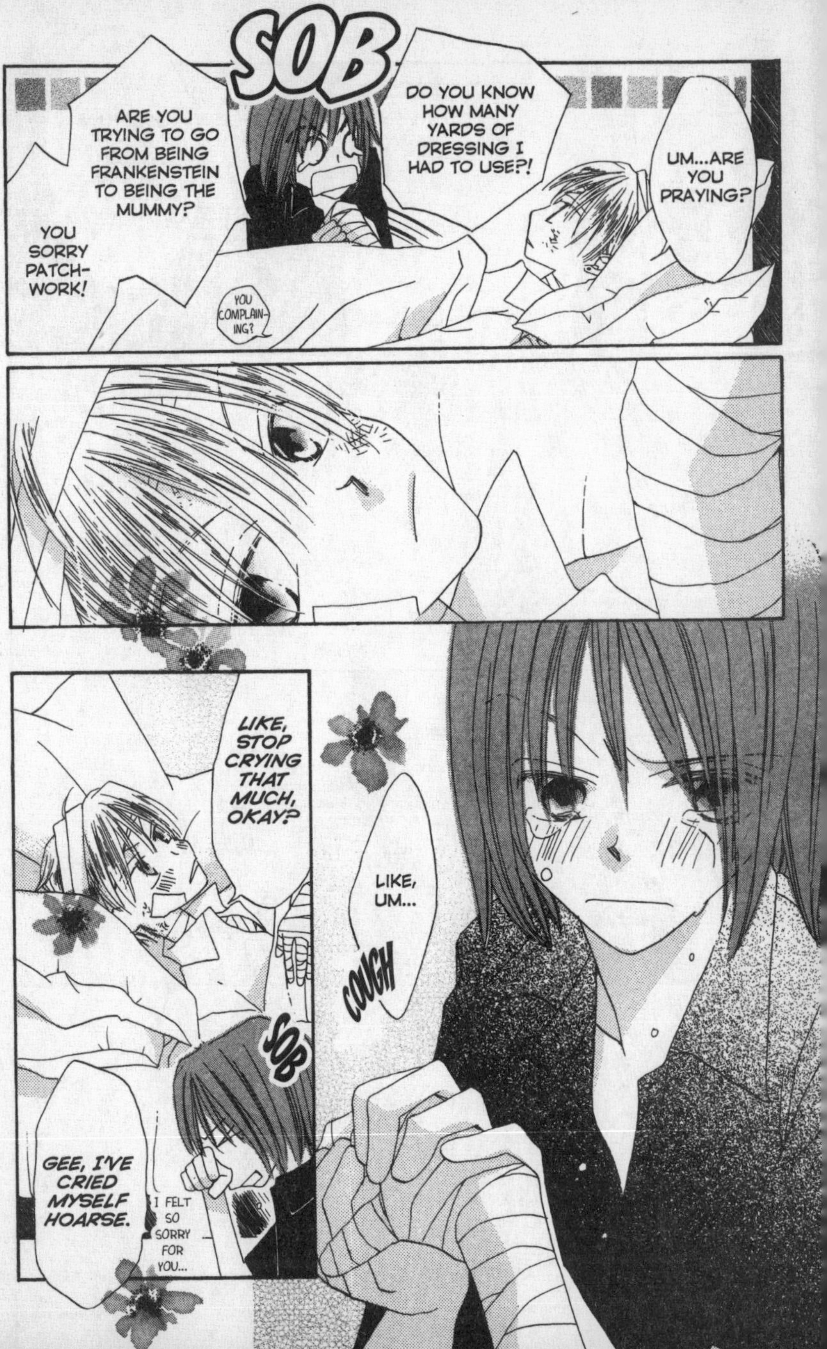
UM...ARE YOU PRAYING?
SOB
DO YOU KNOW HOW MANY YARDS OF DRESSING I HAD TO USE?!
ARE YOU TRYING TO GO FROM BEING FRANKENSTEIN TO BEING THE MUMMY?
YOU SORRY PATCH-WORK!
YOU COMPLAIN-ING?
LIKE, UM...
COUGH
LIKE, STOP CRYING THAT MUCH, OKAY?
SOB
GEE, I'VE CRIED MYSELF HOARSE.
I FELT SO SORRY FOR YOU...

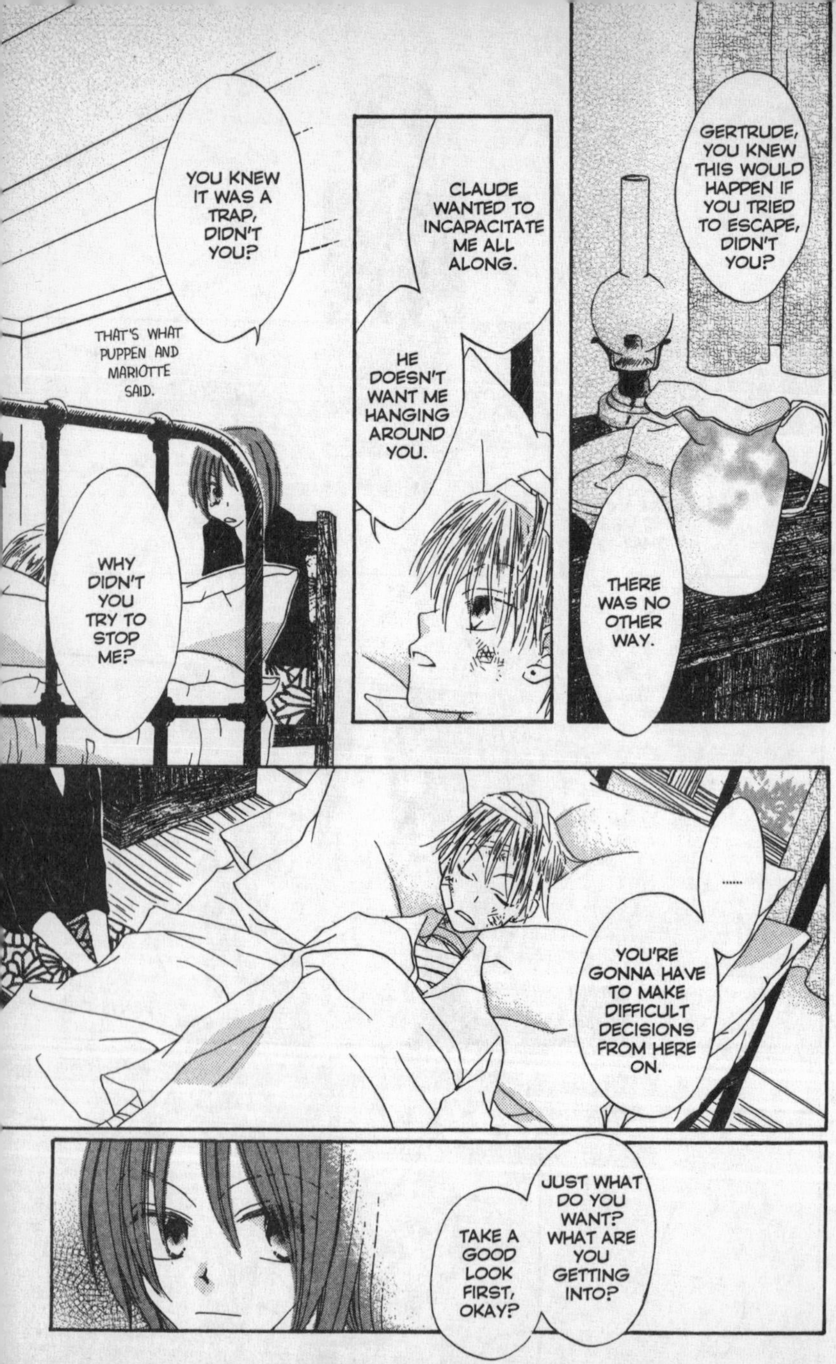
GERTRUDE, YOU KNEW THIS WOULD HAPPEN IF YOU TRIED TO ESCAPE, DIDN'T YOU?
THERE WAS NO OTHER WAY.
CLAUDE WANTED TO INCAPACITATE ME ALL ALONG.
HE DOESN'T WANT ME HANGING AROUND YOU.
YOU KNEW IT WAS A TRAP, DIDN'T YOU?
THAT'S WHAT PUPPEN AND MARIOTTE SAID.
WHY DIDN'T YOU TRY TO STOP ME?
......
YOU'RE GONNA HAVE TO MAKE DIFFICULT DECISIONS FROM HERE ON.
JUST WHAT DO YOU WANT? WHAT ARE YOU GETTING INTO?
TAKE A GOOD LOOK FIRST, OKAY?

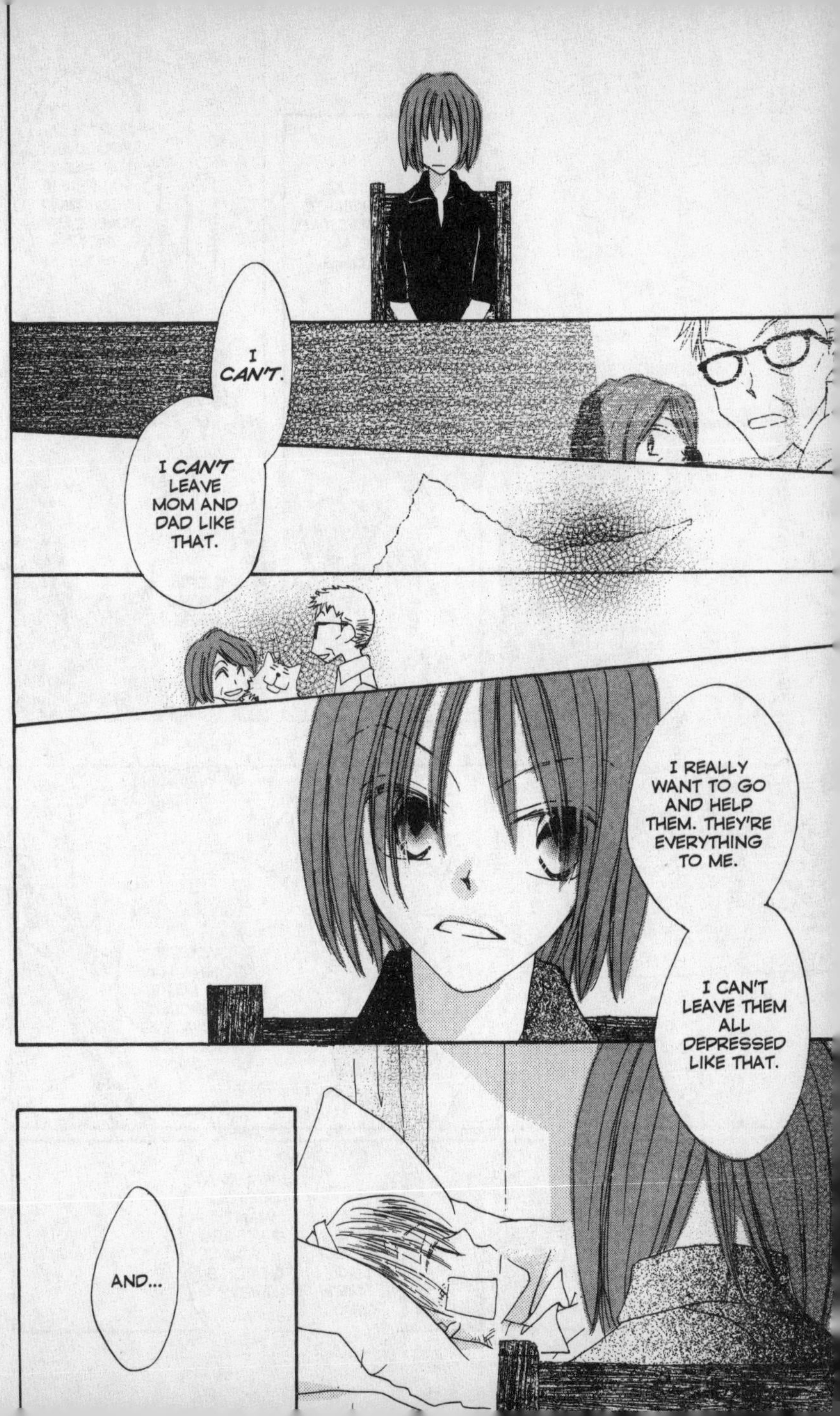
I *CAN'T*.
I *CAN'T* LEAVE MOM AND DAD LIKE THAT.
I REALLY WANT TO GO AND HELP THEM. THEY'RE EVERYTHING TO ME.
I CAN'T LEAVE THEM ALL DEPRESSED LIKE THAT.
AND...

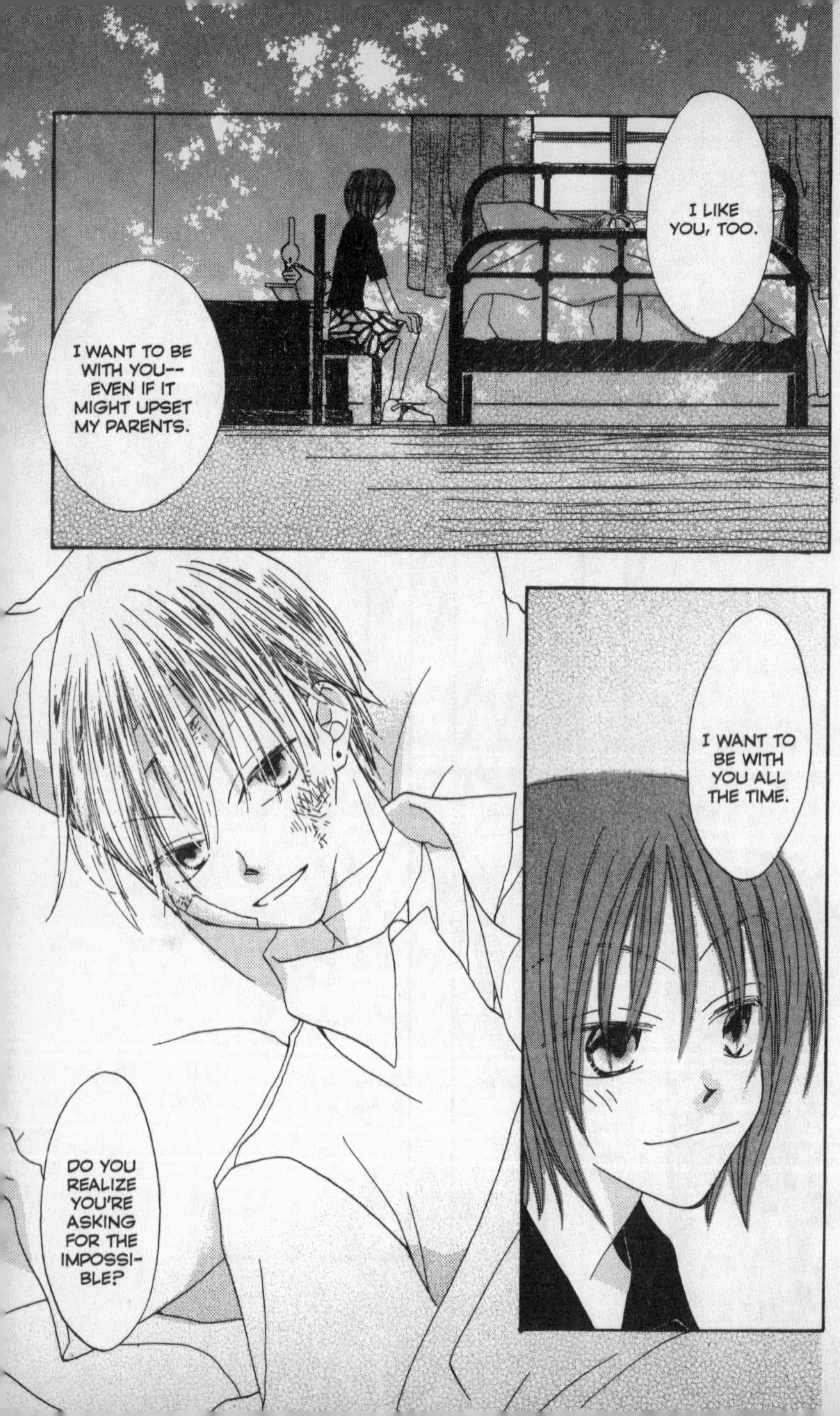
I LIKE YOU, TOO.
I WANT TO BE WITH YOU-- EVEN IF IT MIGHT UPSET MY PARENTS.
I WANT TO BE WITH YOU ALL THE TIME.
DO YOU REALIZE YOU'RE ASKING FOR THE IMPOSSI-BLE?

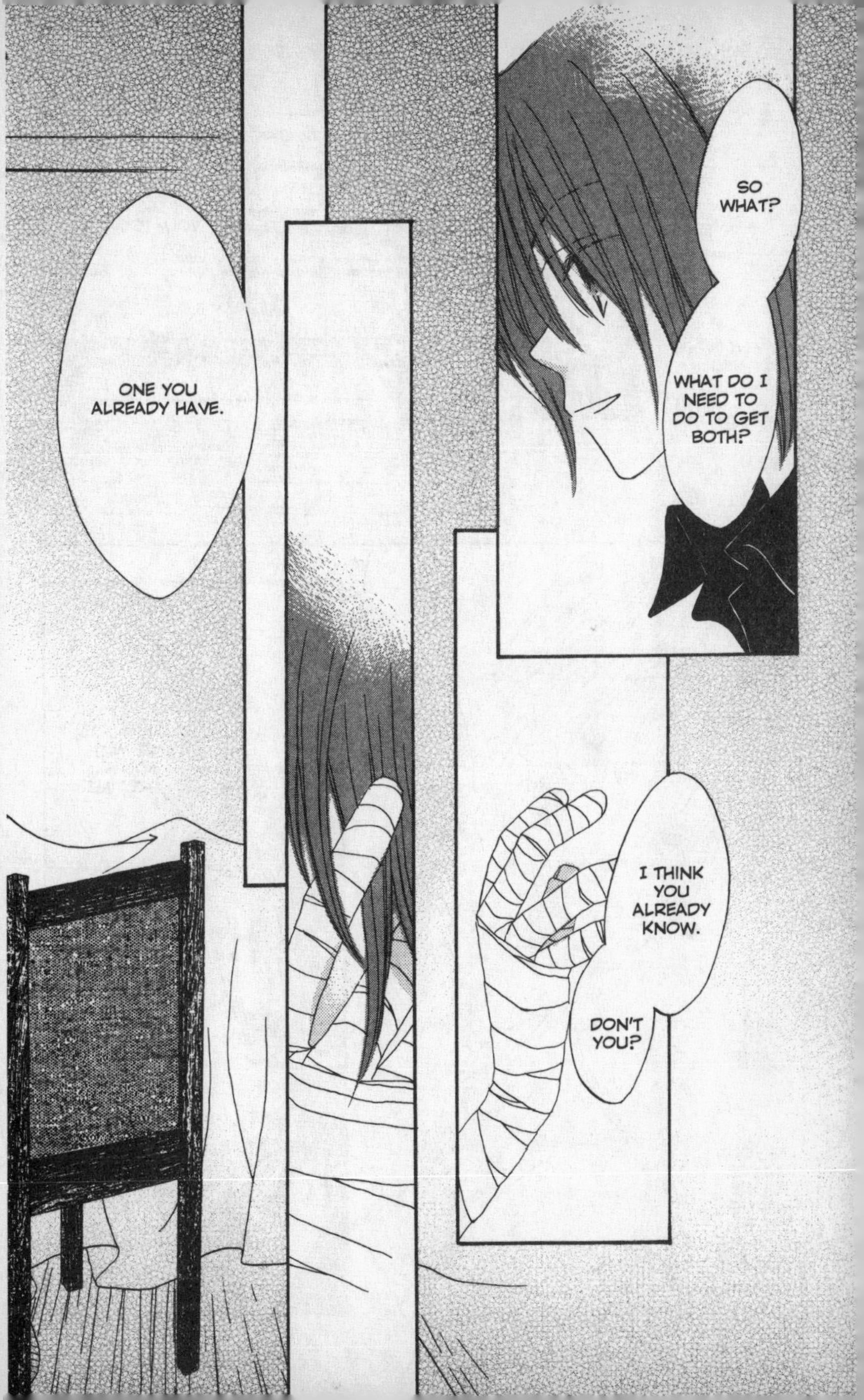
SO WHAT?
WHAT DO I NEED TO DO TO GET BOTH?
ONE YOU ALREADY HAVE.
I THINK YOU ALREADY KNOW.
DON'T YOU?

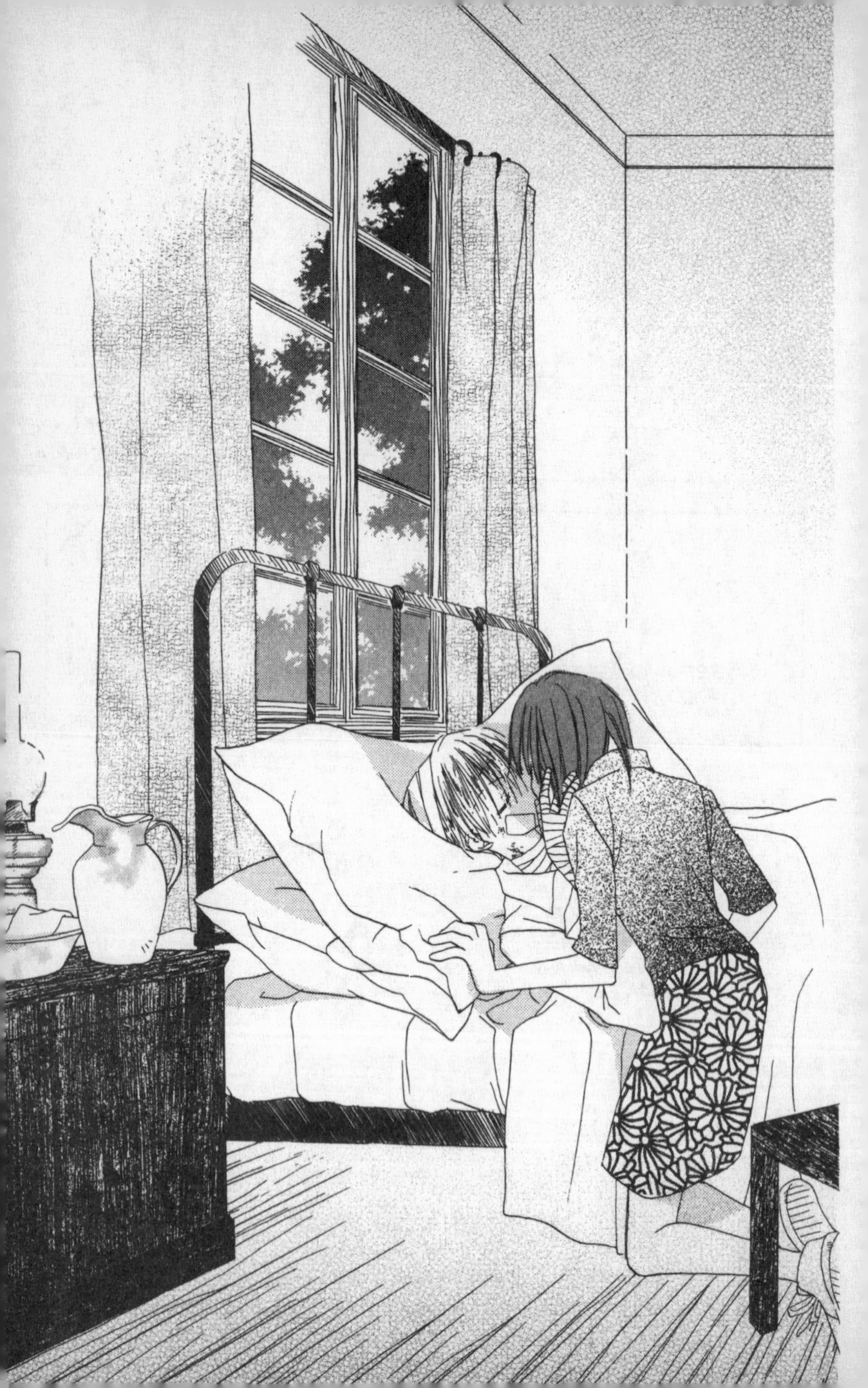

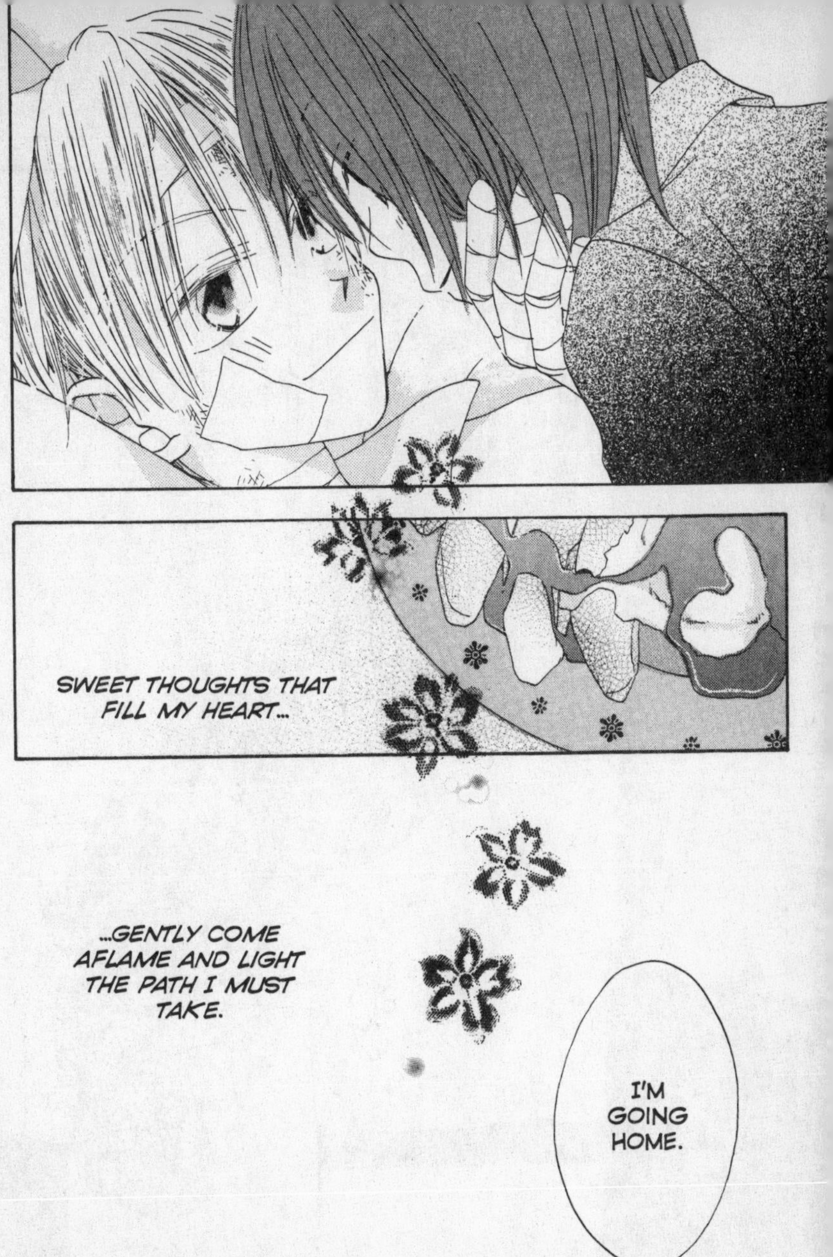
SWEET THOUGHTS THAT FILL MY HEART...
...GENTLY COME AFLAME AND LIGHT THE PATH I MUST TAKE.
I'M GOING HOME.

THE RECIPE FOR GERTRUDE 2--END

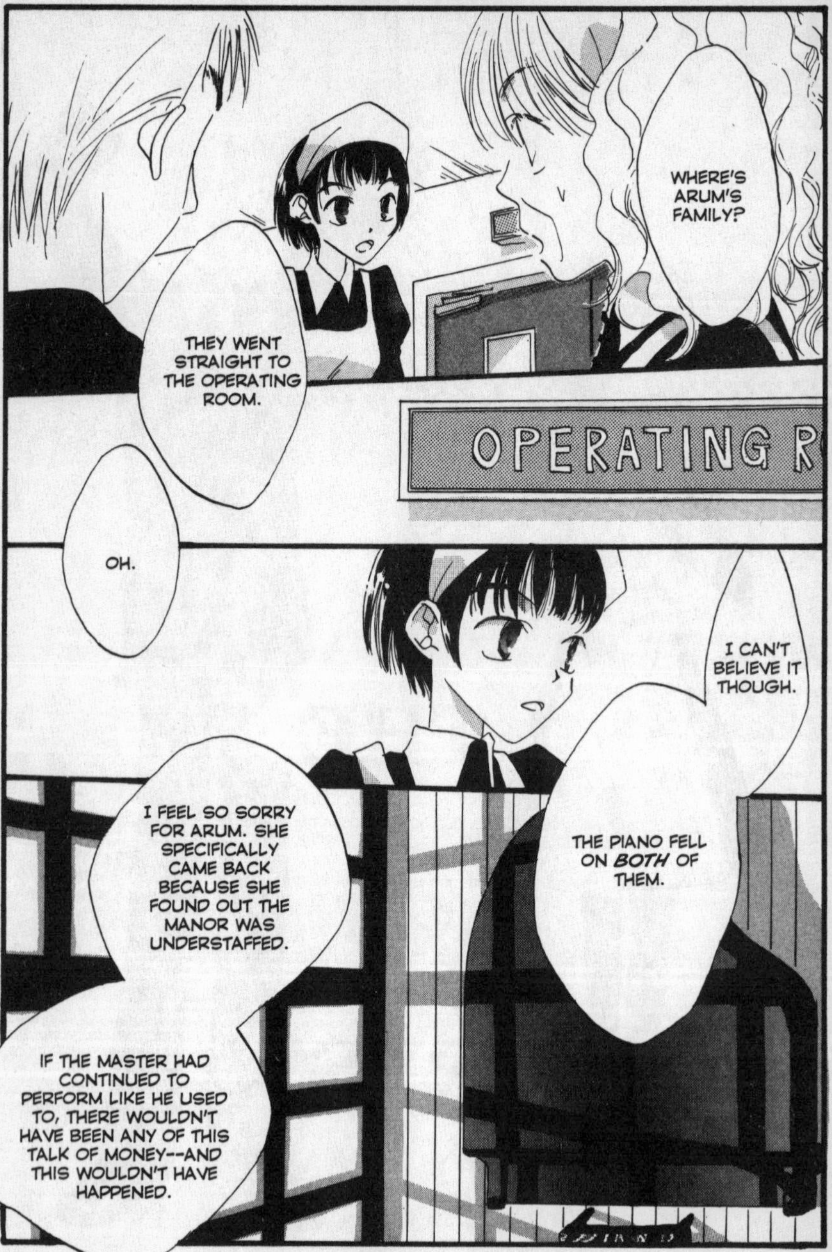
WHERE'S ARUM'S FAMILY?
THEY WENT STRAIGHT TO THE OPERATING ROOM.
OPERATING R
OH.
I CAN'T BELIEVE IT THOUGH.
THE PIANO FELL ON *BOTH* OF THEM.
I FEEL SO SORRY FOR ARUM. SHE SPECIFICALLY CAME BACK BECAUSE SHE FOUND OUT THE MANOR WAS UNDERSTAFFED.
IF THE MASTER HAD CONTINUED TO PERFORM LIKE HE USED TO, THERE WOULDN'T HAVE BEEN ANY OF THIS TALK OF MONEY--AND THIS WOULDN'T HAVE HAPPENED.

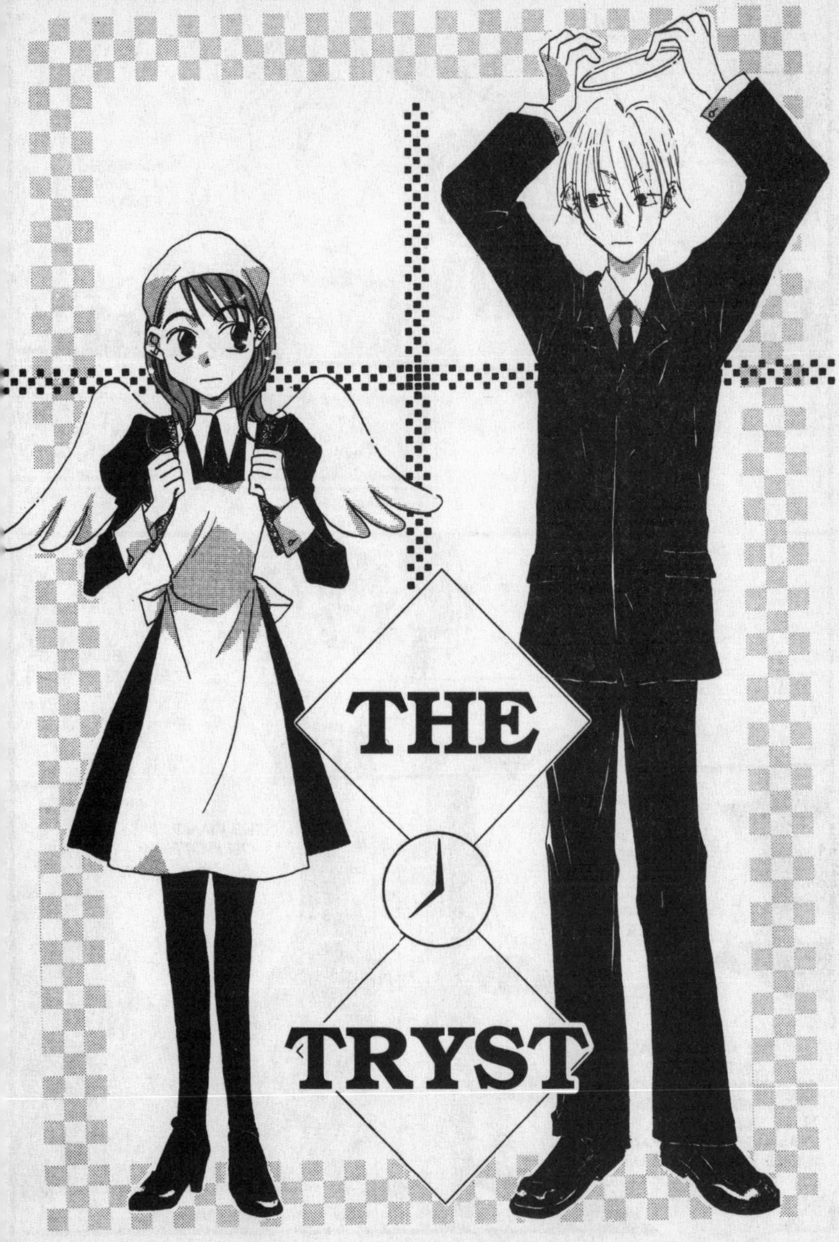
THE
TRYST

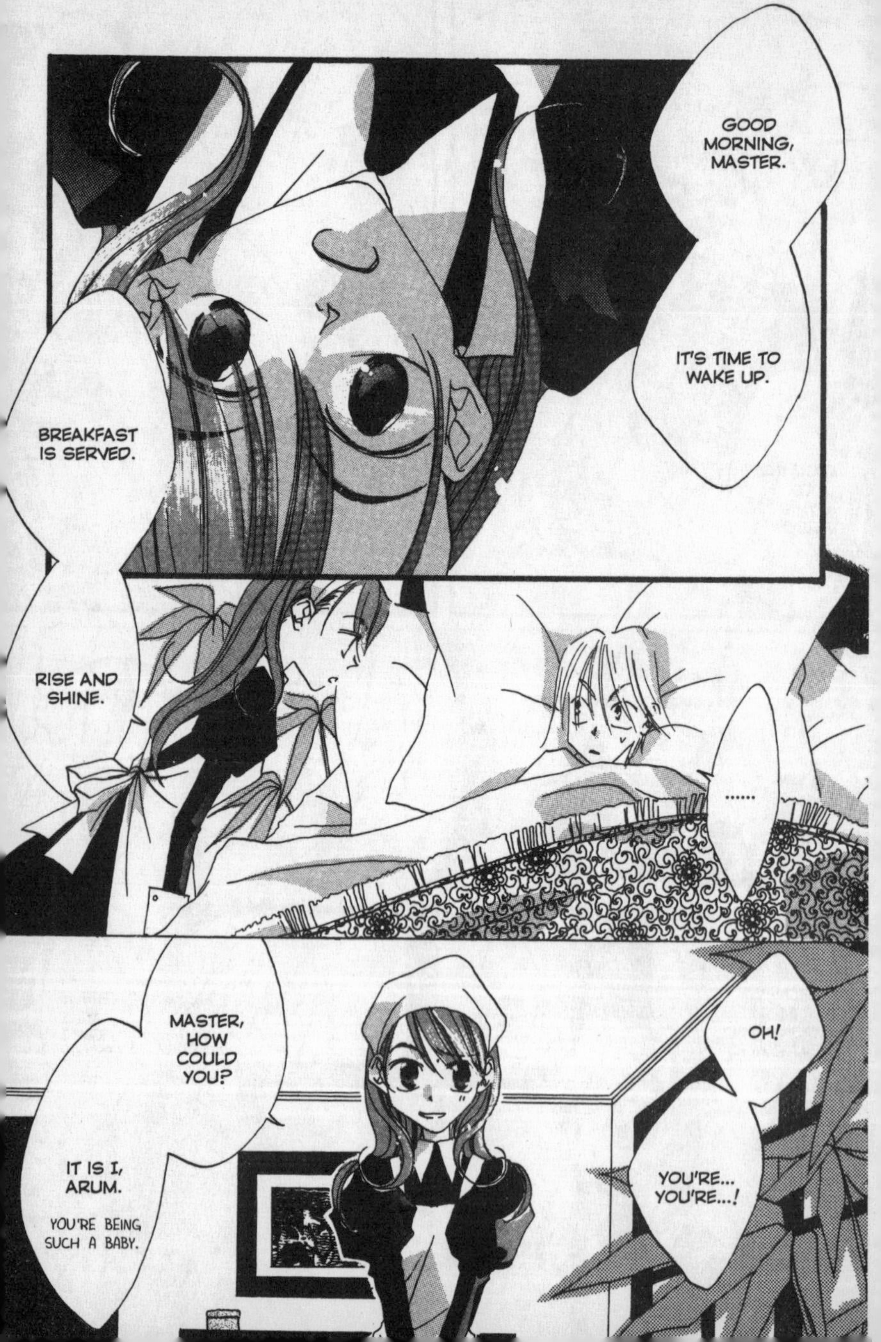
GOOD MORNING, MASTER.
IT'S TIME TO WAKE UP.
BREAKFAST IS SERVED.
RISE AND SHINE.
......
OH!
YOU'RE... YOU'RE...!
MASTER, HOW COULD YOU?
IT IS I, ARUM.
YOU'RE BEING SUCH A BABY.

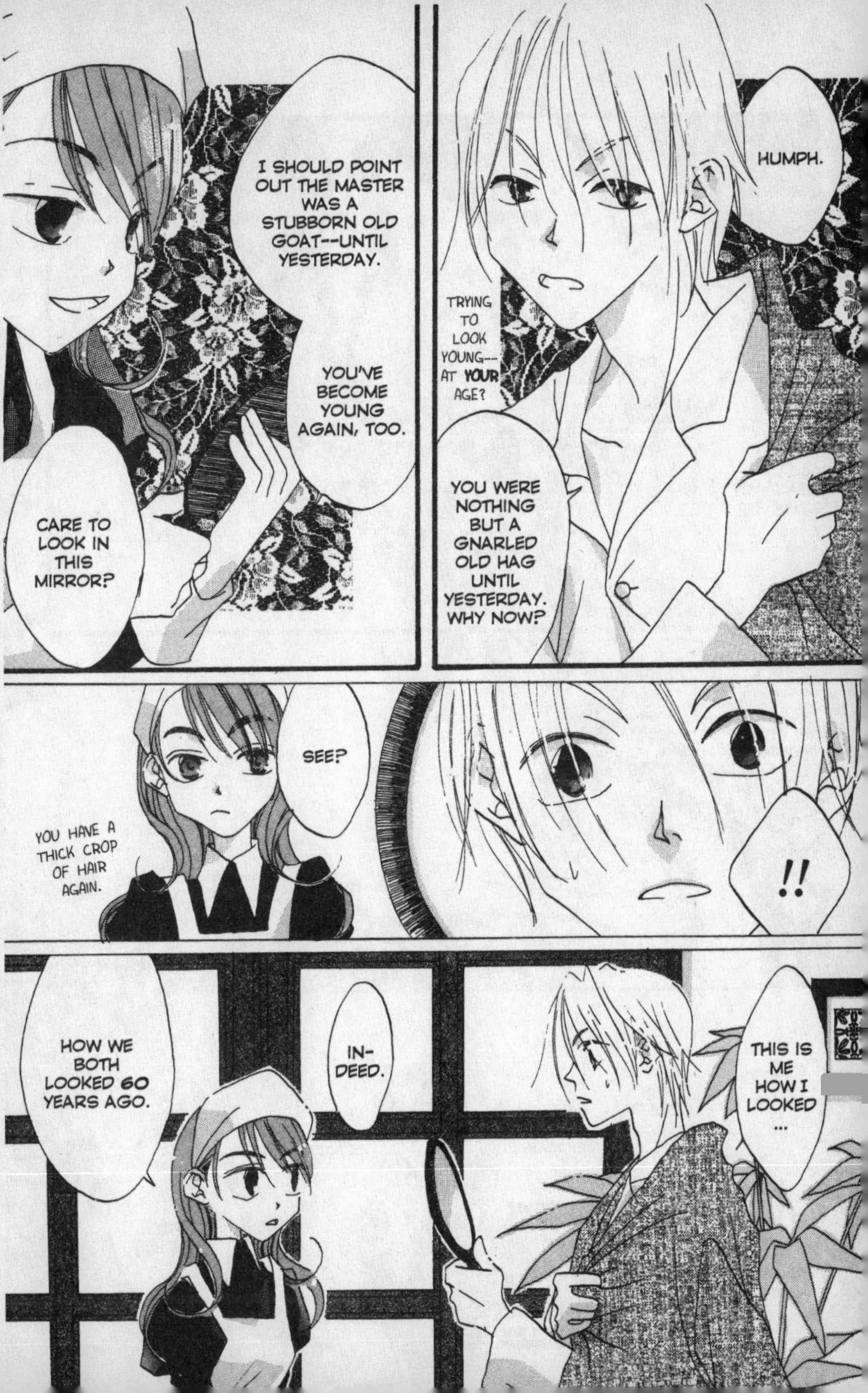
HUMPH.
TRYING TO LOOK YOUNG--AT YOUR AGE?
YOU WERE NOTHING BUT A GNARLED OLD HAG UNTIL YESTERDAY. WHY NOW?
I SHOULD POINT OUT THE MASTER WAS A STUBBORN OLD GOAT--UNTIL YESTERDAY.
YOU'VE BECOME YOUNG AGAIN, TOO.
CARE TO LOOK IN THIS MIRROR?
!!
SEE?
YOU HAVE A THICK CROP OF HAIR AGAIN.
THIS IS ME HOW I LOOKED ...
IN-DEED.
HOW WE BOTH LOOKED 60 YEARS AGO.

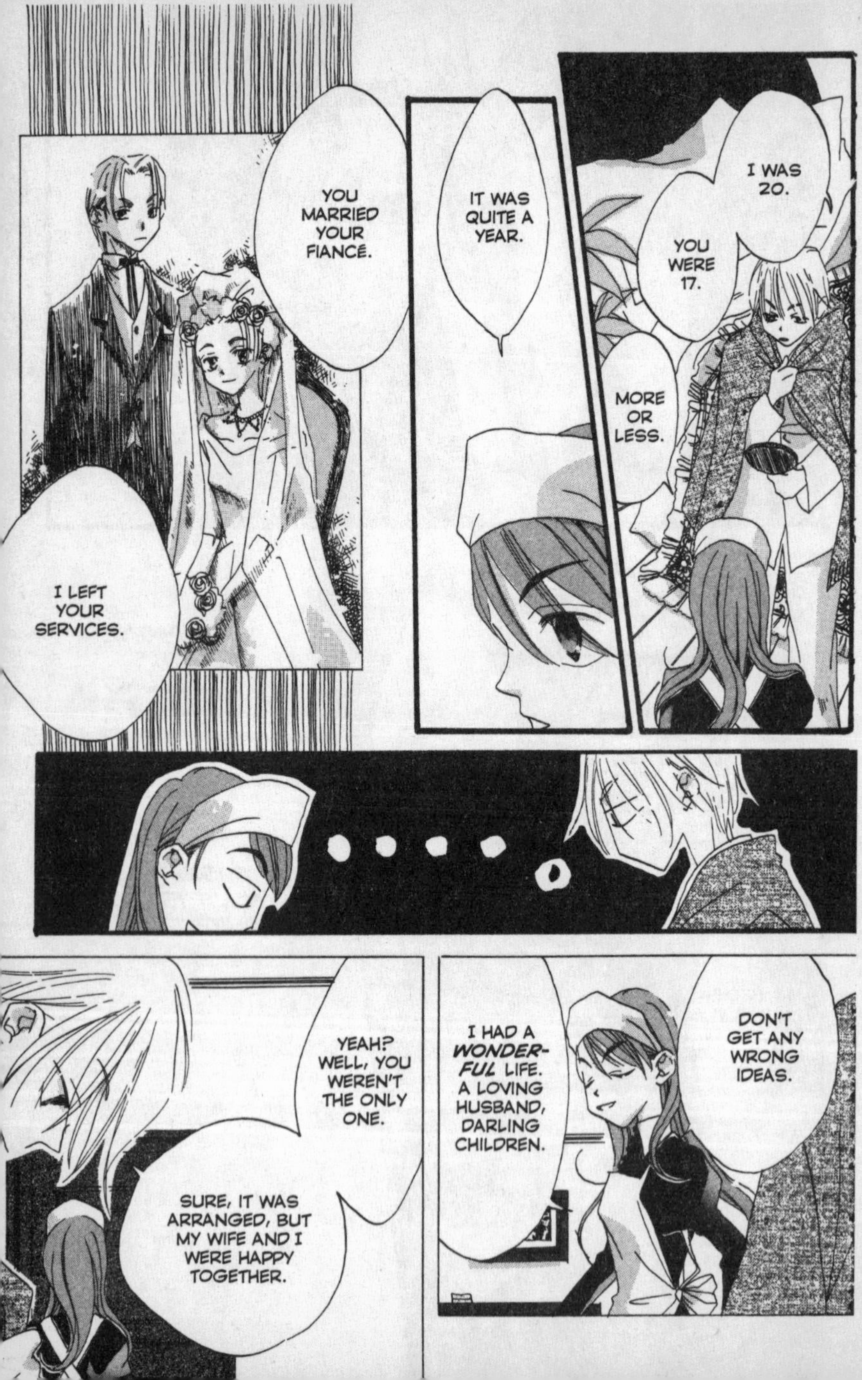
I WAS 20.
YOU WERE 17.
MORE OR LESS.
IT WAS QUITE A YEAR.
YOU MARRIED YOUR FIANCÉ.
I LEFT YOUR SERVICES.
.....
DON'T GET ANY WRONG IDEAS.
I HAD A WONDERFUL LIFE. A LOVING HUSBAND, DARLING CHILDREN.
YEAH? WELL, YOU WEREN'T THE ONLY ONE.
SURE, IT WAS ARRANGED, BUT MY WIFE AND I WERE HAPPY TOGETHER.

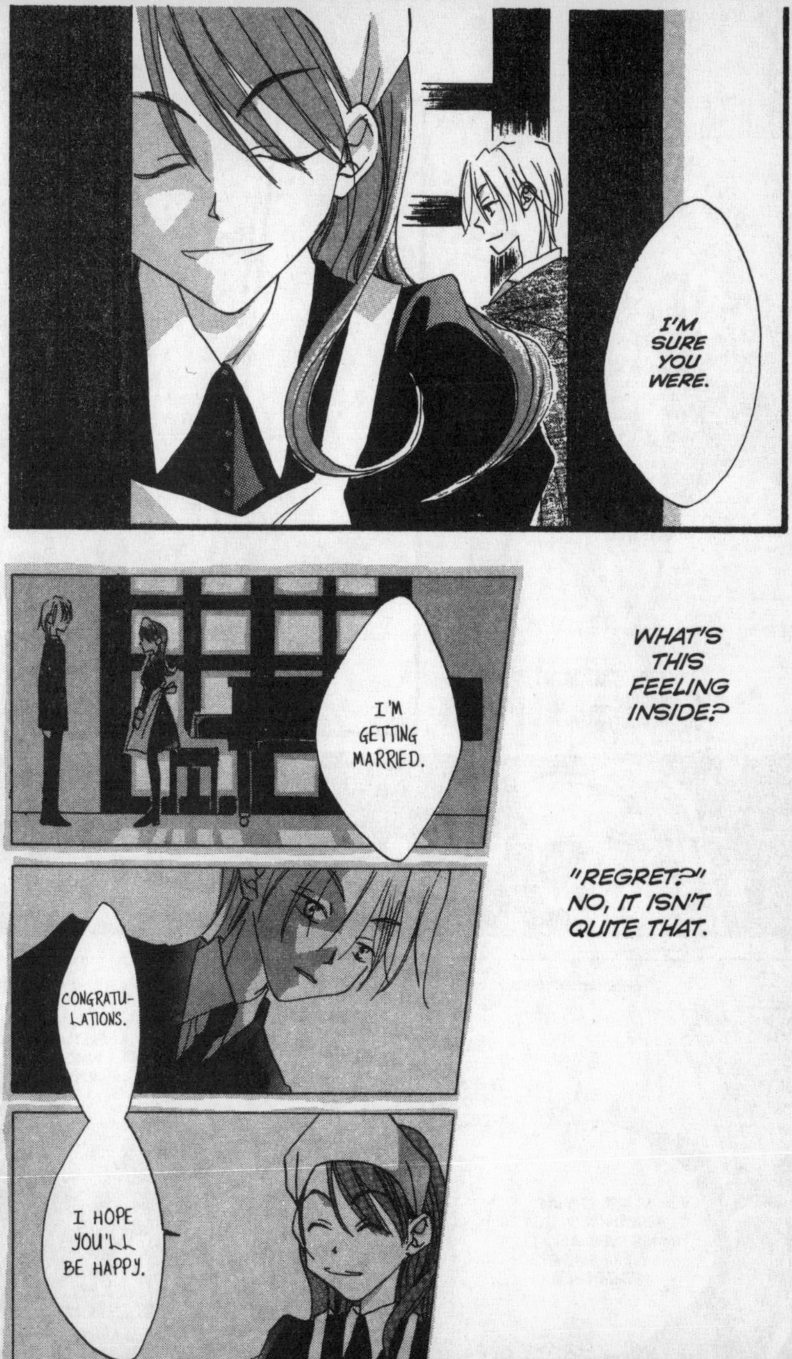
I'M SURE YOU WERE.
WHAT'S THIS FEELING INSIDE?
I'M GETTING MARRIED.
"REGRET?" NO, IT ISN'T QUITE THAT.
CONGRATU-LATIONS.
I HOPE YOU'LL BE HAPPY.

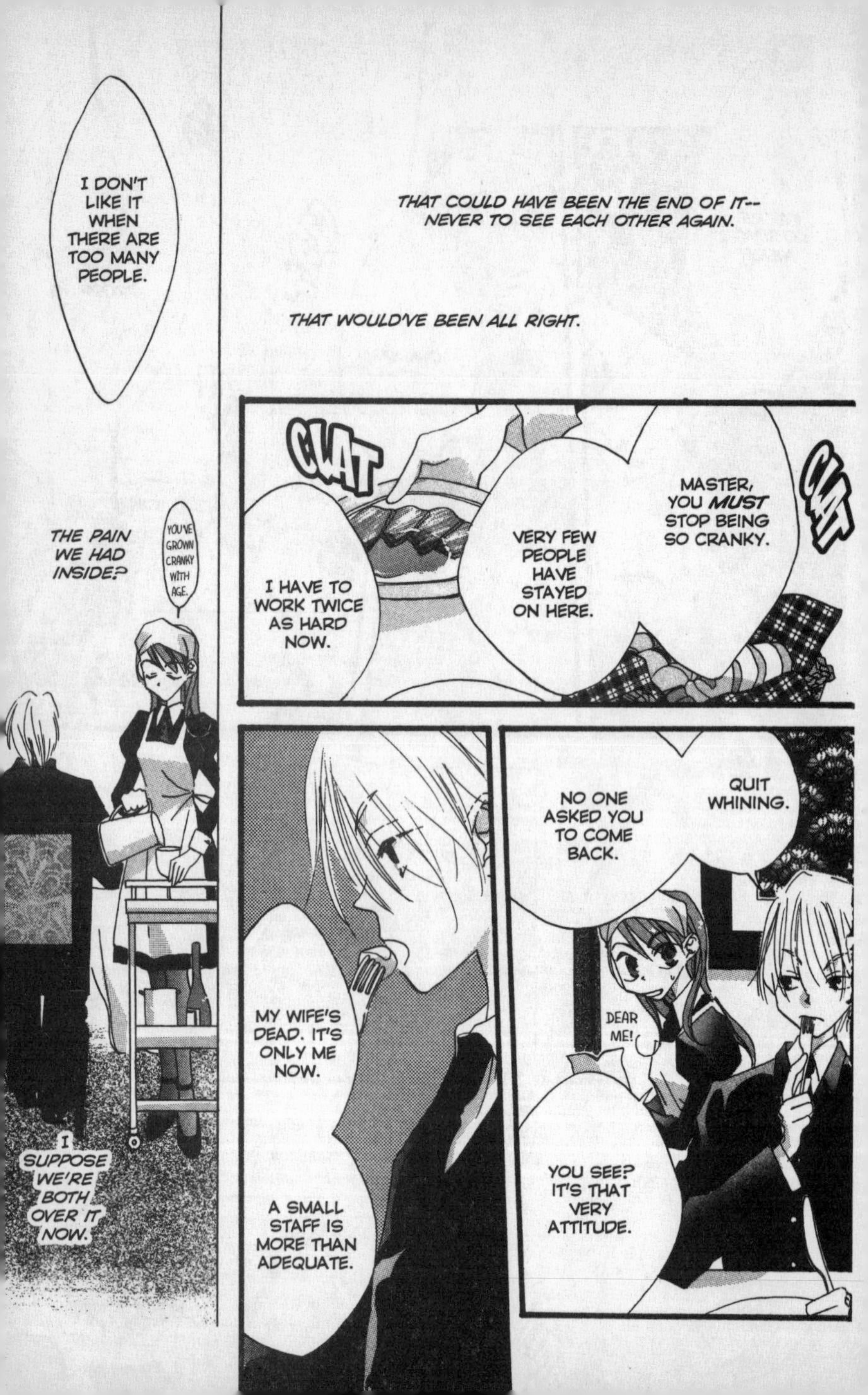
THAT COULD HAVE BEEN THE END OF IT-- NEVER TO SEE EACH OTHER AGAIN.
THAT WOULD'VE BEEN ALL RIGHT.
CLAT
MASTER, YOU *MUST* STOP BEING SO CRANKY.
VERY FEW PEOPLE HAVE STAYED ON HERE.
CLAT
I HAVE TO WORK TWICE AS HARD NOW.
QUIT WHINING.
NO ONE ASKED YOU TO COME BACK.
DEAR ME!
YOU SEE? IT'S THAT VERY ATTITUDE.
MY WIFE'S DEAD. IT'S ONLY ME NOW.
A SMALL STAFF IS MORE THAN ADEQUATE.
I DON'T LIKE IT WHEN THERE ARE TOO MANY PEOPLE.
YOU'VE GROWN CRANKY WITH AGE.
THE PAIN WE HAD INSIDE?
I SUPPOSE WE'RE BOTH OVER IT NOW.

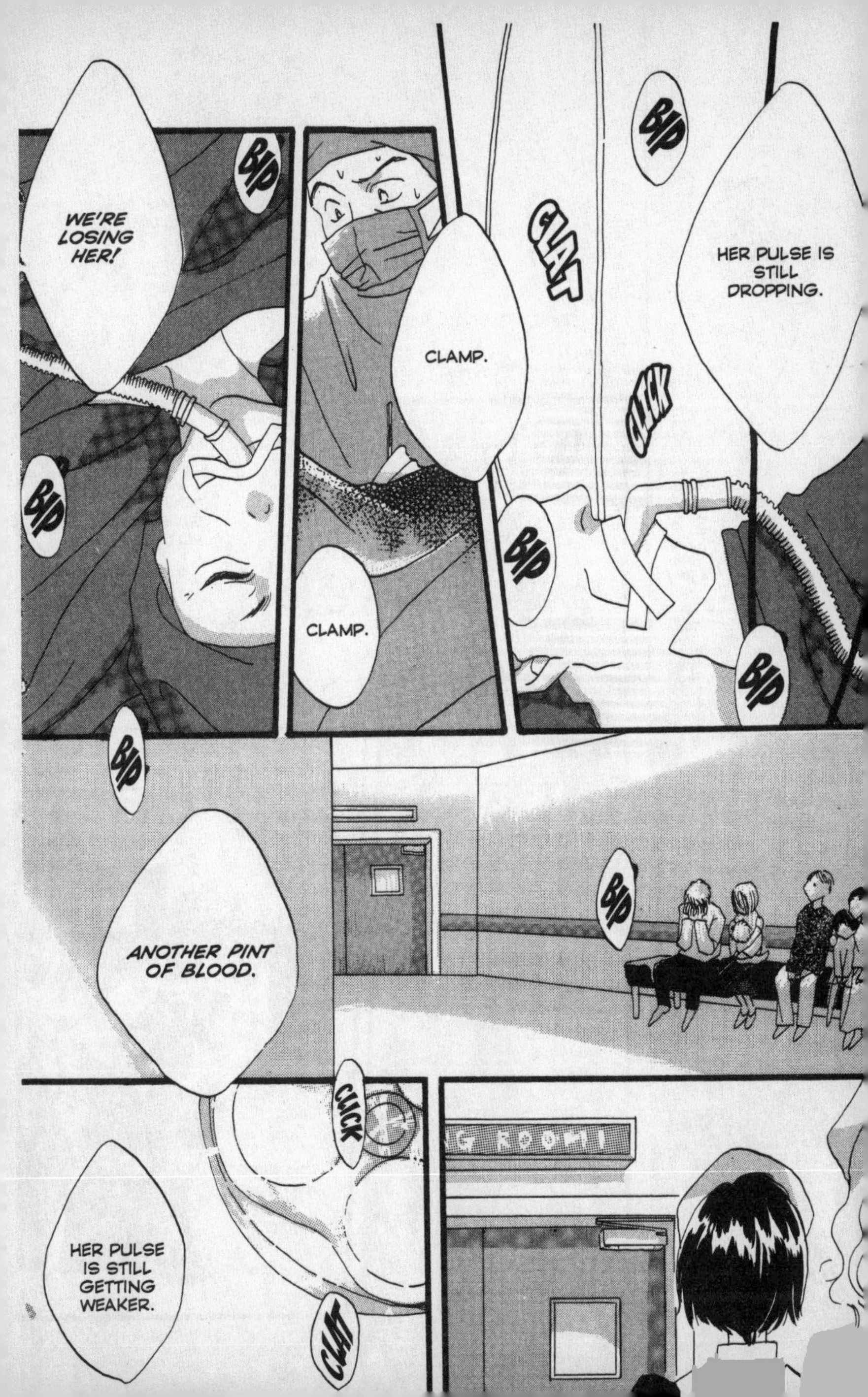
BIP
HER PULSE IS STILL DROPPING.
CLAT
CLICK
BIP
BIP
CLAMP.
CLAMP.
BIP
WE'RE LOSING HER!
BIP
BIP
BIP
ANOTHER PINT OF BLOOD.
CLICK
HER PULSE IS STILL GETTING WEAKER.
CLAT

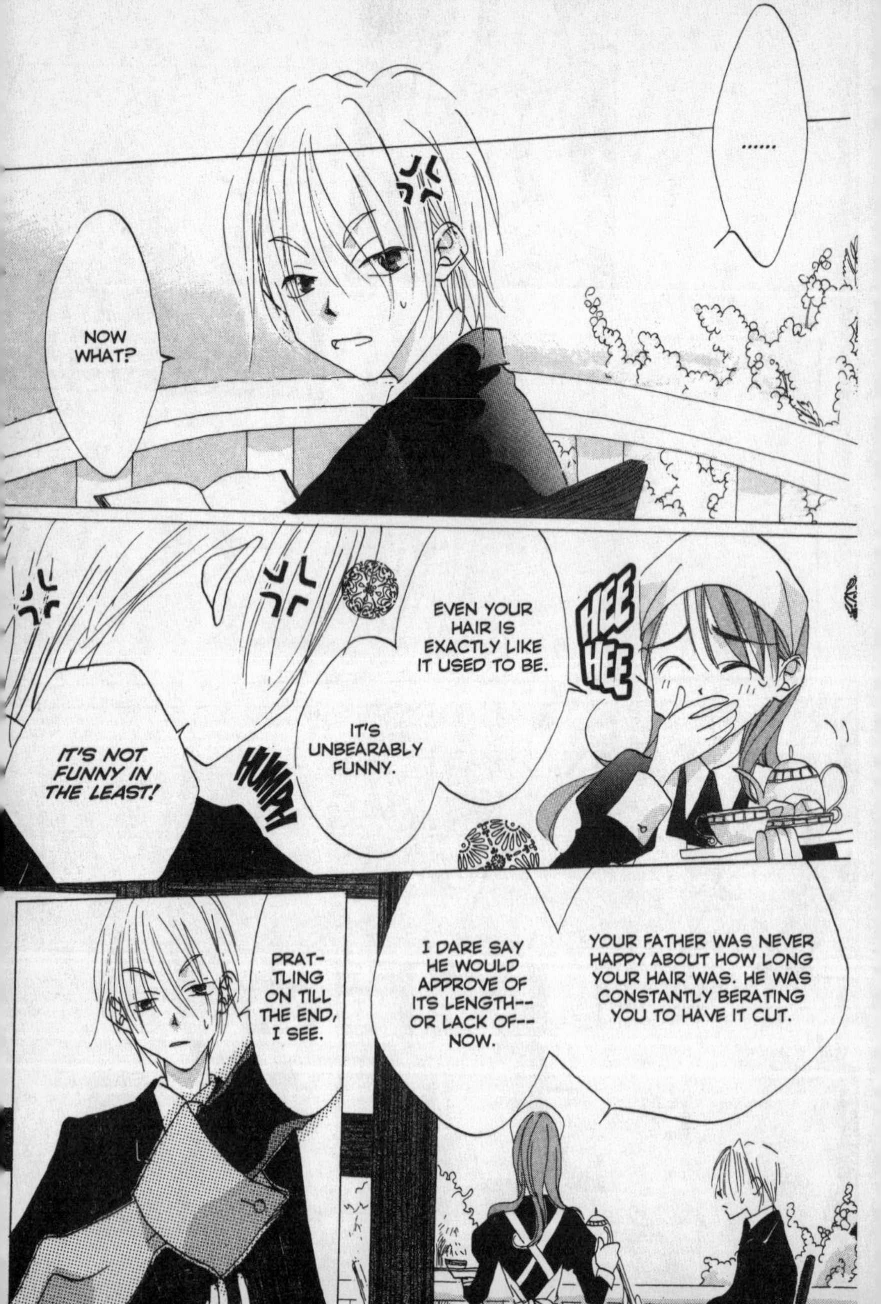
......
NOW WHAT?
HEE HEE
EVEN YOUR HAIR IS EXACTLY LIKE IT USED TO BE.
IT'S UNBEARABLY FUNNY.
HUMPH
IT'S NOT FUNNY IN THE LEAST!
YOUR FATHER WAS NEVER HAPPY ABOUT HOW LONG YOUR HAIR WAS. HE WAS CONSTANTLY BERATING YOU TO HAVE IT CUT.
I DARE SAY HE WOULD APPROVE OF ITS LENGTH-- OR LACK OF-- NOW.
PRAT-TLING ON TILL THE END, I SEE.

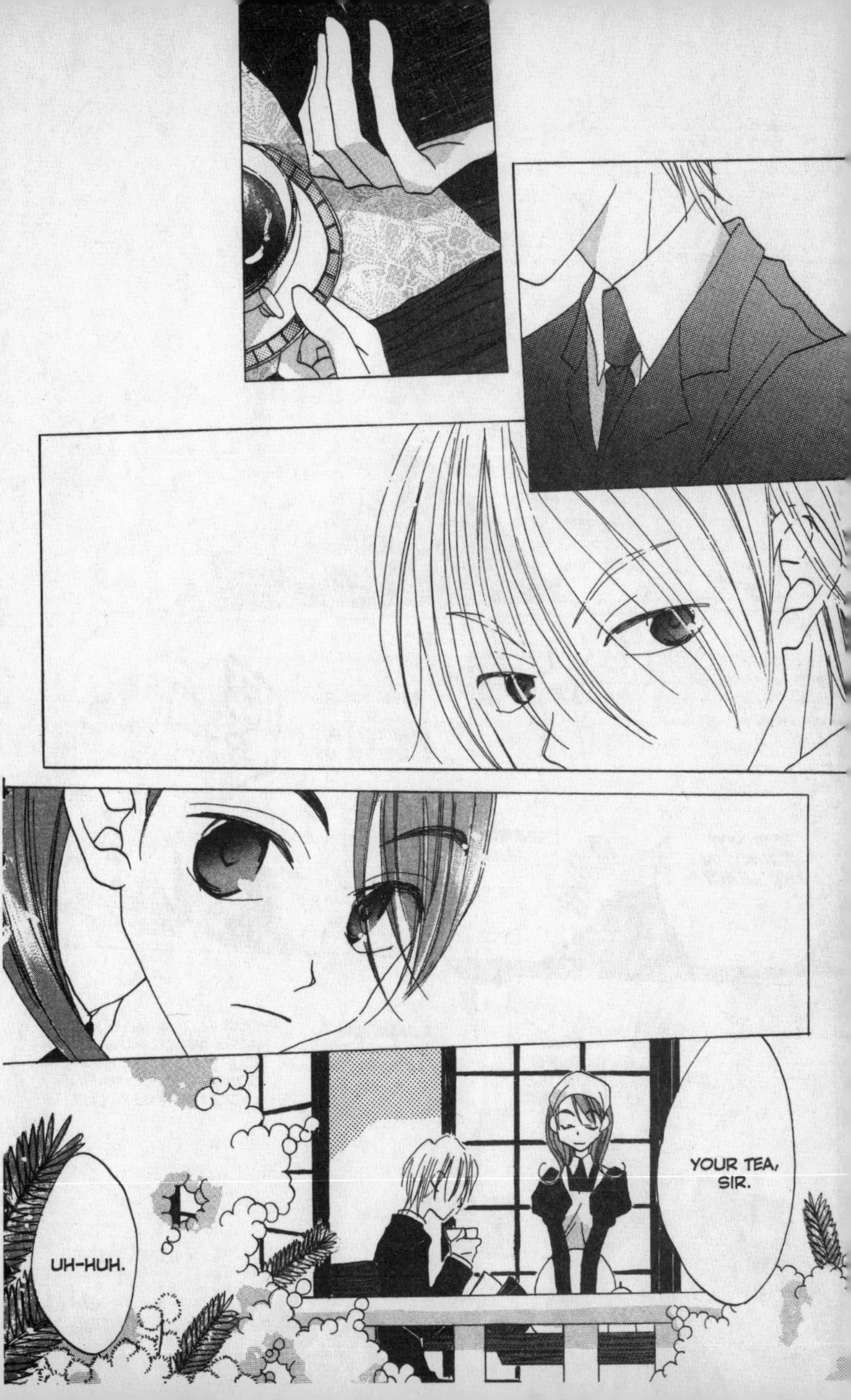
YOUR TEA, SIR.
UH-HUH.

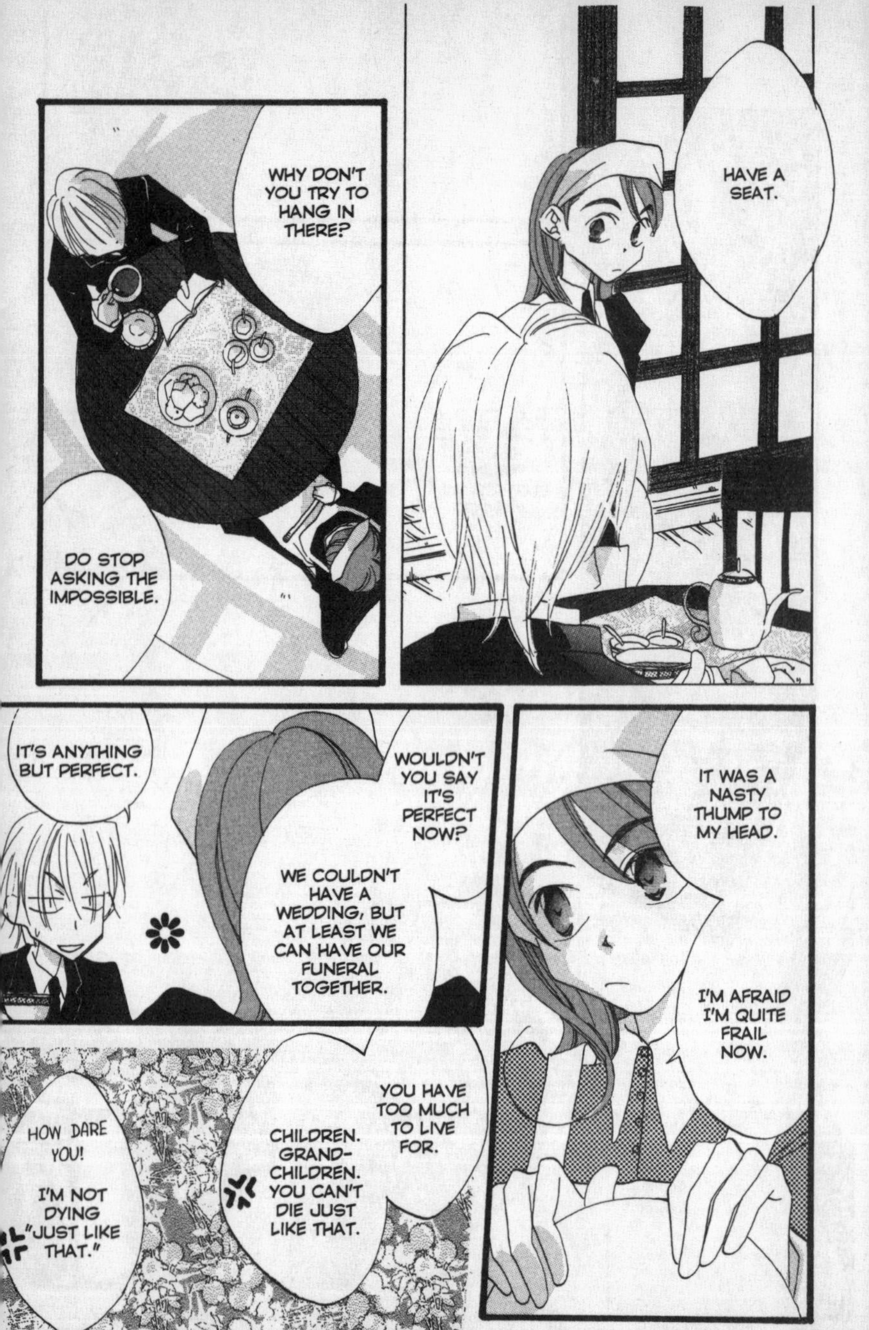
HAVE A SEAT.
WHY DON'T YOU TRY TO HANG IN THERE?
DO STOP ASKING THE IMPOSSIBLE.
IT WAS A NASTY THUMP TO MY HEAD.
I'M AFRAID I'M QUITE FRAIL NOW.
WOULDN'T YOU SAY IT'S PERFECT NOW?
WE COULDN'T HAVE A WEDDING, BUT AT LEAST WE CAN HAVE OUR FUNERAL TOGETHER.
IT'S ANYTHING BUT PERFECT.
YOU HAVE TOO MUCH TO LIVE FOR.
CHILDREN. GRAND-CHILDREN. YOU CAN'T DIE JUST LIKE THAT.
HOW DARE YOU!
I'M NOT DYING "JUST LIKE THAT."

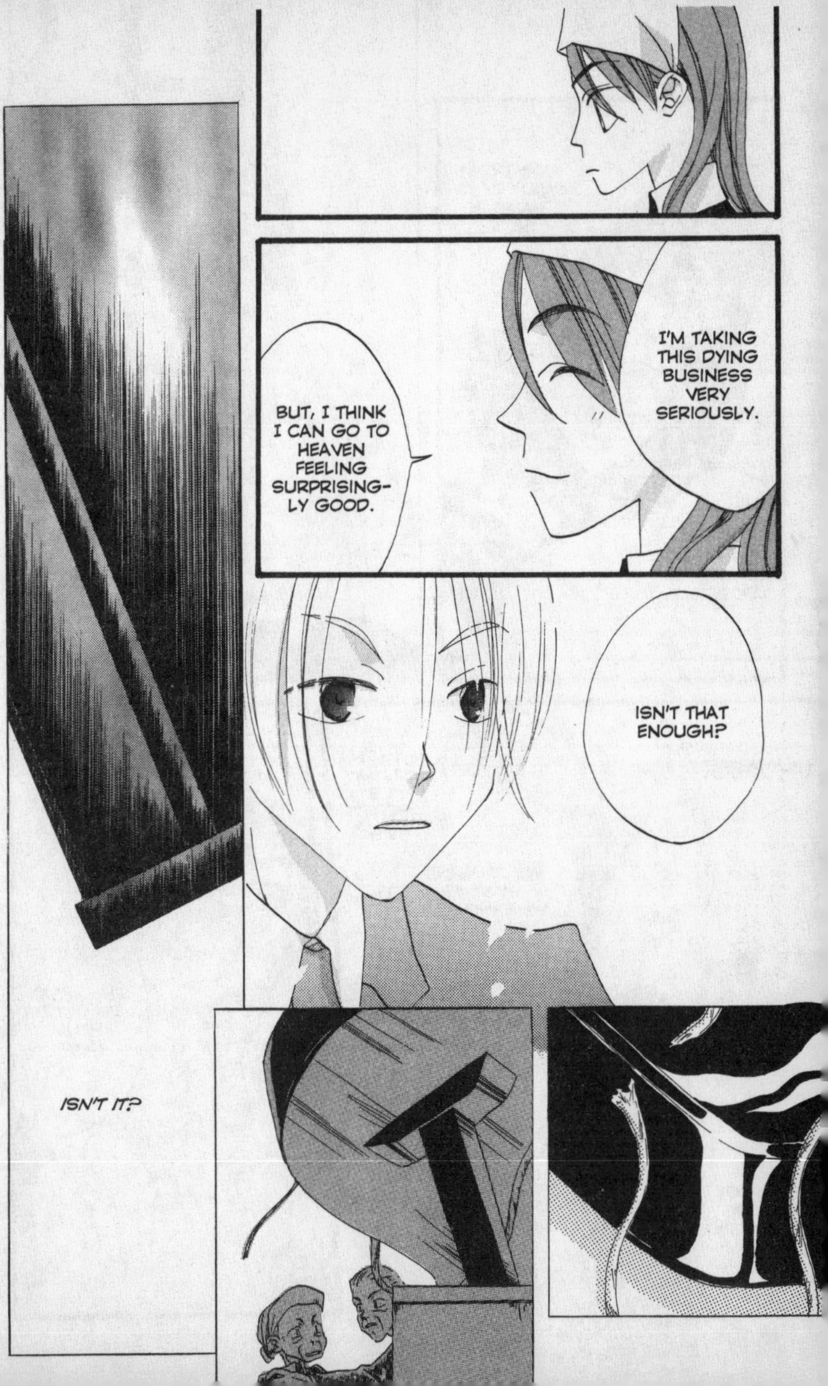
I'M TAKING THIS DYING BUSINESS VERY SERIOUSLY.
BUT, I THINK I CAN GO TO HEAVEN FEELING SURPRISING-LY GOOD.
ISN'T THAT ENOUGH?
ISN'T IT?

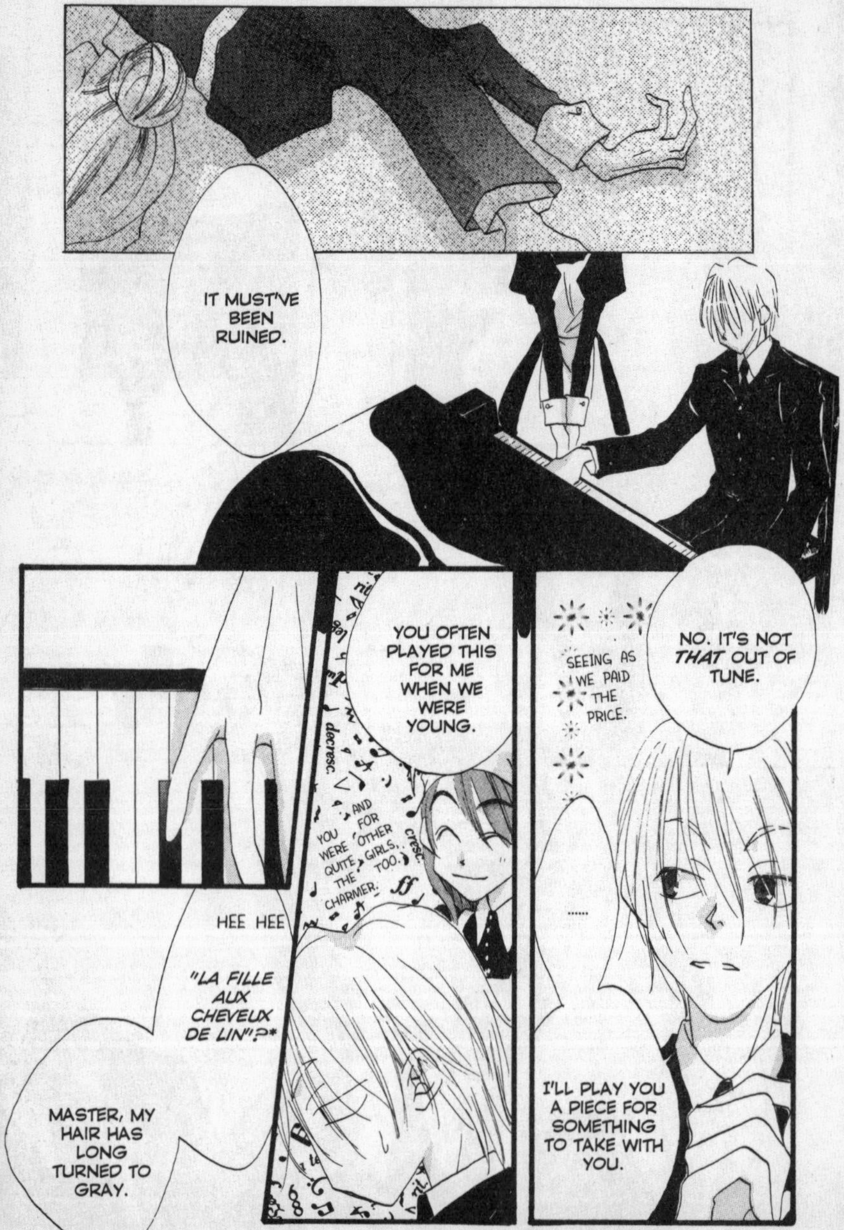
IT MUST'VE BEEN RUINED.
NO. IT'S NOT *THAT* OUT OF TUNE.
SEEING AS WE PAID THE PRICE.
......
I'LL PLAY YOU A PIECE FOR SOMETHING TO TAKE WITH YOU.
YOU OFTEN PLAYED THIS FOR ME WHEN WE WERE YOUNG.
AND FOR OTHER GIRLS, TOO.
YOU WERE QUITE THE CHARMER.
HEE HEE
*"LA FILLE AUX CHEVEUX DE LIN"?**
MASTER, MY HAIR HAS LONG TURNED TO GRAY.

* *"THE GIRL WITH FLAXEN HAIR,"* BY CLAUDE DEBUSSY.

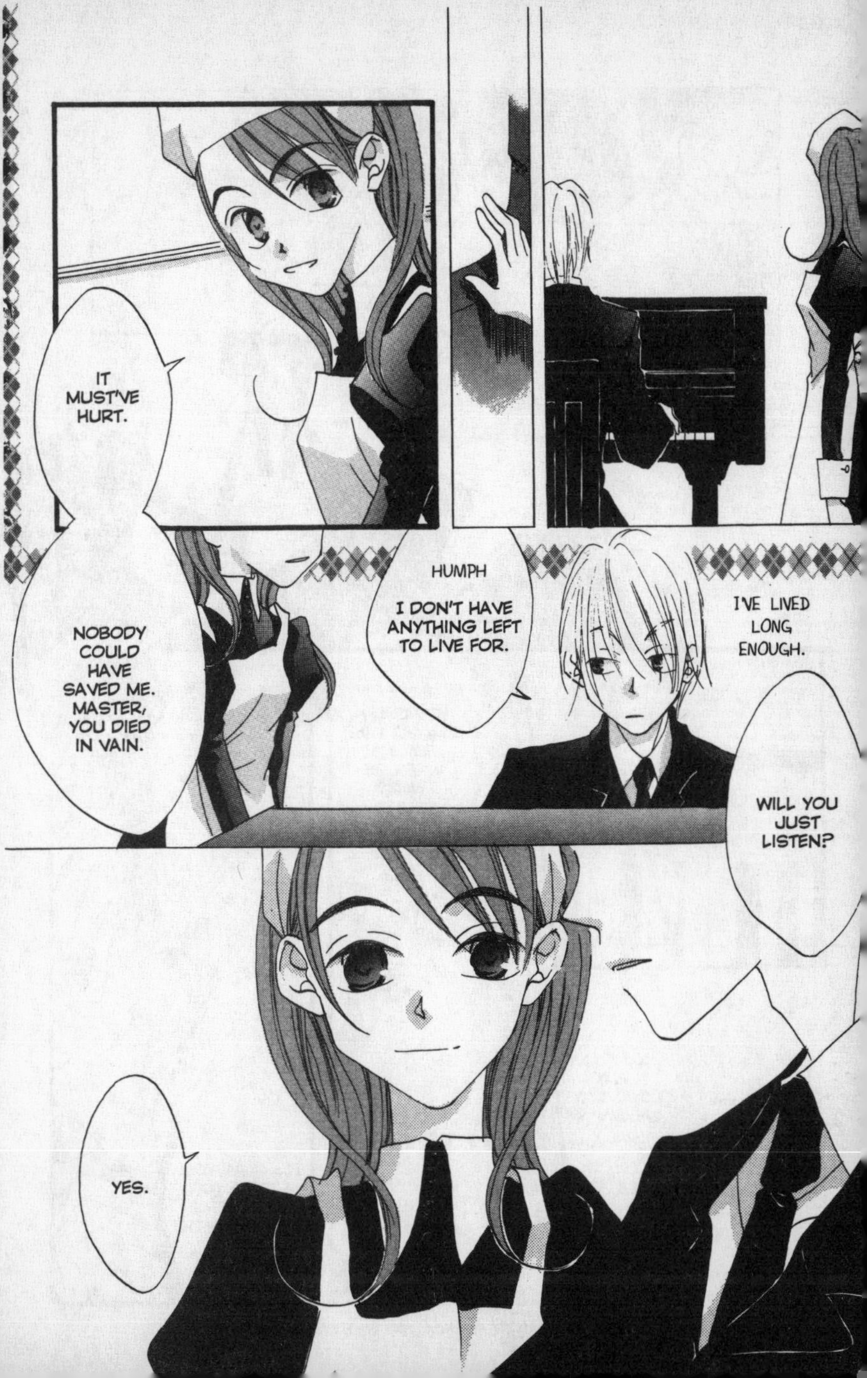
IT MUST'VE HURT.
I'VE LIVED LONG ENOUGH.
HUMPH
I DON'T HAVE ANYTHING LEFT TO LIVE FOR.
NOBODY COULD HAVE SAVED ME. MASTER, YOU DIED IN VAIN.
WILL YOU JUST LISTEN?
YES.

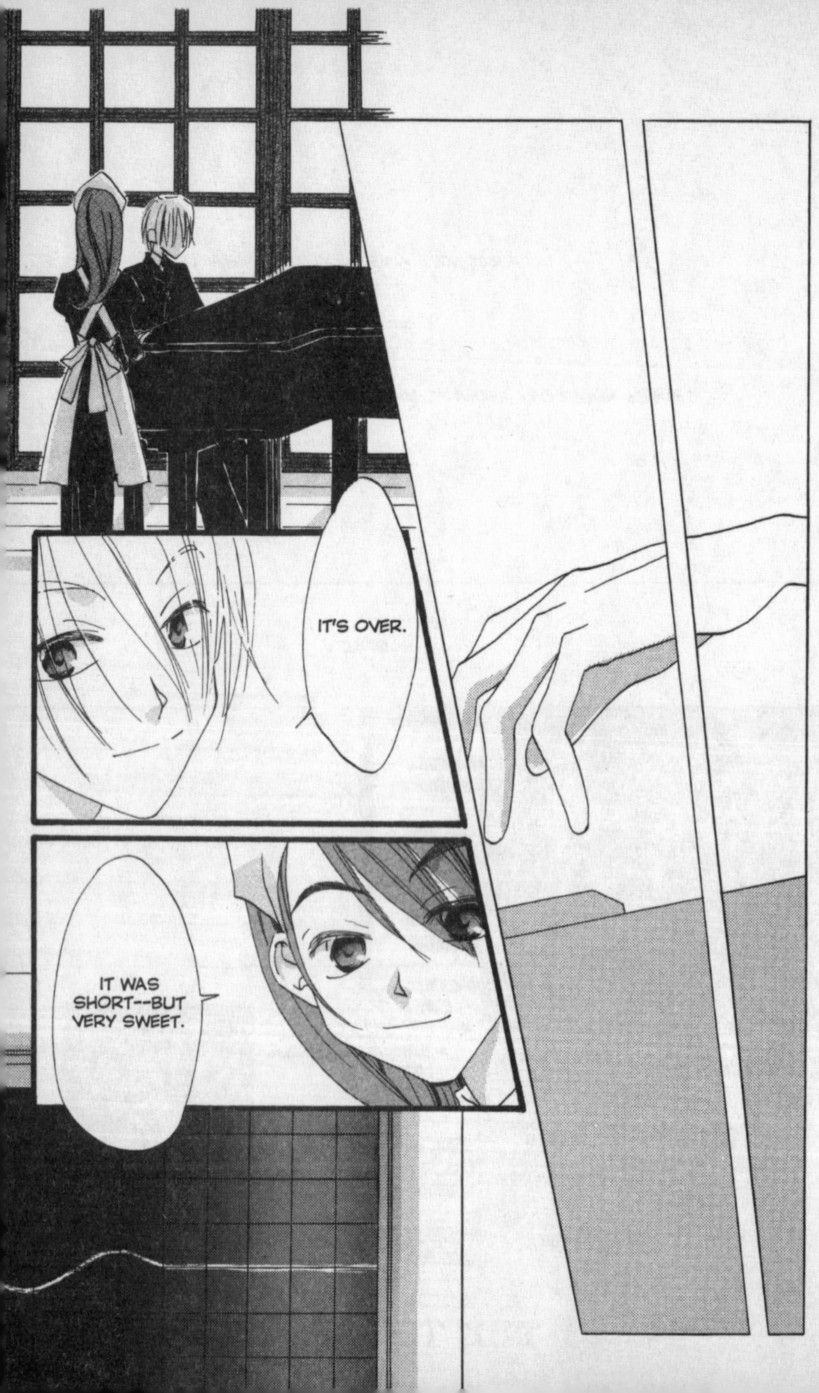
IT'S OVER.
IT WAS SHORT--BUT VERY SWEET.

MY FIRST LOVE WAS SO VERY LONG AGO.

I SHALL NEVER CRY ABOUT IT AGAIN. NOR WILL I THINK ABOUT IT AGAIN.

STILL...

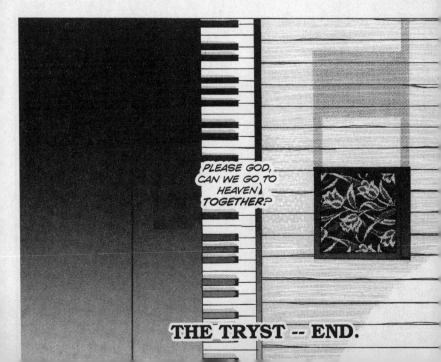

PLEASE GOD, CAN WE GO TO HEAVEN TOGETHER?

THE TRYST -- END.

No.

Date 1998-2001

KUSAKAWA'S NOTES

The records of "The Recipe for Gertrude" and others...

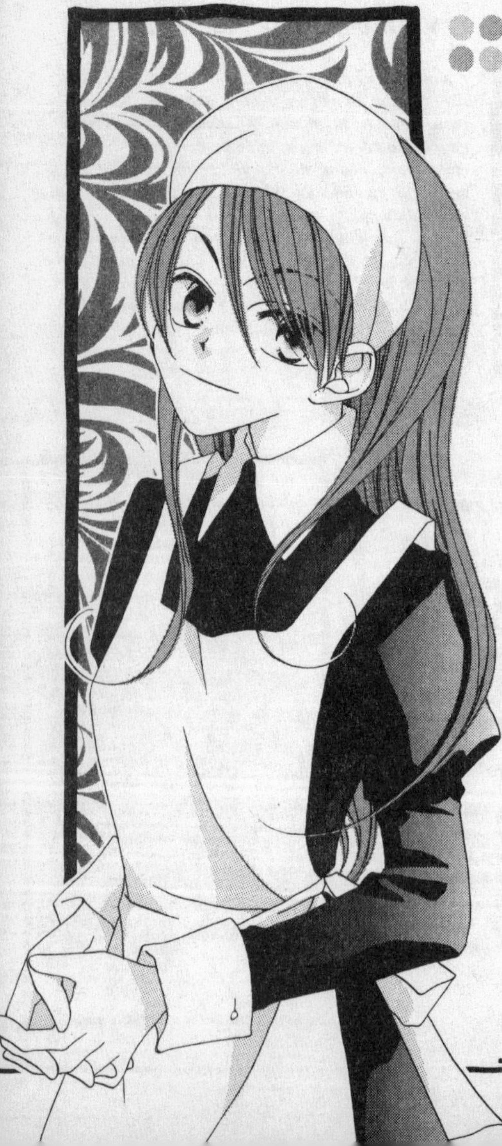

THE TRYST

I'm a little partial to this one. It also won an award, and it came before my official debut story, which you might have read in volume one. My editor (an earlier one) helped me through it. It was my first time in print. It all began with a single drawing of a maid's outfit.

I was working part-time at a library at the time, so the train rides home were relatively quiet--

and perfect for coming up with the dialogue. Back then, I was only able to do one page a day. It seems so long ago now. Around the same time, I applied for a regular job, but instead of "Dear So-and-so" in Japanese, I chose the wrong kanji and wrote "I adore philosophy." That, too, seems long ago. Needless to say, I didn't get the job.

THE STORIES

The Recipe for Gertrude 5

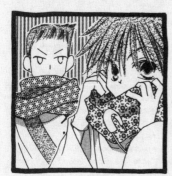

I use a certain screen tone for when Gertrude casts a spell. So, you can imagine how much I panicked when I found out it was discontinued. However, I got through that one okay after I talked to the manufacturer and my editor.
As it turned out, the local stationery shop that I often go to had sheets and sheets of it. Maybe they knew, maybe they didn't. Later on, I found myself saying, "What? This one, too?" on more than one occasion.

The Recipe for Gertrude 6

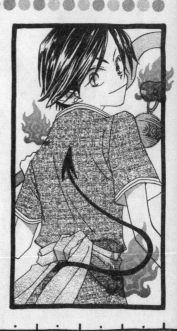

The tail Chelock is looking for doesn't look like a monkey's but like the one on the right. Really. Many people may have the impression it's supposed to look like a monkey's, but maybe it's because it's the way he's dressed. I use a spiky looking screen tone for Mariotte.
Puppen's looks like the pattern used on rice bowls. I also draw bigger food servings for him. I did this one during summer, and I used to snap myself awake when I started getting sleepy near dawn by sucking on a certain frozen sweet. They don't seem to make the white ones anymore...

No.

Date 1998-2001

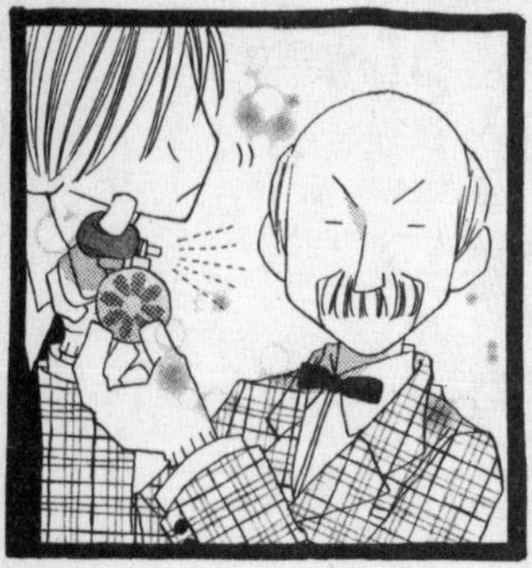

The Recipe for Gertrude 7

I used to work part-time at a bookstore. You can see it in the way the storekeeper acts. The foppish old man is actually modeled on someone, but I made a lot of changes.
While I was shopping at a certain bookstore, this old man came up and started talking to me. He said he was a med school professor. Sure. He was constantly going on about "from a medical point of view..." I wonder...

The Recipe for Gertrude 8

My mother's been helping me. At first, it was really embarrassing when she'd read the dialogue. (It shouldn't have mattered because she'd eventually see it in the magazine.)
But for this story I had her even erase the pencil lines in the kiss scene that comes at the end. With a deadline approaching, you can't afford to be embarrassed.

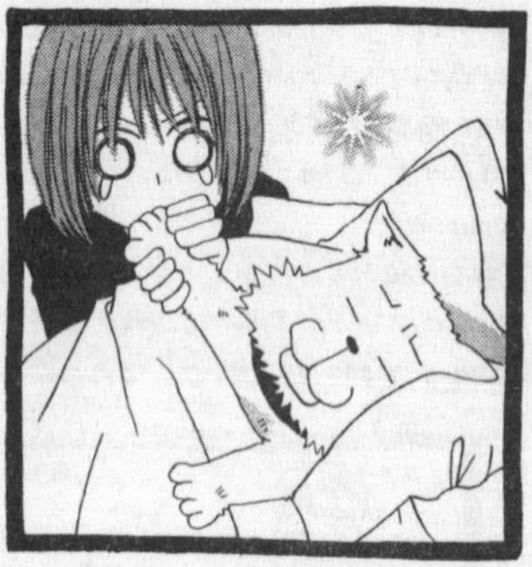

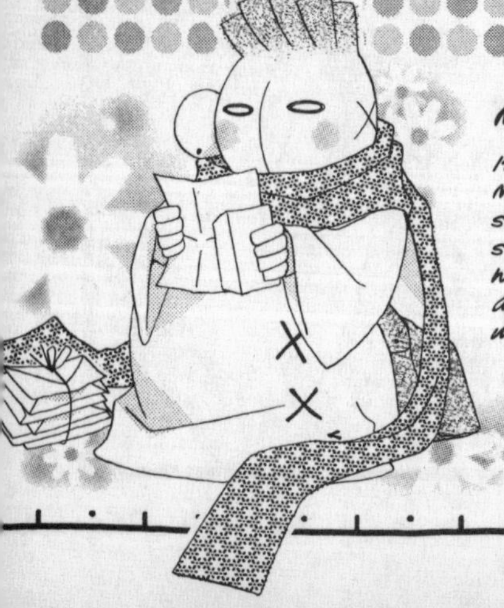

Mariotte's Fan Club

In the first volume, I wrote that Mariotte wasn't very popular. Well, since then I've received letters of support (for him) and letters asking how to join the club.
Anyone who introduces herself is welcome to join (ha ha).

Heights

Gertrude	5'11"
Sahara	5'2"
Puppen About	6'
Mariotte About	6'2"
Sahara's brother	5'10"
Encyclopedia Storekeeper	6'8"

Apart from Sahara's, most of these heights aren't properly reflected in the artwork (sigh). At first, I wanted to make the storekeeper 10 feet tall, but I made him shorter because he wouldn't fit into the panels.

Incidentally, he has huge eyes because he speed reads all the time (I'm assuming here). I gave him long fingers so that he can carry a lot of books.

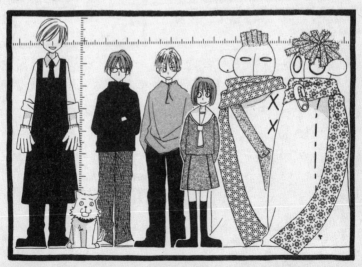

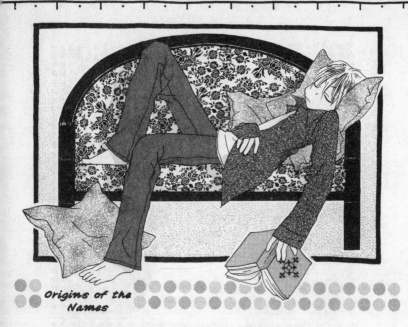

Origins of the Names

Gertrude	*A poet featured in a magazine. Maybe it was an author.*
Sahara Susugi	*The "Sahara" is from the Sahara Desert. I tried to come up with other names based on famous places that could be written in kanji. I gave up. "Susugi" comes from a different reading for the "So" kanji in Natsume Soseki (who was a very famous Japanese author).*
Puppen	*From the German word puppenspiel which means, one, to play with dolls and, two, a puppet play. I liked the way it sounded.*
Mariotte	*A twisting of marionette. There's also a hotel with the same name at the Nagoya train station.*
Kyusaku/ Claude	*"Kyusaku" is from both Yumeno Kyusaku, an author, and Shimada Kyusaku, an actor. We passed around a copy of Dogura Magura among several friends. I couldn't make heads or tails of it. The "Claude" is from Claude Monet, the painter.*

No.
Date 1998-2001

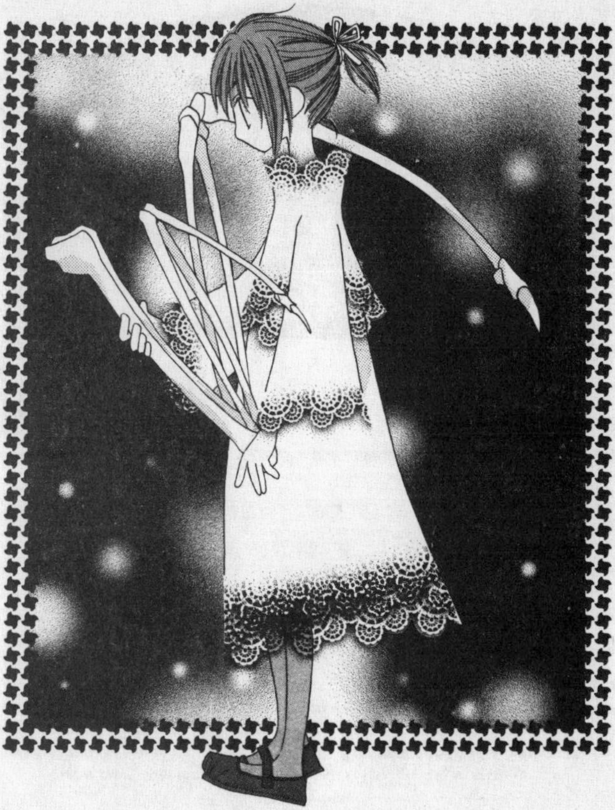

To the readers who've stayed with me,
To my editors and others who helped me get published,
To my family and friends,
To the liquor store staff where I do my photocopying,
Thank you very much.

Kusakawa's notes -- End

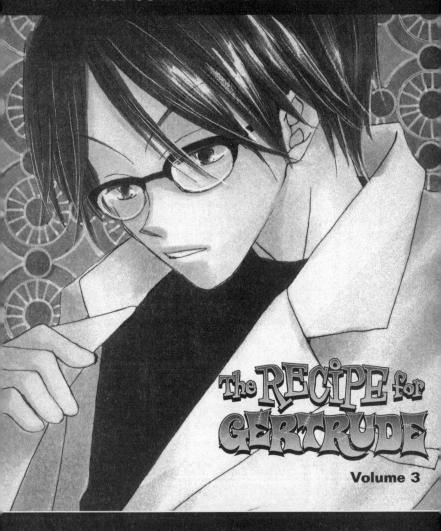

The RECIPE for GERTRUDE

Volume 3

By Nari Kusakawa. With Gertrude injured, Sahara is forced to face her brother and Gertrude's creator by herself. Fearing for her safety, Gertrude is forced to recruit an old nemesis to aid Sahara. Will our favorite patchwork demon be able to pay the price of this bargain? The Recipe is almost within grasp, but first they will have to find out just how Gertrude came to be and how he got his name!

GERTRUDE NO RECIPE Vol. 3 © 2001 Nari Kusakawa/HAKUSENSHA, INC.

DON'T MISS THE TRAIN!

DENSHA OTOKO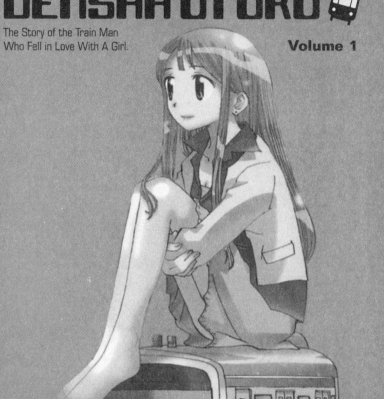

The Story of the Train Man
Who Fell in Love With A Girl.

Volume 1

By Hitori Nakano & Wataru Watanabe. A painfully shy young man's life is turned upside down when an incident on a train brings him into contact with something he's completely unfamiliar with…a woman! In desperation, he solicits the advice of the online community to improve his social skills. But will their advice help the socially challenged Densha Otoko ("Train Man") or just confuse him even more?

 DENSHA OTOKO - DEMO ORE, TABIDATSUYO. - Vol. 1 © 2005 Wataru Watanabe, Hitori Nakano/Akitashoten

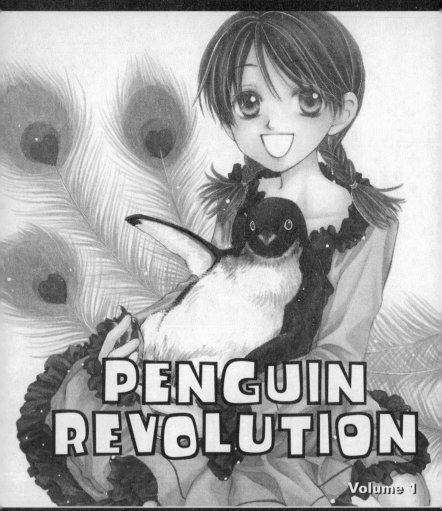

PENGUIN REVOLUTION

Volume 1

By Sakura Tsukuba. A new series from fan-favorite creator of LAND OF THE BLINDFOLDED! High school student Yukari Fujimaru is able to see a potential star from the special "aura" they give off, in the form of angelic wings. A fellow student has a small pair of wings and is one of these aspiring talents, but no one knows "she" is actually a boy in disguise! Now, to make her own down-to-earth dream come true, Yukari has to help her new friend become a star.

PENGUIN KAKUMEI Volume 1 © 2004 Sakura Tsukuba/HAKUSENSHA, INC.

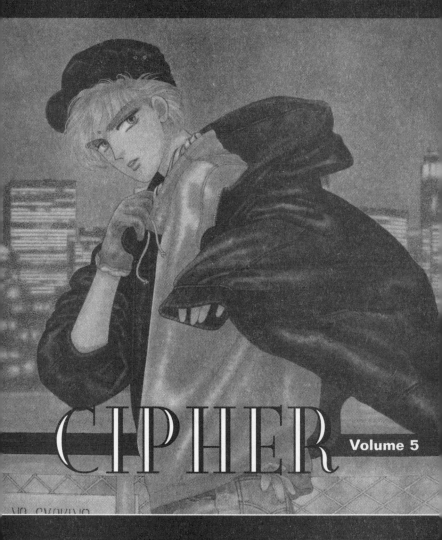

IF YOU LIKE THE RECIPE FOR GERTRUDE, YOU'LL LOVE THESE SERIES, TOO!

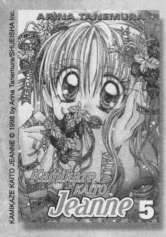

By Arina Tanemura
5 Volumes Available

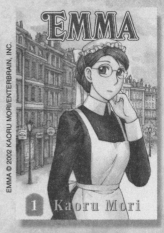

By Kaoru Mori
1 Volume Available

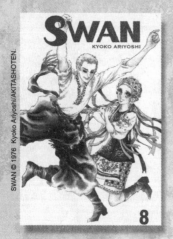

By Kyoko Ariyoshi
8 Volumes Available

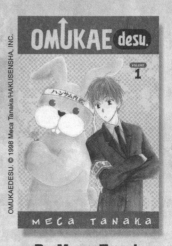

By Meca Tanaka
1 Volume Available

CHECK OUT THESE OTHER GREAT SERIES!

2
OYAYUBIHIME
INFINITY
Toru Fujieda

By Toru Fujieda
2 Volumes Available

7
the DEVIL DOES EXIST
Mitsuba Takanashi

By Mitsuba Takanashi
7 Volumes Available

Volume 1
Naoe Kita
KARA NO TEIKOKU
THE EMPTY EMPIRE

By Naoe Kita
1 Volume Available

Mihona Fujii
GALS! 7

By Mihona Fujii
7 Volumes Available

For more information and sneak previews, visit cmxmanga.com. Call 1-800-COMIC BOOK for the nearest comics shop or head to your local book store.

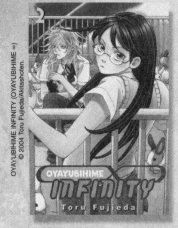

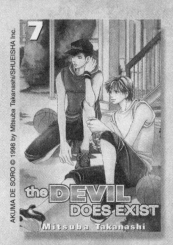

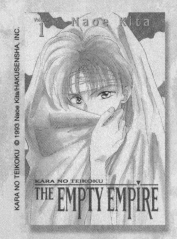

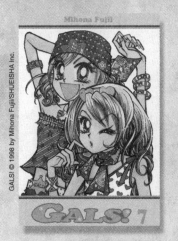

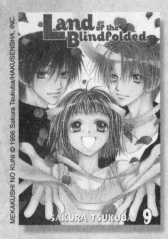
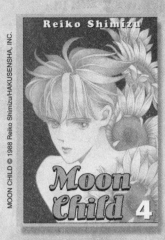
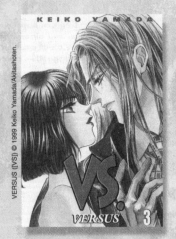
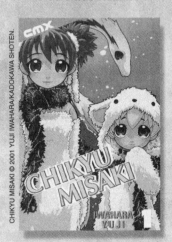

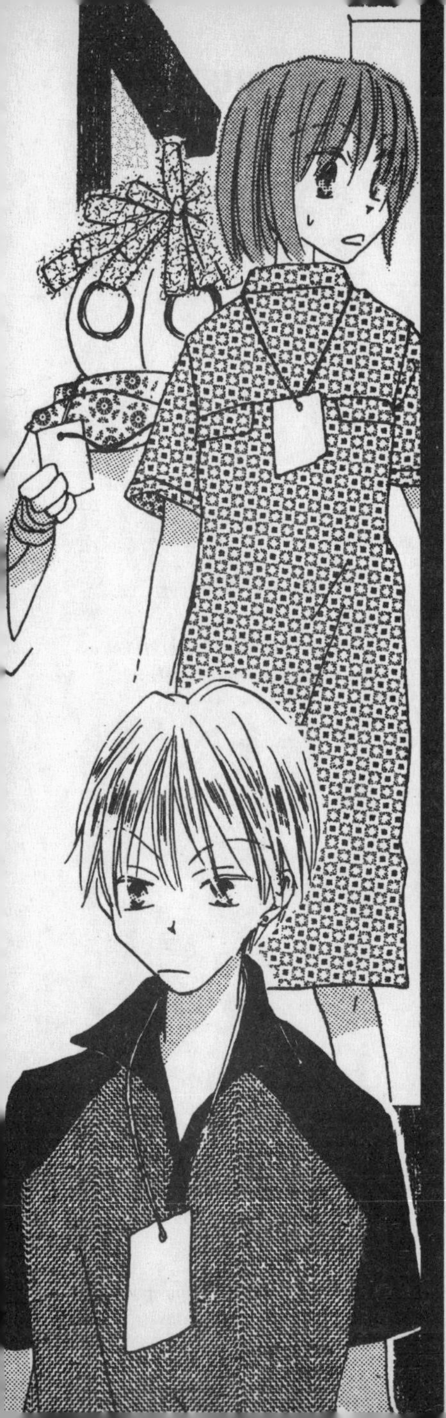

KNOW WHAT'S INSIDE

With the wide variety of manga available, CMX understands it can be confusing to determine age-appropriate material. We rate our books in four categories: EVERYONE, TEEN, TEEN + and MATURE. For the TEEN, TEEN + and MATURE categories, we include additional, specific descriptions to assist consumers in determining if the book is age appropriate. (Our MATURE books are shipped shrink-wrapped with a Parental Advisory sticker affixed to the wrapper.)

E

EVERYONE

Titles with this rating are appropriate for all age readers. They contain no offensive material. They may contain mild violence and/or some comic mischief.

T

TEEN

Titles with this rating are appropriate for a teen audience and older. They may contain some violent content, language, and/or suggestive themes.

T+

TEEN PLUS

Titles with this rating are appropriate for an audience of 16 and older. They may contain partial nudity, mild profanity and more intense violence.

M

MATURE

Titles with this rating are appropriate only for mature readers. They may contain graphic violence, nudity, sex and content suitable only for older readers.

CMX

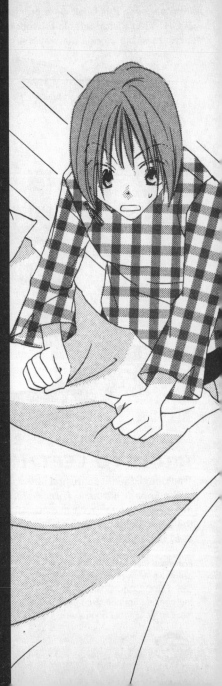

GERTRUDE NO RECIPE Volume 2 © 1999 Nari Kusakawa.
All Rights Reserved. First published in Japan in 2002 by
HAKUSENSHA, INC., Tokyo.

THE RECIPE FOR GERTRUDE Volume 2. published by
WildStorm Productions, an imprint of DC Comics, 888
Prospect St. #240, La Jolla, CA 92037. English Translation
© 2006. All Rights Reserved. English translation rights in
U.S.A. and Canada arranged by HAKUSENSHA, INC.,
through Tuttle-Mori Agency Inc., Tokyo. The stories, characters, and incidents mentioned in this magazine are entirely
fictional. Printed on recyclable paper. WildStorm does not
read or accept unsolicited submissions of ideas, stories or
artwork. Printed in Canada.

DC Comics, A Warner Bros. Entertainment Company.

Tony Ogasawara – Translation and Adaptation

William F. Schuch – Lettering

arry Berry – Design

m Chadwick – Editor

ISBN:1-4012-1111-9
ISBN-13: 978-1-4012-1111-0

All the pages in this book were created—and are printed here—in Japanese RIGHT-to-LEFT format. No artwork has been reversed or altered, so you can read the stories the way the creators meant for them to be read.

FLIP IT!

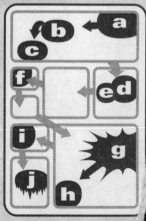

RIGHT TO LEFT?!

Traditional Japanese manga starts at the upper right-hand corner, and moves right-to-left as it goes down the page. Follow this guide for an easy understanding.

a
b
c
e d
f
g
i
j
h

For more information and sneak previews, visit cmxmanga.com. Call 1-800-COMIC BOOK for the nearest comics shop or head to your local book store.